About the author

Ian Wishart has written for magazines, newspapers, radio and television in New Zealand, Australia and the UK. His work has featured in national and international journalism awards 13 times in the past 14 years.

The *Frontline* investigation into European Pacific's winebox, co-produced with Mark Champion, Carol Hirschfeld, Michael Wilson, Shaun Brown and Paul Norris, was acclaimed as far away as New York, where it made the finals of the Film and Television Awards. Wishart is currently contracted to TVNZ.

THE PARADISE CONSPIRACY

Ian Wishart

Howling At The Moon Productions Ltd

First edition published 1995 (Oct) by
Howling at The Moon Productions Ltd,
Box 16-233, Sandringham,
Auckland, New Zealand
Reprinted 1995 (Oct)
Reprinted 1995 (Dec)
Reprinted 1996 (Feb)
Reprinted 1996 (May)

ISBN 0-473-03397-6
Typeset in Berkeley Book
Printed in Australia by Australian Print Group.

Contents

Warning

ALL REFERENCES TO ALLEGED fraud or fraud in this book must be considered in the light of the fact that no criminal charges have been brought against anyone in the European Pacific affair or the bloodstock and film partnership investigations referred to within.

The reader should *not* assume that a person is guilty of any crime until that person has been convicted in a Court of Law. What you read here may be elements of a possible prosecution case, were one ever to be brought, but please bear in mind that you have not heard the defence submission.

INTRODUCTION

EVERY SO OFTEN, a story comes along that cries out to be told. This is one of those stories. It has not been easy. Three years ago I began this journey, aided along the way by bankers, lawyers, investigators – an entire zoo of diverse characters. Some require anonymity in this book – the price of disclosure, they argue, would be broken careers and retribution. But they all tell a similar tale, and they tell it only because they learnt to trust an investigative journalist who became swept up in their maelstrom.

The Paradise Conspiracy had its genesis in an investigation by two New Zealand business newspapers into claims of tax cheating. It quickly ballooned into something much bigger, a three year long hunt for the truth that culminated in a television documentary costing nearly a million dollars to air, and ultimately a Commission of Inquiry into the activities uncovered by the television team and whether some of the law enforcement agencies had acted lawfully or competently in their own probes into the alleged crimes.

The lessons learnt apply not just to the people of New Zealand, but equally to those in the rest of the industrialised world. This is a story from the cutting edge of capitalism, the final frontier of finance. What happened here will happen again. And again . . .

In journeying through this book, the reader should be aware of a number of factors regarding the author's methodology. Firstly, because of European Pacific's desperate efforts to discover the identities of our many informants – in order to gag them with huge writs – I have in many cases altered the names of those people and, where necessary, altered the locations where they were spoken to. Sometimes, to confuse the enemy, nothing has been changed.

Those whose identities have been fudged are referred to in the text by a first name only. To protect those whose information was so sensitive that even a name change won't fool their former colleagues, I have created amalgam characters – a mixture of perhaps two or three individuals whose testimony in this book will be delivered by a single mouthpiece.

What has *not* been altered, however, is what those people said. In the vast majority of cases the conversations were recorded on audio tape for accuracy's sake and appear in the book verbatim, in the remainder notes were transcribed immediately after each interview with a time and date noted. In those cases, the quotes are as close to verbatim as has been possible, and where possible or appropriate the quotes have been reconfirmed with those who made them.

Where possible, all external source material is noted in the main body of the text, with the most significant material reprinted in the appendices at the back of this publication.

A mentor of mine once exhorted his reporters to remember where they came from and why they were there – "*the objective is pursuit of truth,*" he admonished, "*and sometimes the truth may conflict with your own or your company's commercial objectives. Do not lose sight of the truth – it is the reason you are journalists, first and foremost."*

It is with a bitter sense of irony, then, that I write this. The truth I am pursuing has caused me to pause several times, caused me to confront the certain knowledge that what is contained within these pages will create enemies where I had none – it may even cost me my career. To fail to reveal what I know, however, would be a betrayal of those who risked their reputations and careers to help me, and a betrayal of the public's right to know and make up their own minds.

The truth, as defined by New Zealand's defamation laws, is what a jury believes to be true *"in the balance of probabilities"* – in other words, is there more than a 50 percent chance that this story is true? You, the reader, are my jury. These are my submissions. It is time to cast the dice into the air; let them fall where they will.

The Dream Police

"Cause they're waiting for me,
They're looking for me,
The dream police they're coming to arrest me."
– RICK NIELSEN, FROM THE ALBUM BY *CHEAP TRICK*, 1979

THE TIP HAD COME – as they often had recently – late in the evening, a sleep-shattering phone call with a voice speaking in hushed tones down the line.

"The Serious Fraud Office will rendezvous with one of your contacts, 9:00am tomorrow morning, Aotea Square. Be there."

I'd caught sight of my quarry a little after nine – the familiar visage of Spook, a source of mine, standing near the middle of the Square and, with him, senior SFO investigator Gib Beattie and another officer, both looking like they'd been tailored by the FBI.

Retreating from my vantage point I slunk back to the car. The camera was on the back seat. All I needed to do was load the film. Please God, I muttered frantically as I slumped into the driver's seat and swapped the 400mm long lens for a more manageable 210mm zoom, please give me time to roll off a few shots.

I knew Beattie had been talking to Spook for months. I also knew what had been discussed in those conversations. With a Commission of Inquiry underway, a photo of my contact meeting these SFO guys could prove relevant down the line. I hadn't figured on Murphy's Law.

"Look," Spook was repeating to Beattie back in the Square, *"I'm not happy about you bringing this guy Steve Drain down here. I don't know him, and I don't want to talk in front of him. Besides, I'm worried my car might get a parking ticket. Can we go back down there by the street where I can keep an eye on it?"*

And so it was that just as I unpacked the film, Spook walked around the corner with the SFO's Gib Beattie and Steve Drain. My worst stakeout nightmare had just come true. I may as well have hung out a sign saying "Here I Am, Come And Get Me".

Beattie and Drain took a half-step past my car and stopped dead in their tracks. While they couldn't see my face, that could tell that someone in the driver's seat had a camera in his lap.

Drain, in one fluid movement, whirled around and opened my passenger door, leaning in as he did so.

"What the hell are you doing here?," he demanded. I clutched vainly at a straw, hoping that Drain was taking a wild guess, that he wasn't an avid watcher of TV news bulletins which have featured my face every week for five years, and that even if he did know who Ian Wishart was, he wouldn't recognise me behind the Ray-Ban Aviators. Fat bloody chance!

"*Haven't we met before, somewhere?,*" he sneered, before adding "*I know who you are, now tell me what you are doing down here!*"

"*None of your business,*" I retorted, giving up the play-dumb ruse.

Gib Beattie couldn't make up his mind whether to gloat or snarl, so he mixed the two expressions, his ears and nose appearing to twitch in the battle for facial control. His eyes, however, glittered with hate.

"*Wishart, you bastard. You bastard! We've got you now!*"

I barely had time to react – Serious Fraud Office investigator Steve Drain, a former cop, chose that moment to lunge across the seat in a bid to grab the camera and rip the film out. We fought briefly as I lashed out to stop him gaining a secure grip on the Olympus.

"*Back off pal!,*" I warned as menacingly as I could muster, "*You don't have any authority down here.*" Perhaps realising that entering my vehicle and attempting to snatch the camera had overstepped the mark, Drain beat a retreat from the interior. Beattie, too, was backing away by now, the sneer appearing permanently etched on his face.

"*We've got you, you bastard. Your day is coming soon, boy!,*" he threatened.

* * *

IT WAS WAR ON the streets of New Zealand, and the public never knew. Like the plot of a Cold War spy novel, it was a clandestine campaign of dirty tricks, international intrigue, kidnap attempts, death threats, beatings, buggings and break-ins.

In recent weeks I'd become aware that two groups, including a private investigation agency, were shaking every tree they could find to get hold of a draft of this book. Money was being talked about.

"*Would half a million shut you up?,*" queried my security adviser after fending off another inquisitive investigator. "*If you play it real cunning, you can sell these guys the book rights, and then go and write the movie script behind their backs.*"

"*Half a mil's tempting,*" I grinned, "*but I don't know whether I'd be able to sleep with myself afterwards. Nah, what the hell, the story's gotta be told. I'd rather publish and be damned.*"

CHAPTER 1

A Cornered Animal

*"The TV business is uglier than most things. It is normally perceived
as some kind of cruel and shallow money trench through the heart
of the journalism industry, a long plastic hallway where thieves and
pimps run free and good men die like dogs, for no good reason.
Which is more or less true. For the most part, they are dirty little
animals with huge brains and no pulse . . . You can't get away
from TV. It is everywhere. The hog is in the tunnel."*
- HUNTER S. THOMPSON, 1985

IN A TELEVISION NEWSROOM, adrenalin-pumping deadline-beating tub-thumping breaking news stories don't come along every day. When they do, it's like a feeding frenzy of gremlins in a morgue; duck the flying body parts as each cynical hardnose journalist goes snout-first for the jugular.

Thus it was when New Zealand's most popular politician, a man named Winston Peters, strode purposefully into the country's Parliament on the afternoon of June 10, 1992. Inside his briefcase, a fresh corpse for the media pack to feed on.

Peters had carved a name as a maverick, an unguided missile with a penchant for trouble. Named for British wartime leader Sir Winston Churchill, the Maori boy from the far north of New Zealand spent much of his childhood enduring the nickname Winnie the Pooh. The moniker had obviously taken its toll: to his parliamentary colleagues that afternoon, Winston was the teddy bear from hell.

For years he'd been a kind of political Jiminy Cricket, a carryover from the bad old days prior to New Zealand's great economic experiment of 1984. Peters' National Party, then led by a benevolent dictator in the form of Sir Robert Muldoon, had been tossed from power as voters turned instead to an invigorated Labour Party led by the charismatic David Lange.

As part and parcel of jettisoning the baggage of the Muldoon years, the Labour administration moved swiftly to deregulate the economy – left, right and centre. Farmers – traditional supporters of the blue ribbon National Party – lost their taxpayer funded production subsidies, financial markets were thrown open with no restrictions, overseas investors were invited to browse and shop in "supermarket New Zealand", where anything, even citizenship, was up for sale.

Such no-holds-barred tariff reduction and openness were brave/foolhardy, considering that no other Western nations had taken such drastic steps. Not to worry, said the Labour Government, we'll be an example to the rest of the world and lead the way in new right economics. Pretty soon everyone will be doing it.

As a whole, the NZ population fell for it, although a small group, notably people like Peters, cynically compared it to a rather obese, middle-aged individual striding down a beach towards a group of tanned and slim beauties, whilst throwing off every item of clothing in the expectation that the other sexy young things on the beach will do likewise.

In the international game of truth-or-dare, New Zealand was exposing its bloomers to the rest of the world. Unfortunately, other countries misinterpreted this act of magnanimous generosity as a hostile act, and instead, we took an economic hiding in the decade that followed.

Among the few winners in New Zealand: some of the major corporates who took advantage of financial deregulation to act, in some cases almost simultaneously, as advisers to the Government on which state corporations should be sold, and also as purchasers of those same state assets.

New Zealand in the 1980's was regarded by many as the "Dodge City" of the entire western world. Nowhere, not even Wall Street at its worst, came close to the unregulated corporate gunslinging that took place downunder.

It was against some of their nastier excesses that people like Peters railed, often to little avail. After all, the new right lobby group, the Business Roundtable, was largely responsible for the spirit of a lot of the Labour and, post-1990, National Government policy and legislation.

On this particular June day, Winston Peters had the Business Roundtable firmly in his sights.

As he stood in the chamber, using the protective cloak of parliamentary privilege that prevents MPs from being sued over anything they say in the House, Peters talked of members of the Roundtable asking him to swing in behind the right-wing economic policies of fellow National MP Ruth Richardson. Richardson was the party's finance spokeswoman, and a supporter of the freemarket policies begun by Labour's Roger Douglas.

Peters claimed the request had come at a meeting way back in October 1989, shortly after David Lange's resignation as Prime Minister. With an election looming, and Peters the country's most popular politician, the business community was keen to see Peters and Richardson bury their differences.

To waiting parliamentarians and the media, all this was old news. What they had all gathered to hear was the name of a prominent businessman alleged to have offered Peters large sums of money.

We had all gathered around the radio in the newsroom. *"Give us the name Winston,"* snapped a producer beside me, *"give us the bloody name!"*

"He is, Sir, Mr Selwyn J. Cushing, of Brierley Investments Ltd."

It was a bombshell. Speculation had been building for days after Peters appeared on an Australian current affairs show, *Four Corners*, and talked of his dealings with the Business Roundtable, a gathering of the top business leaders in the country and an influential Government lobby group; commercial knights of the realm.

The politician was today informing Parliament what he had told *Four Corners* – that he'd been asked before the 1990 election to visit *". . a certain group in the Roundtable."*

"I was pretty certain as to what the conversation would be about, and it was about that. It was about my swinging in behind a certain economic philosophy."

The programme continued, Peters explained, with his own claim that after his meeting, he'd been approached with an offer of help.

"And, further, I just as a matter of curiosity said: 'Well, what do you mean by help? Do you mean money?' And he said 'Yes'. And I said: 'Well, how much?'

"And I nominated a few figures and each figure was agreed to. And I said: 'Well, look, I'm not prepared to sell out the people I represent in either my constituency or nationwide.'"

The *Four Corners* documentary had played on Australia's state-owned ABC Network on Monday, June 1. In the intervening days, the government MP had been ripped apart by his National Party colleagues over the claims, and his refusal to name names, Prime Minister Jim Bolger telling his rebel backbencher to *"Put up or shut up!"*. Finance Minister Ruth Richardson, a longtime foe of Peters', swung in behind Bolger, saying the allegations were so serious that Peters was *"morally bound"* to produce evidence.

Backed into a corner by his own comments on Australian TV and the reaction of his colleagues, Winston Peters glanced up at the TV cameras in the parliamentary press gallery overhead, gulped once and unleashed the rest of his speech.

"What was important to me then, as it is now, is how I would have felt about it. The three sums of money that go with the answers to the transcript [of the Four Corners programme] are $20,000, $30,000, and $50,000 – not in addition, but alternatively.

"Had I taken the money for my campaign I would have felt no longer free – that there would have been a new element in my mind when considering important economic matters."

Winston savoured his next line, rolling it out like a pièce de résistance.

"I would personally have felt bought. Remember Sir, that the offer of financial assistance was direct: it was a departure from the conventional method of funding for political parties. The man belonged to a company associated with the Roundtable.

"And the man, even if his offer was genuine – and I leave that open and believe it is possible – even if the offer was genuine, was a significant shareholder in a company associated with the Roundtable, and the political tactics of some members of that group had caused me grave disquiet."

In the Auckland newsroom of 3 *National News*, producer Mike Brockie called his gremlins to their battle stations. The Wellington bureau would handle the lead story, a straight report on Peters' revelations in Parliament. Auckland would do the reaction, reporters Steve Christensen and I had our orders: Find Selwyn Cushing.

Cushing was rich. Personally worth an estimated 25 million dollars, he was a senior executive of corporate highflyer Brierley Investments Limited. A company directorship check showed Cushing was on the board of 408 companies; even after eliminating some of the double entries on that list he was still obviously a busy and sought-after man.

Like dozens of other journalists around the country, Steve and I hit the phones.

"Good Afternoon, Brierley Investments."

"Yes hello, Ian Wishart here from TV3 News. We're looking for Selwyn Cushing please."

"You and everybody else. He's out of the office at the moment, can anybody else help?"

"Could you put me through to his secretary please?"

It's at times like this that the heart sinks, the chance of an easy "kill" diminishes and the prospect of locking horns with that most feared of beasts – the fractious, suspicious, protective corporate secretary – grows in inverse proportions.

Luckily, Selwyn Cushing's secretary was not one of these creatures. Although obviously tired of picking up the phone every three minutes to hear a reporter grunting at her, she kept her cool and in my case gave me a bonus.

"If you must know, he's in Tahiti on leave, but that's all I can tell you."

There's an advantage to being last cab off the rank, sometimes. As events unfolded, it became clear she hadn't told anyone else that particular snippet of information. *"Tahiti?,"* queried Christensen, his nose quivering as he adopted a particularly dubious air. *"Why would a multi-millionaire and one of New Zealand's most powerful businessmen go for a holiday in Tahiti?"*

"Club Med?," I joked. I was only half joking, actually. Club Mediteranee Moorea was the only resort I could name in the French territory, and then only because my folks had stayed on the island a couple of years previously. What the hell – this close to deadline we had nothing to lose by trying Club Med.

We raced to the recording suite – I manned the phone while Christensen stood by the mic, ready to start interviewing.

"Allo, Club Méditeranee Moorea."

"Bonjour mademoiselle," I blurted in my best schoolboy French, *"Je voudrais parler à Monsieur Selwyn Cushing, s'il vous plaît."*

"Ah, oui, Monsieur Cushing. Un moment, Monsieur."

When Cushing actually answered the phone, Christensen and I almost let out a big "Oui!" in unison. The gamble, small though it had been, had paid off, and we had ourselves a scoop. While other media were reporting that Cushing *"is currently holidaying overseas at an undisclosed location and can't be reached for comment,"* we had the Brierley boss in his tropical lair veritably hissing his reaction to Peters' claims.

Describing it as *"a disgraceful travesty of the truth"*, Cushing angrily denied ever attempting to bribe the National MP. As he would later repeat to newspapers and other media, Cushing said he couldn't understand why Peters had singled him out, and he found the allegations *"nasty and totally false."*

Others sprang to the millionaire's side, including Peters' former researcher Michael Laws, now an MP in his own right in the National Party seat of Hawkes Bay. Cushing was a friend of Laws, and it had been Michael Laws who introduced him to Peters.

It was, said Laws, *"a tragic misunderstanding"* on Winston's part, and he added that Selwyn Cushing had been one of the few top businessmen to attack the new right economic policies of Roger Douglas between 1984 and '87.

Cushing later issued defamation proceedings against Peters – those proceedings are still before the court.

But in the TV3 newsroom on the evening of June 10, 1992, issues of truth didn't necessarily enter the equation. All we saw were two powerful individuals squaring off against each other – the symbolism was more important than the players, for it reflected a boiling to the surface of tensions that had been building for so long.

After months of watching quietly from the sidelines, we had tasted first blood. I found myself transfixed by the implications, standing in a kind of Aladdin's Cave of Journalistic Wonders. Somewhere, I knew, we would find the Genie.

*　*　*

ON VALENTINE'S DAY 1992, the *National Business Review* published a fairy tale. But it wasn't the hearts and flowers variety.

"Once upon a time, in a land far, far away . . . ", teased the headline. So far so good – in newsrooms and corporate office towers right around the country we all grabbed a gulp of coffee and read on, entranced.

"Were there any such place, Wogistani public affairs would be carried out in a manner not altogether dissimilar to those in this green and pleasant isle. Readers will please keep in mind, as a patriotic article of faith, the fact that Kiwi officials are, and forever shall be, incorruptible.

"In Wogistan dwelt Ali Baba, a man well-known among the republic's pleaders. Ali and his band had friends in high places – in particular a leading legal Vasir ever so grateful to Ali for his help in filling pre-election coffers.

"Ali was a particularly adept tax lawyer – so apt [sic] he could, it was said, get bulldust – if not camel dung – through the eye of a regulatory needle.

"Dozens of well-heeled merchants trod the dusty path to Ali's door in search of a bit of income protection. Ali and his band devised schemes so cunning they did baffle the fiscal fiend until, one fateful day, Ali and his band overstepped the bounds of what we self-righteous Kiwis would call moral rectitude and, in a rash moment, not only dodged the taxman but defrauded their clients as well.

"As was the fashion of the time, Ali's colleagues were in the habit of forming special partnerships for favoured clients and often steered such people towards bloodstock – not ordinary bloodstock, mind, but racing camel bloodstock. But Ali wasn't especially fond of horses. An urbane and sophisticated man, he liked movies.

"So it came to pass that dozens of Wogistani punters were pulled into film partnerships, including one starring the Thin White Duke, who was making part of the movie in Southern Wogistan.

"But unbeknown to the special partners, Ali and his colleagues had persuaded the film commission in a neighbouring country to sink money into the enterprise. Ali was loathe to trouble his clients with this small detail. Their worries, after all, were great enough as it was. It would be so much simpler just to park the money – several million sheckels, it is understood – into his firm's trust account in a tiny tax haven far from the shores of Southern Wogistan.

"But as the years passed it became crystal clear to the Wogistani counterpoint of our fiscal fiend that mischief was afoot. Within his department was a man with more balls than political reticence, who vowed to take Ali and his band to the cleaners."

Get the picture so far? We did.

"Quietly he began to probe – firstly the partnership itself, and then the partners' trust account tucked away in that far-off tax haven. The harder he probed, the more excited he became.

"Ali and his partners had been to the best schools. They had friends in high places and dined with the most powerful of the vasirs, from whence many favours came. The man from infernal revenue was also growing fearful. How would the Wogistani establishment react to fraud charges against its favourite sons?

"But as it came to pass he worried in vain. It reached the ears of one of the top – and, as it happened, one of the silliest – vasirs that Ali and his band were under investigation. Naturally, the Vasir wasn't pleased. A scandal, especially within the patrician classes, was the last thing he needed. A by-election was nigh, and who was to say how the common herd might react and, even more frightening, who could say where his probing might lead?

"There was nothing for it, the Vasir decided. The man from infernal revenue must be stopped. And so, using loyal lackeys so it could never be traced to him, the Vasir nipped the investigation in the bud.

"Such are the politics of Southern Wogistan. It could never happen in New Zealand."

Wrapped as it was in Middle-Eastern allegory, it wasn't difficult to spot the camelprints of one Warren Berryman, or "Wog" to those who knew him well. An irascible, hard-drinking American, Berryman had taken to journalism late in his career – the proverbial jack-of-all-trades. While his stories were sometimes described as a sub-editor's nightmare, a general rule of thumb was that if Wog was digging somewhere, he'd probably found oil. He had a nose for business news that would have made Pinocchio proud.*

Around town, word got out about Southern Wogistan. Ears pricked up, eyes darted and claws were sharpened. The fox was heading for the hen house, and the forecast was blood and feathers on the floor.

We didn't have to wait long. Seven thousand miles and 10 time zones

---

* Berryman had left the NBR in December 1991, but his colleague, Jenni McManus, still worked there. The article was written one afternoon on Jenni's back porch, over several beers and the remains of a curry. It was submitted under Jenni's name. She subsequently left the NBR to join Berryman on his new venture, The Independent.

away from Wogistan, the New Zealand Commissioner of Inland Revenue, David Henry, wrote to *NBR* with a reassurance for readers that *"investigations into the affairs of taxpayers in this country are a matter for the Commissioner of Inland Revenue. They are carried out without external influences being exerted on the process. While investigations might be 'nipped in the bud' for nefarious purposes in Wogistan, that is not so in New Zealand."*

Ouch! Also writing in defence of his realm, the Minister of Justice, Doug Graham.

"Shoeshine's column of February 14, 1992, describing events that occurred in Wogistan, by innuendo at least, implies some improper coercion during Labour's era. I am happy to be able to reassure your readers that to the best of my knowledge no such action, if it ever occurred at all, has been repeated since the election of the National Government."

Ouch! again. This conspiracy theory in Wogistan had me licking my lips in anticipation. The only problem? I had no idea in the slightest what Berryman was on about. While the plot was obvious we had no leads on the players – if they existed – and no real idea where to find them. That defeatist attitude was soon beaten out of us, however, as Winston Peters opened fire in Parliament.

On August 4, 1992, he named Robin Congreve, Geoff Ricketts and Paul Carran – all lawyers associated with the country's biggest lawfirm, Russell McVeagh McKenzie Bartleet and Co. He accused them of *"massive, criminal, fraudulent activity"* in the arranging of finance for the movie *Merry Christmas Mr Lawrence*, a film that starred rock performer David Bowie – the "Thin White Duke". He tabled documentation in the House showing investors who put in a dollar would get more than two dollars back – not from profits but by allegedly raiding the revenue in the form of tax savings.

Peters calculated the New Zealand IRD had been *"defrauded"* of nearly $11.5 million. He also tabled an Inland Revenue letter dated April 7, 1987, which referred to part of the movie's financing as a *"sham"*, and disallowed claimed spending of $4.6 million by the film partnership.

In particular, the IRD letter advised investors that the claimed expenditure *"which represents proceeds from the loan from Charlesbay Ltd is to be disallowed . . ."*

"The loan from Charlesbay Ltd is considered to be a sham, and the purported payments thereto are to be disregarded accordingly."

Later, the IRD warned each investor.

"Finally, in view of the discrepancies disclosed, it appears that an offence against Section 416 of the Income Tax Act 1976 may have been committed. Please let me have, in writing, your personal explanation of the discrepancies and any reason why you consider that penal action should not be taken against you."

Peters, of course, went to town on it.

"What immunity from prosecution do those perpetrators of fraud have?," he asked his fellow MPs.

Even former Prime Minister David Lange waded in to back Peters up, telling Parliament *"There is a very clear body of evidence that indicates a clear conspiracy amongst those people to produce from the taxpayer more than they ever hoped to get through artistic endeavour."*

By the following day, Inland Revenue Commissioner David Henry had rejected the claims of fraud, telling the *Herald* the film partnership had been thoroughly investigated by his department.

"I am not alleging that any tax offences have been committed by the promoters or any of the 300 investors in that film," he told the newspaper. He also backed away from the 1987 IRD letter describing the financing as a sham, saying the letter had later been withdrawn. *"By the end of our investigation we were not alleging that the transactions were a sham."* David Henry repeated what would become an oft-heard refrain over the next two years: the public can have complete confidence in the department's investigations.

Two of the men named by Peters – Congreve and Ricketts – were current directors of the Bank of New Zealand and Fay Richwhite. Peters had only weeks earlier turned his guns on the Bank of New Zealand bailouts back in 1989 and 1990. The 1989 restructuring saw the Crown sell a 30 percent stake in the bank to Fay Richwhite's Capital Markets Ltd, for $300 million, in a bid to stave off a cashflow crisis. The following year, the incoming National Government had to plug $620 million into saving the bank a second time.

He criticised the Government decision to buy $60 million worth of BNZ shares off Fay Richwhite, who might otherwise have struggled to meet their $160 million share of the restructuring cost. He criticised the subsequent payment of fees to Fay Richwhite and Co for advice to the BNZ on the restructuring, and he questioned Fay Richwhite's own restructuring in August 1990, when it merged with its public listed company, Capital Markets, in a highly controversial deal.

By implicating Congreve and Ricketts in his parliamentary claims of fraud in the film deals, the rampaging MP was attempting to tar and feather both the BNZ and Fay Richwhite. Reaction from Russell McVeagh McKenzie Bartleet and Co was swift, as was the response from Congreve, Ricketts and Carran. All parties denied any fraudulent dealings, and pointed to the IRD's assertion that nothing untoward had taken place. Russell McVeagh also defended Congreve and Ricketts, saying they were simply ordinary investors in the schemes, and being unfairly targeted.

But certainly the denials of any wrongdoing, put forward by the IRD's David Henry, failed to halt the Peters steamroller. Within a fortnight of his first claims about *Merry Christmas*, Winston Peters was back in the debating chamber and back on the attack. He accused the IRD of withdrawing its claims that the deal was a sham, only after unlawful pressure from Russell McVeagh.

"The Inland Revenue Department was told to lift the claim, to change it, otherwise the company would bring every Inland Revenue Department case it had and would paralyse the department; it would paralyse that department's operation. Either the department was to change its '87 view that there was a sham or the firm would paralyse the department's operations."

Peters then raked over the old *NBR* article on "Wogistan", asking whether the Vasir in mythological Wogistan, who nipped the investigation in the bud, had an allegorical counterpart in New Zealand.

"Who was the Minister involved, and why did he do it?," he posed. The wily MP also turned up the heat on Inland Revenue Commissioner David Henry.

"For 4 years the Inland Revenue Department had the view that this was a sham. I want to know what happened to change the mind of the Commissioner of Inland Revenue. Why for 4 years did he assert that there had been a sham: fraudulent behaviour – in fact, criminal behaviour?

"If he could substantiate that allegation, why for 4 years did he keep up that assertion, then suddenly in December 1991 change his mind?"

Peters then questioned why, if the scheme wasn't a sham, investors in the partnership were being stung for tax payments by the IRD – a process he alleged began in 1987 – while partners in Russell McVeagh were *"able to obtain a no-prosecution arrangement".*

In a farcical follow-up the next day, the Prime Minister, Jim Bolger, asked all his Ministers to fess up and resign if they had in any way pressured the IRD over the film deal. None confessed.

Again, retaliation from Russell McVeagh and the named partners also came swiftly. While MP's can use parliamentary privilege to say anything they like in the House without fear of being sued, Winston Peters, they claimed, had made some comments at a news conference afterward. The lawfirm pounced, issuing writs claiming $4.25 million in damages on behalf of the firm, as well as Congreve, Ricketts and Carran.

There is an old piece of advice that hunters sometimes give each other – never corner a wounded animal. It would become a lesson that New Zealand's business and political establishment would learn at great cost over the next three years. Nothing drives a person to keep digging as much as the threat of a lawsuit hanging over them.

CHAPTER 2

The Citibank Diversion

*"In public discussion 'conspiracy' was made into a pejorative word,
so that those who dared to mention it were themselves "paranoid' or
'left wing', the contributors of 'theories' and 'scuttlebutt'. This was an
odd attitude. That conspiracies by definition provide predominantly
circumstantial evidence and are difficult to prove in a legal sense
does not make them less true or less likely to happen."*
– JOHN PILGER, *A SECRET COUNTRY*, 1989

THROUGHOUT THE PREVIOUS THREE months, the media pack circling around
Peters and his allegations had, in reality, little to go on. His revelations under
parliamentary privilege had so far caused a lot of smoke, but the flame was
noticeably absent.

While some had speculated on the source of the MP's information about
the Bank of New Zealand, Fay Richwhite and other corporate wheeling and
dealing, Peters hadn't revealed his sources and no one else had discovered
them. One of them, however, died in mysterious circumstances on
September 5, 1992. His links with the popular politician, prior to his death,
made him headline news.

In June 1992 a 26 year old second-hand computer dealer named Paul
White received a phone call. On the line was David Palmer, the owner of a
surplus goods company who'd just purchased a shipment of old furniture
from Citibank Auckland. Palmer told White that the shipment included
some old computer gear – he knew of White's interest in computers and
invited him around to look at it.

White offered $550 for the computer hardware, which included a box of
floppy disks. After making his purchase and shipping the gear to his office,
Paul White made a discovery: banking data was still present on the floppy
disks. Floppy disks are like cassette tapes. They magnetically record
information – in this case computer data – to be recalled at the touch of a
button. There were 90 of these disks,* discarded by Citibank during a
refurbishment of its office. Also included in the haul, 10 paper files of
banking information and correspondence.

It took White some days to work through the information, not all of it
could be read on his older computer system. But what he found astounded
him. He told friends he'd discovered information on the disks linking
politicians to big business.

Realising the significance of the data – at the very least it was
commercially sensitive client information belonging to Citibank – White

---

* White testified on oath to the High Court that he had taken possession of 90 disks.

hired a lawyer on July 2, 1992, to act as an intermediary with the bank.

High Court records show he asked the lawyer, Mark Blomkamp, *"to negotiate the return of the diskettes and literature to Citibank in return for a finder's fee or reward"*.

Earlier in the day White had phoned a colleague at Growth Computers in Sydney, Australia. As White wrote in his court affidavit, he told his friend about the Citibank diskettes, and the information on them.

"His immediate reaction was that of concern, as he was aware of similar situations in Australia and the aggressive tactics taken in some instances. He pointed out that contacting the bank itself might not be wise, they might become somewhat aggressive, and he suggested that I should contact the bank – but through a lawyer. He also brought to my attention a case in Australia of a somewhat similar occurrence, and underlined the fact that large multi-national corporations often use whatever means possible to protect themselves."

Mark Blomkamp took the case. A South African by birth, he'd grown up in New Zealand. Former schoolfriends described him as arrogant and tough, traits that would serve him well in the cutthroat world of law.

After meeting White, and getting a printout of the information on one disk to illustrate the general nature of the data, he contacted Citibank executive Mike Farland by phone five days later, on the morning of Tuesday, July 7. Farland later told the court what transpired.

"He spoke to me about a client of his whom he refused to name. He advised me that his client had recently purchased some computer hardware, which I now know had been sold through Office Clearance Company Ltd.

"Mark Blomkamp advised me that when his client took delivery of the hardware he discovered that there was also some software which contained confidential information from Citibank's records. Initially I acknowledged my gratitude to Mr Blomkamp for bringing this to my attention, and sought to make arrangements for the return of the information. At that time he advised me that his client required a 'gratuity' before the goods would be returned.

"He also advised me that if the gratuity was not paid, his client would be providing the confidential information to the Herald, National Business Review, or another 'interested' journalist."

Citibank Auckland normally followed the same data protection rules as other Citibank branches throughout the world. Diskettes with sensitive information requiring disposal would always be *"magnetically cleared and then physically destroyed – they would never be sold in any circumstances."*

A "stunned" Mike Farland says at that stage he didn't really believe the confidential information existed, so he asked Blomkamp to send him some examples. When that was done, Citibank realised there had indeed been a security breach, and bank officials agreed to meet Blomkamp on the Thursday morning.

Brushing off suggestions from Citibank executives and lawyers that he was trying to extort money, Mark Blomkamp said his client was seeking $50,000 as a finder's fee for the return of the information. To back up his position, he cited an Australian court decision involving the Brambles company, which was ordered to pay $62,000 to secure the return of computer data it had accidentally sold.

Citibank knew it had a major problem. Failure to pay the money asked meant the disks could fall into the hands of "investigative journalists", and yet the bank felt it was being blackmailed. Farland decided to stall for time, telling White's lawyer it would take seven days to get approval from the United States to pay the $50,000.

Blomkamp agreed to hold off for a week, and gave an assurance that he would instruct his client not to disseminate the disks or information for seven days. Despite repeated questioning, the lawyer refused to divulge his client's identity.

As soon as Blomkamp left, the bank went into overdrive. Phone calls to the Office Clearance Company's David Palmer revealed Paul White was the purchaser of the disks and computer gear. Armed with that information, Citibank's lawyers went to the High Court on July 10 seeking an injunction forcing White and Blomkamp to hand back the booty. In support of the application, Citibank NZ Vice-President Mike Farland told the court that the printouts Blomkamp had supplied him with contained *"very sensitive information"*, and, apart from the impact on the bank's relationship with its clients, *"I cannot begin to estimate what damage could also be done to the clients themselves by disclosure of this information."*

It is important to remember that Citibank was approaching the issue out of concern for its customers. The bank dealt largely with corporate clients who wouldn't appreciate having their financial transactions publicly scrutinised. The classification of such data as *"very sensitive"* applies to its nature as a commercial transaction, not to the legality of the deals which Citibank, as simply a banking facility, is unlikely to be aware of.

They didn't get an order for the immediate return of the disks, but Citibank did succeed in getting an injunction. Justice Tompkins instructed White, his solicitor and any associates not to disseminate, sell or otherwise deal with the software and information held on 10 document files. The battle lines had been drawn.

Citibank now moved onto the attack, seeking legal advice on whether it could lay criminal charges against White or his lawyer. The police files on the case show that on July 16, Citibank made a formal complaint to the Auckland police fraud squad, alleging theft by conversion and/or demanding with menaces.

The complaint followed discussions between Citibank lawyer, Sheila McCabe, and the Deputy Director of the Serious Fraud Office, Denis Pain, a former District Court Judge. According to McCabe's written comments she didn't tell Pain the identities of any of the parties involved, only the scenario.

"He advised us of the procedures to follow should Citibank wish the Serious Fraud Office to consider the case formally. However, he advised that it was unlikely that the Serious Fraud Office would be in a position to investigate and suggested that Citibank should contact the police," McCabe wrote in a letter to Citibank.

The fact that Citibank had even discussed the case with the Serious Fraud Office (SFO), however, seemed to impress the police when the bank contacted them. Fraud Squad Detective Sergeant Mark Churches later reported to his bosses *"Mr Payne [sic], a former District Court Judge, obviously considered that there was sufficient evidence to warrant a criminal investigation as he suggested that the matter be referred to the Police."*

The police swung into action. Despite the fact that civil proceedings between White and Citibank were now in train in the High Court to determine the ownership of the disks and the information, the police decided not to wait for the Court's decision on those points.

"Having read the various affidavits and correspondence supplied by Citibank, I was of the opinion," wrote Churches, *"that an offence had been committed and therefore that a criminal investigation should be undertaken."*

The Police Legal Section would later recommend: *"Neither WHITE nor BLOMKAMP have committed any criminal offence and the investigation into their actions should now cease,"* but by the time his name was cleared, Paul White would be dead. Instead, at this early stage in the police inquiry, it was full steam ahead. Detectives began making preparations to get search warrants.

Paul White, meanwhile, wasn't exactly taking it easy. Publicity in the news media since the injunction was granted had given his case a certain notoriety, coming as it did in the midst of Winston Peters' parliamentary crusade against alleged big business/political corruption. With 90 disks to peruse, some on different formats to his own computer, he sought help, and the man he went to was another computer dealer.

Chris Cotton, a quietly spoken and essentially private individual, made a small fortune from his computer business, a shop in downtown Auckland called Dr Floppy. Paul White told his parents that Cotton helped him examine the disks, that he saw the information.

Interviewed after White's death by Television New Zealand's *Holmes* programme, Cotton said he'd been told by White that the disks showed a US$50,000 payment by a multi-national company to a member of Parliament. The money, he said, had been deposited in the Bahamas. Discoveries like this frightened White.

"He just saw it as perhaps corruption," Cotton told TVNZ, before he added the only comment to date that comes close to an admission that he too saw the disks. Chris Cotton said White appeared to be an opportunistic businessman, and he didn't trust him until he had checked everything himself. It was Cotton who told Paul White to contact Winston Peters.

"I offered the name of Winston Peters, who had been using parliamentary privilege on other matters . . . I believe he spoke to Winston Peters."

In fact, they spoke on a number of occasions, in a number of places, and they were seen by a large number of people. It was an odd pairing. The popular politico with the penchant for conspiracy theories, and the 26 year old who was later likened by one police witness to the TV comedy character Mr Bean – an awkward, gangly and somewhat naive creation portrayed by Rowan Atkinson.

One rendezvous took place after dark in the office of Peters' lawyer, Auckland barrister Brian Henry, and they were worried they might have been under surveillance.

It's not yet known what was revealed in those first discussions. Winston Peters has never publicly admitted meeting Paul White, but it's clear that information was being passed to the MP. He and White were seen at Auckland pubs like the Chelsea Park Inn during the weekend of the National Party's annual conference in the city. The bar manager, Barry Collard, stumbled across Peters and White in a shadowy corner of the hotel closed off to the public. They were locked in discussion, speaking in hushed tones. The manager didn't know who White was at the time, but he instantly recognised the prominent visage of National's most outspoken MP.

Others saw Peters and White drinking at central city pubs like the Birdcage and nightclubs like the trendy "Grapes". Not all the eyes watching were friendly. Police files show Detective Sergeant Churches received a phone call on Wednesday, July 29, shortly before 4:00pm. The call was from Citibank's Mike Farland. Churches took a note of what he said.

"He stated that he had received information from an anonymous person that a Member of Parliament, namely Winston Peters, was interested in what information White was holding and they had dinner together at Hammerheads on Monday night."

The chances of that tip being the result of a random sighting by a member of the public are about as high as the chances of finding an ice cream in Hell, but I don't for a moment believe that Citibank had White under surveillance. The expense of keeping physical tabs on a person for two months is huge, and certainly not justified for such a minor matter as a squabble over the disks.

At $50 an hour, private investigators watching Paul White 24 hours a day would have clocked up nearly $76,000 per person in fees – far in excess of the $50,000 White was seeking from Citibank. It would be patently obvious to a 10 year old with a calculator, let alone a major bank, which one of those options would have been the most economic with the least hassle. No, if anyone was watching White, I'd place good money on the fact that it wasn't Citibank.

Despite the publicity over the court case, no media organisation had published Paul White's photograph at this stage. How would the "anonymous person" realise who Paul White was, to know that he was Winston Peters' dinner guest? How would that person know to contact Citibank? The issue is an important one, however, because Paul White told a number of people that he was being watched.

White's neighbours had noticed a white van with tinted windows often parked across the road from White's North Shore apartment. The van was seen a number of times in the weeks leading up to his death. A similar white van with tinted windows was parked outside journalist Fran O'Sullivan's central Auckland apartment during a 1993 meeting with a key source on the BNZ's dealings with Fay Richwhite. They took a note of the registration number, NE 9118, which came back on the motor registration computer as a white Toyota van belonging to a woman from Gore, in New Zealand's South Island, 1300 kilometres away.

Ann Meikle thought someone was pulling her leg when a journalist rang in October 1993 and asked where her van was?

"*It's right here on my front lawn. I'm looking at it out the window now. Why?*"

"*A white Toyota Hiace van with tinted windows and the registration number was seen in Auckland yesterday in suspicious circumstances. Its registration was NE9118,*" I explained.

"*Well, my van is a Hiace, and it is white, but it doesn't have tinted windows. Instead it's got bullbars and a mesh shield running around the bottom of the windscreen. But my registration is NE 9118, yes.*"

"*Is there any chance,*" I ventured, already knowing the answer, '*that your van was in Auckland yesterday?*"

"*No way. It's been here with me.*"

Apart from the obvious similarities between the van outside Paul White's place and the van outside O'Sullivan's, there's also another factor that tends to rule out private investigators in this instance. The registration plate on the van was obviously false, yet based on a real Toyota van. Using false number plates is illegal in New Zealand and difficult, unless, of course, you're with an agency of some kind that has a big budget and access to a number plate factory. The private security firms I know of may use vehicles registered to Acme Dynamite Company or other similar noms-de-plume, but they're still real registrations, not copies of someone else's.

Winston Peters says somebody phoned the computer dealer up just after he'd arranged to meet him, and the anonymous caller told White that meeting Peters would "*not be such a good idea*". Figments of White's paranoid imagination? Perhaps, but the circumstantial evidence tends to suggest otherwise.

On the night of Tuesday, July 21st, Paul White received a visitor. In fact the caller knocked at the door of a graphic design office below White's apartment. Designer Geoff Rowe answered it.

"*It was about 7:00pm, pouring with rain, and there was this guy standing there, dressed in a suit and coat. He wouldn't come in, but he asked to see Paul. When Paul came down the two of them went for a walk in the rain, I watched them go up the road.*

"*The guy never came back, but Paul did and he was shaking like a leaf. He said the guy claimed he was with the SIS, and he told Paul that if he didn't hand over the disks to them, there'd be a search warrant executed on the flat in two days time by the police.*"

At this point in the discussion White's landlord, architect Paul Higgins, returned to the office he shared with Rowe, and the story was briefly recounted for Higgins' benefit. He recalls White appeared "unnerved" at the course events were taking. White did not hand over the disks and, exactly two days later as predicted, the police marched in with search warrants.

Higgins and Rowe have little doubt that whoever White talked to in the rain that night, he must have been someone in a position of authority. The two men are adamant that they knew two days in advance exactly when the police were planning to raid – information that was only known to a handful of people.

Was it someone from the Security Intelligence Service, as claimed? If he wasn't SIS, who was he and how did he know the date that police would search White's apartment? It was unlikely to be a police officer, as they had no reason to impersonate an intelligence operative, and even less reason to blow their own operation by tipping off White in advance. Could it have been an SIS agent who'd followed White to his dinner with Winston Peters at Hammerheads restaurant the following week – the man who then made an anonymous phone call to Citibank warning executives there that White was meeting Peters.

Lieutenant General Don McIver, the Director of the SIS, reportedly laughed when the allegation that White met an SIS agent was first raised on television after the accident.

"I can't confirm anything. I don't know what you're talking about. No, I've got no idea what you're talking about. It's the first I've heard of it," McIver told *The Dominion.*

"I remember the story about the fellow who drove into the harbour bridge or had an accident, yeah. I know no more than that. I've read that in the newspapers."

But rumours of SIS involvement wouldn't die so easily. It was already known that White was meeting Winston Peters, and Peters' barrister, Brian Henry, believes his office was already under some kind of surveillance because of a high profile criminal trial he was working on involving executives of the collapsed investment company, Equiticorp. A computer disk relating to the case was stolen from Henry's office but there was no sign of a forced break-in. The only spare key had been in the care of a security firm. The key was discovered missing the morning after the disk was stolen.

It's my belief that the security company employed former SIS agents and soldiers from the elite Special Air Service – the army's commando force. The Justice Department's security licensing division did confirm a military connection but refused to comment further. Brian Henry didn't discover this claim until the start of 1993, the night before a crucial court hearing where Peters' was challenging the National Party over moves to expel him. That night, the lawyer decided to get his office swept for bugs – the eavesdropping kind not the ones with hordes of legs. Henry brought in a firm of private investigators.

They were partway through the procedure when a security guard burst into the office without knocking. Henry told the man to leave, and after the guard did so one of the security staff conducting the electronic sweep pulled himself back out from under a desk he'd been examining.

"You may as well forget about doing this sweep, because that guy's SIS! You'll never detect any bugs if they're behind it!"

The security man, himself a former intelligence operative, revealed that a large number of upper echelon security firms now have former spooks and troops on staff, and he knew personally the man behind this particular company. He also explained the "symbiotic" nature of relationships between former intelligence staff and their previous employers – favours done and returned on a regular basis; spy-catching back-scratching.

The next day, the day of the Peters vs National Party court hearing, staff in Henry's office saw what appeared to be a boom microphone or a large telephoto camera lens pointing at the office from a room in an adjacent hotel. Hotel staff put it down to a camera-happy tourist. Henry put it down to staff jitters. He hoped.

The intrusions didn't stop, however. On another occasion the computer system in Henry's office crashed. A computer expert brought in to troubleshoot discovered that the system had crashed during the previous weekend as well and, at the time, someone had been using it.

If computers "crash" while in use they usually automatically save the current file in use. The expert discovered one of these backup files, and Brian Henry instantly sensed that he was again the victim of espionage of some kind. The file that had been saved by the computer was a sensitive one relating to Winston Peters and his anti-corruption crusade. It had not been stored on the computer previously, but instead was on a floppy disk kept elsewhere in the office. Someone had inserted that disk into the computer and was viewing it when the system collapsed.

It was a "Goldilocks and the Three Bears" scenario – who's been sitting in my chair? Whoever the spy was, they obviously didn't realise they'd left electronic micro-footprints behind.

Paul White meanwhile was also continuing to attract unwelcome attention, or so he claimed. He was also starting to become unsettled. His father Peter recalls being phoned by Paul at 1:30am on the morning of July 24th, to be told of a mysterious phone call he'd received earlier in the evening.

"He stated he'd been told to meet a flight at Auckland airport, arriving at 4:20pm on the 24th. He said he was supposed to meet a representative from the Prime Minister's office* to be escorted to a meeting of importance on a national basis.

"Now I wrote this down verbatim as he talked to me. There were certain things when he rang he wanted me to write down. He was becoming paranoiac, there's no two ways about it, but he was very upset. The airport was fogbound the next day however, and the flight was cancelled."

Peter White was woken four days later by another early morning call – this one at 2:15am on the 28th of July. Paul talked of how he'd been to dinner with Winston Peters the previous evening – the 27th – at a restaurant down on Tamaki Drive named Hammerheads. It was the same restaurant

---

* White may have meant Prime Minister's Department, which has certain intelligence responsibilities.

where the pair were spotted by an anonymous informer, and obviously the same occasion.

"While we were speaking he was using his cellphone, and we were cut off. He went out and used a phone box down the road and rang me, and I said 'What the hell's going on?'

"He said 'well, during the conversation on the cellphone, someone came across the line and used one word: DESIST. That's all they said, 'desist'." The interruption had come during a discussion about dinner with the MP.* *"Winston had been blowing his top off about Paul flying to Wellington and presenting all these disks within parliamentary privilege, which wouldn't apply to Paul. But the way Paul got it, Winston was definitely inferring that Paul would have that privilege also. We're not quite that stupid!"*

Peter White continued reading through the notes he'd taken at the time of the conversation. *"What else have we got here? . . . Winston, SIS – I can't remember what the reference to SIS is about – barrister, phone tap, house under surveillance, great danger, phone number on receipt."* An interesting collection of subject headings.

When the self-proclaimed SIS agent told White on the 21st that his apartment was about to be searched, the decision to do so had only just been made by the police. Records show the officer heading the inquiry, Mark Churches, consulted police lawyers on the 18th over whether to apply for search warrants against White.

"The result of our discussion," wrote Churches in a report to his superiors, *"was that there was sufficient evidence to make application for a search warrant. The matter of the interim injunction (which had been granted at that time) was discussed and our advice was that the existence of the injunction was not a bar to obtaining a search warrant."*

On July 23rd, the search warrant was executed, citing theft as the alleged crime. Detectives didn't find the disks or files, but White did eventually tell them he'd stored the disks at Brambles Record Management using a security guard as his agent. There was a certain touch of irony to this: Brambles was the Australian company ordered to pay $62,000 after it accidentally sold some of its computer records at an auction. Police found the storage receipt, and began making their own enquiries.

The question of police powers in the face of a High Court civil injunction would later become a bone of contention, but for the police it was a minor hurdle at this stage.

Alarmed at the raid, White's new solicitor John Carter rang the police and spoke to Detective Sgt Churches' offsider, Peter Preece, telling him that the theft allegation simply would not stand up in a court of law, because White had ample evidence that he had paid for and purchased the computer disks openly and in good faith. Carter even sent witness affidavits to the

---

* There is no evidence of cellphone interference beyond the anecdote itself. It may be significant however that other evidence already exists that White was under surveillance of some kind that night, which brings White's claim further into the realms of possibility.

police to back up his point. His arguments fell on deaf ears.

Using the storage receipt for the disks, detectives tracked down Thomas Cotter, a security agent at New Zealand Guard Services. It was Cotter who had deposited the disks with Brambles on Paul White's behalf, on July 7th. He told police that he'd uplifted the disks only a few days later without White's knowledge. The reason? Newspaper publicity surrounding Citibank's injunction against White alerted Brambles to the possibility they were storing disputed property. They also felt it was an extortion attempt.

Cotter was contacted and asked to remove the disks. Amid much protest he did so, taking the black briefcase-full of trouble to another security company, Armourguard. Just after getting off the phone to Tom Cotter, Mark Churches got a phone call from Citibank's Mike Farland. He asked Farland what he should do about the disks.

"I advised him of the location of the disks and asked him to consult with Sheila McCabe [Citibank's solicitor] as to whether we should take possession of the property. He will get back to me on that," diarised Churches on July 29.

Presumably Citibank's answer to the police came through loud and clear; on August 6, 1992, detectives executed a search warrant on the Armourguard premises, once again listing "theft" as the reason for the warrant on the application to the District Court. Eighty-six of the computer floppy disks purchased and paid for by White were now in the hands of police, called in by Citibank to investigate a complaint of theft and demanding with menaces. White's lawyer was outraged.

"We would like to go on record and say that we are amazed that a second search warrant should have been executed by the Police against Mr White after I spoke to you by phone and after you had Mr White's affidavit to the High Court supplied to you," began Carter's letter to Peter Preece, in prose that almost sizzled on the page. *"Over the telephone you mentioned that you were still investigating the matter with particular regard to section 239 of the Crimes Act. That section says:*

Everyone is liable to imprisonment for a term not exceeding seven years who, with menaces, demands from any person, either for himself or for any other person, anything capable of being stolen, with intent to steal it.

"We understand that Citibank's solicitors may have referred you to the case of R V Hare. That was a case of theft by finding. That defendant had formed the intention of permanently depriving the true owner of the letter which he had found. That case is clearly irrelevant to the situation here where Mr White <u>bought</u> the disks and the literature. Applying section 239 to the facts we have here:

1. *Mr White has made no demand nor made any menaces.*
2. *Even if Citibank's view of the interview with Mr Blomkamp is correct then MrBlomkamp could only be said to have 'demanded' money. He was not demanding the disks and the literature or the information thereon. Nor could he possibly have any intent to steal the money he was asking for. He was there to endeavour to transact a commercial arrangement. Nor could he have any intent to steal the disks or the literature. His client at the time, Mr White, had already purchased that.*

"We hereby require you to return all the materials seized from Mr White to him in the same order and condition it was when uplifted under the search warrant. In the meantime we require your written undertaking that you will not allow any other persons access to it or the computer information stored on it."

John Carter's letter was written on August 11, 1992, five days after the disks had been seized. He didn't know it then, but the police had already opened the stable door and chased the horse out in relation to his final request. On August 7, the day after the seizure, Detective Sergeant Churches contacted Farland again, advising him that police had retrieved the disks under warrant.

"He requested permission to inspect the disks and make a copy of each one," Churches wrote. *"To that end he attended my office with a bank solicitor, Mark Fitzgerald, a computer technician whose name I do not recall, and Louise Perkins, solicitor from McElroy Milne [Citibank's lawyers]. I remained in their presence while the copying was completed.*

"Prior to any copying being done we discussed what the implications were in terms of the High Court injunction. It was generally considered that we would not be breaching the injunction because it applied to White and Blomkamp only."

As I reviewed this information on a wintry Sunday night, with torrential rain pelting on the roof and a crisp draught curling around my feet, I found myself continually coming back to what I believe are two very important points.

Firstly, the police have decided to grant Citibank – a litigant in a highly sensitive civil court case – access to evidence seized under a criminal warrant. The warrant had specified a criminal charge, theft, and – in my experience as a crime reporter – the disks would likely have played a key role in Paul White's defence had he come to trial on the matter. The disks, and the information on them, could have been crucial.

Regardless of the morality of the situation, regardless of whether you sympathise with Citibank or White, under any objective analysis of the criminal justice system, granting outsiders physical access to what is essentially the Queen's Evidence could be seen to prejudice the possibility of a fair trial on a serious criminal matter.* When the evidence is as delicate as a floppy computer disk, where files can be erased at the touch of a button, the need for justice to be seen to be even handed is even greater.

---

* Another high profile extortion case foundered in 1995, also in the wake of allegations that the police had lost evidence crucial to the defence. British private investigator Bryan Cooper was accused of trying to extort US$4 million from NZ millionaire Alexander van Heeren. In Court, Cooper's lawyers claimed that police had given a prosecution witness access to a file seized as evidence, a file that allegedly went missing for a number of weeks. Police documents produced in Court revealed police could not vouch for the integrity of the evidence. Weighing up this and a number of other factors, the Crown legal team abandoned the prosecution of Cooper four days into the preliminary hearing and, in a deal between Crown and Defence, Cooper walked free following conviction and a fine on a restricted weapon charge, and an admission of the intimidation charge with an apology to van Heeren.

This issue is just as important for Citibank's case as well. The last thing the bank would have wanted was seeing legal action founder on a technicality over the handling of evidence.

Secondly, Detective Sergeant Churches – at least on the face of the police file – did not contact the police legal section at this point over his obligations under the terms of the High Court injunction. Instead he appeared to take advice solely from the two Citibank lawyers present. I am certain that, had he been aware of the controversy that was to follow, Mark Churches would have clarified the police legal position before proceeding further. However, hindsight is always 20/20.

The fact of the matter is that Churches appears not to have made that call, and instead has relied on Citibank's advice. The breach – even if unintentional – of a High Court order, which was issued to preserve the status quo pending a full hearing to determine ownership of the disks and the information they contained, could amount to contempt of court, should a Judge or another party to the proceedings choose to take umbrage. Not only did police apparently fail to seek their own legal advice, they also failed to notify Paul White or his solicitor of the plan to let Citibank physically copy all the disks.

When 3 National News interviewed Auckland Police Superintendent Norman Stanhope on these points, he rode out the criticism.

"First of all, Citibank came into the police station at their request. We had to identify that the disks were in fact the property of Citibank. The only way they could actually identify them was, of course, by examining the disks in the first place, otherwise they could have been any disks."

While they could have been, the disks appear at this stage to have been clearly labelled, and for purposes of identification it would have been sufficient for police to simply call up each disk on screen, without letting the bank physically handle and copy the disks.

"As far as we are concerned the information on the disks is the property of Citibank, so I can see no objection to allowing the owner of the information to have a copy of it," Stanhope continued.

Again, another area where police had unilaterally pre-empted the High Court. At the time police decided the data belonged to Citibank, the High Court still had not issued a ruling on the question of ownership. Again, the potential for a contempt of court accusation to be levelled against police by White's lawyer.

3 National News continued to press, interviewer Chris Harrington asking whether police could guarantee that the disks weren't tampered with or even erased. Norman Stanhope didn't bat an eyelid.

"During the time that Citibank personnel were actually viewing the disks and copying the information we had two members of the CIB present at all times, so we're quite confident that it could not be tampered with, and I see no reason why in fact Citibank would want to tamper with it in the first place."

Harrington countered. "Well, allegedly this is sensitive information, so there possibly was a reason."

"It's information which Citibank have always held," Stanhope replied, looking slightly annoyed, *"has always been in their possession, so I don't see why they should suddenly want to tamper with it. They had no reason to tamper with it, and we had no reason to suspect they would tamper with it."*

Detective Sergeant Mark Churches appears to have reached similar justifications for letting the bank have copies of the data.

"The request by the bank seemed a reasonable one in the circumstances. It became apparent that there were literally hundreds of files contained on the disks and to go through each file would take hours. It also seemed to me to be entirely proper and appropriate for the bank to have a copy of the information contained on the disks, as it was after all their information to start with.

"It was not as if they were copying something which was foreign to them and I believe they had a right to know what it was Blomkamp and White were threatening to disclose to the media if the demand was not met. Any suggestion that files were deleted is spurious."

Again, the police decided that, despite High Court orders preventing the disclosure or use of any information from the Citibank files, White and Blomkamp still posed a threat to Citibank publicity-wise and this was a justification for supplying the bank with the disputed information.

Sensitive to the criticism levelled by White's lawyer, Mark Churches reported to his bosses about the discussion he'd had with John Carter.

"During the course of that conversation I raised the matter of Citibank taking a copy of the discs. I assumed that he [Carter] already was aware of this but obviously he was not. He assumes that this somehow confirms some sort of conspiracy between the bank and the police, namely myself, and refers to 'ulterior motive and an abuse of process'.

"Nothing could be further from the truth and my actions were, I believe, in the interests of natural justice and fairness. Citibank's complaint was treated and attended to no differently from that of any other dealt with by Fraud Squad.

"As with all complaints I deal with I take a dispassionate view of the complaint and evidence in support of same. It is my duty to investigate any complaint made if I have good cause to suspect an offence has been committed. Any suggestion to the contrary is spurious and patently untrue."

Churches' report to his superiors contained other interesting observations about the events of August 7, 1992. He indicated that there may not always have been two police officers in the room, and he also gave his explanation on why the copying didn't breach rules governing protection of evidence.

"Allowing Citibank to copy the disks did not breach Section 199(1) Summary Proceedings Act 1957 because the property remained in the custody of the police."

Custody, yes. In police control? It is open for debate whether police took sufficient care. There's evidence in the police files that control of the disks and the information they contained passed effectively, even if only temporarily, to Citibank. Firstly, police apparently failed to keep an accurate record of exactly who was in the room. Churches mentions Citibank's *"computer technician, whose name I do not recall"*. This "nameless" individual was the person who would physically handle the controversial computer disks on Citibank's behalf – the man who would operate the computers to copy the files. Police don't know who he was.

As any computer expert would tell you, the person who's pushing the keys is the person who's in control of the computer. In this case, it wasn't police officers pushing the keys.

Secondly, and even more importantly, the police closed ranks during parliamentary questioning on the issue from Winston Peters. Peters had asked, for example, how many laptops were used in the copying process, what was the capacity of those laptop computers, and were the files transferred into compressed or uncompressed state – computer terminology relating to the size of the files being transferred. The police answer was fulsome and technically correct.

"Two laptop computers were used to copy the disks seized by police under search warrant. One laptop computer had a 40 megabyte hard drive capacity and the other had a 20 megabyte hard drive capacity.

"Approximately 90% of the files were uncompressed when copied and the remaining 10% of files were in backup format in a compressed state and were uncompressed at a later time by Citibank officials. All the files were merely backup word processing files."

The answer, like the rest written by the police, certainly sounded authoritative, but the draft response to that question was nowhere near as complete. *"Two laptop computers were used,"* it stated. **"Further information will be obtained from Citibank."**

Four more parliamentary questions to police on the specifics of the copying process had the same draft answer. The most important question of all, which police should have been able to answer if they'd been in control of the copying process, was Question For Written Answer No. 434.

In it, Peters asked whether the disks were copied, and if so how were they copied, and what was the software used to copy them? The draft answer to Question 434: **"Further information coming from Citibank."** The answer to Question 434, by the time it got to Winston Peters, read: *"The disks seized by police were copied onto a combination of hard disks and floppy disks using two external disk drives. The software used to copy them was a standard DOS command called XCOPY which ensures all files, directories and sub-directories are copied."*

There was no reference to the fact that the information, which Peters had assumed was coming from police computer experts, was in fact being supplied by Citibank itself. The person sitting at the keyboard could equally have used a much more upmarket copying programme capable of erasing selected files as it went, the police may never have known. And yet when Peters also asked whether the police staff in attendance were *"competent in the knowledge of computer operations?,"* the response was reassuring: Yes.

None of this is to say that Citibank's nameless computer expert did erase or alter any files as he copied off the disks. There's no evidence to suggest that he did, and in truth the question of tampering with the evidence is irrelevant to my main point, which is this: it is fundamental to the New Zealand justice system that evidence in criminal prosecutions is kept, and seen to be kept, sacrosanct.

If a mere journalist can find fault with the process, imagine the field day a team of lawyers could have! It doesn't matter to a Court that you can swear on a Bible that nothing was altered – if you can't **prove** that the exhibits of evidence are OK then you've got big problems. The police files released under the Official Information Act show the police supervision of the copying process contained potential loopholes.

The questions that police could not answer without Citibank's help related to – in addition to those already outlined – the total megabyte size of all the White disks together, whether the files were copied onto hard or floppy disks by Citibank, and whether the disks were physically placed in Citibank's laptop computers – if so were they "write-protected" so as to prevent erasure.

In all of those questions, police could not provide the answers. In regard to the last question, police added that they didn't know whether the disks had been write-protected. This answer in itself indicates that police took no precautions to prevent the disks from being wiped.

Police also revealed that Citibank had brought in extra floppy disks to do the copying, but there's no indication in the police file that police kept a record of how many floppy disks were brought in, or whether any had surreptitiously been swapped with some of Paul White's disks. Again, there's no suggestion that Citibank did try to swap any, but police have no way of proving that they didn't – a dismal state of affairs if they'd had to stand up in court at a later date and testify to the integrity of the Queen's Evidence.

Still smarting over both raids, Paul White turned up the heat on Citibank. Lawyer John Carter filed a $350,000 lawsuit against the bank. The statement of claim said White had been *"exposed to adverse publicity, shame and indignity at being the subject of a search warrant, and was exposed to the possibility of conviction, based on false or misleading evidence,"* a claim based on legal opinion that the theft complaint wouldn't stack up in court because White had legitimately purchased the computer disks.

Already the alleged victim of anonymous phone calls, Paul White found his own position getting hotter at the same time. Close friend Richard Poore remembers being told of one call in particular, early in August.

"Yeah, that was really weird. He got a phone from someone who said 'If you ever get the money from this extortion thing that you're trying to pull, you won't live to spend it'. About a couple of days later he arrived home, got beaten up upstairs, once he got up the stairs, basically thrown down the stairs by two guys that quote 'were in ski masks'. I didn't see him after that, so I don't know if it was true or not."

In fact something did happen to White on that occasion. On the morning of August 9, White was dropped home by Winston Peters. Constable Callum Blair filed a police report on the events that followed.

"We were directed to the address to attend to a complaint of assault. On our

arrival the complainant White was spoken to. He was in a very intoxicated state and appeared to be mentally unstable," wrote Constable Blair. The reason for the suggestion of mental instability – White claimed he'd been nightclubbing with the country's most popular politician.

"White alleges that that evening he had been to several licensed premises with the politician Winston Peters. On being driven home by Peters, an unsighted person pulled his arm through his front door window as he attempted to enter his flat. He further stated that whilst walking up the interior stairs he was pulled by the leg, again by this unsighted person, causing him to knock his head."

In White's own words at the time: "I have been out with the right honourable Winston Peters. I am involved in a huge international political situation – look, here's all the media coverage. I drove home sober – I have got this drunk since all this happened – and I was opening my front door when somehow I was grabbed and shoved through the pane of glass."

Blair checked for evidence of a struggle.

"The window in the front door to the flat had been smashed consistent with the complainant's story. There was no apparent forced entry into the premises allowing the alleged offender to have been inside the premises as the complainant has outlined."

Constable Blair noted White had a small cut to his right wrist, but concluded that he was both drunk and mentally ill. His report notes that at one stage the police patrol considered taking him in to see "if in fact a S19 committal would be appropriate."

No one knows for sure what happened that night. White was sober enough to remember the incident, and it wasn't the only break-in. Four weeks later, on the night after Paul White died, landlord Paul Higgins recalls locking the internal door separating his office from White's hallway. It was a conscious and deliberate move – the previous evening he'd caught a man on the balcony of White's apartment. Feeling jittery, Higgins made certain that all the doors were locked.

The next morning, on Monday September 7, 1992, when he returned to the office, the door was unlocked and slightly ajar, but there was no sign of a forced entry anywhere in the building. Higgins immediately rang the police to report the break-in, but the police never came. In fact, they didn't turn up until the following day, Tuesday September 8.

Police had known since Saturday afternoon that $15,000 was missing, but they didn't turn up to search his flat until the Tuesday morning. They paid no attention to the landlord's claim of a break-in – apparently deciding that because there was no sign of forced entry, no break-in had taken place. Higgins still wonders whether New Zealand police have any experience at all in dealing with *professional* crime.

The police file on this last break-in was censored by police before being released under the Official Information Act.

CHAPTER 3

Working on Something Big

*"And it wasn't no way to carry on, it wasn't no way to live,
But he could put up with it for a little while,
he was working on something big."*
- TOM PETTY, THE WAITING, 1981

DURING AUGUST, 1992, events in the Paul White/Citibank spat were gathering momentum. The bank's injunction hearing was adjourned until September 4, and in the interim attempts had been made to settle. On July 23, the day of the first police raid, White had offered to return all the disks and literature to Citibank if legal action was dropped and his $5,000 legal bill paid. Citibank turned him down, coming back with a counter-offer of $2,500. It was White's turn to stick his nose in the air and sniff haughtily.

Detective Sergeant Mark Churches replied to John Carter's earlier complaint over the search warrants with a missive of his own on August 12. He declined to mention that police had already let Citibank view and copy the 86 seized disks, but did hint that such a situation was possible.

"I will give no undertaking to deny other interested parties access to the disks seized, or the information contained thereon."

Churches also included a dig at Carter's earlier letter requesting the immediate return of the disks.

"It is not my practice to take instructions from Counsel acting for a person who is under investigation by this office."

The jousting continued, Carter firing back by fax: *"We note that you will not take 'instructions' from us. That is entirely appropriate and we respect your position. We sincerely hope that you are not taking instructions from Citibank or its solicitor,"* wrote Carter, before taking a swing at the "undertaking" comment. *"You are no doubt aware of the High Court injunction. We presume therefore that the police will not allow third parties access to the information on the disks. Accordingly we construe your letter as meaning that you regard yourself free to provide Citibank access to the disks and the information. If we should take any other meaning from your letter, we would be pleased to know just exactly what that meaning is."*

John Carter was still unaware that Citibank had been given access five days earlier and, despite his hopes to the contrary, the police were asking Citibank for advice, an example being the July 29 conversation between Churches and Citibank's Mike Farland, where the police officer says he asked Farland *"to consult with Sheila McCabe [Citibank's solicitor] as to whether we should take possession of the property [disks stored by White]. He will get back to me on that,"* Churches had diarised.

White's disintegration, meanwhile, was accelerating. He began staying up all night in his apartment, and kept a loaded air pistol beside him. He slept during the days, comforted by the knowledge that five or six people were working in the various offices on the floor below him. His nocturnal activities included ringing people at all hours.

On the morning when White was allegedly thrown down his stairs by some intruders, his phone records show he rang Winston Peters at home 3 times. The first call went through at 3:04 am, 18 minutes before White rang the police to complain about the assault. That call lasted 4 minutes and 16 seconds.

After the police had left, White rang Peters again. Once at 4:32 am, and again at 4:40am – both calls lasted only 1 minute. Who he spoke to is not known; if Peters had in fact been with White only a couple of hours earlier, it is unlikely that he would have been home in Tauranga. Peters would be the beneficiary of another wake-up call on August 21, at 1:30am.

Living like a night owl, becoming manic and paranoid, White also developed a nervous twitch as the pressure took its toll. Something, or someone, was scaring the 26 year old, and friends noticed the changes.

"The house was a total mess. It was a real pigsty. He was drinking extremely heavily – he drank a lot of wine, and at one stage when he had money he had quite a nice little collection of wine bottles, but he sort of reverted to drinking four litre casks each night by the end of it. He was drinking a lot," remembers Richard Poore.

At the same time, he was furiously printing off paper copies of everything on the disks – he told friends it was his insurance policy.

"What he'd done, basically when he had the disks, was he'd run his printer overtime and just printed everything that was on them, because he wanted a hard copy of everything.

"Which is quite interesting because that's never turned up, has it?," said Poore. *"I mean he just had stacks and stacks of stuff."*

Other friends remember Paul claiming to have made several copies of the 90 disks, but all Richard Poore saw were the printouts. Some of the information, he says, related to Cook Islands tax dodges.

"The Cook Islands, yes, that was quite a thing in Paul's bonnet. Some of the stuff I saw, at this stage I wasn't really interested – he was just saying 'Hey, look what I've got', and we sort of read through it and I remember seeing some pretty huge figures and thinking 'My God, that's a lot of money.'

"The clients were all doing the same thing, channelling the money off in the endeavour not to pay tax. And that was around the time, you remember, the Government was saying 'We're going to clamp down on people that aren't paying tax!' "

But even to his mates, Paul White was the boy who cried wolf. Poore and others remember him as something of a maverick, craving attention and willing to showboat to get it. It was a personality trait White maintained to the end.

It is the final 24 hours of White's life that is, understandably, the most well documented period in police files. On the afternoon of September 4,

Citibank's injunction proceedings against White were coming to a close in the High Court at Auckland. It was clear the Judge would make a "King Solomon" ruling – the physical diskettes belonged to Paul White, but the information on them belonged to Citibank.

"The injunction against Mr White should remain in force," decided Justice Blanchard, *"pending further order of the Court. Citibank would appear to have an almost unanswerable case against Mr White, perhaps not for permanent return to them of the tapes [disks], but certainly for temporary return so that the confidential information can be recovered from them and erased from the tapes.*

"I am prepared to assume for present purposes that Mr White has legitimately become the owner of the tapes themselves, but I cannot see how he can establish any right to the confidential information which is on them."

During an afternoon recess in the case, however, there was a significant new development. Citibank already knew that 86 of the original 90 disks were in police custody, and it knew that the Court was likely to continue the injunction against White preventing further disclosure of the confidential information. In addition, Citibank had already turned down one offer by Paul White to return everything if the bank paid his $5,000 legal fee.

The bank had White's balls in the crusher, and they knew it, so why – with all this in mind – did Citibank turn around and offer to pay Paul White $15,000?

From the police files now available it appears the 26 year old computer broker played what he believed was a trump card, suddenly "discovering" two more computer disks that afternoon. His attorney Tracey McLeod – John Carter's offsider – passed that information on to Citibank's lawyer Sheila McCabe. While the legal beagles were doing battle in court, Citibank's Mike Farland made an out-of-court approach to Paul White. In return for the two disks and a bank security manual, and a promise to accept a permanent injunction preventing him from discussing the disks, Citibank would pay him $15,000.

White couldn't believe it. All of a sudden he was being offered money: six times more than Citibank had ever offered him before. Naturally enough, he accepted. Tracey McLeod remembers being surprised at the suddenness.

"When I came out of Court at about 4:00pm I was advised by White that an out-of-Court settlement had been reached. Mr White offered me a ride into town, we went to Citibank. I got the impression that the settlement was to take place at the Park Royal. They (officials of Citibank) pointed several times at the Park Royal."

The deal was done in a private lounge of the Park Royal Hotel in downtown Auckland, a room rented to Citibank from 3:30 pm to 4:30 pm.

During the subsequent police investigation of White's death, Mike Farland told detectives he'd sent a staff member, Michelle Lonerjan, down to a nearby branch of the National Bank at 3:30 pm with a bank cheque for $15,000. She was given two wads of cash, the first a sum of $10,000 and the second $5,000, all in $100 bills.

The cash-for-computer disks swap took place, according to Farland between 4:00pm and 10 past, and he noted Paul White was sober and reasonable, with a nervous twitch.

The agreement recording the settlement for posterity was drafted on the back of an envelope. It was dated September 4, and named the parties as Citibank N.A. and Citicorp New Zealand Ltd, and Paul White.

'It is hereby agreed between the parties that:

1. *Citibank shall pay Mr White $15,000 as a contribution to his legal costs and in full and final settlement of the counterclaim, today 4 September.*
2. *Mr White acknowledges that he or any related party has no proprietary interest in the information contained on the computer software.*
3. *The terms of this settlement shall remain confidential.*
4. *Any information that Mr White has or may obtain in the future that is relevant to the action against Citibank shall be returned forthwith.*
5. *Mr White shall not disseminate or discuss any of the information contained on the computer discs with any party."*

The signatories were Paul White and Michael Farland.

There are differing explanations on why Citibank suddenly decided to pay such a huge sum of money to settle. Citibank says it was to avoid further pointless legal expense, but it could equally have reached that decision much more cheaply back at the end of July when White offered to settle on the same terms for only $5,000.

White, naturally enough, had a different explanation for the bank's change of heart, telling the *New Zealand Herald* the evening before his death that the extra files, which he had deposited with his lawyer on Thursday evening, were a key factor in what he said was the out-of-court settlement.

White's associates remember him commenting that 95 percent of the matters he was concerned about were on those two disks. Even so, the two "new" disks only brought the total to 88, not the 90 Paul White talked about in his earlier affidavits. Where were the missing two disks he had referred to, and why was Citibank "satisfied" that no other disks were outstanding. Citibank's PR consultant, David Peach, offered one explanation.

"We have a written undertaking from Mr White that the two discs that he handed back to us on that Friday outside court were all that were in his hands," Peach told the *Herald.*

"He assured us they were the only ones outstanding." If such a written undertaking exists, it was certainly not handed to police investigating the death. In fact, evidence would emerge later that several disks were indeed outstanding, presumably much to the consternation of the bank.

Certainly there is no evidence that the paper printouts that Richard Poore saw were ever handed back, and the copies of the disks that White claims he'd made were never found either.

White's movements after receiving the cash were very well documented. He was back at his lawyer's office by 5:00pm to crack open the champagne. It appears certain that he did not bank any of the cash that afternoon, telling his lawyers he *"wanted to hold the cash until Monday,"* when he would come back and pay his $10,000 legal bill. Tracey McLeod told detectives she didn't think White had been to a bank.

"Given the time sequence he wouldn't have had time and the banks would have been closed."

There is some confusion over his movements between 6:00 pm and 8:00 pm. Both McLeod and John Carter say White stayed at their office for several hours, Carter saying White was there at least up to 7:00 pm when the lawyer went home, and McLeod adding she was with him until around 8:30 pm.

White must, however, have slipped out briefly. Centra Hotel Assistant Manager Carl Jones was on duty that Friday evening, and told police he remembers seeing White around 6:00 pm.

"A man there wanted someone in authority to count some money. The man was by himself. He was fairly scruffily dressed with beige sports trousers and an off-white business shirt with the shirt tail hanging out. He said he'd just come from a court case where he'd won some money and he wanted it counted."

Jones remembers counting the bigger of the two bundles White had with him. It was $10,000, and he wrote the figure on the back of his business card and signed it before giving the money and the card back to White. The computer dealer said he had $16,000, and he was planning to go out and spend it.

Other hotel employees also recall seeing White there at the same time, from 6:00pm to 7:00pm, and one, Kelly Enoko, told police she'd first seen him there between 4:00pm and 5:00pm. They all remembered White as arrogant, and getting drunker as the night wore on.

Some time after 8:00pm he was joined by a friend, Alan Wisnewsky. White had earlier phoned Wisnewsky from the lawyers' office, around 4:00pm. *"At that stage he confirmed he had bought a bottle of champagne and was enjoying a few drinks with his lawyer."*

White phoned him again later, and they arranged to meet at the Centra Hotel. Wisnewsky says he arrived there around 8:10pm. White was on the phone but, apparently relishing his role as the big-noting big-spender, nonchalantly flipped open his briefcase – giving his buddy an eyeful of the loot.

"I was really shocked. Paul just left the briefcase open while he carried on talking. I felt uncomfortable with it open so I shut the briefcase."

When White got off the phone, they went to the bar.

"He said to me that was not all the cash he had," Wisnewsky later told police.

"He confirmed that he had banked $5,000 with the ASB hole-in-the-wall, I think between the time he left the lawyer's office and arriving at the Centra. He made a joke that he hoped it didn't get robbed.

"He said to me that there are similar bundles of cash at different locations. About an hour later, when Sharon had arrived, he told me how much he'd actually got. He wrote it down on a piece of paper and showed me. It said $75,000."

It would appear at this stage that Paul White was exaggerating to impress his friends. There is no evidence in the police files to suggest that he received $75,000. Staff at the National Bank reported cashing a $15,000 cheque for Citibank, and in earlier conversations with his lawyers and Carl Jones he hadn't mentioned the larger figure.

Wisnewsky's partner, Sharon Young, arrived at the Centra about 9:30 pm to join the celebrations. She immediately noticed two men standing near Paul and Alan as they talked. When White was called away to talk to TVNZ producer Phil Corkery, one of the men came over to Alan and Sharon and *"asked me what I was drinking, which I thought was a bit strange, I told him a martini and left it at that, but they remained there,"* Young stated to police.

When White and the producer returned they asked the two men to move away, but according to Young they stayed close.

At around 10:20 pm, White met another reporter, Tony Berends from the *Herald*. Berends would later describe how White boasted of the settlement *"that has left me a wealthy man."* The idea that within 11 hours White would be dead, and the money missing, was the farthest thing from their minds.

Berends left the hotel after White fell onto a glass table in the hotel lobby, smashing a number of cups in the process. Whether drunk with the elixir of success or just plain alcohol remains unclear – the effect was the same.

"I heard a loud crash, sounded like glass breaking, and I saw Paul sprawled on the floor," Sharon Young wrote in her police statement. In the interim she noted, the two men who'd been hanging around had slipped away.

Paul White meanwhile had picked himself up off the floor and began rearranging his clothes, asking a waiter for a glass of soda to help remove bloodstains on his shirt.

Carl Jones told police that while White didn't appear "falling down drunk," he was beginning to become a nuisance, and Jones told his staff not to serve him any more alcohol. This only provoked White, who then threw $4,000 on the bar with the words *"Will that do?"* An argument began, with White at one point asking Jones *"Don't you know who I am?"*

Without waiting for an answer, and obviously annoyed at the display, one man in a group at the end of the bar piped up – *"Yeah, we know who you are, you're a fuckwit!"* To the accompanying laughter Paul White, Sharon Young and Alan Wisnewsky left the hotel. The barman told police the incident attracted more than a passing interest from the group at the bar.

"One of the group of two men and two women said 'We should follow him out and roll him for his money', in a joking manner." They didn't follow him out, but many of the hotel staff noted White had made no secret of the fact he was carrying a large amount of cash, and many people knew about it.

"His whole attitude was one of being someone of importance, and he came across as arrogant and impolite," wrote one bartender, while a waitress was struck by his nervous tic.

"To me he didn't appear to be all there. He had a twitch which always caused his head to twitch back and forth, which was pretty distracting and really made him stand out. He gave me the impression of a person who I wouldn't trust as far as I could throw him. I don't know why, he just did."

It was a similar story at other establishments White visited that night. He and his friends arrived at the Regent Hotel just after 11:00 pm, but managed to secure a meal in the brasserie. The party ended when White knocked a glass of red wine over Sharon Young – she and her partner left.

Curiously, someone may have followed White to the Regent. Hotel security staff told detectives that the drivers of two different cars had asked if a "weedy" guy with a briefcase had come into the hotel. Wisnewsky and Young had driven to the Regent with White, and they had no reason to ask security if he'd arrived yet. One of the questioners was driving a white Honda Prelude. The other, a little later, was driving a red Honda Civic, and used exactly the same question: *"Has a weedy guy with a briefcase come into the hotel?".*

There is another curious factor involving White at the Regent. A waitress at the Regent Brasserie said White had been dining not just with Wisnewsky and Young, but in the company of two other men also.

Later White left the Regent, arriving at Grapes Nightclub sometime after 1:00am to continue his celebrations. Nightclub manager Sean Peters remembers talking to White on several occasions, and he told police that the computer dealer *"wasn't, or didn't appear drunk, when he came in [to Peters' office]. He was coherent and knew what he was about."*

White spoke to a number of staff, including chef Simon Tabuteau, telling him he'd won a court case.

"This is the first instalment," White allegedly boasted, *"I've got 3 or 4 more lots coming."*

When Tabuteau pressed the point, White told him each of the instalments would be worth $15,000. It was during this time that White caught the attention of an off-duty bouncer. The bouncer and White left sometime between 3:00am and 4:00am, heading for the Customhouse Bar. While they were there, Paul White made a comment about how the lights above the bar were looking strange. Moving on, they arrived at the Galatos Bar a short time later. White dropped some cash on the floor.

"It was embarrassing," the bouncer told police later. *"Someone asked me 'where was that from?'. I assumed he was talking about the money and I said 'I wouldn't have a clue'. I didn't like the idea of getting into a conversation about it with anybody. I suppose the situation was nerve wracking."*

After putting the loot back in a plastic bag, White and his new friend left the bar. They headed back to Grapes, arriving around 4:15am. Theoretically. Once again confusion arises among police witnesses about the exact whereabouts of Mr Paul Gordon Edward White. One staff member interviewed by police says he left Grapes at 4:15am and White was still inside at the time having drinks with other staff. Other staff report White and the bouncer arriving back around 4:30am.

Whatever the exact time, all witnesses agree that the bouncer was out in the carpark trying to convince Paul White not to drive himself home. A waitress leaving the club to go home was watching the discussion.

"I remember seeing two guys walk up and stand behind them, a few paces away, for a minute or so," she told police. *"I turned away for about three minutes*

and when I looked back they had gone. I had no idea where they went."

It was just a passing observation, but it echoed Sharon Young's earlier comment about two men standing close to White at the Centra Hotel several hours earlier.

One police witness says he saw Paul drag a wad of money from one of his pockets and wave it around at one point in the carpark, this would be the last documented sighting of a significant amount of cash on White. Eventually, however, sometime just before 5:00am, only White and the bouncer were left.

Within half an hour Paul White would be deep in a coma and dying. His money would be missing. The last thing he saw was probably a concrete wall.

CHAPTER 4

Just Another Wasted Youth?

"Meier gestured at the equipment line. 'The beauty of controlling the brakes is that, if Horsley survives, he will remember perfectly well that the car deliberately disobeyed the steering wheel. He will be mystified, of course, but not suspicious. Remember, also, that the gear must be as easy as possible to remove quietly and by torchlight tomorrow night.' "
- SIR RANULPH FIENNES, *THE FEATHER MEN*, 1991

MONDAY, SEPTEMBER 7, was a great day. One of those classic cloudless spring days that Auckland can turn on so easily. The morning *Herald*, devoured over a cup of hot coffee, carried a front page wrap-up of White's accident. Headlined **"Computer disc row man dies"**, the article touched on Paul White's legal battle with Citibank, the Friday evening payout and the subsequent crash. It also contained the first public suggestion that the $15,000 cash settlement was missing.

At *3 National News* my specialty was crime reporting, and for that I normally teamed up with cameraman Peter Stones. On any other day we would have been assigned the Citibank story, but we had already been working for several days on a 60 year old murder mystery involving an old rest home matron named Elspeth Kerr, aka the Granny Killer.

Kerr had murdered a number of her elderly patients by slowly poisoning them to death back in the 1920's and 30's. Now workers on a building site on Auckland's North Shore had discovered a skeleton under the foundations of a house being removed. It turned out the house had been built on a property once owned by Kerr.

Residents in earlier years had reported finding what they thought were "monkey skeletons" while gardening. In fact Elspeth Kerr was an abortionist and may also have killed several young children. A big hunt was on for more bodies.

Faced with an easy day in the sun watching cops do hard labour on a building site, or chasing around trying to reconstruct the final hours of an obscure computer dealer, Stones and I chose to stay with the former, a story we were looking at turning into a longer current affairs piece. As history now teaches us, it was the wrong choice.

Instead, reporter Janet Wilson hit the road on the White story. The only new twist to emerge by broadcast time was a vague hint from computer industry sources that the discs might have contained some "devastating" information.

Understandably, Citibank was not impressed at the allegation, and rang TV3 to complain. The following morning, however, the bank had even more to complain about. A banner headline across the *Herald's* front page read:

"**Missing cash, burglaries add to death puzzle**". The first paragraph was even more informative. *"An early morning burglary has increased the mystery surrounding the death of a Birkenhead computer broker involved in a dispute over confidential files."*

The article went on to reveal White's apartment had been broken into professionally the day after his death, the latest in an apparent string of break-ins. It also told of White's claim the night he died that he'd made extra copies of the discs and hidden them. Also of interest: *"Police traffic officers are making separate inquiries into the accident but it is understood that Mr White's blood alcohol level was not high when he was tested after the crash."*

News producers Steve Bloxham and John Hale were getting twitchy; they wanted 3 *National News* to climb into the story in a big way. Peter Stones and I were called back from skeleton duties to cover the country's newest mystery death.

It quickly became apparent, from talking to Paul White's friends and neighbours, that there was a lot more to White's life and death than had so far appeared in print. Among the first people we tracked down was Mark Blomkamp, holidaying in Queenstown with his wife, at the Blue Peaks Lodge.

Blomkamp wasn't keen to hear from us, but a camera crew we sent to his hotel asked him whether, given the disappearance of the money, the accident might in fact have been "invoked". The lawyer's cagey response: *"You might well think that, but I could not possibly comment."*

It was a lead, of sorts. When Stones and I questioned White's associates, even more bizarre information began to emerge. Real estate agents working in an office below his apartment said Paul had claimed to have found dealings on the discs involving the BNZ and other big New Zealand corporates.

White's former associates also remembered him talking of a US$50,000 payment to another senior National MP via an account at Citibank Nassau, in the Bahamas.

In what would later emerge as a significant lead, they recalled Paul White talking also of a secret deal involving a New Zealand company and a Middle Eastern country, they thought he mentioned Saudi Arabia. They talked too of a mysterious white van with dark windows that had been hanging around outside for the past few weeks.

Paul White claimed to have evidence of money laundering, and we discovered he'd been having regular meetings with rebel MP Winston Peters. It was heady stuff.

As we worked our way through the building we came to architect Paul Higgins and graphic designer Geoff Rowe, who'd witnessed White's meeting with an alleged SIS agent.

At midday, we discovered White's funeral was being held that afternoon in Whangarei, nearly two hours' drive to the north. We booted it. In the world of television news speed is of the essence and, when it gets down to the wire, no expense is spared to get the story to air. TV3 was taking no chances with this story – the network flew a charter plane to Whangarei and had it standby on the runway so I could fly back, rather than drive, with the video tape of the funeral.

Journalists hate covering funerals, or at least this one does. It's a popular misconception, fostered no doubt by TV soaps like *Shortland Street* or *The Young Doctors*, that journalists vie for a place on the food chain with creatures like vultures or the rare Outer Mongolian Yak-eating Buzzard. It's not true: the buzzards are much more sophisticated.

In reality, the media only covers funerals where there is an important public interest element. In a case such as this, where the deceased may have had vital information, it is important not only to cover the funeral, but to assess whether the family had anything of significance that they might wish to say.

Peter and Maureen White, Paul's parents, had, as anyone would expect, been hit very hard by the loss of their 26 year old son. No parent wants to outlive a child, and where the loss is sudden and violent it is especially hard to take.

As they buried their little boy, the couple were privately convinced he had been murdered. Bravely, Peter White faced the camera.

"My son was a martyr for what he was trying to do, and there's people in Auckland who'll tell you so. If anybody knows anything, for God's sake get in touch with the police."

Looking into his haunted eyes I could feel the keen, raw edge of his grief, but I could also sense Peter White was sizing me up for another reason. I knew that we would talk again.

As Maureen, weeping uncontrollably, was led away to a waiting car, I found myself wondering about the possible role of the Security Intelligence Service in this man's death. After all that Winston Peters had been alleging about big business and political links; on a chilly grey afternoon, in a Whangarei graveyard, I really began for the first time to give it serious consideration. It was Stones who brought me back to reality, in his own inimitable way.

"C'mon ya tosser, you've got a plane to catch."

* * *

WHEN THE ITEM WENT to air that night, it was like a mini nuclear explosion. Within the hour our report that White had possibly met SIS agents was all over the radio networks, along with Mark Blomkamp's veiled suggestion that someone might have found the information serious enough to kill for. Winston Peters was reportedly refusing to comment on TV3's claims that he'd been meeting Paul White.

Within two hours Police Minister John Banks had lent his voice to the growing chorus of people who wanted a more in-depth investigation of White's death.

Up to this point police had been treating the matter purely as a 1-V, policespeak for a traffic accident. As an indicator of the significance of

White's death on a scale of 1 to 10, the cops had placed their most junior investigators on the case. It was being handled by the Enquiry Office, a branch of the uniform section rather than the more experienced CIB Crime Squad, or even CIB's General Squad.

John Banks, true to his "shoot first, ask questions later" policy, pushed all the right buttons. He told Radio New Zealand the allegations were so serious that he would boost the investigation and provide whatever resource was necessary to get at the facts.

Wellington's *Dominion* newspaper led with the new development the next morning, its headline screaming **"Banks asks for probe into death mystery"**.

"Police Minister John Banks last night asked police to investigate allegations that the death of Birkenhead computer broker Paul White may have been linked to information he gleaned from a bank's computer disks," wrote journalists Phil Taylor and Corinne Ambler.

"Mr Banks said the allegations were serious and he had asked police to make the investigation a high priority."

In Auckland too the pressure was piling on, with the normally conservative *New Zealand Herald* carrying a front page article also revealing possible Security Intelligence Service connections to the case and following up on the Peters meetings.

It was a stressed out Detective Senior Sergeant Graham Bell who fronted up that morning for the daily police media briefing in Auckland. Bell is an affable cop, quick to share a story over a beer and popular with the media. His nickname is "Ding". On this particular morning though, he looked anything but affable. Facing him were three television crews and journalists from all the radio stations and newspapers.

"Let me say from the outset," began Bell, *"that as to the allegations of the involvement of the SIS, we've referred that to Police National Headquarters and there's discussion taking place this morning between Police HQ personnel and the SIS to see whether there's been any involvement or interest from the SIS. The initial indication as I understand it is that the SIS don't have any interest in the man."*

Indeed, the *Dominion* had already carried SIS director, Lieutenant-General Don McIver's, response to the claims. His first comment: *"Who's Paul White? I don't know anything about him"*, and he broke into laughter when asked if the SIS had visited White at his apartment.

"I can't confirm anything, I don't know what you're talking about. No, I've got no idea what you're talking about, it's the first I've heard of it."

McIver later conceded that he did *"remember the story about the fellow who drove into the harbour bridge or had an accident, yeah. I know no more than that. I've read that in the newspapers."*

As to the confidentiality of the information on the Citibank discs, the SIS Director said that unless the data affected national security, he wouldn't regard it as confidential.

But back at Bell's news conference, the questions were flying thick and fast.

"John Banks has asked police to look into this whole allegation that he may

have been murdered because of what was on the tapes," interjected one reporter.

"I've been in touch with the Minister's office this morning," shot back Bell, eyes glittering angrily, "Mr Banks has asked me to reiterate that he has not ordered any police inquiry into any aspect of this affair. What we have here is a motor accident, and the disappearance of a sum of money."

There was a moment's stunned silence at this sudden about-face by the Police Minister.

"He told us," said a genuinely confused-looking Radio New Zealand reporter, his voice beginning to squeak in disbelief, "and we've got him on tape, saying he wants this inquiry. John Banks!"

"Well," countered Bell, "he's asked, through Superintendent Fitzharris, he has reiterated that he hasn't directed that any inquiry take place. He's obviously satisfied that the matters concerning police are being investigated: that is, the motor accident and the possible disappearance of a sum of money."

Under further pressure, Bell phoned Superintendent Paul Fitzharris, the Police Minister's personal adviser in the Beehive.

"I've got all the media gathered here before me at the moment. The problem is, they're all quite happy to accept that police are dealing with a motor accident and the disappearance of a bit of money, but they are more concerned with the contents of these bloody floppy discs, which they believe – and they've got it from all sorts of bloody sources – contained information on payments into Ministers' bank accounts and politicians' bank accounts and various fraudulent and scurrilous activities involving famous people."

Then Bell dropped a clanger on Fitzharris, and judging from his expression he knew it.

"So what's the response from the SIS? Yes, no, they can't hear you."

When he got off the phone, Ding Bell tried to set things straight.

"I said earlier that the indications were that the SIS wasn't interested in him. Well, I'm not allowed to say that, because the SIS want to make their own report to the Prime Minister. But let me say this:

"The police at headquarters level have been in touch with the director of the SIS. who has advised us that he will be reporting to the Prime Minister at midday, and that any comment as to the involvement or otherwise of the SIS should come from the Prime Minister.

"As to the tapes [disks] , let me summarise this whole business as follows: The police are investigating a motor accident. It appears to be a straightforward fatal motor accident with no foul play indicated. Ancillary to that we are investigating the possible disappearance of a sum of money believed to be somewhere in the vicinity of 10-15 thousand dollars.

"We can confirm that we did execute search warrants to recover some floppy disks from Mr White in July and August. That was as a result of a theft complaint made by Citibank in respect of the disks themselves, not the content of the disks.

"Any intrigue in this whole business lies in the contents of the tapes, or appears to. The police position is that they are none of our business. If you want to know what's in the tapes you go and ask Citibank. If there are allegations of foul play indicated in those tapes, then that should be reported or referred to the appropriate law enforcement authority."

I decided to fire my last salvo across Ding's bows, feeling guilty as I did so because I knew he was merely the muggins who drew the short straw this morning.

"The allegation from those who knew Paul White is that he was possibly murdered in an incident made to look like an accident because of what was on those disks." I paused, partly from exasperation and partly for dramatic effect. "How can police now not have an interest in those disks?"

"Because there is no indication in the circumstances of the accident of foul play. We have witnesses, or a witness, who saw what happened. We have a number of witnesses who saw the condition of Mr White before he drove his car. I've already indicated that he'd been drinking during the night, and we haven't yet received confirmation of the blood alcohol level, but I think it's fair to say that it would probably be in excess of the legal limit," sighed Bell, wishing at this point that he'd called in sick all week.

In fact, as police files confirm, there were actually no witnesses to the impact of White's car with the motorway bridge abutment. The car immediately behind White's was being driven by the bouncer who – in a statement to the police – said he had followed White's car from the nightclub. This witness gave police three different versions of what happened.

In version one, a statement taken by police at 3:02pm on Tuesday September 8, the bouncer indicated he'd come across an isolated wreck, about 25 minutes after last seeing Paul at Grapes The bouncer said he'd been for a drink at another pub in the interim. He was driving home in his Honda Integra.

"When I got to the bridge on-ramp I saw a car sitting in the middle of the road, steaming. As I arrived a van pulled up behind me. We arrived at the same time. The occupant of this van was an Armourguard officer in uniform.

"We both went over to the car. I saw the occupant lying partly in the car and partly on the road. I realised it was Paul. I think the Armourguard man felt for his pulse, I heard him gurgling. At no stage did I touch him."

Version two was taken by police the following day, nearly eight hours after Graham Bell's news conference. The time on the statement was 5:04pm. Again, after leaving White at the nightclub the bouncer said he'd been to another pub before finally leaving for home.

"As I went past Grapes I looked over to see if Paul's car was there. It wasn't. I kept going down the hill, I turned right into Halsey Street and then left into Fanshawe Street. I can't remember any cars on the road at all. I can't remember any cars in front of me or any behind me. To be honest, I'd had a few to drink.

"As I went along Fanshawe St the lights were green to cross Beaumont St and go onto the motorway. As I came around from the traffic lights I saw the car in the middle of the road. I basically saw a smashed car in the middle of the road, steaming. It was at rest when I first saw it. It's hard to say how long it had been there.

"It could have happened right there and then, or it could have happened half an hour ago, but probably not that long – maybe a couple of minutes. There was a lot of steam coming out of it. Coming across the scene of an accident you freak a bit. It was a red car, the make was unrecognisable.

"The on-ramp where the car was is roughly two lanes wide. The car was in the middle of the road. I pulled up and parked to the left of the accident. I got out and had to walk about a lane and a half across to the wrecked car. Straightaway after I pulled up the Armourguard guy pulled up. He pulled up behind somewhere.

"I went over to the wrecked car. It was side on to the lane and the driver's door was facing back down towards the city. When I got out of my car it crossed my mind that it might be Paul's car. When I got over to the car I recognised him. The Armourguard guy called out to me when I got out of my car and he was practically behind when I got up to Paul."

Version 3 contains major changes to the previous two, and was recorded by police later the same Wednesday evening, at 8:17 pm. In this third and definitive version, the bouncer says his previous two statements were untrue in some places.

"I didn't go to the Terrace Bar, I stayed with Paul at the club in the carpark. I was trying to talk to him about not driving but he wouldn't listen to me. I asked him for his keys, he wouldn't let me have them.

"He reversed out of the parking space and then drove out onto the road. I decided to follow him, I was going over the bridge as well. He was driving and swerving because he had too much to drink. It was quite obvious from his driving that he had been drinking.

"As we went along Fanshawe Street I was behind him. I would have been four or five car lengths behind him. The way he was driving I didn't want to get too close. As we approached the lights across Beaumont St they were green. He accelerated off Fanshawe Street, he was accelerating on to the on-ramp.

"The on-ramp goes to the right, I lost sight of him for a moment. As I came around the corner I saw the car in the air just after it hit the wall. I pulled over and stopped. Everything that happened after that was as I have told you in my last statement.

"The only things that were untrue in the previous statement were about me going to the Terrace Bar and about me saying I didn't see the accident when I did. Everything else is true."

Hardly the world's most reliable witness. And again, at the crucial point – that of impact – the bouncer didn't see what happened.

The second police witness was an Armourguard officer, Dennis Manson, driving home after working the nightshift. Manson had been with the security firm a relatively short time – he'd spent most of his career in the Armed Forces, serving as a medic in the Vietnam War. Manson's statement was also taken on Wednesday, at 11:34 am – two hours after the news conference.

"I saw a red car go through a green light at the Beaumont Street intersection. It then began to accelerate at high speed. He then began to veer to the right. I wondered where he was going as he continued to veer to the right. I then lost sight *of him as I went through the bend. The red car when I lost sight of him would have been no more than 6-7 car lengths ahead of me.*

"There was a white car ahead of me but behind the red car as the red car went through the lights. The white car was in the left lane. It did not accelerate off at high speed like the red car.

"The white car was about 3-4 car lengths behind the red car as it went through the intersection and the driver would have seen the accident happen.

"As I rounded the bend I saw darkness, thinking that the driver of the red car may have turned his lights off. I then saw two red lights about 10 feet in the air. I thought that a car had come off the viaduct. I then applied the brakes and noticed the white car in front of me had applied his brakes also. I noticed then that the red car had crashed into the wall of the bridge.

"I parked my vehicle on the left hand side of the road directly opposite the crash. The driver of the white car parked his car about 20 metres further up the road on the left hand side."

In a brief comment to police earlier in the week, Manson had added the rider — *"To the best of my knowledge, no other vehicle was involved."*

Two witnesses, both of whom had failed to see the actual moment of impact, despite the fact that both were accelerating on a motorway on-ramp almost right behind Paul White's vehicle. On a wet road, in the dark, what kind of evasive action would the two drivers have had to take, especially as White's car had hit the wall and literally stopped dead, right in front of them?

Paul Owen-Lowe, a TV3 news producer, visited the crash site a few days later. He found long skid marks down the motorway and ending at the abutment that White's car hit. Neither of the witnesses reported seeing White applying the brakes. Instead, Dennis Manson believes White was accelerating heavily at the time. Both witnesses claimed to have lost sight of White's Nissan Pulsar at exactly the same moment, even though they were several car lengths apart.

In fact the police were having trouble with other witness accounts of what happened as well. A motorbike rider, Michael Owen, was third on the scene, but says the only other person there was the Armourguard driver, who was beside the wreck, and a gold Trans-Am just pulling up on the left. Manson sent him back to a nearby service station to call an ambulance, and when he returned Owen says he parked behind a white car which had pulled up 10 metres behind the crash.

Dennis Manson stated to police that the bouncer's white Honda had been parked 20 metres in front of the crash, while the bouncer himself says he pulled up and only had to walk across one and a half lanes of the road to reach the wreck. Manson, a combat medic in the Vietnam War, says he felt for White's pulse but couldn't find one and assumed he was dead. He later told 3 *National News* he may have *"looked in the wrong place"* for the pulse, in the heat of the moment.

Confusion appears to have reigned also within the emergency services that attended. Police Traffic Senior Sergeant William Steedman remembers going "*around to the passenger's door which had sprung open at the time of the accident. It was open far enough for me to put my body in.*"

But Traffic Officer Kieran McGonigle remembers it differently.

"*The Senior was trying to get in the passenger's side but the door was jammed, so he asked one of the fire guys for a crowbar. He used it to open the door. He started looking through some of the documents on the back seat to get a name for the driver.*"

Confused? Then let firefighter Roy Breeze add his statement to the mix.

"*After checking for petrol leaks and things around the car I went around to the passenger side. I found the door easy to open, so I don't think it was secured closed.*

"*I have worked on the rescue tender for 7 years and in that time have attended a lot of accidents, and so that's why I can clearly remember that the door was easy to open and wasn't jammed locked, closed, like they normally are.*"

None of this serves to indicate anything untoward took place, but what it does illustrate – as is well known to anyone who investigates accidents or crimes – is that, even with the best of intentions, witnesses – professional or otherwise – often give totally different versions of events.

But there's a more significant contradiction locked in the police files that detectives didn't pick up. It's a mistake that could have cost them a lead to the person who took the money and, if the dark suspicions of White's friends are correct, it may have let a murderer slip away unnoticed.

Senior Sergeant Steedman, after opening the passenger door and gaining access to the vehicle, discovered White's leather briefcase on the footwell in front of the passenger seat, probably thrown there by the force of the crash. In the hunt for something to identify the victim, he tried to open the case.

"*It wouldn't open when I pressed the fasteners to release them. It had combination numbers for each of the two fasteners. I tried two or three times to get it open but without success. I put it back in the well and then started to look through a large number of documents in the back seat.*"

At the accident scene, the briefcase was not opened. Senior Sergeant Steedman put the case back **in the footwell**.

Police, at this stage, were not aware of the missing $15,000. It wasn't until Paul White's parents were notified of the fatality late that afternoon – and queried where the money was – that anyone realised the Citibank payout was missing. A police patrol was dispatched to a towing yard to search the wreck for it. They found the briefcase in a different location, and partially open. Constable Colin Ware didn't realise the significance at that stage but, being a good cop, he noted everything he found.

"*I went to the passenger's door and opened it. I noticed sitting on the front passenger's seat was a black briefcase with a piece of dash panel with a radio attached sitting on top of it. The handle was facing forward, I think it was the correct way up. I removed the briefcase and placed it on its end beside the vehicle.*

"*I thought I had better open the briefcase to check if the money was inside. The left hand lock combination was 000 and it opened. The right hand numbers were muddled so I turned them to 000 and the right hand lock opened,*" Ware wrote in his official report.

Who had opened the briefcase in the 12 hours following the crash? What had they found inside – extra computer disks? Fifteen thousand dollars? Did that person take money or disks from the briefcase?

Vital questions, but they were never investigated by the Auckland Police team that Police Minister John Banks had promised would get to the bottom of the case. Instead, Banks was now playing down the death, calling it an *"unfortunate accident,"* and nothing more.

At a news conference he noted that the pathologist had described White's injuries as being *"consistent"* with those sustained in a high impact vehicle collision, and joked that the international intrigue that had built since White's car crashed had all the makings of a good novel.

Was this the same John Banks, Minister of Police, who 24 hours previously had heard all of the same allegations and called for a full and frank investigation of all the claims? Banks had changed tack rapidly, apparently after Citibank assured him there was nothing of note on the disks.

Also back-peddling rapidly, Detective Senior Sergeant Bell. He rang us that afternoon begging us not to use any videotape of him referring to either the SIS or the Prime Minister. His superiors, he said, had been summoned to Parliament for a dressing down, and he'd been ordered not to make any mention of the intelligence service or the PM in any future sentences containing the words "Citibank" or "White".

"Prime Ministers," he implored, *"can have senior sergeants sacked at the stroke of a pen."*

We rang the Prime Minister's office to find out more about whether any pressure had been in fact applied to the police – without mentioning Bell or even Auckland Police – only to get a string of denials. Ten minutes later Bell rang back, sounding terrified and angry.

"What the hell do you think you're doing? Are you trying to get me fired? Why did you ring the bloody PM's office?"

It was interesting that, despite the denials, the pressure had come straight back on an Auckland police officer involved in the investigation. When we pushed the PM's button, it obviously rang in Ding Bell's office. Intriguing.

Meanwhile, the most junior squad on the force, Enquiry Office, plodded on as best they could, ignoring clues like the opened briefcase.

There's evidence that Enquiry Office were themselves feeling under pressure, if not from their superiors then certainly from the media, to quickly close the case and move on. In a letter to Police National Headquarters, Sergeant Karen Wilson noted:

"The matter is receiving great media interest and is obviously very high profile. We have received many media enquiries in relation to this matter and so seek to quickly eliminate any avenues of enquiry and avoid even more publicity."

In their haste to stamp the file "CASE CLOSED – ROAD ACCIDENT", Wilson's team instead targeted the bouncer as the probable thief, surmising that because he had lied to police about his involvement, in two earlier statements, he was likely to be guilty of robbing a corpse – or damn near to it.

It is, however, highly unlikely that the bouncer could have done it. Detectives searched his home and his place of work. They searched his bank accounts and talked to his colleagues – even his girlfriend. They maintained a six month alert on his activities. Nothing was found.

The police files, however, indicate it's pretty unlikely that anyone had the opportunity to take the $15,000 in cash that White had stashed on his person.

Dennis Manson says he left the bouncer at the scene for maybe 30 to 40 seconds while he shifted his van from one side the road to the other, but it's important to remember that Manson would probably have had the wreck in view during this time because it was only a few metres away in his headlights as he manoeuvred.

Even if the bouncer did have an intention to steal the cash, could he in that time have rifled through White's bloodstained clothing and retrieved that much cash in such a short time, without dropping any or attracting any attention. Witness reports had indicated the money was loose in a plastic bread bag or in White's briefcase – did the bouncer really have a chance of cleaning that out in such a short time, especially when the case was locked and around the other side of the wreck?

Likewise, could he have cleaned out 15 thousand dollars loose in White's pockets without dropping any money at all, or causing any other disarray? The evidence would tend to suggest two possibilities: that White's money was missing before he crashed, or was taken from the briefcase at the towing yard.

What are the odds against being paid $15,000, being robbed of $15,000, and colliding with a concrete pillar and killing yourself – all in the space of 12 hours? What are the odds against all of that happening to a person who claimed to have received death threats a few weeks earlier, telling friends he'd been phoned by a man who told him if he ever received any money he *"wouldn't live to spend it."*

What was the likelihood of White being robbed of $15,000, and then driving directly home without calling the police? Who had access to the tow yard? Could a burglar who knew what they were looking for have broken into the yard after the car was dropped off but before the yard opened later on Saturday morning?

Assume for a moment that the bouncer did take the money. He was, after all, the only person at the accident scene who would have known about the cash. Even the police didn't find out about the missing money until much later in the day. If the bouncer took the money, who went to the tow yard and rifled through the briefcase? Why would they bother? The tow yard staff did a lot of police work. These were all questions that raced through our minds, but they were questions without answers.

There was ample evidence that White had been drinking, but how much? Blood samples taken on the operating table indicated a blood alcohol level of 102mg/100ml, slightly over the 80mg legal limit but not what police or experts would call raging drunk.

Police and the coroner made mention of the fact that White's blood alcohol level was probably much higher, because the reading would have been diluted by transfusions. The police file however tells a different story.

Following enquiries by Sergeant Karen Wilson of the Enquiry Office, a Dr John Gowardman wrote back to confirm the procedures for measuring White's blood alcohol.

"I was actually the attending Critical Care doctor for the admission of the above patient when he was initially admitted. Presumably the blood sample that you are referring to was a blood alcohol level. This would have been taken off on admission with his initial bloods. This would have been processed in the hospital laboratory.

"This patient was given no other drugs that would interfere with this measurement during his initial resuscitation," wrote Gowardman.

The hospital's files paint a matter-of-fact picture of Paul White's final hours. He arrived at Auckland Hospital at 5:50am in a deep coma. His condition was described as very unstable and there were signs of heavy internal bleeding and liver damage. All limbs except for his left arm were fractured. For some reason, which not even police could explain, he wasn't wearing any socks or shoes.

He died at 9:35am, September 5, 1992.

CHAPTER 5

Defence of the Realm

*"Everyone who deals with arms, officially or unofficially,
can expect to be tripped up once in a while."*
– ARI BEN-MENASHE, *PROFITS OF WAR*, 1992

AS PRESSURE MOUNTED FOR a quick solution to the mystery, the police gave
their inquiry into his death an operational codename, MR BEAN. It derived
from a comment made by a hotel patron who watched White trip over a
table at the Centra Hotel. The witness told police that White looked like the
well known comedy character, Mr Bean.

As police pursued the enormous number of people who'd come into
contact with White the evening of his death, the media too were pursuing
their own investigations, speaking to their own informants.

Among the more bizarre and crazy rumours to do the rounds, a claim
that White had been assassinated on the orders of some mysterious official
in the Government. The informant told a number of media outlets,
including Radio New Zealand which broadcast some of the claims, that
White's disks were said to contain information that could prejudice national
security. He claimed the SIS had called in military heavies from Army Group
6, better known as the elite Special Air Service, to do an unofficial hatchet
job on Paul White. And what was the "information" that was so prejudicial
to "national security"?

Our informant, a small, hairy man whose paternity – judging from his
appearance – might be traceable to a werewolf, looked me in the eye without
blinking.

*"A major company has been trying to reduce the amount of money it's owed by
a former Iron Curtain country. Apparently they may have accepted an offer of
Soviet-made arms instead of cash. It seems the company is said to have bartered
weaponry to some Middle Eastern countries in return for oil, which was then sold
for dollars. One of those transactions was supposedly on the disks."*

As sure as God made little green apples, the man was mad. But, with
nothing better to do, we heard him out. For some time, he continued, the
Soviet Union and some of its former satellites had been finding it difficult to
pay cash for a whole range of products from various countries around the
world, and yet the regimes remained substantial New Zealand customers on
a number of industry fronts.

The bright-eyed boys at this particular company hatched a plan so
cunning you could stick a tail on it and call it perestroika – their own crafty
debt restructuring plan. With war brewing in the Middle East between Iraq
and the rest of the world, and conflicts in other global hotspots, there was a
market for weaponry and munitions.

As an example, he said, the country involved might trade $30 million worth of AK47 assault rifles for the NZ goods. The company's offshore entities would then flick the armaments on to buyers in the Middle East in exchange for oil, which would then be sold on the international market for $30 million in cash. The profits could naturally be stashed in one of the company's international Citibank accounts.

As he finished his briefing, I flipped the notebook closed, mentally leap-frogging in several directions at once. If it were true, it didn't take a hell of a lot of imagination to work out why the disks might pose a national security threat if leaked to the media or even foreign intelligence agencies. The international arms trade often has sovereign Government involvement or support – especially as the trade involves by its very nature the sale of classified military secrets.

Even if the New Zealand Government was not involved in this particular deal, a tetchy Government overseas somewhere might overlook the niceties and use the information regardless to cause diplomatic trouble. Was Paul White a man who knew too much? Was he killed because of that know-ledge? If he was, at what point does the security of New Zealand or its embarrassment on the international stage warrant the murder of one of its citizens?

On the flip side, other countries deal in weapons all the time – many of New Zealand's main trading partners are open buyers or sellers of armaments on the international stage. Would New Zealand really have suffered retaliation if caught out? Soviet-bloc countries had been heavily involved in secretly supplying weaponry to both sides in the Iran-Iraq war during the 1980's. In an effort not to be seen to be doing it, third parties like Israel were used as brokers. As former Israeli intelligence operative Ari Ben-Menashe explained in his book *Profits of War*, Israel was in fact also acting as a secret arms broker in Iranian attempts to procure American weaponry.

So convoluted were the shipping and money laundering routes that even Australia had been used as both a transit point for the weaponry and a banking centre to transact the deals. Some of the weapons had been in storage at the port of Fremantle, in Western Australia, in 1987 – the year of the America's Cup campaign there.

"In 1982 I first visited Australia to hire an accounting firm and open accounts in four major banks," wrote Ben-Menashe. *"Eventually monies deposited in Australian banks reached the amount of approximately $82 million US. Starting in early 1986, 12 C-130 aircraft we had purchased from Vietnam were shipped to Western Australia for repairs and refurbishment.*

"In 1987, while the Iran-contra hearings were going on in the US Congress, some of the arms going to Iran were temporarily parked in Western Australia." And the list went on, shipment after shipment, with Ben-Menashe implicating Australian business and political figures in the arms smuggling.

Painted against that backdrop, it wasn't quite so difficult to imagine New Zealand involvement in the massive trade, somewhere, but one thing was certain – if we couldn't find the disks or someone who could testify to having seen their contents, this would be one story we could probably never tell. It is to my eternal embarrassment that I failed to make the connection at this point between this fanciful tale, and the earlier comment by real estate agents Ross Walters and Letitia Reddington, who worked from an office below Paul White's apartment. They had told us on the day of White's funeral that he'd talked of a secret deal involving this particular company and a Middle Eastern country, but at that stage in proceedings it had meant nothing to me.

Back in 1992, as I listened to our mysterious informant, I had completely forgotten my earlier interview with the real estate team. Instead, I was focussing completely on assessing the informant's credibility.

What if this hairy guy was just, and this was entirely probable, another fruitloop. There was no hard evidence to support his claims, and quite possibly that evidence just did not exist. Society thrives on rumour and speculation, they are the undercurrent of democracy and autocracy alike. When Governments or private corporations indulge in it, it's called "intelligence". When the public do it it's called gossip, and when the media does it, it's called "defamation", and results in hefty lawsuits from the aforementioned Governments and corporations. I knew that these claims were defamatory in their raw state, so I opted to file them under X – for unexplained.

Some journalists might dismiss out of hand claims like these and the people who make them. But I also knew that not everyone dressed in a suit and tie tells the truth, and not everyone dressed in combat fatigues and looking like Leon Trotsky is necessarily a liar. The world is not black and white, and truth is often camouflaged in several shades of grey. Through bitter experience of missing out on leads I had long since learnt to listen to everything first and ask questions afterward. I couldn't afford to turn any potential source away.

We nicknamed him "Spook", in view of his claims to be linked to a foreign intelligence cell in New Zealand and also in light of his apparent ability to haunt the media with his conspiracy theories. Spook* claimed to have a military background – something I doubted, given his appearance – and one of the reasons the SAS had stuffed up this operation was because they'd lost several of their best strategists in a combat operation overseas around the time of the Gulf War. Now this was an interesting diversion. I leaned further forward in the seat.

"What do you mean the SAS lost guys fighting overseas? The NZ Special Air Service hasn't been in combat since the end of the Vietnam War!"

"Buzz, wrong answer Wishart. How do you think the SAS train and stay at combat readiness? They're attached to the British SAS and they've fought in every

---

* Spook, I later learnt, had done contract work for several Government agencies, and some private ones. Dressed, as often as not, like some "oik" from the mean streets, and driving around in a car full of rubbish and weaponry (he was a collector), I was doubly surprised to discover that he was raking in up to a thousand dollars a week in fees.

major conflict since Vietnam and a few minor ones as well. They fought in the Gulf War, and they're in Northern Ireland too."

"You're trying to tell me that New Zealand soldiers are serving in secret wars without public knowledge? That kiwi troops are dying on foreign fields while we publicly play the role of a non-aligned, nuclear-free, clean, green Pacific backwater?," I queried, my voice betraying my incredulity.

"Yes," said Spook, adjusting his glasses and rubbing his beard.

"Bollocks!"

"Take it or leave it, I'm telling you the truth. If you've got a problem, don't bother listening. But if you don't listen, you won't know where to look for the answers you're seeking."

For a hardbitten, cynical journalist who thought he'd sussed out the world and his own place in it, it was like being baptised in a pool of molasses. Everywhere I turned I was getting bogged down in conspiracy theories that each seemed to deserve their own fullscale investigations.

As I briefed Christensen on the bizarre conversation, I left out the part about the New Zealand company selling Soviet-made weapons. Accepting that our SAS might be active overseas was difficult enough, but I couldn't reconcile in my own mind the idea that kiwi business executives were out there in the international marketplace outbidding Adnan Kashoggi for the latest arms shipments. I sure as hell knew the boss wouldn't buy it!

Together, Steve and I approached Rod Pedersen with a sanitised version of the possible scenarios. To this day I'm not sure he believed any of it, but he obviously figured the best way to keep us out of his hair was to go along with our crazy schemes. We left his office with approval to stay working fulltime on the White case for the next two weeks, and *60 Minutes* field producer Chris Harrington would fly up from Wellington to oversee our investigation.

One of our first discoveries was the fact that police had secretly given Citibank officials access to the floppy disks, without telling White or his lawyer. It lent weight to our belief that something wasn't right with the way police were handling the case. At this stage the Serious Fraud Office had indicated it wanted to look at the disks because of the allegations being made, but it hadn't yet taken delivery of them. I rang the SFO and spoke to director Charles Sturt's personal assistant. By way of explanation, Chas Sturt doesn't generally answer phones. All his calls are usually screened by a team of highly trained secretarial guard dogs. I explained to his assistant our concerns about the police decision to let Citibank copy the seized disks – something we felt had compromised the perceived integrity of exhibits of evidence. Evidence, as I have noted earlier in this book, must be **seen** to be free from interference if it is to be relevant to a criminal trial. I suggested that the SFO might like to get an independent computer expert to evaluate the disks and see if any evidence of tampering existed.

When I spoke to her later that day, she told me how grateful Chas Sturt had been for our tip and to be sure and pass on anything else that might be relevant. Being a naive person, I seriously believed that the SFO might take that kind of information seriously when analysing the computer disks. As arguably the most powerful law enforcement watchdog in the land, I expected the SFO to at least share our concern about the integrity of the evidence. Instead, we made our second discovery.

In a two page news release issued on Friday, September 11, 1992, The Serious Fraud Office director, Charles Sturt, suggested that his office had looked at the police disks. *"The information contained on all 86 computer disks held by the Police and the two disks returned by Mr White to Citibank have now been examined by the Serious Fraud Office."*

In fact, the Serious Fraud Office never looked at White's files at all. We were later to discover the SFO never uplifted the original disks from the police. Not knowing this at the time, we read on. After an inquiry that lasted several hours, Sturt and his team were pouring cold water on White's allegations. *"I am now completely satisfied that these disks do not contain a scintilla of evidence to suggest that any company mentioned on them was involved in any fraudulent activity nor that any Member of Parliament was involved in any form of corruption. In fact, there was not even mention, directly or indirectly, of any Member of Parliament on any of the computer disks."*

Hold the line! Back up three spaces, my mind was screaming to me. Paul White told some of his friends the name of the Government MP who received a $50,000 payment into his account in Citibank Nassau. We knew the name ourselves. Was the SFO trying to say Paul White had plucked the name and details out of thin air?

Sure enough, a few lines further on, *"I am fully satisfied that Mr White and those with whom he had discussed the matter, had either totally misinterpreted information or had been misled."*

Having made a point of telling the SFO of our concerns about the potential for evidence to have been interfered with – because of the nature of the copying process – I now looked through the two page statement for any mention of what we believed was an important public issue, but there was no reference to this being considered. How could the SFO ignore something as serious as potential tampering with evidence? I didn't understand. Each disk was capable of holding between 300 and one thousand pages of text information and, as we now know, most of the disks were full and all the files were word processing rather than banking transaction data. To read a thousand pages takes longer than six or eight hours, and here there were 88 computer disks with a potential total of between 30 thousand and 88 thousand pages of information.

The Serious Fraud Office was **seriously** asking us to believe that it had thoroughly read through all that data in one day? It didn't seem to me to be humanly possible. It had taken White several weeks to go through them. Besides, I thought, the SFO itself had boasted about taking months to thoroughly investigate Equiticorp's document trail, yet here we were being told the office had completed this investigation in what must only have been a matter of hours without needing any follow-up of the information on the disks?

The SFO's statement is contradicted by an internal police memorandum written by Detective Sergeant Mark Churches. *"It became apparent,"* Churches had written in a report to his superiors, *"that there were literally* **hundreds of files** *contained on the disks,* **and to go through each file** *[author's emphasis]* **would take hours."** Were the SFO and Police even looking at the same disks? I began to seriously wonder. I spat and hissed and stormed around the office. Harrington and Christensen couldn't believe it either.

There was a final twist that firmly drove a nail into the SFO's coffin in my eyes, and it didn't emerge until some weeks later. In his statement of September 11, 1992, Sturt had set out his reasons for launching an independent investigation of the matter. *"The Serious Fraud Office has completed its investigations into the serious allegations arising from information said to have been stored on computer disks formerly held by the late Paul White. These allegations relate to both the possible fraudulent dealings of corporate entities through 'money laundering' and the suspected corrupt activities of a Member or Members of Parliament.*

"These allegations are of a very serious nature and clearly fall within the purview of matters requiring investigation by this Office. Central to these allegations and the intrigue surrounding this entire matter, are the computer disks believed to have been in the possession of Mr White."

So far, well and good. The SFO is confirming that the allegations were serious enough to warrant full investigation, and that central to them were the disks held by Paul White.

The whole point of my calls to the SFO in preceding days had been to pass on information or our conjecture to what we believed to be the primary example of an independent investigatory force. If anyone had the power to investigate the actions of police or politicians, it was the Serious Fraud Office. Imagine my surprise then, to discover that the SFO investigation had been carried out with Citibank's help – a party to the whole dispute. It transpired that it was Citibank staff and Citibank computers that were used to show SFO investigators what was on the disks.

If the investigation was to be truly independent, the SFO should have hired one of the many independent computer companies to provide the experts and equipment. Citibank had made no secret of the fact that it considered there was nothing worthy of investigation on the disks and, furthermore, that it did not want the information on the disks disclosed to anyone. I had no argument with Citibank's position: the bank had a duty to its clients to make that stand. But surely that would make the bank appear publicly to be a less than impartial "co-investigator" for the SFO to team up with? I thought so, anyway.

But most importantly, we discovered, via the police, that the Serious Fraud Office had not even examined Paul White's disks at all. Detective Sergeant Mark Churches confirmed to me that Paul White's disks – the ones seized by police – had remained locked in a police storage facility. The police had expected a request from the SFO to look at them but, according to Churches, that request never came. Instead, the Serious Fraud Office had gone directly to Citibank for help. The disks and data being examined were the material Citibank had copied from the files held by police.

It's a very important point. The only disks that Paul White had ever touched were still in Police custody, and if the SFO had ever intended a serious investigation, it should have looked at those disks and those disks only. The Serious Fraud Office, according to police, never once asked to see those original disks. *"Central to these allegations and the intrigue surrounding this entire matter, are the computer disks believed to have been in the possession of Mr White,"* wrote Charles Sturt in his press release. But contrary to those suggestions, neither the Director nor any of his staff had investigated Paul White's disks at all, which made the investigation extremely doubtful, in my view. To further muddy the waters, it now appears that the SFO may not even have looked at the computer file copies made by Citibank, but only at paper printouts of those files provided by the bank. Citibank executive Michael Farland told me the SFO had gone through the *"paper printouts"* extensively. If it was only paper printouts that the SFO saw, then the investigators were one step even further removed from the disks at the centre of it all.

There's no evidence to suggest that Citibank did anything wrong. There is no evidence that Citibank failed to provide full copies of the original files. However, that is not the point. The SFO said it was going to carry out an independent investigation and, as a result of its actions, I can't see how it's in a position to prove the contention that Paul White's disks contained nothing of significance. Therefore, the SFO's confident assurances that the information on the police disks had been looked at were worth nothing.

Two years later, in September 1994, we tried to clarify exactly what the SFO had done on the Citibank case. *60 Minutes* researcher Carolyne Meng-Yee fired in an Official Information Act request to Charles Sturt.

"Could you please tell me whether the SFO actually obtained the original disks themselves from the police, or whether they were the copies made by the bank, or whether the SFO only saw paper printouts of the information on the disks? If it was paper printouts that SFO staff saw, could you please tell me how many pages there were?

"I would also be grateful if you could clarify what assistance Citibank was able to give logistically – ie, were the disks or printouts examined in the SFO office or at the bank, were the disks loaded in Citibank computers or SFO ones, and finally, how long did it take to complete the investigation?"

I had used Carolyne as a "front" because I had previously crossed swords with the SFO, and wanted to see if a different personality attracted more cooperation. It didn't. In a reply dated September 27, 1994, Sturt refused to answer the questions.

"I regret that because of the secrecy provisions of the Serious Fraud Office Act it would be totally inappropriate for me to comment on the matters you have raised in your letter. I can only again emphasise that the investigation of the Citibank disks by this Office conclusively established that there was no evidence suggesting criminal wrongdoing by any person."

It's fair to say that we never discovered evidence of criminal wrongdoing either, and there's nothing to suggest there ever was any but, again, that's not the point. Given the nature of what, in my opinion anyway, deserves to be called an "investigation" by the SFO, I don't personally believe the SFO could find a three-leafed clover at the bottom of my garden, let alone "conclusively".

Back in 1992, however, our Paul White inquiry was continuing to run into major doses of the wild and wacky. Late on Wednesday, September 16, I was woken by a phonecall at quarter to midnight. I'd been asleep for an hour and, in that strange manner that happens when your first hour of sleep is disrupted, the trill of the receiver on the wall beside my ear sounded like a team of workmen with a jack-hammer.

It gives you a heightened state of awareness, and I can still sharply recall the first thing I heard, before anyone spoke. It was the crackle of a police radio in the background, and the word "Citibank" came spinning out of the ether and thumped into my dazed mind. The voice on the phone spoke, it was TV3's *Nightline* producer Alan Thurston.

"Sorry to wake you up old chap, but there's a real drama going on at the Citibank building. There's cops all over it and we heard a report there were two guys on the roof."

In a nano-second the sleep dropped from me like a slinky shift on a virgin's wedding night. I was wide awake and listening as Thursty continued. *"Do you want to call a camera crew out?"*

As he spoke I heard a cop on the radio, *"Speaking to one at the moment, trying to find the other".*

"Forget it," I answered Thurston's question, *"They've just caught one. By the time we get there it'll be over. I'll chase it up in the morning."*

The next morning, when I rang the police, the incident didn't exist. No one in the police media section could find a record of it, and no one in the police control room could locate one either. And then the phone rang. On the line was Robert T, a criminal contact who at times had proved a useful source on other matters.

"You won't believe what went down last night," he said, a short way into the conversation.

"Try me."

"One of SK's boys was asked to get someone into the Citibank building."

"What the hell do you mean?"

"There was some job on at Citibank last night, to get in, that's all I know."

I was speechless. Here was an incident that police said hadn't happened, that I had heard myself on the police radio, and here's a crim at 8 o'clock in the morning telling me about it. On pressing him further, "SK" referred to burglary mastermind Simon Kerr, the man behind the infamous "Hole in the Wall Gang", which made a name for itself in the late 1980's by bashing holes in buildings and banks and dragging the safes out using heavy machinery in the middle of the night. Subtlety was never their strong point. Rob suggested that it was an SIS job.

Peter Stones and I hit the streets, trying to find anyone who might have seen the incident or seen police cars attending. Nightshift staff at a nearby restaurant had certainly seen the police activity but weren't told what was happening. The police, however, were still denying that anything had happened at all, and so were Citibank. Citibank executives invited us up to talk about it, then warned us that nothing had happened, and we'd be sued if we said anything had. The bank had a barrage of security cameras and alarms, all of which had been checked following our inquiries, all of which showed nothing.

"If someone so much as pisses on the front door, our perimeter security system would tell us immediately," boasted one of them. Well that was incredibly useful to know, I thought. Remind me not to piss on Citibank's front door in the future. Although itching to run a story that night, the Thursday, we couldn't. Without confirmation that an incident had taken place we had nothing, and yet to us the refusal of the police and Citibank to admit that something had occurred was even more bizarre.

That night I fired an unofficial request in to a friendly detective. The next morning he had an answer. He too had found nothing on the log, but one of his colleagues did remember the call out. Apparently some street kids had trashed a money machine on the ground floor but escaped before the cops could catch them. We knew that that version of events couldn't be true either. I'd heard the report that at least one offender was caught, and we'd been at the ground floor money machines the morning after and nothing was untoward.

That evening, at quarter to midnight, I phoned the police control room, hoping to strike the Senior Sergeant who'd been working the same shift on Wednesday. He confirmed that police were called to reports of someone being on the roof of Citibank, but says it was discovered they were street kids so no action was taken. For the first time we had official confirmation that there really had been a callout. We ran the story the next day, Saturday. A *Herald* reporter who enquired was also told that street kids had trashed a money machine and escaped.

A few days later, we tracked down Dave Sheridan, the nearby resident who actually called police to the scene. His version of events was markedly different. He recalled seeing three men dragging what looked like a safe or a metal box across the roof of the Citibank carpark. *"They were trying to open it. One of them got so frustrated he picked it up and slung it down the stairs. I thought what a bloody idiot, making all this noise. And he picked it back up, brought it back up, and the other guy started hammering it, hammering the top with a hammer and having no joy, getting very frustrated with it."*

Sheridan called the police and directed them into position. Fortunately all police radio traffic and emergency calls are kept on audio tape. Copies of the police tapes of both Sheridan's call and patrol car radio traffic shed some light on what was going on.

"Control calls a free unit in the city."

"City-I [incident car]."

"Yeah, City-I, possibly three offenders on the roof of Citibank. Can you 10-2 please."

Other units nearby also call in for instructions to head to the scene – patrol cars are sealing off the area. Somehow, within 60 seconds, an Armourguard vehicle is on the scene, its presence noted by the first patrol car to arrive at the bank.

"Control, AVC."

"AVC."

"Yeah, we're off at Citibank with the Armourguard."

A minute and a half later a beat cop radios in to say he has all three offenders, although his controller is having difficulty getting accurate information from him, a point made doubly clear by an aside comment to another patrol asking what's going on at the scene.

"Yeah, I'm not quite sure what the guts is here, this guy's not giving me much info. AKB 11, Control."

"Go ahead."

"Yeah, can you tell us exactly what's going on there, do you have all the offenders, is anyone else required?"

"We have got three guys here, nobody else is required. It appears they have just walked from the carpark down the stairs and onto Fort Lane."

The controller had good reason to feel confused. So did we when we compared notes with Dave Sheridan's description of what happened.

"I watched the whole action, what they did, they caught them red handed with the box in their hands. But I think one of them legged it down the road and took off. They got the two guys – one on the top here, one down the bottom – talking to em for quite a while, and that was it."

"Then took them away?"

"Then took them away, yeah."

So what happened to the one that Dave Sheridan watched get away, and what happened to the safe or the metal box that they'd been attempting to break into? Sheridan watched as police loaded two suspects and the box into a patrol car and drove off. Why did the beat constable simply report that the men had been walking across the carpark and there was nothing further to it? How did an Armourguard vehicle apparently beat police to the scene, and why did police initially tell the media nothing happened, then later change the story to say street kids had attacked a money machine but they escaped? Clearly two offenders were bundled off in a police car, and clearly they weren't attacking a money machine. Why would police make up such a story for the media's benefit, instead of simply telling the truth?

Sheridan reckons the men he saw were in their 20's, although he describes them as idiots for trying to open the box in public. They certainly didn't sound like SIS agents, and despite the confusion we'd managed to ascertain that they weren't on the roof of the tall building, merely on the roof of the two storey carpark.

But why the apparent cover-up? Why did Citibank claim to have checked its whizz-bang surveillance system and found nothing, when clearly police were crawling all over the perimeter for, according to Sheridan, up to 20 minutes. And it still didn't tell me how the criminal fraternity had picked up on this apparent non-event by 7:00am the next morning, and why they'd picked it as an SIS break-in. All questions and no answers. Nothing made sense. It was a feeling I was getting used to. In the end we filed it away as just more unexplained phenomena. We didn't know what it actually was, but we could prove it <u>wasn't</u> what the cops said it was. As for Citibank's attitude, we wrote that off as a bad case of being over-sensitive.

While Stones and I had been chasing the phantom burglars at the bank, Steve Christensen had also been digging. He met a friend of his, a Government intelligence operative he'd known for some time. He dropped into the conversation a casual question about whether Special Air Service troops really had fought in the Gulf War and other combat areas. The answer astounded us: Yes.

Further detail would take another two years to collate but, for the sake of literary cohesion, now's as good a time as any to tell the story of New Zealand's secret wars.

They are New Zealand's combat elite and, officially anyway, they haven't fired a shot in anger since the end of the Vietnam War. In one of the more democratically challenging issues to arise from this long investigation however, clear indications have emerged that the New Zealand Special Air Service has been repeatedly active in foreign wars and disputes throughout the 1970's, 80's and 90's, despite Government denials.

One of the first people to confirm SAS involvement in ongoing covert operations overseas was a senior politician, a man not unfamiliar with the Cabinet room, who we rang on November 30, 1992.

"Just a background enquiry. We've discovered the Special Air Service actually served on covert operations in Iraq, apparently on attachment to British SAS. I'm just wondering whether you were briefed on that?"

"Hang on a minute – say that again?"

"The New Zealand Special Air Service, SAS, served in Iraq during the Gulf War, apparently on secondment to British SAS and American Special Forces. Were you briefed on that, or are you as much in the dark as we were?"

"All I'll say is this: I was briefed."

Within 24 hours of that call, the politician had rung back in a blind panic to retract his statement. He asked me not to ring him *"on these phones"* to discuss the matter again. Which raises the question: why are the phones of senior politicians being listened to, and by whom? On the main issue, however, it was confirmation that, despite the Government's promise that no New Zealand combat troops would be deployed, some obviously had been. The evidence continued to stack up.

Former cabinet minister David Thomson, a Minister of Defence in the Muldoon administration from 1980-84, broadly hinted at covert SAS operations in his time at the helm. *"Well, they're a pretty responsible lot, and they keep their noses clean. I've not heard of any Minister being embarrassed by them. All I can say is they would be really daft if they didn't take every opportunity of sharpening up their act. It is a fact that there was nothing but approval from me in my time for that sort of responsible efficiency. It's important that the Minister himself should know where they are, because he's got to be answerable. All I know is that I left my job as Minister of Defence convinced that our SAS were as good or possibly even better than any other similar troops in the world."*

It goes without saying that if the SAS were not not on covert international operations, they would be in their barracks in New Zealand, and the Minister wouldn't have to *"know where they are"* nor would he have anything to be *"answerable"* for.

There was praise too, from a senior American defence analyst, Noel Koch. Koch had been a Deputy Assistant Secretary, Defence, for special operations and low intensity conflict. He was basically in charge of running special operations forces throughout the first Reagan term and halfway through the second. With contacts in special forces units around the world, Koch had moved into the private sector, with his own firm in Washington DC, International Security Management.

He confirmed that Commonwealth Special Forces (SAS) had served in the Gulf. He said, however, that information regarding their activities was still classified.

"The Kiwis never get the kind of publicity they deserve, unfortunately, but if they were in it I'm sure they acquitted themselves well, and I'm sure we're not in a position to elaborate on that."

The comment that the NZSAS *"never get the kind of publicity they deserve, unfortunately,"* I took as an extremely strong indication that NZSAS have been combat active in the recent past. After all, if they were as inactive as the NZ Government claims, how would a high ranking US defence adviser know of their abilities, and why would he say that they don't get the publicity they deserve?

"Do you know anyone who is able to confirm that they were part of the Commonwealth Special Forces?," I continued.

"I don't know anyone who has the authority to do it who will do it on the record."

"Still a classified operation at this stage, then?"

"Ah, yes. For all practical purposes, one might say it's not over yet."

Classification would turn out to be a major bugbear during investigations into New Zealand's secret wars. SAS troops who took part in a secret mission in Indonesia during the Malaysian Confrontation of the 1960's had been ordered by their commanders never to refer to the mission ever again, not even in their personal diaries. The cat was only let out of the bag when an Australian officer broke silence two decades later, in 1989, in an article for an Australian journal.

From that, *Dominion* journalist Michael Field, now with *Agence France Presse*, managed to track down the commanding officer of the NZSAS detachment in Indonesia, former Colonel David Moloney, who explained the reason for 20 years of official denials.

"Obviously the political ramifications of the whole thing are not lost on you. It's not such a hot issue now, but then it was."

Field noted that while the New Zealand public remained oblivious to *"one of the deepest post-World War 2 military secrets,"* the Indonesians had known about New Zealand involvement all along.

Perhaps the most significant revelation to emerge was that successive New Zealand Governments had been prepared to lie to the media and the public about the NZ involvement to safeguard a national secret. It is a trait that continues to this day.

Australian journalist John Pilger had run into similar difficulties during his investigations into British SAS operations training Pol Pot's Khmer Rouge guerillas during the mid 80's. British Foreign Secretary Douglas Hurd had told Parliament, *"We have never given, and will never give, support of any kind to the Khmer Rouge."*

"The Hurd statement," wrote Pilger, *"failed to satisfy a great many people and caused one of those curious disturbances in the House of Commons when Tory MP's have to deal with postbags overflowing with letters on a subject they wish would go away.*

"Several debates on Cambodia ensued, minister after minister denied that Britain was indirectly backing the Khmer Rouge – until William Waldegrave, then a Foreign Office minister, made a slip and gave away what the opposition interpreted as a 'tacit admission' that the SAS were indeed in Cambodia."

As a result of the furore that followed, says Pilger, the SAS operation was given *"total deniability"*, by removing the SAS instructors in Cambodia from the ranks of serving personnel – ie, they were no longer "employed" by the British Government.

"In operational terms that made no difference whatsoever, as SAS personnel normally 'disappear' from army records whenever they go on secret missions. What was important was that the Government could now deny that British servicemen were involved," concluded Pilger in his book, *Distant Voices*.

This, I would soon discover, is how the New Zealand Government and military establishment may have been able to deny the existence of New Zealand's "secret wars". Following an Official Information Act request in December 1992, I received back the following answers from the New Zealand Defence Force.

*"No soldier of the New Zealand Army, serving on the **posted strength** [author's emphasis] of the 1st New Zealand Special Air Service Group, has been involved in any active service or been in any combat operations, including those related to intelligence or reconnaissance, since the conclusion of the Vietnam War.*

*"Given that, the answer to your first question is **no serving** New Zealand Special Air Service soldier since the Vietnam War has been attached in either a combat or advisory role to any foreign military unit involved in combat operations.*

*"Following from that, the answer to your next question is that **no serving** New Zealand Special Air Service soldiers operated in the Gulf Area in any capacity whatsoever during the period of the Gulf War hostilities, either under the New Zealand or any other nation's flag."*

Defence Force spokesman, Dr Malcolm McNamara, went on to confirm that any activities the SAS got up to overseas would have to be approved by the New Zealand Government before adding:

"No serving New Zealand Special Air Service soldier has served in any official capacity with the Khmer Rouge . . . . We cannot make a categorical statement that no discharged ex-New Zealand Special Air Service soldier has ever served in a private capacity with the Khmer Rouge."

The key words in all cases have been highlighted. A further request pushed for information on the exact nature of the secondment arrangement that allows NZSAS to be attached to British units. The request was refused.

"Because of the role of the Special Air Services of New Zealand, Australia and Britain in addressing the terrorist threat, and because of the nature of that threat, a substantial amount of information shared between these three countries' SAS organisations is accorded a very high degree of protection.

"For New Zealand to release information about aspects of SAS work (including information about SAS personnel) which an alliance partner would not release (or would neither confirm nor deny) would be likely to prejudice the entrusting of further information of a similar degree of sensitivity to the Government of New Zealand or our alliance partners."

In essence, any revelations about the activities of NZSAS could be considered as revelations about all three SAS organisations, an implication by omission in some respects. As to suggestions that NZSAS troops "disappeared" from the records whilst on active service overseas, McNamara disagreed.

"It has never been a practice of the New Zealand army to have a soldier's records 'vanish' from the official files," he retorted. *"You have asked us to elucidate the expression 'on the posted strength'. All soldiers are held against an established post for employment within a unit – that is, on its 'posted strength' – except when they are undergoing certain categories of extended training."*

I attempted to get further definitions – such as what constituted extended training – but the requests were stonewalled in military legalese.

It is interesting to note some of the behind the scenes machinations that accompanied my Official Information Act requests on these matters. A week before my first request to Defence I had fired in an OIA application about the UK/USA Treaty,* a top secret military intelligence treaty that New Zealand was a signatory to. That request had resulted in a call to TV3 news director Rod Pedersen's office from defence officials representing the Minister of Defence, Warren Cooper.

Pedersen's executive assistant, Carol van Stockum, told me they'd asked

---

* The UK/USA Treaty is classified on the "If I told you, I'd have to kill you!" level. Its existence is neither confirmed nor denied, but essentially it relates to interception of radio and phone communications. Virtually all international calls, cellular calls and radio transmissions can be and are intercepted – those containing certain keywords are captured by computer for further analysis.

for an urgent meeting with him in Cooper's Beehive office, and they were prepared to fly Pedersen down to Wellington at their expense. Rod and Carol stalled for time – eventually the follow-up calls dwindled and stopped. Thus, when I faxed off my first request on the SAS operations the following Friday, Defence chiefs had already been rattled.

On Friday afternoon I got a phone call from a businessman I'd met through Spook, a man he claimed had intelligence links – although the person concerned denied it vehemently. However, our mutual friend gave me a warning on this occasion.

"Your Official Information request is creating waves. This is a dangerous business, so I want you to be extremely careful and vigilant around your house and car. You'll get a letter on Monday denying the existence of the information you're seeking. I wish we'd had a chance to discuss this before you put the request in, but what's done is done."

I could feel the goosebumps rising as he spoke. What made it even more chilling was the fact that on Monday, as predicted, a letter turned up from the Ministry of Defence turned up denying the existence of the information I was seeking. It was the fastest reaction to an Official Information Act request that I'd ever had.

Further letters met with further denials, and I eventually appealed to the Office of the Ombudsman over the matter. Over a period of months we still got nowhere, but the Ombudsman's case worker handling my correspondence revealed some interesting experiences of his own.

He told me that Defence officials had been absolutely insistent that the Ombudsman's inquiries do not deviate by so much as a dotted "i" from the exact wording of my requests. Any attempt to rephrase my questions was stonewalled.

Defence officials were also arguing with the Ombudsman's Office about what constituted "official information". I had asked for information, including what Defence officials knew but had not committed to paper. Defence took the view that the Act applied only to paper records, and refused to comply with arguments to the contrary.

Contrast the official position with the testimony from the next witness we located. His name – David Mason, a former British SAS officer made internationally famous in a book called The Feather Men by Sir Ranulph Fiennes. Mason had led a team known as the "Feather Men" to safeguard the lives of SAS soldiers from the many enemies they may create during a career. One of those enemies was an Arabian Sheik, whose son had allegedly been killed in clashes with the Special Air Service in Oman.

The Sheik hired his own team of contract killers to identify the SAS men involved and murder them – the only stipulation being that the deaths had to look either accidental or of natural causes. For 13 years, between 1977 and 1990, the assassins hunted down and killed four British soldiers, two of them ex-SAS. For 13 years Mason and his men had followed the killers around the world, trying to establish a motive for the killings and work out who was on the list. They managed to save the life of the last victim, and they managed to catch the killers. David Mason was in a good position to know about NZSAS operations in Britain.

Mason was in New Zealand in July 1993 to promote his first book, *Shadow Over Babylon*, a docudrama about a plot to assassinate Iraqi leader Saddam Hussein a year earlier. I managed to corner him at the TV3 studios for five minutes.

Born in 1951, Mason had joined the SAS in the early 1970's, his record including tours of duty in Northern Ireland and the Arabian state of Oman from 1974 to 1976. He recalled fighting alongside two New Zealand SAS personnel in Oman who, he recalled, were on extended secondment to British SAS and who fought in "A" Company.

Mason showed no reluctance to answer my questions, and happily explained that he'd served alongside New Zealanders on many campaigns. NZ SAS, he said, were sent regularly to Britain on secondment, often a troop (four men) at a time. Not only do they train at the British SAS Headquarters at Hereford, but according to Mason they're also attached to British units and serve in combat roles in Northern Ireland and everywhere that Britain goes.

Although retired from active duty, Mason understood that New Zealand SAS were involved in the Gulf War, as were the Australians, and in answer to another question he confirmed there have been New Zealand and Australian casualties on secret missions in the past.

It's worth noting that Mason, according to his service record in *The Feather Men*, hadn't served in Vietnam – the only place he could have legitimately come across NZSAS in combat if one accepted the New Zealand Defence Force claims. And here I was, torn between who to believe. I also took into account the confirmation given by TV3 journalist Steve Christensen's intelligence agent, who also mentioned service in Northern Ireland and other theatres of war.

Then there was another of my own intelligence informants, who warned me about the consequences of digging all this up.

"You are 100% bang on with your information on the SAS fighting overseas, except you're wrong in assuming they were killed in the Gulf War. Three of them were killed in one incident a couple of years back, but it wasn't in the Gulf.

"The boys in Defence are going to try and stymie your Official Information Act requests* – my advice to you is to let the sleeping dog lie. They're like the bloody Brotherhood – you don't want them coming after you. I'm told that if it looks like you're getting close to cracking it you'll get a visit. Don't push it."

In January, 1993, during a routine video news shoot, I'd posed a question to a senior Royal New Zealand Air Force officer at Auckland's Whenuapai Airbase. Whilst unaware of any major SAS mobilisation during the Gulf War period, he did recall one SAS trooper heading up, a soldier whose part-

---

* As noted earlier in this chapter – even the Ombudsman's staff remarked that they were being stonewalled at every turn.

Maori heritage would help him blend into the Arabic scenery. The NZ SAS trooper ended up attached to British SAS.

It's worth noting, also, that one of the SAS men featured in the book *Bravo Two Zero* – a chronicle of the British SAS team of the same name who fought in the Gulf War – was named *"Mark the Kiwi"*. Co-incidence, I'm sure.

Officially, the New Zealand Government denies all of this. And perhaps that's the way it has to be for a force that is New Zealand's only counter-terrorism unit and which has to stay up to world standards – the price the country pays for its isolation, although it's an anachronism in a country that publicly professes its neutrality and relative non-alignment.

Unofficially, it's acknowledged that the secret warriors are a credit to their country, a group who deserve more recognition, recognition they're unlikely to get as long as the New Zealand Government insists on maintaining the pretence that they don't actually do anything.

Why am I concentrating on the role of the Special Air Service?, you may ask: simply because the NZSAS are, on the basis of information passed to me, becoming increasingly involved in civilian intelligence work as practised by the Security Intelligence Service. Some of the private sector security companies are owned, run and staffed by former members of the SAS and the SIS, and these agencies still have very close contacts to those services.

The Security Intelligence Service, for example, may hire one of these agencies to carry out some work or, on the extremes, perhaps carry out surveillance or bugging that the SIS either will not, or cannot by law, do itself. Certainly that's the case in Britain, on which the NZSAS and SIS are modelled, to a large extent. In his book, *Enemies of the State*, former British MI5 agent Gary Murray sets out just how incestuous the relationship between state and private security agencies has become.

Murray quotes former MI6 officer Captain Fred Holroyd, now retired, who testifies to the extensive use of the British Special Air Service as intelligence "heavies". SAS roles have included acting as watchdogs while intelligence staff plant bugs in a house.

"The whole area is screened by the Special Air Service in civilian clothes, who keep watch and intercept anyone who might visit the house," says Holroyd. *"The SAS in this country have become an adjunct of the Security Services. They are no longer regarded as purely military troops. They now have a political role which is very much in the forefront with 22 SAS, and that is covert operations for the Security Services."*

Could the men who confronted Paul White in his apartment one August evening in 1992 have been NZSAS troops keeping watch while the SIS tried to burgle the unit in a search for more disks – the disks we now know he had kept hidden from the police?

But while all of this was intriguing, and no doubt something that will be hotly debated and denied for a long time to come, it wasn't getting us any closer to what lay behind the Paul White mystery. Once again it was Spook who caused the next diversion, in a phone call to the office at TV3 a few days after the fuss over the police callout to the Citibank building. It was mid-September 1992.

"Can you come down and meet me. I've got some information on the SIS meetings with White. Be at the kiosk in 15 minutes."

Steve drove me down, but stayed in the car, parked 50 metres away. It was just after 6:00pm, and most of the businesses and shops had long since shut. As I walked into the entrance to the downtown tour bus terminal, a guy in a suit and coat, aged in his 40's walked out. When he saw me he visibly flinched. Strangely, I jumped at exactly the same time. With his trench coat and shifty look he damned well looked like a spy. I cast a second glance back over my shoulder and he was looking back at me as well. *"Nah, just paranoia on my part,"* I told myself, but when I got to the kiosk Spook was even more spooked than I was.

"Did you see that SIS agent?," he growled. *"The guy arrived about 10 minutes after I called you. All he's done for the past 10 minutes is just linger around the kiosk. When he saw we'd sprung him he took off."*

We raced back to the doorway. I could see the man walking along Quay Street towards the Ferry Building, his features quite distinguishable in the crowd. A hundred metres away by now, he was heading for the entrance to a café. I shrugged and was about to go back inside when the man turned his head. Of all the things to look at, again he was staring straight back at me.

When he saw me standing there he casually turned back and went in to the café. Suspecting this man might be interesting to watch and follow, we waited out of sight behind a bush. Five minutes later the suit appeared at the café doorway, once again staring at where we'd been. Apparently satisfied that we'd gone back inside the man started walking back towards us, so I decided to really test the lie of the land.

Figuring that if he was an ordinary punter he'd keep on coming, Spook and I gradually let ourselves be seen, carrying on a face-to-face discussion while watching the guy's approach. He looked up a couple of seconds later. He was still 50 metres away and across the other side of a four lane road, but when he saw us he stopped, paused to look out at the harbour and then walked back down the road.

"That," I muttered under my breath, heart thumping like an express train, *"is not the behaviour of an innocent man."*

We followed him for 20 minutes, a circuitous, zig-zagging route across the city and through back alleys, sometimes crossing the same road twice. He never again turned openly to look behind him, but he always made sure we were in the corner of his vision during a casual glance. Another mark of a professional. He finally vanished into the Centra Hotel.

To a passer-by, or a film crew with time lapse cameras, it would have resembled one of those ubiquitous cartoon chases where Sylvester and Tweety-bird are constantly ducking in and out of doorways down a long corridor. To us it was an adrenalin rush; apparent proof that the intelligence agencies were indeed listening in. I say apparent because they don't leave calling cards.

"What took you so long?," bleated Christensen when I got back to the car. I had to laugh. For a trained observer and investigative journalist, he'd managed to miss the great spy hunt of '92, although we'd passed him four times. Even Steve saw the funny side.

That week, the hunt began in earnest to find the disks. First port of call was Paul White's father, Peter. He agreed to meet us at the family home in Ruakaka, just south of Whangarei.

I think that, for Peter and Maureen, the shock still hadn't really set in. Sprawled on couches and chairs, Stones, Christensen and myself felt every bit the intruders we obviously were as we listened to this couple pour out their grief and suspicions, and yet we were perhaps more determined than anyone else in the country to find the truth about their son's death.

We talked for hours into the night, trying to persuade Paul's parents to part with all the information they had. They too had been advised of contact with the SIS on two occasions, and they'd been concerned at how paranoid and scared Paul was becoming. It was out of character, they said, for Paul to drive home drunk. On numerous occasions they'd been aware of, Paul had left his car and caught taxis home after a night on the town.

The same point had been made by others close to White. But none of this was getting us any closer to finding the disks. We'd been desperately hoping that White might have hidden a set with his parents.

"If you have any disks," I ventured, *"now would be a good time to tell us. We are committed to finding out why your son was killed, but we can't do that unless we can find a motive."*

It was the question Peter and Maureen White had been both expecting and dreading. You could see it in the guarded looks they threw each other.

"Alright," responded Peter, *"we'll trust you. We have one disk, Paul sent it to us as a sample. You can look at it, but you can't take it away. It's our only copy."*

Anticipating just such a moment, we'd packed a big computer in the backseat of the car before leaving Auckland.

"Just co-incidentally," I said, *"we do happen to have a computer with us. We can copy the disk off and research its contents back at TV3."*

Five minutes later we were downloading files furiously, hoping beyond hope that, having finally laid hands on one of the 90 disks, we'd actually find evidence to back up some of the claims White had made. As we scrolled through however, disappointment set in. The disk contained a series of analyses of company accounts managed by Citibank. Included in the lineup, the BNZ, the giant Australasian brewer Lion Nathan, and the Rural Bank of New Zealand. Nothing of startling significance in those reports. There was also a file on the New Zealand Dairy Board.

It was a series of letters dated April and June 1989, addressed to the Board and written by Citibank. It was confirming a foreign exchange transaction described as *"a Nassau Sweep agreement."* Under the terms of the deal, Citibank was to shift surplus funds in the accounts of two subsidiaries, at the end of each trading day, into an offshore account in the Bahamas tax haven. The two subsidiaries involved were Dairy Investments (Bermuda)

Ltd and New Zealand Dairy Board Finance Ltd – a company based in another Caribbean tax haven, the Cayman Islands. Just a couple of the 170 associate and subsidiary companies that the Board has set up around the world.

Where the hell were the other 89 disks? Was this the best or just a disk chosen at random? We had no way of knowing. I continued my perusal of the files, looking in vain for any mention of arms deals or politicians, but there wasn't any. With the pressure on from work to produce results, we turned over every single rock we could find. It was a case, noted Christensen, of simply shaking the trees until a gorilla fell out. We tracked down as many known associates of White as possible, none could help. We located and interviewed his former fiancee, Joanne Clark.

She threw two spanners into the works. In the first instance, she claimed to know where copies of the disks were but said they'd been removed when she went looking for them. Clark claimed they'd been hidden in a swamp close to White's apartment.

Stones and I duly equipped ourselves with steel prods and went stalking through the swamp for any sign that something may have been hidden there. For a pair of muckrakers, we were in our element. Coming up empty-handed and dirty, we returned to Clark for round two.

She was at the time a volunteer worker with the St Johns Ambulance service in Auckland, and she reckoned she'd been told the inside story on White's crash by her supervisor. According to Clark's version of events, when the ambulance first arrived on the scene there was nobody there, no other cars and no witnesses. I spoke to her supervisor on the phone. He said what he'd told Joanne had been correct, but he wouldn't say what he'd told her, and therefore couldn't corroborate or deny the story she gave us.

When we tried to raise the ambulance crew who attended, one had been sent to Seattle, Washington for several weeks, and the other refused to talk to us, closing his door in our faces. Pursuing the lines of enquiry raised by Joanne Clark wasted a considerable amount of our time. It was a matter of weeks before we were able to establish, on the basis of probability, that her version of the ambulance arrival was confused and erroneous. It may not have been a muddy swamp, but the end result was the same.

By the end of September 1992, after three weeks of full time investigation on the case, we'd come up with nothing we could stand up in a Court of Law with and prove murder. We had one more name to check on our list, North Shore car dealer Wayne Dunn, the man who had sold Paul White the vehicle that became his tomb. We were staggered to find Dunn was still in possession of Paul's wrecked Nissan Pulsar EXA Turbo. As we examined and photographed the wreck, we came across damage that could have been significant if police had bothered to do a thorough criminal investigation.

On the passenger side of the vehicle – the side of the car that according to official records never hit anything – there were horizontal scratch marks along the rear quarter consistent with scraping from another vehicle's bumper, consistent with the possibility that Paul White's car had been nudged into the wall by another vehicle.

The vehicle inspector who originally checked the car for police doesn't believe White was knocked off the road, and he points to the trajectory at the moment of impact as proof of this. However, this argument does not take into account the steering over-correction that a driver would make to compensate for such a knock: it is likely that the tail would firstly slide to the right then back to the left and so on. The trajectory at the moment of impact would be dependent on how far back the nudge had come and how much steering correction the driver had dialled in.

In addition, the motorists who were following Paul White claimed he was accelerating around the corner. The centrifugal force of such a manoeuvre should have seen White skid off the outside, left-hand, edge of the corner – not skid off on the *inside* of the corner, especially if, as alleged, White was so drunk that he fell asleep at the wheel.

The car was sold for scrap soon after the 1992 accident; the photo's are the only remaining evidence of the scratch marks. There is nothing in the police file to explain the existence of scratch marks in that position.

Dunn had kept in close contact with White by virtue of the hire purchase deal on the car, and was aware of the meetings with Peters and some of the claims of what was on the disks. None of this was new, but he did have one lead that subsequently proved important. On Friday, September 4th, Dunn remembered being contacted by a Larry Johnson, a former BNZ big-wig who was desperate to get hold of White that day.

It took several days of accessing computer records and phone books to locate Johnson, and when we went to see him we were secretly wired, so that our conversation could be recorded by Stones, waiting around the corner in the camera car. This was done not for broadcast, but for security and accuracy reasons. It would also become policy throughout the two year investigation to wear a hidden recorder at every interview. With suggestions of death threats, official "hits" and the need to get every fact straight, having taped interviews and full transcripts stored in a number of locations added up to a more effective insurance policy than Paul White had managed to muster. For all his boasts of making copies, none had turned up, and I wasn't about to repeat the mistake.

Speaking in hushed tones, Johnson explained his own background as the former Property Services Manager for the BNZ who'd been made to walk the plank. He wouldn't say why, but suggested it was because he knew too much about certain BNZ deals.* He claimed to have been bankrupted and hounded, but indicated he belonged to some kind of underground group that was keeping tabs on business and political corruption. We knew, although he wouldn't talk about it, that he had met Peters from time to time, but he said it was pure co-incidence that brought him into the White affair.

---

* See Chapters 6 and 27.

"I just happened to know the guy that sold him the car. There I was trying to dial White's home telephone number, and within 24 hours he was dead in his car.

"There's just no way in the world you can convince me, you know, that the big rally driver in the sky pulled him off the track! That didn't happen. I just can't believe it. There's just too much shit going on right now. Everybody feels too scared and there's too many people who are too close to too many things. There'll be a big explosion soon, and hopefully we'll start seeing it all."

There was an ironical twist in our meeting with Larry Johnson. After his sacking from the BNZ he'd taken a personal grievance case through the Employment Court. The lawyer acting for the BNZ against him was Julian Miles QC, a very accomplished barrister with a tongue like a surgeon's scalpel. He was also a cousin of mine through marriage.

Miles' presence turned into a kind of running gag throughout the investigation, everywhere I went he was there.

Johnson was extremely bitter at his treatment in the Court hearing. His evidence on why he'd been sacked had been permanently sealed from public view on order of the Judge, and he harboured a lot of resentment towards Miles. He also harboured major doubts about the competence of the Serious Fraud Office. He was told to go and see them for his own legal protection, and spill the beans on what he knew about impropriety within the Bank of New Zealand. *"So I went and gave them the 'Once upon a time', and after 10 minutes I could tell they weren't interested. So I said 'if you haven't got the time, I haven't got the time', and after that I just can't take them seriously."*

Unfortunately, Johnson's caginess and apprehension – he gave the impression of wanting to dive for cover every time the police helicopter flew within a kilometre of his house! – didn't add much to the sum total of our knowledge on the White scenario. In fact, that issue didn't become slightly clearer for us for another two years – towards the end of 1994. We discovered a lawyer who had been told by White himself, back in mid-1992, about an alleged arms deal on the disks.

On a warm spring evening in 1994, the lawyer and I took a walk. He recalled White telling him about a counter-trade deal involving a New Zealand company bartering its export products for Soviet-made arms, in lieu of cash. He'd thought nothing more of it. Nothing more, that is, until he met a man at a business function two years after the turbulent events of 1992.

It was May 1994, and the death of Paul White was a fading memory. The function was a seminar that touched on the role of bartering in international trade deals. During a coffee break, the lawyer struck up a conversation with another on the course, a man who wished to continue the discourse on the finer points of barter. It was then that the man across the table revealed a secret. He talked of how a New Zealand company had entered into barter arrangements to move product that otherwise might sit around gathering dust. As an example, he explained, this particular company had struck up a deal to exchange product with an Iron Curtain country in return for arms which were then sold on the international market.

The lawyer's nerves were on fire. It had been nearly two years since he had heard this story first. He would have dismissed it out of hand but for one important fact: The man across the table was an executive with the company allegedly involved.*

Listening to this in September 1994, I could feel the circle finally closing around me. Here was a man who could testify to being told of the arms deal by Paul White, but who also claimed to have been told the same story by an executive of the company concerned. Was it true? Or were they all just re-circulating rumours?

In the months following the car crash, there'd been suggestions of a complaint to the Law Society to get Paul White's solicitor, Mark Blomkamp censured or even struck off for his role in what was maintained was an extortion attempt. Blomkamp, I knew, had consulted a prominent barrister on the issue, and their defence went like this: If the complaint wasn't jettisoned, Blomkamp would go back to the High Court to get the injunction lifted, and would spell out in no uncertain terms what he had seen on the disks. The complaint was dropped. I wondered whether the alleged arms deal was a factor in that issue as well. Mark Blomkamp, however, wasn't co-operating.

"It's not that I don't want to help, but unless the injunction is lifted I cannot speak to you or anyone else about what Paul White showed me, or what I saw on the disks myself. And going back to your first question, I'm certainly not going to disclose my discussions with the Law Society."

There had, I knew by this time, been at least two other witnesses who had allegedly seen the disks. One was Chris Cotton, the computer dealer. Cotton was a frightened man. He never admitted it in the meetings we had, but it was easy to see in his manner and the guarded way he spoke.

Richard Poore, White's parents and even Paul White's fiancee Joanne Clark had named Cotton as a key witness, a man who'd helped Paul analyse the disks and make copies. For about the fourth time in two years he denied it, again. He also denied seeing what was on the disks. Chris Cotton appeared to know a lot more than he was saying, but he certainly wasn't going to let on.

Which brought me to the last potential witness, a journalist who'd accessed the disks about a fortnight before White's death. He too was scared. I tried to explain that he wasn't the only witness, and that I was now also chasing the company named by White with a series of written questions.

"What I need to know is whether you saw that arms deal as well?"

"Ah, no. No. No, I mean no, as in I want to try and stay well out of it," he finally responded. Talk about a half-hearted "no". Sensing I was, after two strenuous years, within striking distance of a possible motive for Paul White's death, I didn't let up.

---

* I have spoken to the executive concerned. He denied making the statement attributed to him but, significantly perhaps, he had already contacted his superiors after learning I was making inquiries. His response to my questions mirrored the response given by the company.

"Just so I know in my heart whether the damn thing was there — "

He was silent for a few seconds. All I could hear was my heart thumping in my chest like a bat was loose in my rib cage. It all came down to this. And then he spoke.

"It's there."

Gotcha! *"It's there, on the disks?"*

"It is there on the disks. I saw it, I didn't actually get to read it, but I saw it and I was told it was there as well. I didn't really understand what I was looking at until it all blew up later. I didn't really understand the significance of what I was looking at, I thought it was just some private notes or something — I didn't realise they were official business."

"But at the time, you understood it was a guns for product deal?"

"It had [the company] mentioned in it, and the basic gist of it was that to pay for [product], [the company] accepted weapons which they then flicked on to a third party." The floodgates had opened. *"There was no identification of the third party, but it said the debt was huge and it said that there had been an offer of military weapons, and the party who had offered these military weapons had already had a buyer. So basically what it was, was the party with the weapons was going to give them to [the company] and set up a deal for [the company].*

"[The company] didn't have to do anything, it was just going to wipe out their debt. The weapons were going to be given to them and then given by them to a third party. That was it. [The company] didn't have to touch the weapons, it didn't have to ship them themselves, it didn't have to do anything like that. It was just basically a transfer of assets into the name of [the company], and pass them straight to the third party. The money that changed hands would go straight to [the company], wipe out the debt."

So here we were on a facts basis: An Auckland lawyer had been told by Paul White in 1992 about an arms/barter deal and a company executive had allegedly recounted a similar story in 1994.

A journalist said he'd been shown the alleged Citibank disks a fortnight prior to White's death in 1992, and saw details of an arms/barter deal.

Ross Walters and Letitia Reddington, the real estate agents working below White's apartment, had themselves been informed by White of a "secret" transaction involving the company and a Middle Eastern country.

What inferences could reasonably be drawn from this handful of facts? As I saw it, there were three options at first glance. The first was that the company had indeed offloaded some of its overseas debt by transacting a deal that somehow involved a weaponry barter, and that a large number of staff knew of it.

The second was that a junior executive, or executives, whilst on business somewhere in Outer Mongolia or the Middle East, had dreamt up the deal but camouflaged it so that even their bosses didn't realise its true nature. The New Zealand company is a respected international trader, and even though there's nothing illegal in arms dealing — even though most of our largest trading partners are regular buyers or sellers of arms — the company itself would have frowned on any involvement in such activities.

The third option is that the company did not get involved in any arms/barter deal, and that the allegations made by Paul White and apparently repeated by an executive, had been based on either misunderstandings or idle rumours. Perhaps someone had dummied up some documentation on a computer disk and passed it off to the journalist, and the rumour simply grew to the point where the executive heard it and assumed it was true.

The concept of the former communist nations bartering weaponry wasn't new: at one time the Soviet Union had publicly suggested that it could pay for New Zealand butter imports by trading unwanted Soviet warships in return. A much cheaper option, the Soviets noted, than the billion-dollar ANZAC frigate project.

As an example, the Soviets were flicking off submarines for US$150,000, and warships like destroyers and cruisers were selling for only US$1 million or less. For the outstanding Soviet butter and wool contracts at the time, around $50 million, New Zealand could have had an entire Soviet fleet!

The offer, however, had been turned down by the New Zealand Government. When we put the latest allegations to the head office of the company named by White, in late 1994, the response was terse.

"I am able to advise that neither [the company] nor any affiliate or subsidiary, either based in New Zealand or off-shore, has ever accepted weaponry or armaments from any country as barter payment for products," wrote the company's legal counsel.

"You should be aware that any statement, suggestion or innuendo stating or implying that [the company] or any of its subsidiaries or affiliates has ever traded directly or indirectly in armaments or weaponry of any sort whatsoever at any time, at any place, will substantially damage the reputation, the good name and the business interests of [the company] and those of its subsidiaries and affiliates."

Them's fighting words – although we considered we had a legitimate right to at least investigate the allegations surrounding the company, given the public importance of the matter.

There is no basis in fact for the allegations. I simply raise the matter because it is pertinent to any investigation of White's death, and would provide one possible explanation for the apparent interest shown in White by security agencies.

It would, however, be unfair for the reader to draw a conclusion that the alleged guns/barter deal ever happened. There may well be an innocent explanation behind the allegations, including an original misunderstanding that's been amplified along the way.

At most, all that can be said is this: Paul White died in a vehicle accident. As with every unexplained vehicle crash, his wrecked car was examined by a mechanic for signs of any defects that may have caused it. None were found. Claims were made by those who knew White of possible foul play, but those allegations were not investigated because police were satisfied that the evidence pointed to a random accident involving a drunk driver.

I should also point out that there were three separate police investigations involving White, each independent of the other. The first was the extortion inquiry headed by Detective Sergeant Mark Churches. The second was the accident inquiry dealt with by the police traffic section, and the third was the inquiry into the disappearance of the $15,000, which overlapped to some extent into the circumstances surrounding the accident.

It was not, for example, the job of the extortion inquiry team to investigate the accident – they were entirely separate issues.

However, the police overall failed to spot certain clues like the opened briefcase and, in my opinion, mishandled the Citibank disks held as evidence for the trial of Paul White on criminal charges.

The Serious Fraud Office promised to investigate White's claims but, to all intents and purposes, didn't.

The Security Intelligence Service was implicated in the White affair, but denies it, and Paul White made claims that issues of *"national importance"* were up for discussion. I have absolutely no doubt that New Zealand's – or someone's – security agencies were monitoring White. What I don't know is why.

It is entirely possible, even probable, that Paul White's death was entirely coincidental to all the intrigue swirling around him. However, in my opinion, a lot of public confusion could have been cleared up back in 1992 if the police and Serious Fraud Office had undertaken more robust investigations in view of that public concern. Instead, the unspoken questions have been left to hang in the air.

I believe there should be an official inquiry into the way the White case was handled, if only to put to rest some of the intrigue and to come up with clear guidelines on how such highly-charged matters should be investigated by the authorities.

All of this, of course, is said with the benefit of 1995 hindsight. Back in 1992, with no Citibank disks illustrating the kind of transactions that White had apparently been concerned about, our own investigation had come full circle: we'd arrived back into the BNZ controversy courtesy of Larry Johnson.

But the Citibank story was an important stage-setter for two reasons. Firstly, it was our first experience of law enforcement agencies not doing the kind of job you'd expect them to do. As events later transpired, this wouldn't be the first time that happened.

Secondly, Citibank was a doorway for us into the European Pacific investigation. If we hadn't cut our teeth on the story of Paul White, we wouldn't have made the contacts that enabled us to eventually break open the winebox. For those reasons, the mysterious death of Paul White was a very important starting point for all that was to follow.

CHAPTER 6

Larry's Theme

*"Every financial deal has a key. You have to keep thinking
until you find the key to unlock the door."*
— MICHAEL FAY, 1979

ALTHOUGH WE WEREN'T AWARE of it at the time, Citibank had in fact been
named three years earlier in the United States' biggest ever money laundering investigation, Operation Polar Cap. Polar Cap identified a number of
banks harbouring hundreds of millions of dollars of Colombian cocaine
profits. In fact a *Los Angeles Times* report in April 1990 described how US
Justice officials had frozen 754 accounts in 173 different banking institutions across the US, in just one phase of Operation Polar Cap. Among the
banks mentioned were Bank of America and Security Pacific National Bank,
at the time some of the largest institutions in America. *"There is no
information,"* said a spokesman for Attorney-General Dick Thornburgh, *"that
the banks are anything other than unwitting service providers."*

Compared with the high drama of being named in America's biggest ever
drug money laundering investigation, Citibank executives at the bank's New
York headquarters must have been quaking in their Gucci's to hear that TV3
in New Zealand had suggested some of their customers might have been
laundering cash.

"New Where?," one Citibank US staffer might have said to another as they
gazed out over a Manhattan sunset.

"Who gives a damn?," the other would have said.

Unlikely as it seemed, however, Citibank bosses in New Zealand were
indeed upset; they were threatening to sue for libel. The reference to White's
allegations of "money-laundering" had stung the big American bank, even
though it's a commonly recognised fact that any bank or financial institution
can be unwittingly used for laundering illicit funds.

For TV3 bosses, the Citibank episode was a journalistic exercise of the
Icarus Principle; in other words we came damn close to burning our wings
off. Certainly the feathers of some had been ruffled and, in places, singed.

Several years on, it's clear that Citibank's New Zealand division didn't
have a leg to stand on in a libel suit but at the time, back in late-1992, the
ploy was extremely successful in gagging the television network.

Lawyers' letters were exchanged over allegedly defamatory claims made
in one of our first stories after White's death, and Steve Christensen and I
were hauled in for questioning by Pedersen and TV3's legal beagle, who just
happened to be Julian Miles QC. Miles peered down his spectacles at me. I
mentally crawled under the table, but my body seemed unwilling or unable
to follow.

"I can't get up in a court of law and defend this! Money laundering? Where's the proof?"

He glanced across at Pedersen, I gazed up at the roof. I had known from Day 1 that White's death could be a litigation danger zone. The trick in these things is to write the story in such a way as you can justify that everything you say is a fact. Factually, I could prove that White <u>did</u> claim his disks contained proof of money laundering, so where was the problem? Furthermore, we hadn't linked any companies or individuals to the alleged laundering, and the idea of Citibank getting its nose out of joint, when it's common knowledge that any bank can be used for such purposes, was ridiculous. Just because a jockey may throw a horse race doesn't mean the TAB is in on the plot. And yet here we were, sitting around a table, picking the investigation to pieces because of two lousy words.

Miles took the view that the story implied Citibank was doing the laundering, and as the conversation developed I began to wonder whether he was our lawyer or theirs.

"SIS meeting White? Rubbish!"

"Whatdayamean rubbish?," I countered, *"We've got two professional people saying they saw a man talking to White, then White came back and told them he claimed to be SIS. More importantly, this guy told White — and ispso facto the others — that if he didn't hand over the disks the police would be through in two days time, which they were. Who the hell else — apart from the SIS — could have access to that sort of information!?"*

But it was falling on deaf ears. Julian Miles is a very successful Queen's Counsel, and part of that success lies in his cynicism. He is not a fan of conspiracy theories, and was having pleasure savaging this one. I felt like a treed cougar running out of branches to seek refuge on. But there was another dimension to the problem. Because of Miles' earlier demolition in the Employment Court of the BNZ's Larry Johnson, neither Christensen nor I felt entirely comfortable spilling the beans on everything we knew, especially as some of those beans belonged to Johnson. The irony of the situation didn't escape me as my own beans went through the wringer in place of Larry's. Julian could barely contain the annoyance boiling up within.

"How the hell can I defend this story if you won't even tell me all the details?"

He turned to Pedersen. *"I'm wasting my time here, this is ridiculous."*

Still, I mused as I bounced through the branches in a free fall to the ground, better to get a mauling from my own counsel first — it'll give me a taste of what the opposition will be like.

Under normal circumstances I would have had my ass kicked from here to next Christmas, but as it was I did have an insurance policy. The story had been okayed and cleared for transmission by Keith Slater, at that time the Executive Producer of *60 Minutes* for TV3 and Rod Pedersen's second-in-command. He'd been brought in specifically to oversee it for legal reasons.

As I explained to Rod, what's the point in a journalist getting stories checked by the boss if the boss won't take the rap when the proverbial hits the fan.

There was one other little detail that we didn't notice at the time. In all the fuss about the alleged money laundering, no one had bothered to ask just how Paul White would have known what money laundering was. With White telling Richard Poore of all the Cook Island money dealing on the disks, it's probable that the excitable computer dealer mistook normal foreign exchange transactions or tax avoidance for money laundering. I mean, what does laundered money look like? White was not a banker, and he couldn't have picked the difference.

There may have been another factor in TV3's reluctance to pursue the White story. The tip came from a former Cabinet Minister, Aussie Malcolm, now a private immigration consultant. He'd made the front page of *The Dominion Sunday Times* with a claim that he was the victim of a police vendetta. He revealed that, late in 1991, he'd been approached by a group of backbench National MP's wanting him to stand in the upcoming Tamaki by-election, caused by Sir Robert Muldoon's retirement from politics. The backbenchers wanted Malcolm to win the seat.

"The game plan," he told the newspaper, *"was that having got me a selection, I would then go through the election saying that I was going to go to Wellington to get the right wing of the National Party. This was the objective, with a view to upsetting the leadership with a challenge around about late January/early February in the first caucus meetings."*

But like the best laid plans of mice and men, Malcolm and his supporters hadn't bargained on trouble. It came first in the form of a raid by the Inland Revenue Department, a complete audit of his business and his wife's business. They found nothing. Then it got dirty.

At the time, Malcolm and his family had taken under their wing a teenage boy who claimed to be fleeing abuse from his mother and stepfather. Suddenly police descended on Malcolm, accusing him of attacking the teenager. Not only did the allegation come as a surprise to the former MP on the comeback trail, it came as an even bigger surprise to the teenager, who was still living with the Malcolms.

The boy was taken away by police to be interviewed; he returned to the Malcolm residence more than three hours later claiming to have been beaten by police officers intent on obtaining evidence to support their accusations. In a subsequent official complaint, the Police Surgeon confirmed the injuries to the youth, and Aussie Malcolm accused police of assaulting the boy and of trying to jack-up charges to discredit his chances of a return to politics. He also suspected his phones had been illegally tapped.

"Then, at the end of leaving me sweating under all this pressure, they then mounted a search operation which involved about 14 cops, as far as we can make out, in a coordinated operation involving Helensville police district, the water police and Newmarket police for surveillance of a boat that I own, and simultaneous searches of the Kaipara [harbour], my house and the boat.

"Pulling the places apart, going through every drawer of every bloody cupboard."

Malcolm told the newspaper that while he couldn't prove any link between his planned political coup against the Prime Minister and the police and IRD raids, he had his suspicions.

*"Now you'll pardon me if I just get a little paranoid sometimes and wonder if all those events are connected. Now I'm not saying they are, but sometimes when I'm falling off to sleep at night I just bloody wonder."**

My curiosity was aroused and I phoned Malcolm up. On further discussion I learnt the name of the cop heading the investigation against him – a man I knew had himself been accused of beating foster children to the point of hospitalisation on a number of occasions. I offered him an internal police file on the officer, and in return he gave me an important and timely warning. *"I think you should know, the head of TV3 has suddenly got an immigration problem he didn't have three weeks ago. I think it might be related to your inquiries."*

In essence, when TV3 had emerged from virtual bankruptcy earlier that year, it had been purchased by Canada's Canwest Global company. The New Zealand Government had loosened up restrictions on foreign ownership to accommodate TV3's rescuers, and part of that deal included clearing the immigration path so senior Canadians could settle in New Zealand and get the network back on its feet. The TV3 executive in charge of handling the immigration issue had been told by a Government Minister that those permits were *"guaranteed"*. Now, it seemed, the position had changed.

"Yeah," said Malcolm, *"Ken Clark has just hired me to sort his problem out. I can't go into any detail with you, but suffice to say it's serious enough that if he doesn't get a Cabinet Minister's signature on a piece of paper, he won't be allowed to stay in New Zealand."*

There was no evidence to link Clark's green card problem with my Citibank enquiries, but I later learnt that all kinds of pressures were being brought to bear on the network chief up until the time I quit TV3.

The Citibank lawsuit never eventuated, although it cast a shadow over my remaining months at TV3. But here, in mid-September 1992, the investigation team of myself, Christensen and Harrington found ourselves stood down and back on routine duties. For Harrington that meant a return to Wellington and working on *60 Minutes*, for me and Steve it was back to general news. But the drama and intrigue of the previous three weeks couldn't be just forgotten, and the sense of something "big" slithering through the murky depths where politics and business meet was almost palpable. Yet there is a big difference between knowing something and proving it.

The economic upheaval of the 1980's had left big business firmly in control of all news and current affairs in New Zealand. While that meant

---

* It is not the first time that someone having a run-in with a Government Department or Cabinet Minister has suddenly found themselves ambushed by the IRD. I am aware of at least two other known cases. In one of those instances, a senior Government figure is alleged to have instigated the IRD investigation. If the IRD has ever been used as a "terror" organisation, it is a matter of grave concern.

things looked flashier, the reality was that newsrooms had been slashed out of existence up and down the country as newspapers and radio stations folded or purchased their news prepackaged from poorly resourced networks.

Those journalists left in the industry at the end of all the retrenchment found their hands were full just chasing fire engines all day and processing press releases. There was no time and certainly no money in the meagre budgets for real investigative journalism, and perhaps that's the way their big business masters wanted it. If the media could be diverted to covering crime and other "spot news", they'd be less likely to dig into business or political foul dealing.

For those of us who still remember the days of investigative reporting into important New Zealand issues, this new brand of shallow "McNews" was like working in a tropical fish tank, with our audience swimming around with us. Inside the tank everything is warm and brightly coloured, and we all have a sense of our beneficent leaders and masters throwing a few crumbs of food in at the end of each day to keep us happy.

Our fish tank is illuminated by powerful lights, so that we reporter-fish can clearly see the goings-on of the audience-fish, but there's so much glare that we can't see beyond the tank's four glass walls. And here we live out our lives, well fed, well watered, content in the knowledge that this is our world.

The reality is that beyond our fish tank is a darkness, a chasm where the powerful congregate and scheme, their machinations beyond the scrutiny of journalists or the public trapped in that carefully constructed glass cage.

The crumbs of food and information that trickle down to all of us in the tank are but remnants left over from the feeding frenzies of the corporate sharks and the political remora fish that accompany them. Of all this, we remain blissfully unaware.

And so it might have remained, but for the fact that Paul White's death effectively shot out one of those bright lights surrounding the fish tank. Just for a moment, Steve Christensen and I had glimpsed into that small patch of darkness and caught sight of our own Loch Ness monster – a disturbance in the currents that indicated there was more to reality than the daily doings of our fish tank.

The tricky part would be finding a way to tell the audience-fish of our experience without being laughed out of the tank.

* * *

WHEN PEDERSEN DISBANDED THE investigation team, it was done for economic reasons. The rest of the Citibank disks had not turned up, and without those there was no hope of taking the story any further. Certainly it would be unwise to give Citibank more reasons to litigate. In addition, 3 *National News* producer Mike Brockie was feeling the strain of putting a bulletin together without two of the more senior reporting staff contributing on a daily basis. When it finally came down to calling their dogs off, it was these factors that were uppermost in Pedersen and Brockie's minds.

On the flip side of the coin however, White's death was the latest in a seemingly unconnected series of events. We'd had *NBR's* mysterious article on Southern Wogistan – apparently relating to film fraud investigations in that mythical realm allegedly closed down after political interference on behalf of those being accused.

"Such are the politics of Southern Wogistan," the NBR had noted, *"It could never happen in New Zealand."*

We'd had Winston Peters in Parliament, alleging he was offered a bribe by big business to come on-side, and now we also had parliamentary allegations that Sir Michael Fay had abused his position as a BNZ director to obtain a massive mortgage loan on the Fay Richwhite tower. Peters hadn't yet named his source on the BNZ matters, but Christensen and I were convinced it was Larry Johnson, and possibly Paul White

The fact that Johnson had tried to get hold of White the day before his death lent credence to the possibility that the Citibank case might be linked to all that had gone before. And yet so far I had seen no hard evidence that anything untoward had taken place. This could all be someone's misguided nightmare. When I wasn't filing daily news stories I was spending every other spare minute trying to sniff out leads on what quickly became dubbed "Project X", trying to discover the truth or lie of all that had gone before.

We kept in touch with Johnson, a man we were convinced had important information, despite his caginess. Still, even we were surprised when Peters got up on his hind legs in Parliament one Thursday evening, and let rip with what Prime Minister Bolger would later describe as *"Winston's king-hit"*.

It was an affidavit sworn by Johnson earlier that day, October 15, 1992, in Auckland. Curiously, the Government already appeared to know the contents of Johnson's document, despite the high security surrounding its swearing and subsequent fax transmittal direct to Peters' parliamentary office.

The MP would later allege that either the Security Intelligence Service or a private agency working for big business was carrying out illegal wiretapping of his phone and fax lines – *"There's no other way they could have obtained a copy of that affidavit before I'd even read it in the House,"* he challenged later.

As Peters read the document and its allegations into the Parliamentary record, it became obvious that Johnson certainly had been one of his main sources on the BNZ. Chief among the claims was that Johnson, in charge of the bank's property portfolio, attended a meeting in February 1990 where a loan to one of Sir Michael Fay's companies was being discussed. According to Johnson, Fay was there, despite being a director of the Bank of New Zealand at the time. In his eyes it was a clear conflict of interest.

"The loan application," stated Johnson, *"was for a sum of $42 million, for the purposes of refinancing the building known as the Fay Richwhite Building in Queen Street."*

According to Johnson the BNZ had a rule where property loans couldn't exceed more than 50% of the value of the property. The building itself was worth $116 million, but Fay Richwhite only owned half of it – or property worth $58 million. The giant NZI corporation owned the other half.

A quick calculation showed Fay Richwhite should only be allowed a maximum loan of $29 million, not the $42 million they were seeking. Johnson spat the dummy.

"The processing of the loan application involved my attendance at meetings where Sir Michael Fay was present on two occasions; the second occasion he was present for the duration of the meeting, which he in fact chaired.

"At this time I was summonsed to a meeting at the Fay Richwhite Building. At this meeting there were present Sir Michael Fay; his Financial Manager, John Balgarnie; Jonathan Arthur of the Bank of New Zealand, the account manager for the Fay Richwhite and Co. Ltd; Roger Kennedy, the Bank of New Zealand solicitor; and two other lawyers from Russell McVeagh McKenzie Bartleet and Co who I understand were acting on behalf of Fay Richwhite and Co. Ltd.

"During the course of this meeting, I advised Sir Michael Fay that before I would approve the loan, he would have to alter the structure of the lease. A discussion then took place between Jonathan Arthur and Roger Kennedy and myself in respect of the $900 million current exposure that Fay Richwhite and associated interests had with the Bank of New Zealand.

"In the course of this discussion Sir Michael Fay became highly agitated and I was called a 'little effing God'. I personally advised Sir Michael Fay that he had a conflict of interest as he had his customer's hat on, and asked what he would do when he put on his director's hat.

"I told him that I was hired to clean up some of the mess at the Bank of New Zealand, and now he was arranging his own loan which would be far in excess of the loan to value ratios that had currently been fixed by the full Board of the Bank of New Zealand, and that what he was doing involved a major conflict of interest."

It's worth re-iterating at this point that Johnson was an American, and the US is very strict on issues where conflicts of interest arise. Brian Henry once recounted an incident where he attended a cocktail function at the US Consulate in Auckland while acting as the lawyer for a major US airline.

He ended up in a corner with his client, a consular official and a representative from a rival US carrier, chatting. When the diplomat left to mingle, the rival had to leave the conversation as well. The reason? Under tough US regulations he couldn't be seen to be talking to officials from a competitor without an independent person present. Henry, as the other airline's lawyer, didn't qualify as independent, under the laws that safeguard American corporate ethics. New Zealand on the other hand is almost entirely unregulated and, according to Johnson's affidavit as read out by Peters, Fay didn't take kindly to being told he had a conflict of interest.

"Sir Michael Fay became very irate and told me that it was, quote, 'my effing bank' and 'I will do anything I want to'."

Stalemated, the situation allegedly deteriorated even further. Another meeting two days later failed to resolve the central issues, and Johnson remembers being summoned to another meeting in the Auckland BNZ Tower the next day.

"At the meeting were Sir Michael Fay's financial advisers; Mr Peter Thodey, a very senior officer of the Bank; Jonathan Arthur; lawyers from Russell McVeagh; Roger Kennedy and myself.

"Roger Kennedy and Peter Thodey asked me to step inside Thodey's personal office. Once inside Thodey advised me he had received a phone call from Sir Michael Fay saying I was being unco-operative 'given the time restrictions to make the deal work'. He stated, 'We can't let Michael Fay fall'."

After more haggling, Johnson claims he was told the loan would be brought back within the existing ratios, and other areas he had problems with would be ironed out. On that basis, he says, he signed an approval form for the loan handed to him by Jonathon Arthur, but was subsequently surprised to see the loan remained at the ratio of 72% of the value of the property, not the 50% set down in the guidelines.

When Peters finished reading the affidavit, he attempted to table it – a move that would allow media organisations to print the document without fear of defamation lawsuits. The Government objected, back bencher Tony Ryall – himself a former BNZ employee – blocking the tabling of the affidavit and then launching a counter-attack on behalf of the Government.

Ryall went on to attack Larry Johnson's credibility, saying Johnson had himself ignored a personal conflict of interest when seeking a loan to build his house on the sought-after Whangaparaoa Peninsula north of Auckland. Ryall said Johnson had valued his home at $1.2 million, while other property valuers placed its worth considerably lower. Johnson, he said, was also a bankrupt, a man who was fired from the Bank because he couldn't handle his own finances. Ryall's broadside was matched the next day by BNZ CEO Lindsay Pyne, who called a news conference to discredit Johnson.*

"I have to say, both personally and professionally," said Pyne, "that what I am about to say is deeply distasteful. It goes against my principles as a professional banker. Regretfully, I have been placed in a position where I now have no option but to expose a former employee. But that is now the level of Mr Peters' campaign.

"We have already rejected Mr Peters' allegation of irregularities in the procedures surrounding a Bank loan involving the Fay Richwhite building in Queen Street. We suspected at the time, and Mr Peters now confirms, that the source of the spurious and slanderous allegation was Mr Johnson."

Pyne released documents that, he said, exposed Johnson as a *"proven liar"*.

---

* Ironically, Inland Revenue investigators questioned the roles of Lindsay Pyne, Robin Congreve, and Fay Richwhite's Bill Birnie in a document tabled at the 1995 Davison Commission of Inquiry. All three had been directors of Postbank when it undertook an alleged tax avoidance transaction using European Pacific and Capital Markets. The IRD told the new owner of Postbank, ANZ Group, that *"it may be in the interests of the ANZ to take statements from such persons as Dr Congreve, Mr Birnie, Mr Lindsay Pyne and the Postbank company secretary as to their level of knowledge of 'downstream events'."* The transaction involved was of the same type alluded to in Johnson's allegations of excessive BNZ lending to the Fay Richwhite Group. See Chapter 27.

These related to Johnson's bankruptcy, where he allegedly tried to hide a runabout boat – one of his assets – from his creditors, and also to statements he made to the BNZ in March 1990 relating to the value of his house. Pyne went on, accusing Johnson of mismanaging his personal finances to an incredible extent.

"In 1990, interest payments alone on his borrowings were more than $400 a day and exceeded his total net income. Mr Johnson, supposedly an expert in property valuation, lost total credibility when it came to valuing his own house. In a signed statement to the bank, he valued his property at $1.3 million in March 1990, while at the same time a registered valuer of Mr Johnson's own choice assessed the maximum value at only $775,000.

"My only regret is that the Bank employed Mr Johnson in the first place. We fired him because patently, by his own statements, he could not be trusted. Also his gross mismanagement of his personal financial affairs was totally unacceptable for a banker in his position.

"The New Zealand public should also not trust the claims of Mr Johnson. Joining me here today are a number of Bank staff who were named by Mr Johnson. They are all prepared to testify on oath regarding his allegations."

Contrary to Lindsay Pyne's tough-sounding promise, none of the executives named by Johnson was prepared to testify on oath at all, at least not for the media's sake. In the wake of the 1994 *Frontline* exposé of the alleged European Pacific tax fraud, I wrote to Jonathan Arthur and Peter Thodey, both of whom were still working for the Bank of New Zealand, requesting that they provide affidavits "as promised" rejecting Johnson's allegations. The first reply came from Mark Dowland, Head of Legal Services at the BNZ.

"While the gentlemen concerned remain prepared to testify on oath no circumstances have arisen which would require them to do so," he wrote, at the same time suggesting I direct future correspondence to the Bank's Head of Corporate Relations, Wayne Weston. Undeterred, I fired a missive in Weston's direction – arguing that as the promise had been made at a news conference for the benefit of journalists, and presumably with the intention of giving extra credibility to the bank's position, that affidavits should be forthcoming if so requested.

The reason for requesting affidavits was that it would force all witnesses to tell the truth about the meetings or risk possible perjury charges in Court. Denying something at a news conference is very different from making the same statement on oath. That's not to say that the BNZ's version of events wasn't correct, it's a case of comparing apples with apples – all parties should be prepared to back up their position with affidavits.

"Should the BNZ or its staff be unwilling to furnish the testimony as requested," I wrote in the final line of my letter to Weston, *"I would have no choice but to mention such a refusal in any subsequent story addressing the pro's and con's of the matter."*

The response was equally brutal.

"The Bank has no reason to comply with your request. We treat the matter to

which you are referring as history," stated Weston in a two paragraph letter.

I had already approached two other people present at the alleged meetings. One, Roger Kennedy, the Bank's former lawyer, was like a cat on a hot tin roof when I phoned him and suggested that the allegations in Johnson's affidavit might actually be true. He drew in his breath and there was a silence on the line for 11 seconds before he answered.

"I can't comment on it. I uh, obviously, um, no I can't comment."

Eleven seconds is a long time. Kennedy appeared to have backed away from the BNZ's original total denial of all Johnson's claims, if only because now he refused to offer an opinion one way or the other. I pushed him harder.

"Would you be prepared to testify before a Royal Commission if you had immunity?"

"I don't need immunity."

"Would you then be prepared to swear an affidavit in support of the allegations contained in the Larry Johnson affidavit?"

"I can't comment."

"Well that's a decision that obviously you're going to have to come to at some stage."

"I may not."

"There's only a few people who were in that room at the time. Why is there still a reluctance by people to talk, do you think?"

"I have no idea."

The second interviewee I located had not been mentioned in Johnson's affidavit. He – like Roger Kennedy – had worked for the BNZ's lawfirm Buddle Findlay and had attended at least one of the meetings. His name was Shean Singh, and I'd been told that he would back up Johnson's version of events.

Singh, however, was reluctant to say anything publicly and, like Kennedy, justified his silence by citing legal privilege. I asked about his attitude to testifying before a Parliamentary Select Committee.

"If I am subpoenaed, and I am to answer questions under oath, then obviously the truth will be revealed – unless of course I believe that they do not have the right to know that."

"I suppose Shean what I'm saying is: At what point does one's duty to one's country transcend one's duty to a commer–"

"When I am," he interjected, *"As you say, when I am commissioned before the Parliamentary Select Committee. Then I will."*

"Then you will tell?"

"Yes."

I wasn't the only person keen to see everyone named by Johnson provide sworn affidavits testifying to their role. An Auckland police officer, aware of some of the internal drama at the BNZ, on one occasion bailed up one of the men after a social function to discuss the matter. Things got heated, and the cop left believing there was a lot more to the case than had so far been revealed.

Larry Johnson, himself a Vietnam war veteran, was also far from impressed at the way Lindsay Pyne had lined up the witnesses, describing it as a *"reminder of the way the Iraqis paraded shot-down US fliers."*

"If I am such a flake," he told the *National Business Review*, *"Why did the bank employ me in the first place?"*

It was a fair question, and *NBR's* probing at the BNZ failed to turn up any dissatisfaction with Johnson's performance as Property Services Manager. The paper quoted the bank as saying Johnson had a significant role in quarantining off bad property loans and preventing them having an even bigger impact on the troubled bank. So how much of the picture Lindsay Pyne painted was out of sequence? In fact, the sequence of events was this.

In February 1989, a year before the row blew up over the Fay Richwhite loan, Johnson refinanced an existing AGC Finance mortgage with a $450,000 mortgage from his new employer BNZ which, at discount staff rates, would be much cheaper to service. Johnson later obtained a second mortgage from Westpac and the BNZ came to the party again just before Christmas that year with a third mortgage top-up.

A couple of months later, in February 1990, Johnson attempted to block the Fay Richwhite loan until it met credit guidelines. Within weeks, during March 1990, the BNZ was putting Johnson through the third degree, "discovering" that he'd overvalued his own property. In June 1990 he was dismissed from his $200,000 per annum job; the Bank of New Zealand calling in his extensive loans, cancelling the cheap staff interest rates and ordering him to refinance.

A neighbour, Geoff Hammond, remembers Johnson and his wife Dawn became very withdrawn after his dismissal.

"There were obviously pressures there," Hammond told the *Sunday Star* newspaper, *"It became obvious to me something was grossly wrong. His life came apart."*

Not surprisingly, by November 1990 Johnson was in serious financial trouble, with another finance company getting a Court judgement against him for unpaid debts of nearly $46,000. By January 1991 the plush clifftop mansion had been placed up for mortgagee sale by the BNZ. It eventually sold for $505,000.

Johnson was subsequently bankrupted, and took a personal grievance case against his former employer alleging unjustified dismissal. He claimed he'd been sacked, for reasons that would later emerge in his parliamentary affidavit, but during the December 1991 Employment Court hearing that evidence was suppressed and sealed.

Downtown in the big bronze edifice that housed the Fay Richwhite empire, reaction to the latest skirmish was swift. Just after 11:00am the next day, Sir Michael Fay issued a news release headlined **"FAY CALLS PETERS A LIAR AND A COWARD"**.

"I categorically deny all the claims made by Winston Peters late last night in Parliament on the basis of a supposed sworn affidavit," wrote Fay.

"Once again, as he has so many times before, Mr Peters has got his facts wrong,

his times scrambled and is now producing perjured testimony in his on-going vendetta against myself, Fay Richwhite and the Bank of New Zealand. To avoid any doubt on anyone's part, I absolutely deny any improper conduct on my part, I absolutely deny any impropriety in the roll-over of the loan on 151 Queen Street, I deny pressuring Bank employees to my own advantage and I deny the absurd claim that the BNZ ever had a $900 million exposure to Fay, Richwhite.

"Mr Peter's [sic] behaviour in this matter is vile. The man is a liar and a coward."

In case anyone had missed it, the gloves were well and truly off. By comparison the exchange between Peters and Selwyn Cushing had seemed almost civilised. Sir Michael Fay, however, was sick of being the patsy, and the strain was showing. In the final sting of his news release, he invited the MP to *"take his lies and false evidence and lay them before a court, so that I may defend my reputation."*

As I interviewed Sir Michael on camera that afternoon, I felt almost sorry for the man. Perhaps it was the Dale Carnegie-style habit of referring to me by my first name in the interview – a trick that can backfire in television because producers want such things edited out, creating extra work at the expense of the deadline.

Sir Michael was also very keen that we run his claim that Peters was a liar and a coward. Very keen. I explained to him that the producers had already expressed reservations about that phrase, fearful of a defamation lawsuit from Peters.

When I returned to the newsroom with the videotape, debate on whether to use the claim was again in full swing. I argued in favour of using it, reasoning that Peters was unlikely to be sucked in by such a blatant slap in the face from Fay, and pointing out also that Fay deserved a right of reply.

Legal advice, however, was to drop the phrase. When I rang Sir Michael to tell him, he implored us to reconsider, saying he would pay any legal costs or damages if we were sued by Peters as a result. I was stunned. This guy obviously wanted a courtroom showdown with the MP desperately.

3 *National News* Director Rod Pedersen and senior producer Mike Brockie considered the options. Would Sir Michael, they wondered, be willing to give TV3 a written indemnity? Once again, in my capacity as go between, I expressed doubts that Sir Michael would be dumb enough to put such a request in writing, and naturally enough the Fay Richwhite chief executive agreed with me. He did, however, what he does best. He cut out the middleman and phoned Mike Brockie direct, offering his word that he would personally indemnify the television network from any potential repercussions.

His word was accepted. We ran the liar and coward comments and, as expected, Peters didn't bite. We never found out whether Fay had offered indemnities to other media outlets.

As the mad scramble began to find Johnson and nail down an interview, Christensen and I figured we'd have no problem, given our existing relationship with the guy. Johnson, however, didn't want to be found.

A Television One camera crew allegedly became involved in a car chase in their efforts to grab a word with him, an incident which heightened our feeling that TV3 would get the exclusive. In the end however, without prior warning, Johnson went to TV1 and agreed to appear on *Holmes*.

It didn't exactly boost our own credibility back in the TV3 newsroom.

"Jeez Wishart," sniped one erstwhile colleague, *"if that's the kind of exclusive interview you can get us after several weeks on the case, I'd hate to see what damage you could do after several months."*

Slinking out of the office that evening, I had to agree. With no hard evidence so far on the Citibank case either, the whole imbroglio was getting depressing. Instead of leading the pack, we were dancing like puppets in reaction to other peoples' agendas. Carpe Diem – the Latin phrase meaning Seize the Day – had been one of TV3's foundation stones, and yet so far all we'd seized were shadows.

It was a brick wall in a journalistic maze, and there appeared to be no way out. For the next couple of weeks we quietly stewed, but it was a fortuitous phone call from my uncle that provided our escape route.

Des Wishart was a senior partner in another big Auckland lawfirm, McVeagh Fleming – not to be confused in any way with Russell McVeagh. Des had seen our coverage of the Citibank case, and knew of my interest in the other matters. He suggested I meet a colleague of his, Chris Dickie, who'd been working on the bloodstock cases.

At the time it seemed just another insignificant development, but I think on that particular day God had been playing around with loaded thunderbolts and accidentally dropped one on we mortals below, for our meeting would lead to one of those history-making developments – without which this story might never have been written.

CHAPTER 7

A Little Dickiebird

*"The goodness of gunpowder, and consequently the intensity of its
explosive power, depend entirely upon the purity of its constituents,
and the proportions in which they are mixed."*
— HOME COMPANION, 1853

IF YOU'RE LOOKING FOR legal hit-men, Chris Dickie doesn't exactly spring to
mind as the archetype. Rather than the clean cut Armani-suited creatures
who frequent the small screen, Dickie is short, middle-aged and swarthy
looking. He gives the impression of being a man who has been on intimate
terms with the Four Horsemen of the Apocalypse and, in view of his current
project – the bloodstock investigation – quite possibly one or two of their
horses as well.

I was aware, from prior media coverage, of Dickie, and some of what he
was up to. Dickie, a partner at Auckland lawfirm McVeagh Fleming, not to
be confused with Russell McVeagh, had been pursuing Challenge Corporate
Services and Anzon Capital – two of the 1980's high flyers – and their
solicitors, Russell McVeagh, for several years, on behalf of 300 investors in
bloodstock and film partnerships from the mid-1980's. These partnerships
had been set up essentially as investments, with promises of profits and – at
least initially – apparently enormous tax benefits, back in the days when
Governments gave incentives to produce movies and the like.

The incentives had resulted in a whole string of B-grade movies, from a
whole string of different promoters and film companies, whose raison d'être
appeared to be not to make money but to lose it, and incur valuable tax
writeoffs in the process. Some of these partnerships, according to the media
coverage I'd seen, contained alleged fraud within the schemes.

In the bloodstock partnerships there was a hidden element, allegedly not
disclosed to the investors in the prospectus or anywhere else. It was a secret
company controlled via Hong Kong called Zorasong, which was acquiring
the horses from the overseas studs and then allegedly flicking the nags on at
vastly altered prices to New Zealand investors in the bloodstock partnerships. In one example highlighted in a High Court Statement of Claim,
Zorasong allegedly purchased five horses for just over $791,000, but onsold
them to the bloodstock partnership for $1.7 million, on or about the same
day. The investors were apparently never told of the secret deals and
assumed they were buying their horseflesh direct from the top stud farms in
Australia and the Republic of Ireland, featured in the various prospectii for
the deals. Zorasong, it was alleged, was not independent, but in reality was
a mask worn by the scheme's promoters.

As investigators probed further and deeper, the financial links between the three partnerships [Ermine and Buckingham were later joined by Wicklow] became so confusing it was almost impossible to work out where one finished and another began. To add to the difficulties, the money trail was wending its way through a string of offshore entities in tax havens and financial centres around the globe. In the end, even the Irish stud farms supplying the horseflesh were treating all the partnerships as one – they effectively gave up trying to keep it separate.

"*It was,*" Dickie told me, "*a complete shambles. The accounts were a disaster.*" In the course of his investigations, he had come across links to the BNZ affair and also European Pacific. We began comparing notes.

His own brush with the tax havens began in 1989, when he stumbled across a Cook Islands bank account being used by one of the companies implicated in the bloodstock deals. The bank account belonged to a Cook Islands company, Investment Management Services (CI) Ltd. Dickie wrote the name down on a scrap of paper, and for three years it teased him. What was its significance to the bloodstock money trail?

As he later pointed out, "*My clients were buying horses in Australia and Ireland: What the hell did the Cook Islands have to do with it? What were these bastards doing with my clients' money? The clients were certainly never told anything about it.*"

It was Chris Dickie's introduction to the Cook Islands empire of European Pacific.

While searching for witnesses to the deals, Chris had found a couple of real gems, not directly related to his area of interest however.

One was a Bank of New Zealand executive meeting in the late 1980's, where a senior executive allegedly explained how to do deals that were criminal whilst maintaining the facade of legality. He drew an example of one such deal on a whiteboard, a wiring diagram of a Cook Islands-type tax loop. "*Everything above this line,*" said the executive drawing an arbitrary line across the middle of the diagram, "*is illegal. Everything below the line is what we show the authorities. It's legitimate.*"

On another occasion a banker had been present at a training seminar thrown for the bank's financial whizzkids by lawyers, who allegedly told them how to remove file notes and memo's that might become awkward at a later time. He was advised to use sticky, yellow "Post-It" notes. These could be removed, if necessary, to strengthen the bank's position in disputes with customers or legal action.

Dickie also told of threats resulting from his enquiries – the first two of a personal nature and urging him to back off.

Undeterred, but beginning to feel a little bit like Ebenezer Scrooge being haunted by the three Christmas ghosts, Dickie thought he was mentally prepared for his third shock, which came in the form of friendly, but extremely serious, advice. He wasn't prepared at all.

He was in Hong Kong, investigating the involvement of an international accounting firm, and liaising with a senior commercial lawyer in the colony.

"*I had been planning to approach the Hong Kong fraud office to ask for assistance. My lawyer, a prominent figure in the city, warned me that if I made that approach, I would not leave Hong Kong airport alive that night. He was deadly serious. He went on to tell me that there were certain entities in Hong Kong that were known to be involved in massive money laundering, drugs, tax evasion and arms deals, and that New Zealand, he said, was minute in relation to the total picture."*

But perhaps the most serious threat was a constitutional one. In a meeting at McVeagh Fleming's Auckland office tower, a man involved in one of the partnership deals allegedly told Dickie and Tony Molloy QC how they planned to force the Inland Revenue Department to back off on the *Merry Christmas Mr Lawrence* investigation.

Up to this point, the IRD had been vigorously pursuing the promoters and investors in the movie, a point Winston Peters had alluded to in his parliamentary allegations that the IRD investigation had been nobbled. In support of his claims he'd produced a letter dated April 7, 1987, and written by an IRD Senior Inspector, Denise Latimer.

During the investigation of Mr Lawrence Productions Ltd – the special partnership behind the film *Merry Christmas Mr Lawrence* – Latimer revealed that a loan arrangement had been assessed by the Inland Revenue as *"a sham"*, and went on to warn the investors that they could be prosecuted for illegal tax evasion.

"In view of the discrepancies disclosed, it appears that an offence against Section 416 of the Income Tax Act 1976 may have been committed. Please let me have, in writing, your personal explanation of the discrepancies and any reason why you consider that penal action should not be taken against you."

Two senior tax investigators in the IRD's Auckland office, Ms Latimer and a colleague named Allan May, had travelled the world trying to gather evidence about the film's financing arrangements. The essence of it was that while the promoters had declared to investors and the tax authorities that the movie had made a loss, a profit of $2.5 million had allegedly been secretly shunted into a tax haven bank account in the Channel Islands, between the UK and France.

Latimer and May had come very close to clinching the crucial evidence they needed, but not close enough. At the accounting firm in Hong Kong, after several days of failing to get an appointment with one of the partners, they gained entrance to the building with a form of subterfuge. Within two minutes of their unmasking as IRD officials, they were shown the door.

Following in their footsteps, via Hong Kong and London, Dickie and Molloy managed to uncover the evidence they needed, and they brought the documentation back to New Zealand. At a meeting with Latimer on their return, Dickie took the IRD inspector the documentation she needed.

"She literally danced a jig in her office," Dickie remembered later. *"Their mouths were going like goldfish. I was left in the clearest impression that they now had the evidence they needed to prosecute and planned to do so."*

It was shortly after this that Dickie and Molloy had their meeting with the film partnership man. He stated that no money had been stolen in the

Merry Christmas Mr Lawrence deal. He said that his organisation would force the IRD to back off as well. If the Revenue challenged the scheme, Russell McVeagh would be asked to bring a legal challenge on behalf of every investor, a process that could tie the IRD's legal and accounting teams in knots for the next three years.

The man also stated that he would not be prepared to discuss the merits of any argument presented by the Revenue – whether in respect of Merry Christmas or other film partnerships in which his organisation had acted and which was now under investigation. To Dickie and Molloy this was a mind-numbing suggestion.

If most individuals or companies told the Revenue authorities to effectively "get knotted", they could normally expect to be turned over by an audit team faster than most people can say "jack rabbit". No such fears for this gentleman, apparently.

He also told Molloy and Dickie that a matter of acute embarrassment regarding an Inland Revenue staff member would be raised, if necessary. Above all, he was adamant, there would be no IRD investigation of *Merry Christmas Mr Lawrence*.

The man also tried to get Molloy and Dickie to back off, saying that the stirring up of the case would only end up costing the investors more if IRD ended up challenging their tax assessments as well. Far better, he said, to let Russell McVeagh sort out a deal with the IRD and save everybody money.

Dickie immediately warned the IRD Head Office of the threats he'd just heard, but it appears the threats may have been put into effect.

Latimer and May, the IRD inspectors from Auckland, had taken the new evidence gained from Dickie and Molloy to Head Office. Instead of a pat on the back they were summoned to Wellington, and shortly afterward a senior IRD executive allegedly demanded that the Auckland officers sign a deed of settlement on *Merry Christmas Mr Lawrence*, including, effectively, a non-prosecution deal. When they refused to sign, the IRD superior allegedly did so on their behalf.

Molloy and Dickie were stunned. The organisation that was meant to enforce Revenue collection had just walked away with their hands in the air. The two lawyers suddenly realised they were alone in their battle. It was becoming relatively clear that, despite the hype from the National Government and its Business Roundtable cheer squad, all was definitely not well in Gotham City.

The alleged bloodstock and film frauds spanned the globe. From their origins in New Zealand, I learned of money trails weaving through tropical paradises like Rarotonga, through the spice laden bustle of Hong Kong and the *Bergerac*-like setting of Jersey in the Channel Islands. I learnt of a law firm in Jersey that had so many documents relating to the operation of Zorasong Ltd, and other offshore entities, that *"you couldn't see the top of the bald head of the partner concerned because there were so many documents in front of him on the lawfirm's library table."*

The sojourn to the Channel Islands by Dickie and Molloy was actually history-making in a global sense. They went there to obtain what's known as a "Norwich Pharmacal" order. It allows the plaintiffs in a fraud case to force third parties – in this case the Jersey lawfirm – to identify further parties to the alleged fraud. Such orders are rare anywhere; they're unheard of in tax havens – bastions of banking and financial secrecy. But the two New Zealand investigators beat the odds and gained a world first – a Norwich Pharmacal order in a tax haven jurisdiction, with the extra bite of an order requiring production of the documents.

Zorasong's operations through the Channel Islands must have been huge. Following the successful legal battle, Dickie was advised by a lawyer from the Jersey firm that he now had a major logistical problem to deal with: how to get the documents back to New Zealand.

"You will have to hire a jumbo jet, I'm not joking!," the Jersey lawyer had explained. There was an extra problem as well. The cost of collating and copying the documents was **quarter of a million New Zealand dollars!**

In 1995, as I write this book, I can report that the 63 filing boxes of documents still have not been shipped to New Zealand. Russell McVeagh is taking legal action to prevent their release. Russell McVeagh and its lawyers were also vigorously denying any wrongdoing in relation to any of the bloodstock or film transactions. Once again Aladdin's Cave of Wonders was opening before me, its hidden secrets beckoning me through a savage maw that had the word "LITIGATION" plastered all over it in neon letters 3 metres high.

In the intervening days my path had crossed that of an Australian, John McLennan. McLennan had been a former top manager with the Westpac Banking Group and he'd become a kind of self appointed banking ombudsman in Oz – a financial Jiminy Cricket if there is such a beast. McLennan's latest claim to fame had been helping to expose the so-called "Westpac Letters", a series of documents which disclosed alleged fraud and prompted a national debate.

With the Bank of New Zealand up for sale to National Australia Bank in November, 1992, McLennan was on a flying visit to sound out corruption issues on this side of the Tasman. His talks had led him to a man named Stephen Lunn, a dapper wheeler-dealer whose name meant nothing to me but whose topics of conversation drew me like a magnet. He claimed to have some first hand knowledge of the film and bloodstock partnerships, but McLennan also told me that Lunn claimed to have access to the Citibank disks. Every alarm bell in my head was ringing.

After speaking to Lunn on the phone that evening, I knew he could tell one hell of a yarn about the bloodstock deals – he used to work for Challenge Corporate Services, one of the companies involved. The next morning I phoned Dickie.

"I'm sorry," trilled the very obliging receptionist at McVeagh Fleming, *"Mr Dickie's line is busy. Can I have him ring you back or will you hold?"*

First major mistake. When Chris Dickie's line is busy, never <u>ever</u> offer to stay on hold. I later heard rumours that some clients had grown old and died whilst waiting for Dickie to take a breath. If Dickie has skeletons in his closet, they're probably unfortunate visitors that he shooed in there while he took a phone call. Twenty-seven and a half minutes later, I was put through.

"How would you like to meet the man who can describe to you how the bloodstock money was laundered?"

As Chris Dickie would later joke, it was like asking if he wanted a date with Elle McPherson.

"Fine," I responded, *"I'll pick you up in half an hour, we're meeting him outside the Empire tavern."*

It would be fair to say that by this stage in proceedings paranoia had firmly taken hold of all the players. This was manifested in different ways, but in my case it was an acute sensation of being watched, listened to and followed.

As I pulled out of the TV3 garage driving Pedersen's new Mazda 626, I wasn't really aware of the hot spring day. My attention was more on the rear view mirror, or the guy on the corner with the dark glasses. I was pleased to discover Dickie and Lunn shared my affliction.

Stephen Lunn turned out to be a familiar face. Only a couple of weeks earlier I'd seen him turn up at TV3 for a meeting with Pedersen, Slater and a bunch of lawyers. I'd assumed at the time that it had something to do with Citibank, but Lunn revealed he'd been trying to get TV3 to do the European Pacific story.

He explained he'd had a hand in TVNZ's 1990 *Frontline* programme "For The Public Good". The team that produced the programme had alleged links between the Labour Government and big business.

There's two ways of killing big game. One is a good, clean shot right between the eyes which drops the beast instantly, and the other is a grievous wound that may or may not be eventually fatal – the problem being that in the interim a lot of damage can be wrought. Unfortunately for the production team, those named in the programme were fighting back furiously. When hunting elephants it pays to shoot the beast first, and make sure it's dead, before bagging it.

In this particular case not only had they failed to ensure it was dead, but journalistically-speaking they either hadn't pulled the trigger or their ammunition wasn't big enough. Whatever the reasons, on the night it was not a clean kill. Naturally enough the elephant, in the form of the Labour Government, came charging back out of the bag – trampling the *Frontline* team in the process – before making off into the sunset trumpeting wildly about scumbag journalists and its own innocence.

The result was a programme that attracted millions of dollars in defamation writs, all of which have been settled out of Court, and which saw the production team that worked on it fired. An internal inquiry by TVNZ bosses – not wanting to admit anything that could later be used in Court against the company – instead focussed on the use of "sinister music" as one of the big problems with the programme. In another of those little twists of fate, journalist Murray McLaughlin – who created *For the Public Good* –

ended up working for Australia's ABC network on the *Four Corners* programme about Winston Peters and his allegations.

I found *For the Public Good* was a useful form of personal shock therapy throughout the European Pacific investigation, a reminder that there but for the grace of God . . .

Lunn spent the morning denying to me that he knew anything about the Citibank disks, but he was more forthcoming about the bloodstock deals to Chris Dickie. In fact, he turned out to be crucial.

Lunn had made a habit of being first into the office each morning, first to clear the fax machine. On it were regular messages from Hong Kong to Challenge Corporate Services relating to the partnerships, regular messages also from the Channel Islands.

He proceeded to calmly relate what Dickie had only hitherto suspected, some of the inner workings of the elaborate partnership schemes and a run down of who allegedly knew what. Dickie was one happy puppy, but Lunn threw me a bone as well. He casually mentioned that I could have the European Pacific winebox documents if I wanted them, and I could pick up a set tomorrow. I leapt at the chance. Dickie, too, was impressed, but more so at having discovered a potential new witness who could help him crack the alleged partnership frauds.

Until that day neither man had known of the other but, as we left the Birdcage tavern on a hot spring afternoon, we had no idea that within 36 hours the convergence of all our paths would have repercussions that would shake the very foundations of the country.

CHAPTER 8

From Lunn, With Love

*"The bulk of better reporting consists of information that does not meet
the courtroom standards of proof. Journalism is not a court of law; it
is a process of weaving together, often from necessarily anonymous
sources, the strands of history. If legal standards were applied to news
reporting, the public would have learned nothing of the Watergate
scandal and President Nixon would not have resigned in disgrace."*
— WILLIAM PINWILL, *NATIONAL TIMES ON SUNDAY*, 1988

IT DIDN'T TAKE LONG for the first tremors to hit: they came the following
evening. Stephen Lunn was relaxing at home on Waiheke Island in
Auckland's Hauraki Gulf, pondering his next move in the European Pacific
chess game, when his opponents forced his hand.

From out of the dusk came a helicopter, its blades thumping the still air
ominously as the craft plummeted down onto the beach in front of Lunn's
house. Too stunned to move, he could only watch open-mouthed as a man
came running toward him and slapped a legal document into his hands. It
was an injunction order restricting Lunn from any further dissemination of
the European Pacific documents or discussion of them.

To his island neighbours it was like a scene from *Apocalypse Now*, or in
Lunn's words *"a James Bond movie"*, but to Lunn at the time it was the
beginning of a nightmare. He rang European Pacific boss and old friend
David Lloyd — what the hell's going on? Lunn later told *Metro* magazine
Lloyd's response: *"We have to injunct everyone"*. Shortly afterward came a
phone call that resulted in armed men being called in to protect Lunn's
home. It was a woman's voice on the end of the line, cultured and measured.

"Stephen?," she asked down the line.

"Yes."

*"You must stop what you are doing. You must stop now. What you are doing is
no good to any of us. If you don't stop now, we know where you are, at Onetangi.
We will send some guys to break your fucking kneecaps.*

"We know where you are, where Anna is, where the boys are."

A shocked and frightened Stephen Lunn interrupted, *"Who is this? What
are you talking about?"* The woman ignored him and continued.

"We will arrange for your boys to fall off the harbour bridge. Just stop it." Then
she hung up.

Terrified for the safety of his family, Lunn sent them to spend the night
at a friend's house. He then called police, and he called Chris Dickie. It was
Dickie's house that was used by police as a control point while they decided
whether to send reinforcements to Waiheke to protect Lunn's family.

The decision had already been made for them, however. By the time police had arranged a launch, Lunn phoned to say 20 or so of his neighbours had gathered with guns and dogs to protect the property and the family. The police, reluctantly, accepted the situation. Lunn's neighbourhood vigilante squad, armed to the teeth, would be allowed to stay in place.

Instead, police turned their attention to tracing the call. Naturally enough, the woman hadn't used her own phone – she'd called from a phone booth in Browns Bay. There the trail ended. Lunn and Dickie knew it was highly unlikely to be a crank call from the public given Lunn's non-existent public profile. As to the caller's motives and real intentions – given the highly charged atmosphere and the dramatic turn of events – they could only speculate.

It wouldn't be the first time that a mystery woman played a threatening criminal role behind the scenes as events gained momentum in later months. Someone, somewhere, appeared to have Lunn and others in his immediate circle of possible contacts under surveillance.

The previous week, on Tuesday October 20th, 1992, *National Business Review* journalist Fran O'Sullivan had taken possession of an envelope full of documents delivered to her hotel room. The following day she was attacked in a lift in Auckland's BNZ tower by a man who tried to snatch documents and computer disks she was carrying up to the newspaper's office. Some of the disks fell down the lift shaft and had to be retrieved later by maintenance staff. The offender escaped.

The documents she was carrying related to the so called "Magnum" transaction in the European Pacific winebox. At this point no one in the media realised the significance of that particular transaction. Magnum was the deal that would later be referred to in Court as a *"criminal fraud"* on the New Zealand Revenue to the tune of $2 million. Obviously someone had realised its devastating potential.

Whoever it was, they were undeterred at failing in the lift. O'Sullivan later went back to her hotel room, only to find evidence of a break-in, and her remaining documents had been ransacked.

Coincidentally, perhaps, Lunn was phoned up by a European Pacific executive around that time, and asked whether the Magnum deal was in the winebox. When Lunn replied in the affirmative, the tax haven banker couldn't hide his concern.

"I was afraid you'd say that!"

It was mid-evening on the 28th when I rang Dickie at home to chew over our discussions with Lunn the previous day. When he answered the phone Chris was panicky.

"I can't talk now, the shit's hit the fan, the cops are here, I've got guys with guns and dogs running around Waiheke –"

"Slow down Chris, I'm not with you. What's happened?"

"It's Lunn. They've served an injunction on him and he's had a death threat. I've rung a friend of mine who's a senior cop, we've got it under control."

I hung up the phone, stunned. Guns, dogs, death threats. To come so close to the full winebox and have the damned thing snatched out from under my nose. I was convinced then – somewhat egocentrically, I now hasten to add in hindsight – that the SIS must have bugged TV3's phones; they must have known I was meeting Lunn and decided to act. Shit!

Within hours journalists Warren Berryman and Jenni McManus of *The Independent* business newspaper were experiencing exactly the same thoughts. Lunn had phoned them to warn of the impending injunction. Naturally enough, they freaked. Fearing their own homes and phone lines were bugged, the two met on Jenni's front lawn to decide on their next move. Like squirrels on speed they did what came naturally, hiding their nuts – in this case their documents – in the ceiling of their office.

As dawn broke on the 29th, Dickie and Lunn were already plotting their next move. A court appearance at 10:00am left little room to manoeuvre, and the possibility of an immediate court order to return the winebox left even less room for choice. On Dickie's advice they dropped the winebox in the lap of the Serious Fraud Office, ensuring firstly that the authorities would now have to investigate them and, secondly, kicking the box out of reach of EP. But if they thought the SFO was glad to see the box they were very mistaken. Within the hour, a Serious Fraud Office investigator was on the phone to Chris Dickie.

"What are you trying to do?," he hissed, *"set us up?"*

It was Dickie's turn to be shocked. This didn't sound like the attitude of our top fraud investigators who'd just been handed the key to a tax haven treasure chest – something their counterparts in the US would have crawled across broken glass to obtain.

By this time Stephen Lunn was in the Auckland High Court trying to defend himself against European Pacific's scattergun injunction. Also named as defendants were Pauanui Publishing, publisher of *The Independent*; Fourth Estate Holdings, publisher of *National Business Review*; George Couttie, a former European Pacific employee; and Louis McElwee, an Auckland lawyer. Hearing the case was Justice Peter Hillyer, a hardnose judge with a passion for late model Lotus sports cars.

Hillyer refused to hear any detailed argument for or against the granting of an injunction, citing a lack of time. Stephen Lunn tried to make an impassioned plea for the injunction to be discharged, outlining the events of the night before and begging Justice Hillyer to allow publication of the documents. Lunn figured whoever was threatening his family might back off if everything suddenly spilled into the open. The Judge however disagreed, and issued an order banning publication of anything Lunn had said in Court. Justice Hillyer adjourned the Thursday morning hearing until the following Tuesday, and issued interim orders forbidding the defendants from publishing, using, copying or disseminating any European Pacific documents.

The battle line had been drawn in the sand, but ironically as the two sides squared up for Round 2, it was Justice Hillyer who became the first casualty. The Judge had been an investor in one of Russell McVeagh's controversial partnerships, sinking $4,000 into the venture. None of this is to suggest that Justice Hillyer had done anything wrong. He hadn't. But it's an example of how easy it is to inadvertently get a conflict of interest in a country as small as New Zealand.

The next morning in Court saw a change of presiding judge. In the hotseat, Justice John Henry. First of all he had to examine European Pacific's demands. They included not only prohibition orders on publishing or copying the documents, but also orders for the defendants to hand back any documents still in their possession; to reveal the names of the person or persons who supplied the documents in the first place; and a list of all the documents the defendants had held.

European Pacific's arguments were based on the principles of breach of confidence, breach of copyright* and conversion of personal property – the company arguing that the documents had been stolen from the firm by Couttie when he left EP in 1989.

Where information is confidential, New Zealand law provides automatic protection against publication unless one of two possible defences exist. The first is where the information has already been published or placed in the public domain: in this circumstance the document is no longer confidential because its secrecy has been blown.

The second possible defence to a breach of confidence action is where a defendant can prove that the document discloses an iniquity. This can be either a crime, or on a lesser scale perhaps only something immoral or unethical. The Courts recognise that the public has a right to know if a document discloses iniquities, and in addition Judges are loathe to be seen protecting the perpetrators of an illegal act.

As Justice Henry noted in his interim decision, the newspapers were relying on the iniquity defence to beat the injunction. The papers cited public interest in:

1. **Transactions enabling foreign companies to avoid the provisions of the Land Settlement Promotion and Land Acquisition Act 1952;**
2. **Transactions involving the Bank of New Zealand and possible breaches of s 62 of the Companies Act 1955; and**
3. **Transactions designed to avoid or circumvent New Zealand tax laws.**

"The alleged involvement of the Bank of New Zealand in such matters," wrote Justice Henry, *"is relied upon presumably because of the present controversy surrounding some of its activities. Those matters can, in my view, properly be described as matters of public interest. The question which then arises is whether that overrides the need to protect the confidentiality of the information.*

---

* The copyright issue quickly fell by the wayside: copyright belongs to the author of the document, so European Pacific couldn't claim a blanket copyright on, for example, all the Fay Richwhite, BNZ or Brierleys documents in the winebox – those companies would have to take actions themselves. In short, a legal and logistical nightmare.

"That exercise creates some difficulty in the present case, because all parties have adopted something in the nature of a standoff position and have chosen not to disclose any of the documents to the Court."

Indeed, "difficulty" didn't begin to describe it. Before judging whether a document disclosed iniquity, the Court obviously had to see the document and make its own decision. *NBR* and *The Independent* didn't want to bring their documents into Court and run the risk that they couldn't prove iniquity. If that happened, the Court would issue a permanent injunction and probably order the papers to return all the documents. It was far safer to fudge the issue and hold on to the EP files, in the hope that time would find a way to beat the injunction.

European Pacific, on the other hand, didn't want to give the winebox of documents to the Court for much the same reasons. The company didn't want a Court poking its nose into the transactions, and it certainly didn't want to risk having the news media publishing transaction details gleaned from legal argument in Court. In addition, there was always the risk that a Court might decide that the documents did disclose iniquity, and allow full publication.

With the Bank of New Zealand sale due to be finalised in a matter of weeks, lawyers for the newspapers argued the injunction should be discharged so that BNZ shareholders could make informed decisions. Justice Henry considered the small number of shareholders wasn't sufficient to establish a major public interest factor.

"Moreover, such relevance as this information may have to share value, which I find difficult to discern, is to my mind of marginal significance and could not warrant the permanent loss by the plaintiffs of the prima facie right to protection of confidential information.

"The whole issue of public interest and its effect on that right can better be determined at the substantive hearing of this action, provided that is expedited as it should be and as the Court will assist in achieving."

The Judge paused briefly to wind back the scope of the first, Hillyer, injunction, and left the two business newspapers unable to publish, copy, disseminate or use any of the documents they'd received so far. In regard to Couttie and Lunn, the same restriction applied, but included not only the documents but also any information they knew about European Pacific.

Cracking this little Pandora's Box was going to be difficult – everyone publicly identified with it had been gagged. Once again, Spook re-entered the picture. Like a real-life Walter Mitty, he claimed to have found a European Pacific employee who hadn't been injuncted, and who could spill the beans on some of the company's operations.

We met the man in a darkened basement carpark, no prior phone calls amid Spook's fear that our lines were tapped. Escorted from there to a nearby city apartment, the sense of anticipation was palpable as I flicked on the microcassette recorder. Who the hell was behind European Pacific? What the hell did the company really do?

"What do I call you," I asked.

"You can call me John, I'll give you my real name further down the track."

In a dishevelled former warehouse, the late afternoon sun streaming through the windows and highlighting the dust swirls, the story of what became a planet-circling financial empire unfurled before me.

It was the story of a company whose name was synonymous with discretion, secrecy, concealment, evasion, avoidance, reticence and seclusion – all of those '80's yuppie bywords. It was a time when the doing of the deal was what mattered, not what was being dealt or who was being dealt to.

The European Pacific concept was born at the bottom of Sydney harbour in the late 1970's, a time when a group of corporate raiders made their money by purchasing profitable companies, flogging off all their assets and disappearing with the cash, leaving the now empty shell company unable to pay a bean to the tax authorities.

To make sure they weren't caught, the raiders dropped the records and documents of the cashed-up targets into Sydney Harbour, where tax inspectors couldn't get at them. A novel – if somewhat simple – approach to filing a tax return.

Two of the many people accused of those early tax-dodging schemes were John Wynyard and John Connell. They'd left Australia and ended up in the tropical Cook Islands, helping David Lloyd set up his tax haven.

On Christmas Eve, 1981, the Cook Islands Trust Corporation came into existence, and with it the official opening of the Cook Islands as a tax haven. It was like letting poachers write the gamekeeping laws. Lloyd and his two tax-dodging henchmen had persuaded the Cook Islands Government not just to create a haven, but to actually let them draft the laws required.

"These statutes," a European Pacific brochure later noted, *"establish the off-shore regime as a separate and distinct regime from the domestic jurisdiction of the Cook Islands. Entities established within the off-shore regime are not subject to the ordinary laws of the Cook Islands.*

"This exemption extends beyond taxation and fiscal matters to other obligations, duties and responsibilities imposed by domestic laws."

In other words, they were a law unto themselves. Not even the Cook Islands Government would have the power to police them.

"Strong confidentiality provisions apply in the off-shore regime, requiring Government officials as well as trustee company and bank employees to observe secrecy. These provisions are backed by penal sanctions. The Registries are not open for general search (including by Government officers) and may be inspected only by officers, members, debenture holders or any other person with the written permission of a director or the liquidator."

With all those powers, the Cook Islands Trust Corporation was ready to do business. For a few thousand dollars, you could buy yourself the name "Bank" and do nefarious financial deals the world over. For a little bit less you could set up secret companies and secret accounts to hide your money from creditors or the Inland Revenue. It was a licence to burgle Government treasure chests around the world.

At least, that's the way it was supposed to be. Unfortunately, back in early

1982, no one else in the world had heard of the Cook Islands and, after spending all their money setting up the haven, Lloyd and his partners didn't have much cash left. The Trust Company was, by all accounts, going broke.

The two bottom-of-the-harbour schemers from Australia flew the coop again, selling their shares to Lloyd. It's worth noting what eventually happened to Wynyard – their past caught up with them. John Wynyard died in jail in Australia in 1985 while protesting his innocence of tax fraud charges, while John Connell had been extradited back there from the United States to face charges. In all six men had been arrested and charged with fraud, but with Wynyard's death and the decision by another to turn State's Evidence, only four stood trial.

It was one of life's ironies that saw 800 people screened for jury duty before 12 could be selected, only to have the 1992 trial abandoned forever six months later after the jury failed to reach a verdict. The reason?

"The foreman was deeply concerned about the behaviour and attitude of one of the jurors," reported the *Sydney Morning Herald* on August 20, 1992. The foreman had written a letter to the trial judge.

"According to the foreman, the juror appeared to have problems understanding English; in the jury room she had stuck cottonwool in her ears, put her head on a cushion, and refused to take part in reasonable jury room discussions about the case.

"She had cottonwool in her ears in Court during some days of the Crown's closing address and she had apparently already made up her mind about the outcome of the case. This could make it impossible for the jury to reach a unanimous decision, the foreman wrote, thus making 'a mockery of the jury system'."

I didn't know it then, but before my investigation ended two years later, I too would feel like inserting cotton wool in my ears and banging my head on a cushion. John Connell and his three co-offenders were acquitted, the State of New South Wales decided not to re-try the men after discovering the soonest trial date would probably be two years away.

Back in 1982 though, the possible fate of his colleagues years down the track occupied David Lloyd's mind for a nanosecond. Of far more importance, where was he going to get the injection of capital and clients that he desperately needed to make his tax haven work? Enter Stephen Lunn. Lunn was working at the time for Challenge Corporate Services, a subsidiary of New Zealand's industrial giant Fletcher Challenge, specialising in investment banking operations.

Like two other executives whose names would become intertwined with European Pacific, Lunn had begun his New Zealand career in 1976 at a company called Securitibank. The bank was memorable for imploding violently in a multi-million dollar collapse a few months later. Those other two executives who worked alongside Stephen Lunn? Their names were Michael Fay and David Richwhite.

Curiously enough, Securitibank seemed to be a common thread connecting many of the players. Apart from Lunn, Fay and Richwhite,

Securitibank also employed Rod Petricevic and John Paine, who both went on to become associated with Fay Richwhite, Anthony McCullagh, who later joined European Pacific, and a man named John Hicks, who later became the investigator for the SFO in charge of the winebox inquiry. They were, if you like, the Class of 76.

When Securitibank collapsed, Hicks stayed on to help official liquidator Charles Sturt – the man later to become Director of the SFO. A junior lawyer on that investigation was a man named Brian Henry, who later became Winston Peters' barrister.

Early in 1982, Lunn picked up his morning paper, and noticed a tiny article about Lloyd's new tax haven. Intrigued, he made contact with David Lloyd.

"He didn't have a lot of money left," Lunn would later tell NBR, *"It had taken him a few years to put the whole plan together and he'd run out of steam. He was about to give the whole thing away."*

Sensing a business opportunity, Lunn convinced his superiors at Challenge Corporate to buy a half share in the fledgling tax haven company. Lunn had saved Lloyd's ass – it would be one of the more ironical twists of the saga that Lunn eventually became "the Alpha and the Omega", the part creator and part destroyer of European Pacific. Twelve years would separate those events.

In 1984, Fletcher Challenge decided to pull out of the finance game, jettisoning a raft of associate finance companies and merchant banking subsidiaries, including its half share in the Cook Islands Trust Corporation. David Lloyd found himself once again the sole owner of the company, and in need of a new partner.

It was the same year that ushered in free-market economics in New Zealand, when the David Lange-led Labour Government swept to power on a tide of hostility towards the incumbent National administration of Sir Robert Muldoon. By devaluing and floating the currency, at the same time removing all foreign exchange controls, Labour Finance Minister Roger Douglas unleashed the forces of international money markets and corporate high finance.

The up and coming thrusters of the business community were eager to spread their wings, and a tax haven on the back doorstep seemed like a very good idea.

"Rumour has it," said EP "deepthroat" John, pausing to draw on his cigarette as the late afternoon shadows deepened around us, *"rumour has it Lloyd met Ron Brierley. David was a man who always travelled first class. He liked the high life, drinking champagne and the like.*

"He was a short guy and he always wanted to have an attractive woman – you know – he always had these dolly-birds working for him, traipsing after him. He liked champagne, big fat cigars – immaculately dressed – all that. Anyway, he was travelling first class between Australia and New Zealand on his way up to the Cooks and he happened to sit beside Ron Brierley.

"Ron asked what business he was in, and it all went from there. He just

happened to strike it lucky. The world economy, deregulation, was taking off, everybody was looking for ways to rort the system, and Lloyd had it. Cook Islands Trust Company, first trust company in the Cook Islands. He met the right people through Ron – he met the Fays people, and it was all on."

By 1986, New Zealand investment conglomerate Brierley Investments Ltd [BIL] and merchant bankers Fay Richwhite had gone halves in their own tax haven banking operation, based in Rarotonga. They called it European Pacific Bank. Later that year they merged their bank with Lloyd's trust company, formed a parent company called European Pacific Investments and listed EPI on the Luxembourg stock exchange that Christmas. BIL, Fay Richwhite and a new partner – the Bank of New Zealand – each took a 28 percent holding in EPI, with the public being given a chance to purchase the remaining 16 percent when EPI listed on the NZ exchange in January 1987.

European Pacific's public launch coincided with the America's Cup yacht races off Fremantle, Australia, a challenge organised and sponsored by two of European Pacific's shareholders, Capital Markets and the BNZ. Donations to the cause were turned into even more money by being channelled through the Cook Islands tax haven.

European Pacific Investments shares had a par value of US$2.00, but they climbed to nearly $45 as investors scrambled on board.

As the Capital Markets/BNZ sponsored yacht *KZ 7* thrashed all comers to reach the semifinals of the America's Cup, punters on an already-overheated sharemarket were betting *KZ 7* would eventually win the trophy. Speculators ran wild, bidding up the Capital Markets share price to unprecedented heights and sending property values around the Auckland foreshore – where the next America's Cup might be staged – soaring.

A television current affairs crew following the phenomenon attended an auction at the summer resort Whangaparaoa Peninsula, some 40 kilometres north of Auckland, where an old holiday shack was up for sale. Its Government valuation was in the region of $25,000, the real estate agent felt it might fetch $75,000 in the heated market for property with sea views. A staggered camera crew watched in utter disbelief as bidding climbed through the $100,000 barrier, on through the $500,000 barrier and eventually through the $900,000 barrier. All this for a shanty made of corrugated iron and fibrolite.

The yuppies who purchased it were badly burned a few weeks later when American skipper Dennis Conner, sailing for the previous Cup holder San Diego Yacht Club in *Stars and Stripes*, knocked *KZ 7* out of contention in the challenger finals and went on to win the Auld Mug back from the Australian defenders. The evening of the final race between *KZ 7* and *Stars*

---

* David Richwhite tells a slightly different version. He says he was introduced to Lloyd by Robin Congreve of Russell McVeagh. At the same time, Fays were trying to do a Brierleys deal, and Richwhite and Paul Collins ended up in the Cooks, talking to Lloyd. "That ultimately led to the formation of European Pacific Banking Corporation and the start of what became the European Pacific group," he told the Davison Commission in August 1995.

and Stripes – a race Fay had to win to stay in contention – was an evening when you could have fired a machine gun down Auckland's Queen Street and hit nothing. All the streets in the city were deserted, everyone was watching the live coverage of the make-or-break race. When Fay's *KZ 7* limped home last, three million hearts sank, and the next few days saw a mini sharemarket crash as punters unloaded their now overvalued stock.

Among those to benefit from the European Pacific listing were a number of executives in the state-owned Bank of New Zealand. They were given the chance to purchase EPI stock at par value, they made a financial killing. Even Lunn was given the chance to sup at that trough, he held two thousand shares from the initial float, worth $90,000 dollars at their peak.

One senior BNZ manager remembers the philosophy behind the BNZ's involvement in European Pacific.

"I was told there were two reasons that EPI was set up. One was to enable the bank to do deals which they didn't necessarily want to go through the bank books or the bank board or whatever, so they could do it off from the side without anybody really knowing.

"The other thing was that it was to produce an income for those executives involved in those transactions, that the bank didn't necessarily worry about. Because, you see, the bank was facing enormous competition in the market for good executives and they had to pay those executives well. But the bank pay scale didn't allow them to do that, so they were at risk of losing their key executives, especially in the investment banking area, which was Ron Diack's area.

"I was told by Peter Travers at that time that the second reason for setting up EPI was to enable him to pay bonuses to the guys that he liked, such as Diack and Peter Thodey and people."

Peter Travers was essentially the BNZ's second-in-command, behind Chief Executive Bob McCay. Holding the title General Manager, he'd been with the bank since 1954. He was an inaugural director of European Pacific Investments.

Also on the EPI Board, David Richwhite, David Lloyd, Paul Collins of Brierleys and two other EPI staff. These men came riding into the streets of downtown Rarotonga as the latest in a string of corporates and financiers to descend on one of the planet's fastest-growing tax havens. Of all the service providers in the tiny nation, theirs – European Pacific – was the biggest and brightest.

John looked up at me as the last pool of sunlight faded on the wooden table between us.

"It's getting late, why don't we continue this tomorrow."

And with that I was shown the door. I remember coming out into a dusky summer evening, with a view of Auckland city spreading below me and, beyond, the glittering Waitemata Harbour and Hauraki Gulf where the last feeble sunbeams were dancing on the water. Gazing out over all of that, I found myself thinking of palm trees and sandy beaches somewhere far over the horizon, and I felt that, slowly, the enigma of European Pacific was beginning to unravel.

CHAPTER 9

Gold Merchants, Gun Runners and BCCI

"To maintain secrecy, the banker suggested that I utilise a code name. 'How about Mr Gold?' I asked. That seemed in character with my fantasies. He furrowed his brow and replied, 'No, we already have a Mr Gold.' "
— DENNIS LEVINE, CONVICTED INSIDE-TRADER, 1991

WHEN I NEXT MET John, he was with a friend – a man clutching a box load of documents. *"Before you ask,"* he muttered as he waved me to a seat, *"No, it's not the bloody winebox!"*

Using the pseudonym Andrew, the man with the box turned out to be a man with family ties to the Cook Islands, although no ties, apparently, to European Pacific. He did however have access to a box being kept in safe storage in New Zealand, and this was the cardboard grail in question.

"It's something I think you'll find interesting," John remarked cryptically. "Interesting" turned out to be an understatement. It appeared to be a box of confidential Cook Islands Government documentation dating back to the mid 1980's. Its contents were dynamite.

Confidential diplomatic cable traffic between Rarotonga, New Zealand, Britain and the United States reveals international attention was focussed on the tiny Pacific state. In late 1986 a political scandal was raging through New Zealand over secret plans by the Maori Affairs Department – a Government ministry – to obtain $600 million worth of funding from some dubious Hawaiian business figures utilising the Cook Islands.

While the media, courtesy of Winston Peters, didn't find out about the plot until mid-December that year, cable traffic as early as late-November indicates New Zealand intelligence agencies were already trying to find out who was behind it.

Stamped "CONFIDENTIAL", marked "priority" and sent to the Governments of Tonga, the Cook Islands, the United States and Britain, a diplomatic transmission was fired out by the Ministry of Foreign Affairs in Wellington on November 26, 1986.

"The Department of Maori Affairs has been approached by an Hawaiian group with an offer of a low interest loan (4 percent for 25 years) of USDLRS 300 million. The loan is envisaged as a source of funding for the proposed Maori Resource Development Corporation.

"The Department has been in communication with Hawaiian-based Michael Gisondi, who claims to have acted as an adviser to the Kingdom of Tonga (making reference to the Hon L L Kavaliku and Hon J C Cocker).

"There are also claims that investments have been made in Tonga and the Cook Islands, using the same source of funds.

"We have been told that Gisondi acts on behalf of Max Raepple based in West Germany who in turn is the agent for the original source of the funds in Kuwait. The purpose of the funds is reported to be to counter Soviet influence in the South Pacific, and the total sum for this purpose was thought to be USDLRS 10 billion.

"As far as the Department of Maori Affairs knows the Kuwaiti Government is not involved. Could you please check on Gisondi's activities in Tonga and the Cook Islands, and the validity of the claim that investments have been made. He describes himself as a certified financial planner, and appears to have experience in insurance.

"If London or Washington have any leads on Gisondi, Raepple or the source of funds, please let us know. Reedy from Maori Affairs will be travelling to Hawaii on Sunday 30 November where he will meet with Gisondi and Raepple, so we would appreciate a response by our Friday."

"Is this stuff for real?," I asked John, already knowing the answer.

"Yeah. I think it's important that before you try to understand European Pacific, you understand the climate and culture it operated in. At the time most of these documents were drafted, there were only two trust companies in Rarotonga. Cook Islands Trust was one, and the other was South Pacific Trust Corporation, run by a lawyer named Reuben Tylor.

"A lot of this stuff doesn't directly involve EP, but you'll find it gives one hell of an insight into the way the Cook Islands operate."

I read on. We could find no immediate response to the New Zealand plea for help, but another telex was sent from Rarotonga to the Bank of England, by Cook Islands Auditor Richard McDonald on December 1st.

"You will note that this telex comes from a different number," McDonald begins. *"This is because it is most sensitive, so have used our highest security telex number."* The cable talked of Cook Islands investigations into two characters, named Armin Mattli, a Swiss bullion trader; and Samir Bashout – alias Khalaf Bashout – who were both seeking to be appointed as overseas financial agents for the Cooks Government.

"He [Mattli] was introduced to our Prime Minister by a [man] who was involved in stormy Cook Islands politics in 1970's and who was then alleged to have been involved in a plot of violence [gun running] against the then Premier.

"A Michael Gizondi, based in Hawaii, appears to be linked with Mattli, and Gizondi is reputed legal adviser to Morris who was associated with Bashout and also closely involved with Marcos aides and visited this country in company with three of them – Agdeppa, Fideldia and Pimentel."

Bashout turned out to be an American of Arabic descent and, according to the documents, an alleged con artist of the highest order. He was also a client of the Cook Islands Trust Corporation. In November 1985 Bashout and some dodgy Americans had visited the Cook Islands purportedly to obtain an offshore "B" class bank licence from CITC. To meet the requirements of a $10 million capitalisation, he waved a telex from Metrobank Los Angeles, which stated he had that sum on deposit.

Anthony McCullagh, a Cook Islands Trust Corporation employee, fell for the ruse hook, line and sinker. "Dr" Samir Bashout was introduced to an equally gullible Cook Islands Prime Minister, Sir Thomas Davis, who was conned into appointing Bashout, on December 2nd that year, as the Cook Islands *"official representative in the United States of America on Cook Islands banking matters."*

"Dr Bashout, as the Government representative, is empowered to speak for and act on behalf of the Cook Islands Government."

Sir Thomas was obviously feeling exceedingly generous that particular evening, or perhaps it was Bashout's offsider, Eldon William Morris, who persuaded him. As Sir Thomas noted in a covering letter of introduction to the State Governor of Hawaii, *"Mr Morris and I share many common experiences from our past careers."*

Given Sir Thomas Davis' reported links with the US Central Intelligence Agency – forged during his career as a NASA employee and top US Army research scientist – and Morris' own background – he was also described at the time as a retired General – it wasn't difficult to speculate on possible CIA involvement in the scam somewhere.

Bashout named his new Cook Islands bank the Midland International Bank and Trust Limited, and proceeded to travel the world trying to open branches and con deposits out of people. The US Treasury quickly tumbled to Bashout after finding out the $10 million he claimed to have on deposit in Metrobank was in fact $10 thousand, and a cheque he was trying to cash for nearly $5 million was repeatedly bouncing. Treasury agent John Shockey alerted Richard McDonald, the Cook Islands internal auditor, and the Cook Islands police were called in.

By misrepresenting how much money they had in order to get a banking license, police decided Bashout had attempted to defraud the Cook Islands authorities. As the heat went on, CITC tried to paint itself as squeaky clean. In a letter to the Cook Islands Monetary Board, the tribunal in charge of approving banking licenses, CITC director Anthony McCullagh claimed his company had made every effort to ensure Bashout and Morris had properly capitalised Midland Bank – not to be confused with the real Midland Bank operating out of Britain.

"Our chairman, Mr David Lloyd, has met with both the gentlemen concerned in Hawaii and London. On each such occasion we have specifically queried whether the capital has been paid up and each time the response has been unsatisfactory.

"We now wish to advise your Board that on 14 January 1986 our Mr Trevor Clarke wrote to Dr Bashout and Mr Morris setting out in the strongest terms that unless the Cook Islands Monetary Board received the appropriate evidence as to the payment of the share capital within the very near future then in all likelihood the Banking Licence issued to Midland would be placed in jeopardy."

While McCullagh's tough and responsible attitude seemed commendable, the Cook Islands police had a different version of their dealings with McCullagh. A police memorandum dated February 2, 1986, shows McCullagh was confronted on Saturday, November 30, 1985, with documentation from Chase Manhattan Bank and Metrobank showing Bashout didn't have the money he claimed to have, and in fact may have fraudulently altered a document to suit his purposes.

"Mr McCullagh viewed the documents, Exhibit B and Exhibit D, and stated that he was in error and that Bashout did not have the funds in cash, but these documents would suffice, and added that Bashout could 'buy and sell the Cook Islands'."

Undeterred, McCullagh went in to bat for his client and managed to persuade Cook Islands Crown Counsel Anthony Manarangi to not only approve the original one year banking licence, but to offer a four year renewal. With the Cook Islands Trust Corporation's support, Bashout was then given his letters of appointment by Prime Minister Sir Thomas Davis and went on to attempt a rip-off of foreign banks. It was only after international pressure that on February 7, Bashout's banking licence was revoked and the Cook Islands Trust Corporation sheepishly ditched their troublesome con artist client.

But CITC wasn't the only trust company in the gun that month – its main rival, South Pacific Trust, was also promoting dodgy clients who would later embarrass the Cook Islands Government. One such client was the Commercial Bank of Commerce Limited, an entity that later emerged as an alleged subsidiary of the massive Bank of Credit and Commerce International – BCCI.

BCCI collapsed in July 1991 when enforcement agencies around the world seized its assets and arrested a number of senior staff on fraud charges. BCCI was not so much a bank as an international money launderer, drug financier and gun runner, even going so far as supplying nuclear weapons technology to third world countries like Pakistan. BCCI had also played a key role in laundering slush funds for the Iran/Contra arms deals.

This particular alleged BCCI offshoot claimed to have assets and reserves of US$152 billion, and it purportedly banked with the Rarotonga branch of National Bank of New Zealand, later to become European Pacific Bank, using account number 24315-00. Question marks still hang over the exact links between BCCI and the Commercial Bank of Commerce in Rarotonga. The issue surfaced publicly towards the end of 1994, when a copy of this second winebox – or one like it – was handed via Winston Peters to the Commission of Inquiry set up to examine the first box.

As news leaked out that another box of tricks was around, the Machiavellian MP dropped a few pages to the hungry media, including a financial statement for the Commercial Bank of Commerce.

The document included a telex address in the American state of Utah that included the letters CBCCI. Investigators into BCCI's main network had already uncovered a plethora of subsidiaries that usually incorporated the word "Commerce" in their title somewhere. Of course, "CBCCI" could refer to Commercial Bank of Commerce Cook Islands, but somehow I wasn't convinced that co-incidence could produce two dodgy banking networks with similar names and similar asset-backing descriptions (both banks had a tendency to list intangible assets – CBCCI for example reported *"320 Acres of Utah Tar Sands. Checked and proven to contain . . . 340,736,000 Ounces of GOLD in situ [and] 258,133,333 barrels of in-situ OIL.*

"Checked by independent Assayers, Geologists, and Engineers. At one half the estimated values the property is worth: $100,000,000,000.").

My suspicions were further enhanced when, during an orgy of media interest in the released document, I managed to contact one of the men named in it as an associate of the Commercial Bank of Commerce, American Robert Suazo.

"Hi, my name's Ian Wishart, a journalist from New Zealand," I introduced myself over the phone to Ohio. *"There's been a bit of publicity here relating to the Commercial Bank of Commerce, in Rarotonga – a BCCI bank we understand."*

"Pardon?"

"Was it a BCCI subsidiary?"

"Yeah."

Having established through a further series of monosyllabic answers that this man clearly regarded the Commercial Bank as a BCCI child, I asked what I now have come to realise was one of those blindingly obvious questions that journo's always ask – like "How do you feel?" – in this case I asked what the purpose of the entity was.

"What's the purpose?," Suazo quizzed me back down the phone line, eyebrows raised. *"It's a bank!"*

Yeah, right. OK, let's approach from another direction.

"What advantages did the Cook Islands offer?"

"Who are you again?," he queried, beginning to get suspicious.

"I'm a journalist from New Zealand. Can you remember who the BCCI people were, behind this, who asked it to be set up?"

"No I do not, no I do not. I don't know anything further than that – OK?"

Suddenly the atmosphere had chilled, Suazo realising he'd said too much already.

"Can you remember what advantages the Cook Islands offered?"

"No I do not, I don't remember anything more than that, I can't be answering that to a strange voice on the phone."

Undeterred, but knowing Suazo was likely to ditch the call any second, I kept pressing. *"Billy Beardsley, Bill Beardsley was one of the US directors I understand – "*

"I don't know. I'd say that was the end of the conversation." And with a *"thank you"* he hung up on me.

Beardsley, meanwhile, was denying to all callers that his bank had any links with BCCI. He said it was just a small tax haven bank that had been closed down *"several years ago. It's been checked in the Islands, it's been checked here, it was all done through attorneys. It was clean."*

BCCI was one of the biggest, dirtiest, most dangerous criminal enterprises ever to rear its head in the financial world. Its alleged appearance in the Cook Islands didn't come as any great surprise to me.

As for the National Bank of New Zealand's role, named as it was on the Bank of Commerce document as the company's banker, National denied that its Rarotonga branch had ever provided accounts for foreign banks, especially not BCCI. National Bank, however, had sold the branch to European Pacific in 1986, and with it went all the account details. The mystery of who owned account number 24315-00 remains unsolved.

The documents also showed a surprisingly large number of former CIA or US Defence personnel surfacing in the Cooks in various strange enterprises. One such character was Lawrence John Fahey, at the time a 54 year old American appointed as an aviation adviser to Sir Tom Davis.

Listing degrees in History, Economics and a Ph.D in Government studies, Fahey had at times held lecturing positions in Political Science and Political Behaviour courses at a number of California Universities. His military credentials included service with the USAF Strategic Air Command, USAF Military Airlift Command; Survival Training Courses, Arctic, Jungle and Water; Nuclear Weapons Courses, Planning, Delivery and Safety; and Specialised Courses like Counter Insurgency, Political Warfare and Small Force Tactics, along with Special Activities Aviation Operations for the US Government.

He also had business ties with InterAir, a Nevada-based airline allegedly linked – according to information in the documents – with arms smuggling to Iran during the Contra scandal. He held the status of Lt Colonel, USAF retired, a similar level of command to Iran/Contra mastermind Lt Colonel Oliver North. Which was interesting.

Another figure, William Raupe, was described as a CIA veteran from the Vietnam War whose current "front" was a position with the US Agency for International Development, based at the US Embassy in Suva. US AID was extensively used as a CIA cover during the war in Asia, in conjunction with Air America, the CIA's massive airline.

The documents listed Raupe as an associate of Fahey and one of his staff, Roy Roshto. Confidential cable traffic from Washington to Rarotonga confirmed Roshto had a 1968 conviction for carrying a concealed weapon and false pretences.

"Any evidence," I extrapolated, *"that European Pacific had any links with any of these CIA or arms for hostages types?"*

"Yeah, as a matter of fact there is. Not much mind, but one of EP's big American clients was William Simon."

I didn't need any introduction to Bill Simon. A former Secretary to the Treasury under Presidents Nixon and Ford, Simon was at one stage one of the richest people in the United States, with a fortune estimated by *Forbes* magazine at US$200 million.

A controversial business figure, he landed himself in hot water after persuading friends like US Secretary of State George Shultz to invest in an oil venture that then collapsed. As author Bruce Ross noted in *The Ariadne Story*, Simon had failed to disclose side benefits he received from the promoters of the venture. Now in business with his former Treasury assistant Gerald Parsky, their company in the mid 1980's joined up with Kiwi entrepreneur Bruce Judge's Ariadne Corporation in a US$200 million banking venture called International Financial Services. As Bruce Ross had discovered, tens of millions of dollars of Ariadne money had disappeared down a Cook Islands' plughole when Ariadne collapsed, and Bruce Judge had set up his own shell company through the Cook Islands Trust Company, Willand Ltd.

A shaky empire at the best of times, Bruce Judge's Ariadne turned for advice to the National Commercial Bank of Saudi Arabia. NCB was closely affiliated to BCCI. How come this didn't surprise me.

The fact that Bill Simon had used European Pacific's services piqued my interest, particularly as Simon was a known hardline supporter of the Nicaraguan Contra's and a recognised fundraiser for them.

I remembered seeing earlier in the year a strange document entitled *The Opal File*, which circulates in an underground fashion throughout New Zealand and is sometimes referred to as *The Gemstone File*. Allegedly written by a disaffected FBI agent, the Opal File contained a number of highly defamatory statements about New Zealand businesses and alleged links with the CIA, and also pay-offs to New Zealand and Australian politicians, quoting bank account numbers and amounts. Much of it remains impossible to verify, but among what I had considered its wilder claims was a suggestion that Bill Simon, Gerald Parsky and a senior CIA official named Ray Cline had tried to funnel hundreds of millions of CIA operational funds through the Cook Islands, and in particular through European Pacific Bank.

In fact it would have been difficult for them to avoid using European Pacific Bank – at the times the deals were allegedly done it was the only retail bank in Rarotonga.

"18th October, 1986:," read the relevant section of the Opal File, *"Cline outlines Parsky's plan to 'launder' US$320 million through the New Zealand Treasury for 'Maori Development'.*

"The US$320 million would be part of a US$1 billion package with US$680 million to be funnelled through Cook Islands Trust Corp for construction of a tourist and casino resort in the Cook Islands using five 'financiers' including Ray Cline, Thomas, Keen, Raeppel, Gisondi and Cook Islands' Premier Tom Davis."

Whoever wrote the Opal file couldn't spell names, or maybe it was deliberate. The men publicly identified with the "Hawaiian loan scam" were in fact Stephen Thomas, a 39 year old American with military service; 50 year old Michael Gisondi, a financial planner who also happened to be a former Chairman of the Armed Services YMCA in Hawaii; popular Hawaiian interior designer Charles Heen – a fan of Maori artwork; Robert C Allen, a businessman named by FBI agents in a Television New Zealand report as a CIA agent connected to the CIA front company Bishop Baldwin Dillingham Wong Ltd; and a Rayner Kinney – could the Opal file author have been attempting to sensationalise by corrupting Kinney's name into Ray Cline's?

It certainly sounded wacky at the time, but already today we'd dug up documents on the US$300 million Maori Development Loan. Months earlier

I had managed to establish that Ray Cline had been in fact a Deputy Director of the CIA and, even more curiously, he'd been to New Zealand in 1986 wearing his new hat as an economics and political studies professor.

I'd also managed to unearth a front-page story in the now-defunct *New Zealand Times*, dating back to November 1984. In it, Ray Cline and former Nixon Secretary of State Dr Henry Kissinger – concerned at the New Zealand Labour Government's anti-nuclear position, revealed they were setting up a think tank called the Centre for Strategic and International Studies at Washington DC's Georgetown University.

The Centre would research and lecture on Pacific defence issues, and its advisers included former Australian Prime Minister Malcolm Fraser. Cline said he'd been in touch with *"some friends"* in New Zealand, and was very interested in New Zealand's "geo-strategic" position, *"particularly in relationship with some of the smaller island states"* of the South Pacific. For a former Deputy Director at the CIA, Ray Cline certainly seemed to have stronger ties to New Zealand and the Pacific than one would otherwise expect.

Certainly, Honolulu-based Bishop Baldwin and Co had been a CIA "proprietary", or front company. It had collapsed into bankruptcy in August 1983, but at its peak had been a legitimate company employing up to 50 business executives as a cover for a small number of operational CIA agents. It too had links to wealthy Filipinos, including an Enrique Zobel, reportedly one of the ten richest bankers in the world. The reason for another covert CIA company in the Pacific? Posing as business executives was a perfect cover for intelligence gathering.

"We could hardly knock on doors and say: 'I'm from the CIA, please tell me all you know,' " CIA agent and Bishop Baldwin consultant Bob Jinks told BBC investigative journalist Gavin Esler. The firm collapsed because of fraud on the part of its management, and when founder Ron Rewald was later sentenced to 80 years jail for his part in the swindle, he claimed the missing cash had been funnelled through nearly 100 bank accounts in locations as diverse as South America, Spain, the Cayman Islands and the Cook Islands on CIA business.

Bishop Baldwin also had a New Zealand office, operating in Auckland. Company records show it was registered in July 1983, only a month before the collapse of the parent company. Why were all these Iran/Contra figures, CIA agents and bankers popping up in the Cook Islands? On a hunch I tossed Cline's name into the conversation. John chewed it over for a minute.

"Cline. Now I've heard that name. In what regard I don't know but I have heard that name. Certainly never saw it written down. I can't say really. Ray Cline, that name sounds – I know I've heard it, but in what regard I don't know."

"Did you ever see $680 million come through the Cook Islands Trust Corp on the back of that Maori loan scam?," I pressed.

"No. I mean, as you can see from the documents there were crazy people with telephone number bank balances popping up everyday pushing this scheme or that. I don't recall European Pacific having any role in the loan scam – which isn't to say that it didn't, but I don't think so."

It didn't take us far, and it certainly didn't prove the truth of the wild Opal File claim, but it was another little piece of the jigsaw.

So this was the Cook Islands that European Pacific operated in, I thought as I picked out more papers to read – a veritable hotbed of intrigue, dirty money, arms dealers and spooks. Now I understood why John had wanted me to get a feel for the bigger picture.

We came across another document like the one appointing Samir Bashout as a financial ambassador. This one was a letter dated April 4, 1986, appointing Max Raepple as a *"Cook Islands Government Consultant"* on development projects. Such projects, the letter noted, would be financed by Arab money which Raepple apparently had access to. The letter was signed by Sir Thomas Davis, Prime Minister.

Another document – a Cook Islands newspaper report from May 6 – noted the establishment of the country's largest offshore bank, European Pacific Banking Corporation, with investments of $100 million. On a normal day it might have been the lead story, but European Pacific was beaten from the top spot by reports that Premier Davis was considering giving political asylum to Ferdinand Marcos. The following day the Marcos story developed legs. Opposition leader Geoffrey Henry hit the front page with allegations that Sir Thomas might have had *"underhand dealings"* with *"certain people overseas"*.

"Questions," said Henry, ranged from the Davis/Marcos connection, to whether the PM had any CIA connections and whether Marcos was receiving protection from the CIA who may be seeking asylum for him in any country other than United States territory.

The newspaper carried on, with Henry describing an incident where a Government Minister apparently boasted to a group of people that a large influx of money was shortly arriving in the country for government spending, *"and he spoke of how his political chances for future elections will be greatly enhanced,"* claimed Henry. He noted that earlier in the week US President Ronald Reagan had asked the Philippines Government to grant an official passport for Marcos to enable him to travel to a third country.

At the same time, he said, two Cabinet Ministers were attempting to get an extended lease on the privately owned Manuae Island, to be held by the Government. On a roll now, Geoffrey Henry claimed the Cook Islands Government had done a secret deal with the US to take Ferdinand Marcos out of Hawaii and grant him residency in the Cooks. These latest events, he argued, *"are too much of a co-incidence."*

Marcos was thought to have squirreled some US$10 billion away around the world and, just co-incidentally, BCCI was his banker.

The Opposition Leader had the last laugh, telling Sir Thomas Davis that if he was *"so desperate that he needs Marcos' billions, he should go and live with Marcos and not bring Marcos to live with us."*

The public outcry in Rarotonga was so loud that the Government announced there was categorically no way the ousted dictator would be coming to the Cooks. But it wasn't the end of the small nation's dealings with the billionaire.* When controversial New Zealand gold bullion trader Ray Smith emerged from bankruptcy and jail in 1994, he wrote in his autobiography *Where's the Gold?* of being called in by the Cook Islands Government in the mid 1980's to help launder 1200 tonnes of gold, apparently on behalf of Marcos.

When the Japanese were beaten at the end of World War 2, they'd reputedly left behind billions of dollars worth of bullion plundered during their Asian campaign. Ferdinand Marcos found it. At least, that's Ferdie's version of the story. More cynical souls have suggested the Marcos millions came from fleecing the Philippines Treasury by diverting some of the US Government money paid as rental on the military installations at Subic Bay and Clark air force base.

According to Smith, however, the laundering plan involving his company Goldcorp was simple. *"There were proven traces of gold in certain areas of the Cooks. A bogus mine would be set up and the gold would be 'mined'. Our role was to set up the mine, build a small refinery to process the gold from 99.5 percent to .9999 and then to deal the now legitimate gold onto the world markets.*

"The total value of the metal was about US$15 billion. Our commission was to be four percent."

Smith and a fellow Goldcorp executive flew up to the islands for meetings with Marcos' representatives and the Cooks Prime Minister.

"The deal was agreed to in principle but was dependent on the client being able to get the metal to the Cooks. I was still involved in discussions on this project right up until my sacking in March 1988."

Following Smith's claims, Sir Thomas Davis labelled the claims as "rubbish", although he admitted Marcos had requested asylum there, an approach – he says – that was made in 1986 by a delegation of Filipinos and an American, believed to be from the CIA.

It was shortly after the May 1986 newspaper articles on Marcos and Davis that mysterious financiers Gisondi and Raepple came into their own in the Cooks. Diplomatic messages between the US, Australia and Rarotonga indicated that Bashout's partners, Eldon William Morris and James Centers both had files at the Queensland Special Branch. Morris also apparently featured in FBI files in California and Hawaii.

Enquiries on three Filipinos travelling with them – Dante Dominigo Agdeppa, Leticia T Fideldia and Enrique Pimentel – weren't so revealing. Agdeppa was carrying a US passport and all three were resident in Hawaii. Whoever they were, they may have had access to false passports and identities. An Asian Development Bank officer, Edmond Pereira, came across them on his way out of Rarotonga and back to his base in Manila.

According to confidential cable traffic, he *"identified the group and two of*

---

* Ironically, Marcos had applied to open accounts with European Pacific, but EP Chairman David Richwhite and David Lloyd turned him away. Evidently there are some fugitive billionaires that even tax haven companies won't deal with.

its members, one allegedly as a high ranking executive secretary to Marcos and another man as one of the former President's unplaced staff allegedly involved in financial dealings for the former President, a Dr Roy Tandoc. Tandoc was not the name used here," noted Auditor Richard McDonald in his message to the US Treasury's John Shockey.

When the Maori loan scandal blew up in New Zealand, McDonald fired off a commiseration to a counterpart at the Reserve Bank of New Zealand. The cable was sent on December 17, 1986.

"Understand that an almighty row has blown up regarding Gizondi and Rapaell your end. Indications are that leak would be in Maori Affairs as no mention made of the involvement of these two with Cook Islands."

In the New Zealand Parliament, Winston Peters and his Opposition National Party colleagues were hammering away at a beleaguered Labour Government on the issue, demanding the resignation of Maori Affairs Minister Koro Wetere. The *New Zealand Herald* newspaper was comparing the crisis to the 1975 loan scandal in Australia that saw Labour Prime Minister Gough Whitlam's Government turfed out of office.

On that occasion, wrote the *Herald*, one cabinet minister was sacked and another resigned after it was revealed that the Government was trying to get $4 billion from secret Arab loans.

This too, was interesting. In a searing investigation published in 1987, US *Wall Street Journal* reporter Jonathan Kwitny examined the links between an Australian merchant bank, Nugan Hand, and the Central Intelligence Agency, and their combined efforts to bring down the Australian Government.

Nugan Hand had begun life in the late 1960's as a company called Australasian and Pacific Holdings, based in New South Wales. A large number of its shareholders were CIA agents, as was founder Michael Hand, who'd just quit active service in Southeast Asia.

When Hand met crooked lawyer Frank Nugan, they formed the Nugan Hand Bank. While it had a facade of doing ordinary business, and became a very respectable merchant bank with close ties to politicians and famous figures, Nugan Hand's real business was moving dirty money and financing covert operations for the Central Intelligence Agency. At one stage it became the CIA's global paymaster for illegal operations, and it was also the bank that financed New Zealand's "Mr Asia" heroin smuggling ring.

When co-founder Frank Nugan was found shot dead in his Mercedes on January 27, 1980, his killing took the bank with him in a scandal that saw Hand, and the other CIA operatives running the bank, flee Australia with a Royal Commission of Inquiry in hot pursuit.

Michael Hand hasn't publicly surfaced since the early 1980's, although a man named Michael Hand did feature briefly in the controversial supply of high technology weaponry to Iraq just prior to the Gulf War. This latest Michael Hand was one of three people operating a British company called Euromac Ltd. In 1988 a Californian electronics company alerted officials to the fact that Euromac was attempting to purchase high-speed electronic capacitors known as "krytrons", on behalf of Iraq. Krytrons are used in the detonation circuitry of nuclear warheads.

In their book, *Unholy Babylon*, journalists Adel Darwish and Gregory Alexander described how a sting operation was launched, resulting in the arrest in March 1989 of Hand's two colleagues for attempting to export the krytrons to Iraq illegally. Michael Hand doesn't appear to have been arrested.

There's no evidence proving that both Hands were in fact one Hand, but the telltale fingerprints seemed similar. I digress, however.

It was Nugan Hand's role in the fall of Australian Prime Minister Gough Whitlam that proved intriguing. In his autobiography *Honorable Men*, former CIA Director William Colby claimed that one of the biggest crises of his time as Director was the election of *"a left wing and possibly antagonistic Government in Australia."*

He compared it to the threat of Soviet intervention in the 1973 Arab/Israeli war. Colby later became Nugan Hand Bank's lawyer. The reason for the paranoia was Whitlam's attitude to the American listening post at Pine Gap – a top secret base capable of eavesdropping on phone conversations across a large part of the globe. Whitlam didn't particularly like the deal Australia had been given, and he was correct in assuming the US hadn't told him everything about the base that he felt Australia should know.

It was a similar sort of attitude to nuclear warships that gripped the New Zealand Labour Government a decade later.

In 1975, things were coming to a head and, as Kwitny persuasively argues, the CIA and Australian Secret Service, ASIO, intervened to overthrow the democratically elected Government.*

Ray Cline later told Australia's *National Times* newspaper, *"The CIA would go so far as to provide information to people who would bring it to the surface in Australia. Say they stumbled onto a Whitlam error which they were willing to pump into the system so it might be to his damage . . . if we provided a particular piece of information to the Australian intelligence services, they would make use of it."*

Another top CIA official, Chief of Counter-intelligence James Angleton, was also questioned a few years later about the affair. He told interviewers, *"I will put it this way very bluntly. No one in the Agency would ever believe that I would ever subscribe to any activity that was not coordinated with the chief of the Australian internal security."*

During 1975 Whitlam's Government had been plagued by bizarre Arab loan scandals – a man named Khemlani claimed he was arranging a $4 billion line of credit, and documents – later revealed as fakes – circulated in the media to increase the level of Government embarrassment. The scandal saw the Minister of Energy forced to resign over the fake loan deal. By October 1975, Kwitny reveals, Whitlam was waging unofficial war on the

---

* Also covered in great detail in John Pilger's *A Secret Country*.

CIA in Australia, demanding lists of all American agents operating there and sacking one of his own intelligence directors for not co-operating with his instructions. He was also alleging the CIA had funded the Opposition Conservative parties. In the melee, four CIA agents were publicly identified in the media.

The final straw came on November 8, 1975, and it came directly out of Nugan Hand Bank's stable of spooks. Ted Shackley, a close friend of Michael Hand's and an associate of the dirty bank, fired a memorandum to the Director General of ASIO. In essence, it warned that if the current policies weren't discontinued, the CIA couldn't see *"how our mutually beneficial relationships are going to continue."* Three days later, Prime Minister Whitlam was out of a job, removed from power by Governor-General John Kerr in a constitutional crisis. A very Australian coup.

While most commentators focused on the accompanying financial supply crisis as the catalyst for Whitlam's removal, many didn't know of Governor Kerr's strong CIA links. During his legal career Kerr had been strongly associated with the Australian Association for Cultural Freedom, an entity exposed in the US Congress in 1967 as being *"founded, funded and generally run by the CIA,"* noted Kwitny. Kerr was also the founding president of the Law Association for Asia and the Western Pacific – another group later revealed as CIA funded. He had also served in America's Office of Strategic Services – the forerunner to the CIA – during WWII. Governor Kerr may not have acted solely on the instructions of ASIO and the CIA, but it's unlikely that he was deaf to their concerns.

Now here were documents from the Cook Islands indicating a more oblique attempt to destabilise the New Zealand Labour Government – heavily unpopular with the US administration over the ANZUS warships dispute. The confidential cable traffic shows even the Cooks had twigged to what was going down.

"I personally note similarities between Khemlani affair in Australia in 1975," wrote Richard McDonald in a telex to the Bank of England in February 1987, *"and Raepple affair in NZ. In both cases a Government distasteful to US interests was threatened – in Australia's case successfully, and the basis was financial irregularities associated with phoney international financiers.*

"Certainly the Raepple affair is being used to stir up racial antagonism in NZ which could hurt existing Government very badly."

"Good shit, huh?," gloated John as I looked up from the cable.

"Not bad," I lied unconvincingly.

Ironically, New Zealand had been visited in August 1986 by a 58 year old former CIA operative named Ralph W McGeHee. He'd fallen out with his former employers a long time ago, and he arrived here preaching a warning of what to expect before the 1987 election.

"Unless I'm very much mistaken," he told the *Herald, "A deliberate CIA operation to destabilise or displace a Labour Government with [its] anti-nuclear policies. I can see the early signs of such an operation. And I've seen – and been involved in – too many such operations to be in much doubt about it."*

What signs?, asked the paper.

"*Well, these can range from recent visits from some pretty prominent and hawkish Americans to infiltration and destabilisation of organisations such as labour unions.*

"*You've recently been visited by such people as Ray S Cline, now a prominent American academic but formerly a Deputy Director of the CIA. Under his academic guise of clean, ideological inquiry, such a man is in an excellent position to push official American policy.*"

When dealing with intelligence agencies, it's extremely rare to find smoking gun, bullet and body all in the one easily discovered place. As a rule they try not to leave behind hard evidence that will threaten their cover or remove the cloak of "plausible deniability" – the ability to swear with fingers crossed behind their backs that they weren't involved.

There were no documents in the box signed by the Director of the CIA authorising a campaign against the NZ Government by offering fake loans, but there was enough circumstantial evidence to indicate that the CIA, Ferdinand Marcos and the Cook Islands formed a triangle with enough common interest to leave New Zealand as an unwitting victim.

If this was the high drama that investigating the Cook Islands and European Pacific could provide, then it was going to be one hell of an investigation.

CHAPTER 10

The Empire Builders

*"Mr Bond, power is sovereignty. Clausewitz's first principle was
to have a secure base. From there proceeds freedom of action.
Together, that is sovereignty. I have secured these things and
much besides. No one else in the world possesses them to the
same degree. They cannot have them. The world is too public.
These things can only be secured in privacy. You talk of kings and
presidents. How much power do they possess? As much as their
people will allow them . . . And how do I possess that power, that
sovereignty? Through privacy. Through the fact that nobody knows.
Through the fact that I have to account to no one."*
— IAN FLEMING, DR NO

EUROPEAN PACIFIC INVESTMENTS QUICKLY spread from 1986 onwards. The
company opened offices in New Zealand, Australia, Hong Kong,
Luxembourg, Western Samoa. It was doing deals on nearly every continent,
and certainly in most major Western countries. The Luxembourg office
operated through Britain, the Channel Islands, Belgium, France, Holland,
Germany, Monaco and Italy. From Rarotonga deals reached into the
Caribbean, United States and Canada, while the Hong Kong office looked
after clients from Japan to Indonesia and everywhere in between.

But EP wasn't the only New Zealand money-mover to encircle the globe.
Running parallel was the merchant banking operation Jarden Morgan, a
company based on the worldwide operations of an American bullion trader
called Deak International.

Deak's founder, Hungarian-born Nicholas Deak, had served with the US
Office of Strategic Services (OSS) during the Second World War. The OSS
later became the Central Intelligence Agency and it appears some kind of
relationship was maintained between the spy network and the bullion
network. In *False Profits*, a 1992 expose on the BCCI scandal by journalists
Peter Truell and Larry Gurwin, it was alleged Nick Deak had laundered the
CIA money used to finance the 1953 operation to return the Shah of Iran to
power.

In Jonathan Kwitny's investigation of Nugan Hand, *The Crimes of Patriots*,
Deak and Co featured again. One of the company's international money
couriers, Ron Pulger-Frame, had devised a scheme to launder money across
the Australian border for Nugan Hand, in a bid to beat the tough restrictions
on foreign exchange movements at the time. Pulger-Frame also allegedly
boasted that while with Deak he had handled the delivery of bribes from
Lockheed Corporation to Japanese officials — a controversy that later blew
up on both sides of the Pacific and resulted in the collapse of the Japanese
Government of the day.

Pulger-Frame was also well aware he was carrying the proceeds of narcotics trafficking, and reportedly aware of Nugan Hand's CIA connections. There are also indications that Pulger-Frame wasn't the only Deak employee used by the shady merchant bank. Kwitny unearthed a letter dated July 3, 1979, involving the laundering of US$3 million for corrupt officials of the Thai Government. The Nugan Hand executive writing the letter notes the need for the laundering to be very discreet, and adds *"I really believe it should be a Deak's job. Basically we should alert Deak's or whoever and then give instructions to them verbally here in Thailand."*

In 1984 Deak's had filed for Chapter 11 bankruptcy in the US, seeking protection from its creditors. Deak's problems followed a run on its international banking outlets in South America after the company was summoned to appear before the US Presidential Commission on Organised Crime. In November of the following year, 80 year old Nick Deak, then Chairman of the Company, was shot dead when a woman burst into the company's New York office claiming she'd been cheated, and pulled out a gun. Also killed was a 58 year old receptionist.

Deak's was, at the time, the largest dealer of foreign exchange and precious metals in the US, outside of the established banking system.

In May 1986, the company was rescued from bankruptcy by the "boys from downunder", an Australian entity called Martin Properties Ltd. In fact, Martin was a subsidiary of Bruce Judge's Ariadne Australia, the same company that later tied the knot with former US Treasury Secretary William Simon. Suddenly Ariadne's Martin Properties found itself with 70 offices in 52 American cities, with another 15 branches in Canada. The company's name was changed to Deak Morgan, and expansion was definitely on the agenda.

It took on a sharebroking role as well, buying a 30 percent stake in Canada's Deacon, Morgan; took a 49 percent holding in a Singaporean broker and a 100 percent stake of the Paul Morgan sharebroking company in Australasia. Twenty-three more offices were added to the list in Britain, where Deak took over the foreign exchange business of Erskine Bureaux.

Deak Morgan then acquired the big Johnson Matthey precious metals company's operations in Britain and New York, followed by more purchases in Hong Kong and West Germany. In all, 159 branches around the world, trading 120 currencies. Soon after this, New Zealand's giant NZI Bank corporation bought out Ariadne's stake in Deak. NZI, an insurance company and a banker, already had offices throughout the world. One of the company's major boasts had been its role in helping rebuild San Francisco after the disastrous earthquake and fire of 1906.

NZI peeled off one of Deak's most prized assets, the Swiss Foreign Commerce Bank of Zurich, and incorporated it into its own large banking operation, while Deak Morgan became another arm of the now New Zealand-based NZI subsidiary Jarden Morgan.

Deak's links with shady activities didn't end however. While under New Zealand stewardship, the company was being investigated by US authorities as part of Operation Polar Cap, the big FBI/IRS probe into the laundering of money by the Mafia and South American cocaine cartels.* There was no great mystery in this. Much of the jewellery and bullion business in the United States was, at the time, controlled or used by organised crime, a fact quickly recognised by New Zealand companies doing business in that area.

Ray Smith's Auckland Coin and Bullion Exchange, the forerunner to Goldcorp, had for a long time been dealing with Mafia front companies, although whether Smith realised or not is a different matter.

Auckland Coin and Bullion had also been a Deak's client, and Smith himself was a friend of Deak boss Arkadi Kuhlmann, a Canadian of Russian descent who rose to prominence within the bullion bank after Nick Deak's murder. One of Smith's other suppliers, A-Mark Precious Metals, was named in a big money laundering exercise stateside, while a Goldcorp subsidiary found itself unwittingly doing business with the Mob.

Goldcorp Italia Chain company executive Rex Bosson was taken by surprise. *"Have you ever been to Providence, Rhode Island?"*, he asked me at one point. *"When you go there, you have no idea what it's like. I'd lived in North America for 10 years, and I thought I pretty well knew what it was all like. But you get there, and all of a sudden you realise things are a little bit different. It doesn't take you long to realise that the Mafia stronghold is not Chicago at all – it's bloody Providence, Rhode Island."*

The company Bosson was dealing with was later indicted on drug money laundering charges, according to IRS records. The Mafia family that owned it had a big countrywide jewellery store operation which they later sold off to the Johnson Matthey conglomerate. Not realising the organised crime involvement, Johnson Matthey took a bath when the operation collapsed, and it was some of these firesale assets that Deak eventually picked up as a result. It would have been difficult for Deak to avoid being used for laundering, when a large number of its clients were in the criminal fraternity.

Between European Pacific and the Jarden Morgan/NZI Bank conglomerate, New Zealand financiers had the world in a pincer grip. At one point the two entities came to blows. Jarden Morgan's Monaco office was in trouble and up for sale – European Pacific went in to buy it.

Chief Executive David Lloyd took two trusted lieutenants with him, Guy Jalland and James McKenzie, but Jalland pulled a fast one and purchased the Monaco operation on his own. Former European Pacific staff recall the air being blue with expletives for months afterwards, with Lloyd's rage at the desertion of the man he regarded as *"his golden-haired boy"*.

"David Lloyd was just spitting tacks. He was so angry that Guy Jalland had just split like that, and I think he was also extremely fearful that Guy Jalland knew a lot of the scenarios that were still ongoing," commented one former colleague.

"So a real falling out then?"

---

* There is no evidence that Deak's NZ owners were aware that the company was allegedly being used to help launder cocaine profits.

"Oh shit yes! David Lloyd went white when anybody even mentioned his name. He was his blue eyed boy who just took off, and Guy Jalland was privy to a hell of a lot of David Lloyd's secrets."

European Pacific, however, was big enough to survive setbacks like that. Its owners were corporate heavyweights in their own right. Brierley Investments' stable of companies included holdings in American banks, department store chains and land, as well as a majority interest in TKM, one of the largest motor vehicle distributors in the UK, France and Ireland.

The Bank of New Zealand, a government-owned retail banking operation, had offices in South America, North America, Asia, Australia and Europe, and assets of some $17 billion.

Fay Richwhite, a boutique merchant bank, enjoyed international notoriety as the company behind New Zealand's America's Cup yachting challenges. These included a highly controversial bid in 1988 to challenge the San Diego Yacht Club in a one-on-one racing series. Fay Richwhite put up a 90 foot fibreglass monohull, the largest of its kind ever built. San Diego put up a tiny catamaran, and won.

Fay Richwhite was also a joint venture partner with two of America's "baby Bells" – Ameritech and Bell Atlantic – in the purchase of the formerly Government-owned NZ Telecom for $4.25 billion.

The New Zealand business climate that spawned European Pacific was in many ways vastly different from that which existed in Europe or America. Unlike the US, for example, which has very strict laws on insider trading, there were no laws against that crime in New Zealand until the end of the 80's. Even now the law is regarded as toothless. As an example, Fay Richwhite took on a job as consultant to the Government on the sale of the state-owned rail company. Partway through the proceedings it switched sides and ended up as a joint owner of the rail company in partnership with the US company Wisconsin Rail. Under New Zealand law, such a situation is perfectly legal and lawful.

As one senior American banker remarked after a stint working for a New Zealand bank – not, I might hasten to add, Fay Richwhite, the BNZ or European Pacific – *"I couldn't believe anything I saw. I'd say to my boss 'if this were a Swiss Bank we'd both be facing criminal charges.' He didn't even ask me why. There was stuff going on there I couldn't believe, couldn't believe – still can't believe! Everywhere.*

"It's like, you look under a stone and find a snake. You say 'Shit, a snake!', and pretty soon you're checking under stones all around you and there's snakes under all of them," he remarked sadly. *"The fact of the matter is that business practices in this country are so lax as to permit constant financial irregularities, which in any other country are criminal."*

As another example, money laundering has only just been made a criminal offence in New Zealand. The country's banks have been against proposals for mandatory reporting of certain transactions – à la the US and Australian system – in favour of a voluntary code where a bank would report a transaction only if the bank considered the money flow suspicious.

New Zealand's legal and accounting professions have also tried to get exemptions under any planned legislation. The head of Australia's National Crime Authority, Tom Sherman QC, has been arguing there for Australian lawyers to be included in money laundering laws. He told the *Melbourne Age* that lawyers were an important link in sophisticated money laundering chains. *"I am not talking about people who walk into a bank with a suitcase full of cash, but people who get into back-to-back loans, properties, nominee companies, trusts; myriads of transactions going through many countries."*

The United States placed considerable pressure on New Zealand to criminalise laundering. As one US diplomat noted privately, *"It's a dirty little country when you scrape away the facade."*

Money laundering has also been targeted by the OECD*, which set up a Financial Action Task Force to advise Governments on methods of combating the problem. At a conference in Cairo in 1995, Task Force director Dilwyn Griffiths described how organised crime syndicates including Italian and Russian Mafias, the Japanese Yakuza, Chinese Triads and Colombian drug cartels all laundered money through deposits in unregulated banks or by buying up real estate and companies.

"No one really knows how much money is being laundered . . . a figure I think is plausible is US$300 billion a year – we think it goes on in virtually every country in the world," warned Griffiths. *"A country's need for capital may perhaps lead it to take the short-sighted view that money has no smell, that it doesn't matter what the origin of the money is – it's all coming in for investment and it's all to the good.*

"We stress that taking action against money laundering as part of financial reform is essential. You can't open up your economy without taking measures to protect it from criminal money."

Another specialist, criminology professor Ernesto Savona spoke of how organised crime in Asia and South America took on the appearance of orthodox business executives, *"sending their dirty money anywhere they are able to avoid the control system and can get the best interest rate or investment."*

In the 1994 year, foreign interests invested some $90 billion in New Zealand. Most of that money is undoubtedly legitimate, but some is undoubtedly criminal. Among OECD nations in the Pacific basin, New Zealand's money laundering laws are among the most lax. In 1994 those laws were non-existent in fact. Bankers talk anecdotally of people walking in with $5 million in a suitcase, or transactions running to nine figures zipping in and out of New Zealand overnight for no reason other than to use NZ as a staging point. Given the country's proximity to the drug and crime cartels of Asia and – equally close – Central and South America, it's not hard to see how a lot of criminal cash could be washing through New Zealand, lapped up by an unwitting local business community.

---

* The Organisation for Economic Cooperation and Development. Incidentally, its taskforce publicly criticised New Zealand, Turkey and Greece in July 1995 for not moving fast enough to combat money laundering.

"A lot of countries are signing conventions with one hand and taking the dirty money with the other one," warns criminologist Savona, *"They have very good laws but they don't implement them.*

"These countries need a lot of foreign capital. You think they distinguish what is a criminal dollar and what is a clean dollar? No way. The money doesn't smell at all."

Take those kind of business ethics, wrap them up in a tax haven like the Cook Islands where even fewer rules exist, and you've got yourself a recipe for economic terrorism.

Having painted a composite picture of the beast we were hunting, it was time to load the guns and sally forth. The tricky part would involve getting ahead of the *NBR* and the *Independent* - newspapers at that stage at the cutting edge of the investigation and, with a full team of business journalists, amply qualified to analyse complex financial deals.

Just before the first injunctions were granted by the High Court against the business newspapers, I'd received my first delivery of European Pacific documents. It certainly wasn't a winebox-full, and the papers related to deals that had already been canvassed to some extent in the newspapers or in Peters' parliamentary speeches.

Ironically, it was to be my lack of a solid business-news background that would prove the greatest weapon in cracking the European Pacific case. Examining the few deals I'd been given, nothing jumped out at me yelling "CRIMINAL" or "FRAUD". It was obviously tax avoidance, but avoidance is legal. And yet something had to be in the winebox, otherwise there wouldn't be death threats and break-ins.

In truth, the European Pacific story was never a business story in the traditional sense. As a journalist with more than a decade of experience in investigative and crime reporting, I took the view that I should treat this as a crime story and objectively go through the evidence to see if the various claims and allegations stacked up.

First of all, that meant identifying the crime – if one existed. By going through all the documents we had, we pulled out the names of every European Pacific staff member we could find. Each name represented a potential witness.

I threw those at John for an opinion on each employee.

Anthony McCullagh: *"Great guy. A very scrupulous individual who would always do his best for whomsoever he worked for. But he was very disheartened in the end with European Pacific."*

Trevor Clarke – a former Solicitor General of the Cook Islands, I believe?: *"Yeah, he's Mr Big in the Cook Islands. Very smooth operator. Very highly regarded and ran the Cook Islands operation as quite a separate identity from all the other operations."*

David Lilly?: *"He was the financial controller. He was angry too, really pissed off when he left."*

And so it went on, in all around 30 names being checked, cross-referenced to positions within the organisation where possible and, most importantly, an idea of the person's attitude to the company now. By looking at those who appeared to have no love left for David Lloyd, it might be possible to find someone who'd open up.

We found such an entity in North America – a former senior European Pacific executive with a story to tell, but finding him wasn't easy. We put out feelers in a number of discreet directions – a few days later the call came in. We'll call him Mike.

"I hear you're looking for me. You bastards make enough noise to wake the dead. I thought I'd better ring you today before the other half of the world who don't already know find out about me."

Mike didn't want to go into transactional detail on the phone, sight unseen with a journalist he'd never heard of. He was however, due in New Zealand in mid January 1993 on business. *"We'll talk then,"* he concluded at the end of a 41 second conversation. I looked at the calendar. A six week wait. The guy obviously didn't have a sense of urgency. My initial judgement may have been a little harsh. Mike may not have had a sense of urgency, but he didn't need it – what he had to say carried the same power then as it did when it was finally broadcast to the public 18 months later.

* * *

THE CALL, WHEN IT came, was from an anonymous woman. *"Can you be at the Robert Harris cafe in Newmarket by 3:00pm? Mike's in town."*

"Yeah sure, but how will we find each other?"

"He's been in town a few days, we've already checked you out."

It had obviously been a thorough "checking out". Mike spotted me the moment I arrived and motioned me to a secluded corner.

"You want to know about European Pacific – how good are you at protecting your sources?" It's a daft question really. I mean what scribe with even half a brain is going to answer negatively? I did however pride myself on source protection. During our 1991 investigation of the Government's national identity card plans, we'd interviewed a man seconded to the Prime Minister's Department to work on the project, a man who also carried an official security clearance courtesy of SIS vetting.

Bolger had publicly announced at the time that he'd launched an inquiry to discover our source, and it gave us all in the TV3 newsroom some considerable pleasure to know that all the PM's men had never even come close.

The covering of the tracks was aided by interviewing the man in a different city some time before we actually broke the story, as well as filming only his shadow and replacing his voice with that of an actor. Yes, I liked to think that I could look after a source if I had to.

"Glad to hear it," said Mike, *"because what I'm going to tell you has, I understand, some national security implications. First of all, ignore the bloody winebox. I don't think there's actually much in it. What's got these bastards spinning is another series of deals, and I've been told the shredders have been working overtime at European Pacific to remove any evidence of it.*

"*Let me explain. Large international organisations, like banks and huge multinational conglomerates, finish each business day with surplus funds in their accounts. To minimise taxation, these funds are deposited overnight in tax havens like the Bahamas, then redeposited back in the mainland accounts at the start of each day.*"

This wasn't hard to follow, and I now realised that's what the purpose of the Dairy Board's Nassau Sweep arrangement was. Mike continued his patient explanation.

"*It's a paper transaction only, because obviously money in these amounts cannot be physically moved offshore and back again that quickly. Nevertheless, for legal reasons, the money is deemed to have been moved and this is an accepted common practice.*

"*The Bermuda Government might deduct 15% of the interest made on each overnight deposit as withholding tax, and provides a certificate to this effect so that the companies using the service can tell the IRS they've already been taxed. This too is accepted business taxation practice.*

"*However, when the Cook Islands tax haven was set up, a different thing happened. European Pacific – in connivance with the Cook Islands Government – set up a scheme whereby the Government would issue a certificate stating 15% had been taken in withholding tax, when in fact it hadn't.*"

It took a few seconds for the enormity of the last statement to hit me.

"*You mean these guys were creating fake tax certificates and foisting them on unsuspecting foreign governments in return for tax credits or refunds?*"

"*Yeah. Essentially. The clients for this racket were some of the biggest banks and corporates in the Western world. The major victims in this fraud, which involved hundreds of millions of dollars over a period of years, were not the NZ Treasury – although undoubtedly income was lost – but the Treasuries of foreign governments who lost tax revenue on a grand scale.*

"*Because New Zealand basically administers the Cook Islands, and because the government-owned Bank of New Zealand was involved, it's feared that publication could anger foreign governments to the extent that New Zealand's economy and international reputation could collapse.*

"*Furthermore, some of New Zealand's largest companies would be disgraced internationally, and the political position with the major parties possibly tainted by the fallout could lead to a crisis situation. I think that's why you'll find the SIS is involved, to keep a lid on it.*"

"How do I know this is true?," was the best question I could blurt out at short notice, quickly followed by "and what axe have you got to grind?"

"*You don't know it's true, but you will find that it is. I assure you. I'll give you some more names of staff to check, people who should know. As for my part in this, it's quite simple really.*

"*I don't have problems with tax havens. I mean, they're my job, it's what I do. But I wasn't always a poacher, and when Governments start getting bent and state security organisations become involved, it's time to blow the whistle. I want to be able to bring my family back to New Zealand one day without worrying about it turning into Queensland while I'm gone.*"

Couldn't argue with that. The corruption uncovered in the Australian state of Queensland in the late '80's had been almost unparalleled outside some of the seedier banana republics.

Before he left, Mike passed me an Auckland phone number to ring.

"If you need to get hold of me, pass on a message at this number."

And that was the last I ever saw of Mike, although we spoke many times after that.

The feeling of elation I felt that evening was supreme. Finally we knew what the whole drama was really about and, as we had already figured, it wasn't a business story. European Pacific was allegedly committing criminal fraud against the Governments of a number of countries, in league with a corrupt tax haven Government. The plan was ingenious in its simplicity, breathtaking in its potential.

Steve Christensen had, over the Christmas break, been re-assigned to TV3's parliamentary bureau. His place on the European Pacific investigation was taken by *20/20* journalist Keith Davies. Davies had worked extensively in British television as an investigative journalist before coming to New Zealand, and had plenty of experience working on stories that Governments might not like. One such case came in 1979 when the then Prime Minister, Robert Muldoon, shut down the planned broadcast of a television exposé on drug trafficking. The programme, compiled by Davies, was stopped from going to air and Davies was fired.

On June 6, 1979, a transcript of the programme was read out in Parliament by MP Richard Prebble. It examined a 1975 voyage of a luxury yacht named the *Valkay*, and a crew that included respectable businessmen and lawyers, as well as the brother of a senior National Government MP. According to the script read in Parliament, the *Valkay* ended up in Thailand on a mission to bring back drugs, although the transcript carefully noted that the politician's brother was not involved.

After reading the script, Prebble demanded that television bosses be subpoenaed and questioned over the decision to suppress the documentary.

"Parliament should find out why Keith Davies was sacked, and why he should not be returned and allowed to continue with his plan to investigate the drug dealers. This Parliament should back the courage shown by Mr Davies and follow his brave example. We should take our own initiative and expose these so-called Mr Bigs," he demanded.

Of course, like every seasoned investigator, Davies had also had the occasional slip-up, like his story of cruelty to tortoises in Britain. It went to air as a story about shipments of tortoises, where large numbers of the creatures were dying en-route because of cruelty and negligence by the transporters. Unfortunately for Keith Davies, the tortoises he used as an example were in fact not dead, only in a state of deep hibernation – induced deliberately by the shipping company to avoid any stress to the animals. Within days of the great tortoise scandal going to air, all of the critters were awake and moving around quite happily. Davies would prove to be a useful sounding board on European Pacific.

Within days of meeting Mike, I'd managed to tackle a second former European Pacific executive, returning from Europe on business. We met in the Air New Zealand Koru lounge at Auckland airport. This man, and we'll call him David, acknowledged that a foreign tax credit scheme similar to the one I'd described had been operating, but he claimed that it was legal, and disagreed with my description of it as a "fraud". It wasn't much, but it was confirmation that EP and the Cook's Government were issuing tax certificates while the tax was secretly being paid back under the table.

We discussed the developments with Pedersen on a regular basis, his line was always the same.

"Shit mate. If anyone is going to publish a story like this in New Zealand, it'll be us. TVNZ haven't got the guts."

Over the next few weeks, paranoia and fear set in. I was aware that what we'd uncovered could conceivably be an economic security threat, and I didn't think it was a co-incidence that Security Intelligence Service director Don McIver was asking Parliament for more powers to investigate "economic espionage", or what he described as the theft of trade secrets from large corporations – it could have been a reference to either the Citibank controversy or the European Pacific winebox.

I began to wonder whether I'd see the year out, and became increasingly fatalistic about life in general. I was looking for spooks under beds, behind bushes and in offices with, I would shortly discover, some justification.

As Davies and I continued to dig, it rang alarm bells at European Pacific. A letter arrived at TV3 addressed to Rod Pedersen, dated April 7, 1993. After setting out in detail the existing Court injunction dating from November 1992, EP's lawyer Chris Allan, from the lawfirm Rudd Watts & Stone, fired a warning shot.

"Our clients understand that you are or may be considering preparing a current affairs programme on the European Pacific group and its business activities. We reiterate our advice that although TV3 may not be a direct party to the present High Court proceedings, it may well be liable for contempt of Court if it acts in a fashion which subverts the Court orders, after receiving express notice of the terms of the injunctions."

Later that week, Davies and I were summoned to a meeting with the channel's current affairs boss, Keith Slater.

"I've been told by Rod to let you guys know that we don't want you to work on the story anymore. We don't consider that there's sufficient there for a programme. This also means that you are not to do any more research on this story either during work time or outside work hours – is that understood?"

TV3 was facing two realities. In the first, a multi-national tax haven bank linked to some of the country's most prestigious corporate names had put the channel on notice: we know where you are, we know what you're doing, and if you continue you'll face a very expensive legal fight. The Citibank legal threats would also have been reasonably fresh in TV3's memory.

The second reality was that, as of this moment, Wishart and Davies still didn't have a trump card. Hell, we didn't even have a one-pair hand! Rightly or wrongly, the channel chose discretion rather than possibly suicidal valour, and sounded the retreat.

It was at that moment that I decided to review my future with *3 National News*. To me the channel's decision, whilst reasonable from their perspective, was snatching defeat from the jaws of victory. I'd been with the private network since it started, even taking a pay cut and a demotion from my earlier position as a radio news director at the country's number one rating radio station.

Not being a believer in hasty decisions however, I decided to wait another month before making a final decision on whether to quit. I had a number of other irons in the fire, story-wise, including an Official Information Act request on whether the partial sale of the BNZ to Capital Markets might have breached insider trading laws.

It was a request based on a document which, for four years, the New Zealand Government had denied existed. On May 10, 1993 it was released to us. It was a Treasury report to the Ministers of Finance and State Owned Enterprises, dated May 17, 1989, shortly before Capital Markets purchased a 30% stake in the Bank of New Zealand. Insider trading, in terms of the law applying to this situation, was *"where a substantial shareholder or other person trades in the securities of a listed company after having obtained inside information about the company."*

In particular, the decision to give Capital Markets time to examine the BNZ's finances prior to purchasing, a process known as due diligence, may have breached the law. Certainly the Treasury advisers thought so.

"Although the liability position of prospective buyers who have undertaken due diligence is not yet clear to us, it appears that they or the company may be liable. If so, the Act may effectively prevent sale processes involving due diligence."

It was an important issue that hadn't been tested in Court, and its release came at a time when public attention was firmly focused on the BNZ and Fay Richwhite, courtesy of the ongoing Peters' campaign. *3 National News* network bulletin producer Mike Brockie refused to run it, saying it wasn't a story.

It wasn't the first time I'd crossed swords with Brockie over investigative stories. Back in December 1991 I'd applied for documentation relating to the first Coup d'état in Fiji in 1987. I knew that Prime Minister David Lange had ordered New Zealand military units to go to Fiji, and that Defence officials had, in effect mutinied, stalling the Prime Minister and refusing to commit New Zealand troops.

Through an incredible stroke of bad luck, or a leak somewhere along the way, I found out from Army officials about a month later that another journalist had just applied for the same information, and both requests would be considered together. The military, however, began stonewalling the media, delaying release of the documents for as long as possible. Finally, David Lange stepped in. He'd been asked in April 1992 by the defence officials to review the documentation and authorise its release.

Lange jumped the gun and, in an even more incredible piece of bad luck for me, dumped all the documents in the lap of the second cab off the rank, a newspaper journalist. It was splashed all over the front pages of the country's main newspapers the next morning. Fuming, I rang Lange to find out why he hadn't contacted me as well.

"I looked around for you in the Press Gallery," he boomed into the phone, "but they told me you don't work down here in Wellington, so I gave them to Paul Benseman."

Angry as I was at losing the "scoop", I came in to work on a day off to arrange interviews for what I assumed would be the main story of the day, and briefed the journalist on the significance of what had been released. While the core documents I was seeking on the "mutiny" were not released, those that were, were serious enough. One letter from the Prime Minister to his Defence Minister castigated the military over its foot dragging.

"The [warship] Canterbury should proceed immediately from Cairns in the direction of Fiji. I was very concerned to learn that it had not already taken this action, as it is my recollection that this decision was taken at yesterday's meeting of the Defence Council.

"A C130 Hercules aircraft must be prepared to leave at two hours notice with appropriate army personnel. Again, I was very disturbed to learn that even after yesterday's events it is apparently still not possible to despatch an aircraft with suitable troops at two hours notice!," Lange hissed in his communique.

The 3 National News production desk didn't share my enthusiasm for a story that to my mind went to the heart of New Zealand security – the ability of a Government to order troops into action and the apparent refusal by the military to follow those orders at a time of crisis. The story was banished to a slot well down the bulletin, and wasn't covered again by TV3 after that day. It remained major news for the papers and other media for six weeks, but six months of my work had gone down the gurgler.

Even when the newspapers later revealed senior defence officials had resigned after clashing with Lange over his orders, even with Lange's admission that there was indeed a conflict with defence chiefs over sending troops when the coup broke out – even with all that, TV3 didn't consider it was a news story.

After witnessing the channel's blasé attitude to my Fiji Coup investigation, the decision to call off further work on the Citibank and European Pacific stories, and now Brockie's refusal to run the BNZ insider trading report, I decided that the time had come for a parting of the ways.

I had been earmarked for promotion to the position of Chief Of Staff, a military-sounding description of the person who – in conjunction with Mike Brockie as producer – decides what stories should be covered each day and assigns reporters and camera crews to cover them. The position carried a substantial pay increase, but I knew that if I stayed I would end up in a power struggle with Brockie over editorial issues.

Mike is an excellent journalist and producer, but we both had different agendas to pursue. Brockie's responsibility was to fill an hour of news each night – a job requiring the input of virtually every TV3 journalist. I, however, had my teeth locked, pit-bull terrier-like, into something that to me was far more important than the distractions of general news.

I could understand Brockie's reluctance to throw scarce resource into investigative work, but I knew also that as Chief of Staff I would have been pushing against him all the time to allow it. Clashes would have resulted, and playing Robin to Mike's Batman wasn't my idea of a productive time, nor would it have been fair to TV3.

I entered into negotiations with TVNZ's Deputy Director of News and Current Affairs, Shaun Brown. Over a guiness at one of Auckland's many Irish pubs, we discussed life, the universe, and the big conspiracy theory. To Brown's credit, he listened to the conspiracy allegations and still hired me – sensing I guess that, however confusing it sounded, maybe there was a grain of truth that needed investigating further. I suspect also that the chance to snaffle a reporter from TV3 also played a part regardless.

Pedersen tried to convince me to stay, telling me one of the reasons he wanted me in the Chief of Staff position was to counterbalance Brockie.

"I don't want Mike surrounded by yes-men," he growled, after I'd handed him my resignation. The decision, however, had already been made. I felt the skills that I wanted to offer were not the skills that TV3 wanted me to provide, and – forbidden by TV3 from ever working on the European Pacific case again – I essentially walked the plank from TV3 to continue working on what I considered was the most important story in the country.

CHAPTER 11

Snake in the Grass

"I go checking out the reports, digging up the dirt
You get to meet all sorts, in this line of work
Treachery and Treason — there's always an excuse for it
And when I find the reason, I still can't get used to it."
– MARK KNOPFLER, PRIVATE INVESTIGATIONS, 1982

THE DEPARTURE FROM TV3 took three months — the length of notice I'd been required to give under the terms of my employment contract. Throughout this time I had ignored the order to abandon the investigation — not just because I disagreed with the restriction but also because it was actually impossible to do. So many sources and contacts had by this time been activated that it was not possible to escape the incoming information. The calls usually began as early as 7:00am and continued often through until midnight, from people who had discovered this or that.

There was so much incoming data that my home office quickly became unserviceable — dozens of lever arch files each containing hundreds of pages of research and interviews, scraps of notepaper with phone numbers scribbled in a hurry, endless cassette and microcassette tapes scattered around awaiting transcription. For my family it was hell on earth, a monkey on my back riding me till I dropped. I was becoming overwhelmed with data, and left with no time to sort through it. During the days I was expected to produce stories for the nightly news programme, during the evenings I was chasing up the leads that had emerged on Project X.

Had I been able to claim for it, I would have amassed nearly six months of time off in lieu during 1993, much of it in the first three quarters of the year. By this time the investigation had long since lost whatever lustre or glamour it may have had; it was just a slow, inexorable wade through excrement in search of the truth. It was all-consuming and all-destroying, like riding a huge wave or a runaway train. I didn't know where the ride would end, but I knew that if I didn't see it to its conclusion I would finish my career burnt-out and broken, always wondering about the big one that got away. It also annoyed the hell out of me that various Government agencies appeared indifferent to any of the claims being made. Had there been an Independent Commission Against Corruption in New Zealand, I would have willingly tossed all my evidence at them and said *"go to it!"*

Indeed, I did make some attempt to interest police in some aspects that I was turning up during the course of my inquiries. A Detective Inspector evaluated some of the allegations I was making, accepted that they were very serious allegations, but explained that the people I was accusing had so much clout that *"it would be a very brave cop"* who took them on — the implication being that the people I named – who incidentally don't appear in this book – were virtually untouchable.

The other big factor that kept me going was the smug ignorance in many sections of the New Zealand media. Let me state now, the country is not well served by the sycophantic, shallow, insipid media organs it's been inflicted with. From the moment Winston Peters began opening his mouth back in mid-1992, many leading journalists began bagging the MP for failing to come up with *"hard evidence"* to support his allegations.

Apart from the *Independent's* Jenni McManus and Warren Berryman, and *National Business Review's* Fran O'Sullivan, few newspaper journalists stood back to analyse Peters' claims with anything remotely approaching real intellect. No-one bothered to dig around in the areas he was canvassing to see for themselves whether there was something in it. Instead they resorted to "he said/she said", the sort of journalism usually restricted to kindergartens. In fact, journalism is too good a word for it: it's simply secretarial work.

Faithfully swallowing the utter and complete crap that apologists for the Government and big business were doling out to them by the bucket load, they painted Peters as some kind of mad and lonely shepherd, crying wolf to a world that didn't care. For them, the story wasn't what was being said, it was who was saying it. The whole shebang became an issue of personality and personal credibility.

I'd already developed a healthy contempt for the Parliamentary Press Gallery following a stint as a Cabinet Press Secretary back in the mid-1980's. I spent my life churning out news releases portraying my Minister and his Government in an incredibly positive light, and watching them being reprinted often word for word throughout the country, unchallenged. It was like feeding them baby-food, and while I was keeping the journo's occupied we were covering up scandals and power struggles left, right and centre.

Now I was watching these same journalistic gadflies pontificate on the truth or otherwise of Peters' allegations, without once seeing any of them down at the coal face where a small group of us were trying to do a proper investigation. It made me sick to the stomach to watch.

None of this is to suggest that Peters had any mortgage on truth, accuracy or the ten commandments carved in stone. I had always regarded Peters as a politician, first and foremost, but figured that whatever the pedigree – the allegations were serious enough to be looked at. I'd already seen enough to feel that something was rotten in the Kingdom of Denmark, and the refusal by the rest of the media to either verify or prove it wrong angered the hell out of me.

Of all the driving forces, it was this need to get to the bottom of it, to do the job that no one else could be bothered doing, that kept me going. The Fourth Estate is supposedly there to act as a watchdog and curb on the powers of the state and others who may endanger society – how the hell did I have the misfortune to end up on guard duty the night this phantom came loping up to the city gates?

I found similar sentiments being expressed by an expatriate New Zealand journalist on the other side of the Tasman, David Hellaby. Hellaby, too, had been to hell and back in his investigation of the State Bank of South Australia, which had collapsed owing billions of dollars.

At the time I spoke to Hellaby, he was fighting attempts to have him thrown in jail in Adelaide for refusing to reveal a source in the Auditor's Office who told him criminal dealings in the bank were being investigated. I discovered striking similarities between the corruption in Australia and the alleged corruption here in New Zealand.

He talked of bloodstock syndicates* tied in with the bank:

"These businessmen would put a hundred thousand dollars in each, and form a syndicate, and they would be told 'Right, you've got all this breeding stock – some in New Zealand, some in Australia, some in Ireland' – that sort of thing.

"Now some of it actually existed and was available for them to go and inspect, but of course the other stuff was over the other side of the world, and it didn't exist. The papers existed, the horse was in the stud book even. What they did was, when a stallion serves a mare you've got to put in a service return, then you've got to put in a certificate of pregnancy.

"So they would get that and then they would get a situation where a top stallion served a top mare but then the foal had slipped or died at birth. They wouldn't put in the death return, they would put in a live foal return!

"They already had the first two pieces of paper, now they put in the third piece of paper and they've created a fictitious horse. Beautiful! Entered in the stud book, they leased the horse, and of course it would eventually die.

"A guy was sent to England from Adelaide to find horses valued at $44 million. He found $4 million worth – the rest didn't exist and never had."

Apart from the sheer audacity of selling imaginary horses to gullible investors, some of these Australian crooks had found other ways to commit equine fraud, including the transfer of foal embryos from nags into the wombs of thoroughbred mares whose own foals had slipped. The horse eventually born was a nag, but it had high breeding on paper.

The difference between New Zealand and Australia, Hellaby pointed out, was that in Australia the authorities were fully investigating the huge debts clocked up by the State Bank. In New Zealand, the BNZ's billion dollar bailout was not on top of the Government's list of things to do. Hellaby, I was pleased to note, managed to avoid jail on the contempt of court charge he was facing when he returned to Adelaide the following week.

The most exasperating part was that six months had now elapsed since discovering the fake tax certificate scam European Pacific had masterminded, but still I didn't have any transactions I could pin it on. Both Davies and I knew that, for the story to develop, we had to be able to pin the mechanism to a real life transaction using real money.

We were turning over rocks everywhere, but the snake we were seeking

---

* Not related to the New Zealand bloodstock partnership cases.

was elusive. Frustrated at the lack of success, we did a round of the traps to see what our opposition were up to. For us that meant Berryman and McManus at the *Independent*, Fran O'Sullivan at the *NBR* and, of course, Winston Peters.

After a meeting at the *Independent*, it was pretty clear that the paper hadn't yet tumbled to the tax certificate racket. Warren and Jenni were philosophical about the state of their investigation: the injunction, at $10,000 a day in court, was too expensive to fight and, quite frankly, they hadn't yet found *"the big one"* that they could run to Court with and prove iniquity.

I hadn't spoken to Peters since Paul White's accident, when I was trying to prise out of him any information he may have had on the whereabouts of the disks. Throughout the intervening months, however, the name of Peters' lawyer, Brian Henry, kept popping up. Next stop had to be Brian Henry. I especially didn't want to give away any clues to Henry about how far we'd come – the last thing I wanted was to be pre-empted by Winston Peters in Parliament. It was the mark of the man that he too, like everyone else I'd spoken to, switched on a radio loudly in his office before even opening his mouth to say hello. His own involvement with Peters had begun after the 1987 election, when the pair worked together to turn over an election result in the marginal Wairarapa seat, which had gone to the Labour Government's Reg Boorman on election night.

The plan of attack was simple. Rather than try and recount the votes, they would discover how much Boorman had spent on his election campaign. At the time, political candidates were forbidden from spending more than $5,000 on their campaigns. Whipping out the calculators, they toted up Boorman's spend at $28,000. Boorman lost his seat to National's Wyatt Creech. There was some internal National Party dirt that had to be covered however – during the same investigation they began to suspect that two senior National MP's had spent in excess of $50,000 each. They didn't want Labour to twig to that, so they waited until the last minute before taking on Boorman just as the deadline for such challenges expired. By the time the Labour Government cottoned on, it was too late to retaliate.

In all the electoral petitions up to the Wairarapa one, campaign costs had never been argued. It was as if it was a "no-go area", taboo territory that no party wanted to tread on. But Creech and his counsel, Henry, were seemingly unafraid and unaware of the sensitivity of the situation. By the time the two rival political parties, National and Labour, realised what was happening, and began to appreciate the consequences of campaign expenses being litigated, it was too late. The taboo had been broken. Brian Henry and Winston Peters had worked well as a hit team.

When the National Party campaigned in the 1990 election on a promise of holding an inquiry into the Bank of New Zealand, it was a fair bet in political circles that Peters and Henry would be somewhere in the background, doing the digging. Which explained a certain "commonality of interest", if I can put it that way.

The pair remained in touch with each other and, from what I had seen, Brian Henry wasn't totally unfamiliar with the events of 1992 and Peters' involvement in them.

Now, a year later, in mid 1993, I was trying to retrace Henry's steps.

"How did Peters get hold of the winebox?," I ventured. "Where does it fit in?"

"Good question," Henry whispered conspiratorially, barely audible over the radio, and turning at the same time to look back over his shoulder at the Hotel. "All I know for a fact is that it landed in our laps. There's talk around that it was used to pressure Fay, Richwhite during the America's Cup races in San Diego last year."*

I guess the raised eyebrow must have been obvious.

"Yeah, I know," he continued, "I don't really believe it either. But it's the loudest rumour around on the topic."

Admittedly, the America's Cup story seemed a touch far fetched, but the story surfaced again during the Commission of Inquiry convened in 1994 as a result of our investigation into European Pacific. Serious Fraud Office Director Charles Sturt told the Inquiry of a meeting with Stephen Lunn on September 17, 1991.

"Mr Lunn told me that the documents in question contained evidence of fraud committed by Sir Michael Fay and Mr David Richwhite against Americans in Utah, USA, for whom he was acting. He said that the information had been obtained as a result of investigations carried out by people engaged by his American clients. He said that the Americans were waiting for Michael Fay to win the Louis Vuitton Cup (which would decide the challenger for the America's Cup).

"The timing for the proposed release of the documents was to enable the biggest possible impact when the information was made public."

The strange thing was, when the winebox finally turned up, there were no documents inside relating to anything in Utah.

At this initial meeting between us, Henry and I shadow-boxed a little on the state of our respective investigations, and I could give no hint, in return, of how far we'd got in identifying the crime European Pacific had allegedly committed.

It was soon after this first meeting that someone tried to abduct one of Brian Henry's children. I learnt of it through Peter McCarty, a former jewellery manufacturer who happened to be one of Henry's clients. I'd been talking to him on July 15, 1993, about another matter when he dropped the bombshell. "Listen, do you know Brian Henry's son? Somebody tried to kidnap him from school yesterday."

"Yesterday! No, what happened?"

"They managed to save the kid, and the woman fled."

"How did they try and do it?"

"I don't know. Talk to him. Because he was supposed to be in Wellington today, and he's had to call it off because of this attempt."

---

* 1992.

When I called Henry, he was shaken and wanted no publicity – for fear of prompting a nutcase copycat attempt. In addition, he'd been hounded by the media and refused to talk. A police file on the case had been opened, however. It appears a well-spoken woman had begun asking in the school corridors where she could find the boy, calling him by name. Another student guided her to Henry junior's classroom but, as the woman was about to go in, a teacher came around the corner and the mystery woman took flight. We knew that it was a woman who'd rung Stephen Lunn just after the injunctions were served back in October 1992 and warned him his children would be thrown off the harbour bridge. The question was, was it just an attempt to scare Henry and others in the Peters/Lunn camp, or would the mysterious woman have inflicted real physical harm to a child in a bid to get at the parent?

My initial instinct was to go with the former scenario, but what point would an abduction like that have if nothing came of it? Kidnapping is an extremely serious crime – the addition of a broken limb or some other injury would be unlikely to add significantly to what would already be a stiff sentence if caught. By daring to show up at the school and go through with the attempt, this woman was already risking a jail sentence. There is no reason to think that she wouldn't go through with whatever plan she had hatched.

And yet it was impossible to believe that anyone in this case would harm a child, unless they were mentally unhinged and taking matters into their own hands. Perhaps, rather than some kind of sinister "conspiracy", this was simply a female employee in the other camp who'd become deranged amid the pressure of it all and was roaming around like a loose cannon.

As it was, Brian Henry tightened security around his family, as did others who became aware of it. We'd already seen death threats, bugging attempts, break-ins and even a physical attack on Fran O'Sullivan in a lift. I was shortly to get my own taste of the espionage medicine, although my dose was courtesy of a new lead in the Citibank controversy.

In my final week at 3 *National News* I'd been contacted by Spook.

"*Listen carefully,*" he growled into the phone, sounding like a character from the TV comedy *Allo Allo.*

"*Two names to check. There's a guy named John Doe*, and another guy named John Doe. They're both ex-Special Air Service. They were involved in the White case.*"

A phone call to Defence Headquarters in Wellington was made, with a request to the personnel section that they fax up any details on whether these men had, in fact, been in the military. Three days later on August 5, a faxed reply came while I was out on another story. The first I knew of it was when Chief of Staff Steve Bloxham dragged me into his office and shut the door.

---

* Not their real names.

"There's good news and bad news. This fax came through to you from Defence about some guys named Doe and Doe. That's the good news. The bad news is Paul Campbell has taken a secret photocopy of it."

I hit the roof. The fax confirmed that the military had records of a both men. It went on.

"In terms of the Official Information Act it is usual to provide written permission from the individual concerned before a third party may gain access to information about that individual. Would you please therefore call me on the above number to discuss your access to information concerning these men."

Naturally, I wasn't about to approach these men and ask for permission to investigate their files. If Spook had been correct about their military records, chances were he was also right about them being SAS. But why was Paul Campbell snooping around? Paul Campbell had worked part time for TV3 for about a year. While I knew him, I'd only had to deal with the guy on one previous occasion.

His nephew was a prisoner at the notorious Mangaroa jail in the Hawkes Bay, and when corruption allegations had surfaced there, Campbell arranged for me to call his relative for an interview. We planned to run it as the lead story on the news that night.

Campbell sat in the recording booth and took notes as I questioned the man, before disappearing for half an hour. In that time I had scripted the story and begun editing it for the bulletin, now less than an hour away. Suddenly Campbell stormed in saying his nephew had cold feet and was worried about retaliation from the prison guards. He wanted the story dropped for safety reasons. Being warm, caring and sharing television reporters – not sensationalist vultures – we did so.

No one was more staggered than me to see a front page story in the *Sunday Star* newspaper the next morning written by Paul Campbell and running my interview. Despite a complaint to Pedersen from me regarding the perceived disloyalty, and a severe reprimand, he'd managed to keep his job. Campbell had a charmed existence, as I was about to discover again.

Bloxham explained that when he saw my fax come in he realised how sensitive it was, and put it away in a folder, out of public view. Just before midday he saw Campbell walking back from the photocopier with the fax in one hand and a copy in the other, which he promptly laid face down on the desk and began writing on the back of. Campbell was, at the time, trialing for the Chief Of Staff position that I had declined in favour of joining TVNZ. Bloxham told me Campbell had wrecked his chances of getting the job. I retorted that he'd not only screwed a job, he'd committed either theft or possibly even espionage.

At all costs I had to stop that copy in Campbell's possession from leaving the building with him. Campbell denied it when I first challenged him. I must have been mistaken, he said, all he copied was a job application. I went back to Steve.

"Are you absolutely 100% sure it was this fax he copied? He claims it was a job application."

"It was definitely your fax. I can swear to it."

The adrenalin built for the confrontation I knew was surely going to follow. In a crowded newsroom I was going to have to accuse one of my colleagues of being either a thief or an industrial spy. The repercussions were not going to be pleasant. What if he'd hidden it? What if I demanded a bag search and it wasn't there? What if he'd removed the bloody thing from the building already? I had one shot of getting the proof, and I knew it. There would be no second chance.

"I'm sorry pal," I began my interrogation across the desk, feeling my voice coil up like a whip about to be cracked, *"but I'm going to have to ask you again. Did you take a copy of this fax and then write something on the back of it?"*

"No. I told you before, it was a job application."

"Can I see this job application please?"

"Are you calling me a liar, Wishart?," he warned, his voice taking on a dangerous edge.

"Yeah. I am. You were seen taking the fax to the photocopier and coming back with a copy. Do you want me to say this a little louder Paul? Or is there something you'd like to tell me?"

For an entire minute we stood in silence, staring coldly at one another. Then he surrendered. *"I'm sorry mate. I did take a copy, it was wrong – a gross error of judgement."* And then he invited me into a nearby office to discuss it. He explained how he was in fact a good friend of one of my "John Doe's", a man he confirmed had risen to a high rank in the Special Air Service. Campbell then made a number of wild allegations about his "friend", which I won't bother repeating here. Suffice to say they simply raised further questions about why Paul Campbell had taken a copy of the fax and who he intended passing the information to.

On the back of the copy he'd taken Campbell had written a phone number – the number was not unfamiliar to me, and its appearance in Campbell's handwriting filled me with dread.

He claimed to have some hidden knowledge of the Paul White case, and was insistent, to the point of being over-eager, that there was nothing of national security on Paul White's disks and that I should abandon my inquiries in that direction. He alleged that Paul White had indeed been murdered, but it had nothing to do with Citibank. There were three or four disks still missing, he said, and they had some financial dealings on that were embarrassing to someone.

"What I'm telling you could get both of us killed," he bleated to me.

Pressed further, he gave me explanations that – whilst loosely based around known facts – did not stand up under close scrutiny. For those reasons I am not prepared to waste time going into the detail of those matters, nor am I prepared to name those mentioned by Campbell.

His actions, to me, appeared to be those of someone desperate to lead me off in another direction, urging me to believe a quickly concocted cover story. He had been perfectly placed for the past year to watch my progress on the case. I laid an official complaint with Pedersen, alleging both theft and commercial espionage. Rod defended the guy.

"As far as I'm concerned, the guy was Assistant Chief of Staff for the day and quite entitled to read any fax that comes in to the building and copy it."

Of course, it's one thing to openly copy something in the course of doing one's job, but I had to question the intent of a person sneaking around covertly and then trying to deny it. Rod Pedersen might have considered Campbell had a perfect right to do what he did, but Campbell obviously didn't think his own actions were above board, otherwise he wouldn't have repeatedly apologised for his *"gross error of judgement"*.

Disillusioned but not entirely surprised – given Rod's displeasure at my pending departure to TVNZ – I shrugged Pedersen off.

"Hey pal, it's no skin off my nose. I've got my file back and Campbell can't do anything more with it. If you want to employ someone like this as your Chief of Staff, that's your business, but don't get surprised if you get burnt. I'm sure no one else around here wants to be spied on."

As to the defence fax that Campbell seemed keen to alert somebody about, it was of limited, tangential use in the investigation. The main benefit to me was not the discovery of the military records, but the confirmation that Spook could sometimes access obviously sensitive information. Spook had been correct about the John Does being ex-military, but that's as far as it went. We had no evidence of any other pertinent avenues of inquiry resulting from this.

One thing was for certain – Campbell's claim that several disks were still missing tallied with my own suspicions, based on the figure of 90 disks that Paul White swore on oath to the High Court that he had, and only 88 that had publicly been accounted for.

In addition, Campbell's actions, and the phone number on the back of the Defence fax, indicated that something was still very much unresolved in the mysterious affair of Paul White. What it was I still didn't know, but the belief that White had died in a random car accident was becoming increasingly difficult to sustain.

CHAPTER 12

Closing in

*"Actors come and go. It is the roles that stay,
and that we need to be concerned with."*
— JONATHON KWITNY, 1987

AUGUST AND SEPTEMBER 1993 brought with them not just Spring and a change of employment, but also a substantial breakthrough on European Pacific. Initially slotted in as a *One Network News* reporter, I was instructed by Director of News Paul Norris and his deputy Shaun Brown to continue working on the EP project to bring it up to a point where a decision on whether to begin filming could be made One of the most important discoveries during that period was another key witness – the seventh and subsequently codenamed "Witness 7" on all documentation.

As with nearly all the previous interviews, I wore a hidden microcassette recorder to my first meeting with Seven – not so I could broadcast or blackmail him but purely to ensure I got an accurate record of the points he made. In matters as arcane as tax law, every "i" would have to be dotted and every "t" crossed. Millions of dollars in potential lawsuits were at stake.

The only hassle in the early days of these secret recordings was where to hide the recorder. While slimline, the little Sony packed a lot of weight in a tiny space, and could look a little heavy in a jacket pocket. The only other option was an old pair of leather boots with enough space to slide the machine down the back of my ankle.

Inevitably this left me walking and looking like a cowboy with a limp but, with a little adjustment, it would have to suffice. Despite doing countless such interviews over two years, I never got used to the adrenalin rush that came with fear of discovery. It begins in the pit of the stomach as you climb out of the car and switch on the microphone, a tiny lapel mic on a crocodile clip and a long lead, usually run up inside my jeans and clipped under my shirt somewhere. The sick feeling stays with you during the two or three hour interview. Can they see the outline of the mic if I turn too far that way? Is the bulge in the boot too noticeable?

On one later meeting with Seven, I climbed into the lift, where I'd normally switch the tape recorder on, only to find my quarry in the lift with me. I was surprised he didn't see the panic in my eyes, the surreptitious move to a pocket as he exited ahead of me, flicking on the recorder and hoping like hell I'd already turned on the separate switch for the mic. I had, but in my panic I switched it off again. I came out with five minutes of talk and 55 minutes of nothing on my 60 minute tape. Had I been caught during my first meeting with Seven, the European Pacific tax fraud story may never have been told.

Seven obviously didn't trust me either – he'd brought along a minder for the occasion to sit in with us. I couldn't decide whether this was a good or a bad sign. The obvious starting question: Was there illegal tax evasion?

"*I think not,*" Seven replied, choosing his words carefully. "*It was all avoiding the rules. I guess you could say if the Commissioner of Inland Revenue got to have a look at the schemes he'd immediately put up his hand and say 'Section 99', but I think it's a case where good lawyers saw the loopholes and put together the structures –* "

"*It depends what you mean by evasion,*" Seven's colleague cut in. "*There's some things that Seven told me which were going on and which were tax evasion. The general thrust of what EP were doing though – in terms of their bread-and-butter type work – was good, sharp tax avoidance. Playing with the rules and rorting the system because it was potentially there to be rorted. It wasn't evasion.*"

Now that one had come out of left field. Seven had started out by denying there was any tax evasion, and then his minder contradicts him. This was the kind of minder I could grow to like.

I outlined the false tax certificate scam as I knew it, both men nodding sagely as I went through the mechanism allegedly used.

"*What you're looking for,*" said Seven as I wound up my brief description, "*is a transaction called JIF.*" He paused a moment, glancing across to the nearby Fay Richwhite tower, the merest trace of a smile playing on his face for just a second. It was the only hint of satisfaction he showed about what he was about to say.

"*Back in 1988 and '89, we lured five big Japanese banks down to the Cook Islands and convinced them to loan us a total of US$1 billion. Basically they agreed to deposit the money in European Pacific Bank in the Cooks, and of course we'd pay them interest. The loans were rolled over every six months, and they were to last five years.*

"*Because the Japanese banks were earning interest in the Cook Islands, they had to pay withholding tax to the Cook Islands Government on that interest, at a tax rate of 15%. In return for paying that tax, the Cooks Government issued a tax certificate to the banks so they could claim a refund from the Japanese Revenue in the form of a foreign tax credit.*

"*What the Jap banks didn't know, however, was that we'd done a secret deal with the Cooks Government, who were giving us the tax money back under the table in return for a cut of the profits. Essentially, we were committing fraud against the Government of Japan, in partnership with the Government of the Cooks, and using the New Zealand Government's bank to do it.*"

"*What do you mean using the BNZ – you mean inasmuch as they were a part owner of EPI?,*" I asked, wanting to clarify the BNZ's role.

"*No, I mean the BNZ had to supply the US$1 billion in the first place. You don't think five of the biggest banks in the world are going to lend a tinpot little tax haven operation a billion dollars of their own money, do you? The deal was engineered so that BNZ deposited a billion dollars with the Jap banks, and they used that deposit as security to onlend to us.*

"*Of course, we had to structure the deal so the interest earned by the BNZ wasn't taxed, otherwise we'd have been stuffed. But they're the deals that have caused this ruckus, I know my colleagues still working for EP are determined to make sure the details never see the light of day. The shredders have been working overtime."*

"Can you give me the names of the Japanese banks?"

"I can, but I don't want to. I've told you enough already. You should be able to work the rest out for yourself."

It certainly gave me something to go away and chew on. Now we not only had a mechanism for the transactions, but also a codename. JIF. It was also, I noted wryly, the name of a popular brand of laundry cleaner. What about the BNZ's role – kickstarting a massive rort on a foreign Government, and under whose authority?

I tried working through rough figures on how big the alleged fraud might have been – guessing at the interest rates involved. Using 13% as a ballpark figure for the interest being earnt by the Japanese banks, I calculated they could rake in US$130 million a year in interest, less 15% – or US$19.5 million – in withholding tax. Multiplying that annual tax payment of $19.5 million by five years, it was easy to see nearly US$100 million might have been paid in tax by the Japanese and refunded under the table to European Pacific – a massive amount of money in anyone's book.*

Then I tried working through the other side of the argument. EP would claim, and indeed one staff member already had, that the refund wasn't illegal because the Cook Islands Government could do anything it liked with its tax money, including give it back to European Pacific. Yeah, I thought, a reasonable argument at first glance but it didn't stand up to further scrutiny. For a start, Article 70 of the Cook Islands Constitution limits the ways in which government-owned money can be spent. As New Zealand professor of tax law, Dr John Prebble would later indicate in a legal opinion, *"giving away money is not permitted without specific authority.*

"The problem is not cured by effecting a gift by purchase and sale of a promissory note at an immediate and preordained loss. It follows that the promissory note transactions amounted to theft.

"The relevant provisions of the Cook Islands Crimes Act are sections 242 (1) (a) (definition of theft), 244 (theft by a person required to account) and 118 (contravention of statute)."

It follows that if the tax refund resulted from a criminal act in the Cook Islands, then everything that flowed from that could be held to be fraudulent in a Court of Law. If the Japanese Government knew that the tax was being refunded, it wouldn't recognise the Cook Islands tax certificates presented by the Japanese banks, and the scheme couldn't go ahead. By

---

* A secret witness identifiable only as "Witness A" testified to the Davison Commission in 1995 that Fay Richwhite, European Pacific and the Cook Islands Government split the tax three ways – a third each. He said EP's yearly share was to be anywhere from US$7 million to US$10 million. Over five years, this would take the total profit from JIF to as much as NZ$300 million.

hiding the arrangement from the Japanese they would commit fraud. It was obvious I needed the documents. A further call to Seven did little to help.

"My understanding is there are no documents any more. I had a chat to George Couttie a few months ago about all this, and he told me they'd sent lawyers up to see him in Hong Kong. All they wanted to know was whether JIF was in the winebox of documents he'd given to Lunn. They were panicking about it, but he reckons JIF wasn't in there.

"The other thing is, we usually did these deals at two different levels. On the surface you might get some JIF documentation that's all perfectly legal, but I guarantee you won't find the hidden side of the deal documented. It just won't be there. You could ask Couttie yourself, but he's injuncted and I doubt he'd talk to you."

With nothing to lose, I phoned Couttie and, after a run around, finally located his lawyer, Warren Templeton. He laughed when I said what I wanted.

"George is under a court order. Of course he can't speak to you. Find a way to get the injunction lifted and we might be able to help, but until that happens you may as well give up."

At TVNZ meanwhile, my unexplained disappearances from the daily news roster were starting to raise the interest of my colleagues. Just who was this upstart coming in from TV3 and vanishing all the time to work on some kind of secret project? My responses to questions were also infuriating. *"Can't say too much,"* I'd murmur conspiratorially, *"If I told you, I'd have to shoot you."*

There was also some internal TVNZ politicking to wade through. I'd been asked by Deputy Director of News Shaun Brown and his associate, Paul Cutler, to draft a "best case scenario" – a rough synopsis of what the story might be if everything I'd learnt was true.

Remembering of course that my mind was awash with information and tips, not just JIF, I wrote up a briefing paper encompassing all of the alleged conspiracies I'd heard, and described how they might be loosely connected. It was a nebulous, defamatory document, but it was designed to give my new bosses some idea of a potential bigger picture, so that they could make their own decision where they wanted to dig. It was also full of what I call first-draft facts, information given by witnesses that hasn't been cross checked for accuracy.

Naturally enough, when the team at *Frontline* first saw it, they took fright and bolted. Here was documentary proof that Wishart really was just a "spinner", a conspiracy theorist who'd lost all sense of reality and was going to get them all sued for millions. Added to the fact that I was still an "outsider" from TV3, and not a *Frontline* reporter anyway, life started to become very difficult.

Insults were traded, the delays in getting a research team together stretched into weeks. I bided my time by once more checking the traps and, once more, Spook came up trumps. *"I've got two more names for you,"* he said when we met in a dimly-lit tavern close to the network centre.

"They did the hit on Paul White. They were paid $75 grand for the job. Their names are Papa and Juliet [names changed by author]. They're bad bastards. Whatever you do, don't say you got this from me."

Five minutes later I was on the phone to Auckland Central Police, and a Detective I'd known for some time, Shane O'Halloran. I ran the names past him. O'Halloran knew instantly who I was talking about.

*"That'll be Romeo Papa and Kilo Juliet. They're good friends and extremely dangerous."**

"Yeah, but would they do a hit?"

"They would, and could organise one without batting an eyelid, but I don't think they'd be dumb enough to personally pull the trigger. They've got contacts around the Pacific and they could certainly arrange a hit. They move in the big time. Don't mess with them."

"What's their background?"

"They're both linked to the ————— gang. Juliet's a real upper-echelon crim – he's even got his own company – a very well connected man. An old-time real heavy villain, he's got a big involvement in the drug industry. As for Papa, he's got form for stolen property and drugs."

"Would $75,000 for a hit be out of their league?"

"No, not at all. Most of their jobs would probably earn at least that if not more. What's your interest?"

I explained simply that I'd heard a rumour they may be involved in the Paul White case. O'Halloran's only response was *"Shit!"*, a sentiment I was forced to agree with.

A credit check on the pair followed, and indicated that Kilo Juliet really did move in high circles. He had half a million dollars worth of High Court debt judgements against him, from only a handful of creditors. One debt alone was $345,000.

At this stage there was no corroboration of their involvement in the White case, but as potential culprits they certainly appeared to fit the profile of likely offenders.

Then came the coup de grace I'd been waiting for on the EP front. A chance meeting with Brian Henry resulted in the discovery that he and Peters were working on a transaction called JIF.

"How the hell did you find out about JIF?," I inquired in utter disbelief.

"It's one of the transactions in the wine box we've been trying to figure out," he grinned. *"But don't worry, it'll all be public in a couple of weeks. The winebox is about to be tabled in three foreign parliaments."*

The sense of panic rising up within was hard to quell. Here I was frantically looking for documentation on JIF, only to find it was in the winebox after all, and then discovering the whole lot would be laid bare in a multinational free-for-all within a fortnight.

---

* Another contact of mine, a man with underworld connections, told me a similar story some months later. He claimed the two men were being named in Australian criminal circles as having *"been involved in the hit on White"*.

Even if we'd had the go ahead that day to produce a programme, TVNZ could not have had one ready within two weeks. I needed to stall for time.

"*What do you know about JIF?*," I probed, trying to gauge what kind of spin was likely to be put on JIF if it did see the light of day. That was my second problem. Peters had been criticised previously for not hitting the correct points in some of his earlier Parliamentary outbursts. If he muffed this one, no one would be able to understand it even if TVNZ broadcast the correct version, people would only get even more confused.

"*JIF appears to be a US$200 million dollar loan from the BNZ to European Pacific*," Brian replied, his face now starting to betray some confusion at my line of questioning. "*Why?*"

"*You're looking at JIF the wrong way around*," I told him bluntly. "*It's much bigger than that.*" It took a lot of persuasion to get Henry to try and talk Peters out of Plan A. The wheels had already been set in motion, he said, and two wineboxes were already in place overseas awaiting their fate.

"*Peters has to hold off*," I pleaded. "*JIF could be the granddaddy of the winebox tax evasion schemes. If he goes off half-cocked we'll never be able to get the full story out, and TVNZ is already committed to a one hour documentary on this. What's the best Winnie can do? 10 minutes? He can't do it justice and no one will ever understand it.*"

The November 1993 General Election was only six weeks away. Peters had been planning a campaign for his new New Zealand First Party based on revelations from the winebox. Politicians in a number of other countries, including Australia and the Cook Islands, had been planning to cook up storms of their own based on the documents.

I was asking a lot. I was asking, said Henry, Winston Peters to sacrifice his chances in the upcoming election in return for a promise that the state television network might vindicate him down the track. A state network, Henry reminded me, that had "*repeatedly bagged*" Peters during the setting up of his new political party earlier in the year. It was a point I had to concede.

After the MP had stepped up his campaign for an inquiry into the Bank of New Zealand in 1992, powerful interests had been moving to nobble him. He became increasingly ostracised by his own party, culminating in his expulsion from caucus at the end of 1992. Peters' problems had escalated with a letter on March 4, 1993, from the National Party. It contained his marching orders.

"*I write to advise you the National Executive has decided not to approve you as a candidate for the National Party*," wrote executive director Marg Skews.

The effective expulsion forced a by-election the following month in the Tauranga seat, and during the campaign Peters' lashed out at what he called a "*hysterical analysis of me*" on TVNZ's *Holmes* programme, the previous week. At an 800-strong rally he called it a smear campaign directed against him, and that was the nicest thing he said!

"*Ladies and gentlemen, in 25 years of politics and political involvement that is the most biased, disgraceful and unprofessional TV report I have ever seen. But*

I've got news for TVNZ, and it's this: if you think you are going to get away with that, those that made that decision, I've got news for you and it's all bad."

When the TVNZ camera crew covering the meeting turned their camera off during the monologue, Peters demanded that they turn the camera back on and keep recording.

"Shove it on and give us a fair go here. You're meant to be the watchdog for democracy, not a poodle or chihuahua."

The crowd loved it, joining in with cries of *"shame"* and *"go home"*, directed at the TVNZ contingent.

Throughout the year, a state of undeclared war had remained between TVNZ and the politician. Here I was walking into the middle of it, trying to wave a white flag while both sides were still firing at each other.

"Look Brian," I said wearily, leaning back in the chair, *"You're going to have to trust me on this. I can't force Winston to do anything, and I don't actually want to interfere in whatever shenanigans he's got planned, but hear me out: If he messes this one up, it's going to wreck our chances of getting a well researched, reasoned documentary investigation to air. It's his choice."*

Driving away from that meeting was a white-knuckle experience. I knew Brian Henry would take on board what I'd said, but Winston Peters was a different matter. Only weeks away from an election campaign, and here I was trying to snaffle his election thunder.

The next three weeks would be harrowing as I waited to see whether the box of documents turned up overseas. In the meantime, I did what I should have done months earlier, and went to retrieve the entire winebox of documents from my original source.

I was lucky that my document supplier had not been injuncted along with Stephen Lunn when the first orders went down in October 1992. But then again, it was a measure of our *modus operandi* that very few people knew I was working on the case, and even fewer had the slightest inkling who my sources were.

It had been incredibly convenient to let Jenni McManus and Fran O'Sullivan steal the European Pacific limelight, and attendant legal action, because it allowed us to continue working very quietly but steadily behind the scenes. I had no intention of being injuncted by the tax haven company, I was planning a sneak attack.

The decision not to seek the full winebox after the injunction had been made because everyone I'd talked to had indicated the "big deal" wasn't in it. Now that I knew it was, it became imperative to get hold of it.

It turned out to be, contrary to expectations, a goldmine. "JIF", of course, was there in all its glory. A document dated November 10, 1988, was titled *"JIF/MITSUBISHI"*, and referred to a US$200 million deal with the huge Mitsubishi Bank.

It's important, at this point in the game, to realise how the Cook Islands tax haven works. If you fly to Rarotonga as a tourist, you stay in a hotel and you buy souvenirs from shops. You are dealing with companies based in the Cook Islands **domestic** regime. These companies do not have tax haven status, and they and their employees all pay tax to the Cook Islands Government much like everyone else has to in their own countries.

But the Cooks also has what's known as an **offshore** or **international** regime. You can't see it, but in essence it's another set of totally different laws that apply only to companies registered as "internationals". Companies established in the international regime do not pay any domestic tax, but as a rule they're also not allowed to do any business with companies in the domestic regime either. The two worlds almost never meet, except where European Pacific is involved.

Being the biggest of the tax haven trust companies, and also the one that wrote the original tax laws, EP enjoyed a special relationship with the Cook Islands Government and had a lot of freedom to do deals using both regimes.

If I add the word "domestic" after a company name, it's an indication that the company being used in the transaction is a domestic one, with a commensurate tax liability to the Cooks Government.

The JIF/MITSUBISHI transaction was to begin with a US$200 million loan from the Bank of New Zealand's New York branch. This is the "principal" in the money loop. That money is firstly deposited in the European Pacific Banking Corporation in Rarotonga, an international regime bank. It is then flicked on through a couple of "arms-length" companies before being deposited in the Mitsubishi Bank's Hong Kong branch.

An arms-length company is usually just a front company used to hide the real depositor from any inquisitive tax inspectors or curious bankers. In this case both the front companies had been set up in the Caribbean tax haven of Bermuda, and one of them was owned by Capital Markets Ltd., Fay Richwhite's publicly listed investment vehicle. In this case, the front companies are of no real importance.

Mitsubishi Bank Hong Kong finds itself with US$200 million on deposit, and decides to lend it out to European Pacific Banking Company Limited [domestic], the main retail bank in Rarotonga and subject to Cook Islands tax.

The $200 million principal continues on its merry way, with European Pacific Banking Company Limited lending it on to European Pacific Banking Corporation, which of course repays the BNZ for its original loan.

But the use of the domestic bank in the money-go-round means that any interest earned by Mitsubishi Bank on its massive loan to European Pacific Banking Company Ltd (EPBCL) is subject to withholding tax at a rate of 15%, in much the same way as the NZ IRD takes withholding tax from savings accounts of retail bank customers.

This point cannot be overstressed. Normally you send your money to a tax haven so that you can pay no tax at all! In this case, Mitsubishi bank was deliberately loaning money to the Cook Islands domestic bank, EPBCL, and having to pay tax. This was not what you would call a normal tax-haven transaction. In the JIF document, EP staff Rosemary Healy and Guy Jalland had written:

"*EPBCL [suffers] a withholding tax liability to the Cook Islands Government at the rate of 15%, which is absorbed by Mitsubishi at a cost of 0.35% per annum.*"

The 0.35% absorption cost is essentially the "fee" being paid to Mitsubishi bank for agreeing to take part in the deal. On a loan of $200 million, that worked out at $700,000 per annum. It is the only money that Mitsubishi would have made on the deal, because of course the interest it's earning in the Cook Islands is being balanced out by the interest it's having to repay the two front companies on the other side of the money loop.

But what we couldn't figure out when we found JIF/MITSUBISHI, was where on earth European Pacific were actually making profit on the arrangement. The interest costs balanced out, and we knew EP was paying a US$700,000 fee to Mitsubishi, but nowhere in the document was there any mention of profits for the EP Group anywhere in the circle.

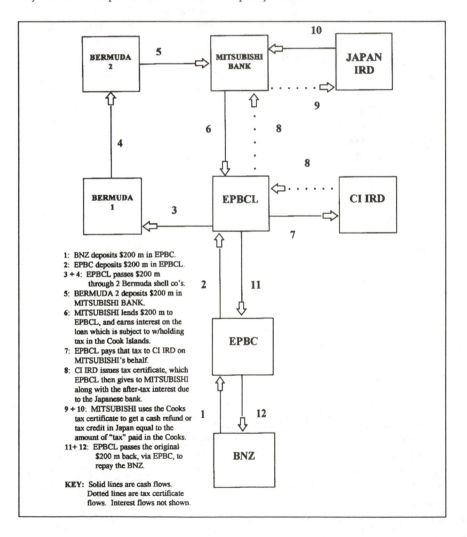

1: BNZ deposits $200 m in EPBC.
2: EPBC deposits $200 m in EPBCL.
3 + 4: EPBCL passes $200 m through 2 Bermuda shell co's.
5: BERMUDA 2 deposits $200 m in MITSUBISHI BANK.
6: MITSUBISHI lends $200 m to EPBCL, and earns interest on the loan which is subject to w/holding tax in the Cook Islands.
7: EPBCL pays that tax to CI IRD on MITSUBISHI's behalf.
8: CI IRD issues tax certificate, which EPBCL then gives to MITSUBISHI along with the after-tax interest due to the Japanese bank.
9 + 10: MITSUBISHI uses the Cooks tax certificate to get a cash refund or tax credit in Japan equal to the amount of "tax" paid in the Cooks.
11 + 12: EPBCL passes the original $200 m back, via EPBC, to repay the BNZ.

KEY: Solid lines are cash flows. Dotted lines are tax certificate flows. Interest flows not shown.

It was also impossible to see any tax rort going on. According to the document in my hands, EPBCL [domestic] was paying withholding tax on behalf of Mitsubishi Bank to the Cook Islands Government. There was nothing there that indicated the tax money was being repaid to the EP Group afterward. It was obvious, as Seven had warned, that we only had one half of the deal.

The elation at finding JIF vanished in an instant. Over the months I'd become very accustomed to the two steps forward-one step back procedure. I was used to the highs followed by crashing lows as I realised that each pinnacle I had finally surmounted was not actually the top of the mountain, only one of the foothills. I made what would be my last call to Seven for the next six months.

"We've got the JIF documentation, but I've got a problem. We've only got the part where Mitsubishi Bank pays tax, we don't have the bit where the tax comes back. How did they do it?"

"Promissory notes."

And that was virtually all he said. He hung up on me. I'd obviously worn out my welcome with Seven in the interim. I looked dubiously back at the box of documents on my desk. Roughly 2500 pages, and I'm looking for some sort of promissory note deal with the Cook Islands Government.

Three hours later it emerged. It was a barely legible, handwritten, wiring diagram, but there – in one small corner – were the words *"C.I. Govt."*

"Yeeeessss!," I yelled, punching the air with a fist. *"Gotcha you bastards! Thank you Jesus!"* As I'd just managed to express so eloquently, my prayers had been answered.

It was a diagram that had nothing to do with JIF, referring instead to something called the *"Magnum transaction"*. I'd been sent some Magnum documentation in October 1992, but this diagram hadn't been part of that delivery. The only thing highlighted in the first tranche of Magnum documentation was a possible breach of Section 62 of the New Zealand Companies Act, which forbids companies from lending money for the purpose of buying their own shares back.

This diagram showed a tax payment to the Cook Islands Government, but then showed the tax coming back out of the Cook Islands IRD and used in a strange little deal with a company called European Pacific Merchant Finance. I looked a little closer, taking note of the figures. It began with a tax payment of $881,582 from an EP company called HACL to the Cooks IRD. My finger traced the arrows marking the money flow.

From the IRD, $831,582 came back out and was given to a company called Govt Property Corp. But this was where it got interesting. Property Corp. then purchased *"P/Notes"*, which I assumed were Promissory Notes – a type of bond – worth $10 million, from another company called Dundee Investments, but instead of paying the $10 million face value, the Government Property Corp. paid Dundee $10,881,582.

Something looked very suspect here – take away the $10 million and you're left with $881,582, the same amount as the original tax payment. I remembered that I don't believe in co-incidence. It was what happened next in the transaction that gave the game away.

Property Corp took its promissory notes – that it had paid $10,881,582 for – and sold them to European Pacific Merchant Finance for only $10,050,000 – an instant loss for Property Corp on the deal of $831,582, and likewise an instant profit for European Pacific of the same amount. Ingenious.

The tax money paid in by HACL that morning of $881,582 had been almost totally laundered back to European Pacific in the afternoon in a transaction where the Government Property Corporation made an $831,582 loss. The difference of $50,000 between the two sums could probably be explained away as some kind of fee or kickback to the Cook Islands Government.

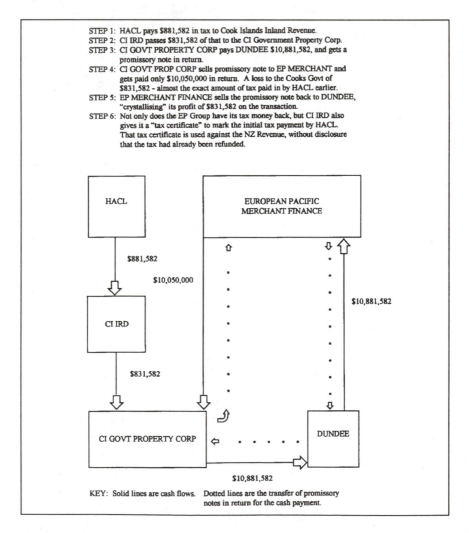

STEP 1: HACL pays $881,582 in tax to Cook Islands Inland Revenue.
STEP 2: CI IRD passes $831,582 of that to the CI Government Property Corp.
STEP 3: CI GOVT PROPERTY CORP pays DUNDEE $10,881,582, and gets a promissory note in return.
STEP 4: CI GOVT PROP CORP sells promissory note to EP MERCHANT and gets paid only $10,050,000 in return. A loss to the Cooks Govt of $831,582 - almost the exact amount of tax paid in by HACL earlier.
STEP 5: EP MERCHANT FINANCE sells the promissory note back to DUNDEE, "crystallising" its profit of $831,582 on the transaction.
STEP 6: Not only does the EP Group have its tax money back, but CI IRD also gives it a "tax certificate" to mark the initial tax payment by HACL. That tax certificate is used against the NZ Revenue, without disclosure that the tax had already been refunded.

HACL

EUROPEAN PACIFIC
MERCHANT FINANCE

$881,582

$10,050,000

CI IRD

$10,881,582

$831,582

CI GOVT PROPERTY CORP

DUNDEE

$10,881,582

KEY: Solid lines are cash flows. Dotted lines are the transfer of promissory notes in return for the cash payment.

After a year of searching I finally had them. Evidence of apparent fraud as defined by two former executives of the company. I looked at the rest of the box – it would need a thorough going over yet again, and the Magnum transaction obviously deserved some special attention. Time for that in the morning, I thought, as I hid the box and flicked off the office light.

For the first time in nearly a year, I had a really good night's sleep.

*   *   *

In the Wogistani sand dunes, a warm zephyr caressing the tethered camel and teasing little eddies of dust from the ground, Aladdin stood gazing at the tarnished bronze lamp he'd retrieved from the cave. Gently rubbing it to remove the accumulated grime of ages past, he wasn't aware at first as deep within a Genie stirred and flexed.

But, in the way of magic, others long fearful of the Genie's coming sensed the moment of his awakening from afar, and they were afraid.

CHAPTER 13

Pandora's Box

"High though his titles, proud his name,
Boundless his wealth as wish can claim;
Despite those titles, power, and pelf,
The wretch, concentred all in self,
Living, shall forfeit fair renown,
And, doubly dying, shall go down
To the vile dust from whence he sprung,
Unwept, unhonoured, and unsung."
– SIR WALTER SCOTT, 1771-1832

EUROPEAN PACIFIC'S WINEBOX HAD derived its name courtesy of Stephen Lunn, who'd returned a box of documents to the apartment of EP boss David Lloyd in Auckland, just across the road from the century-old High Court complex. Lacking any other kind of container to leave the documents in, Lunn had dumped them in an old wine carton.

If I'd known back then the hassle that would follow my retrieval of a set of winebox documents, I'd have probably done what Lloyd's mates did back in Sydney and dropped them in the harbour – tied to a very heavy rock. I, like most journalists I know, prefer my wineboxes to come with wine actually in them, not trouble with a capital T.

Eager young fool that I was, however, I began rummaging through for more pieces of the now half-completed jigsaw puzzle. One of the first to emerge was a document dated November 25, 1987, from EP executive Mark Jones to Robert Hay. It was all about Cook Islands withholding tax, and something called the *"Ribun Issue"*.

"The predominant difficulty in the implementation of the RIBUN Issue is that the Cook Islands tax credits will have a significant impact on the New Zealand/Australian tax base," wrote Jones. *"Antipodean tax authorities will experience a huge increase in the volume of tax credits remitted from the Cook Islands. That apparent increase may make detection an easier task for the authorities."*

And just how big was this *"volume of tax credits"*? Seven would later confirm that European Pacific was talking about more than $1 billion worth of essentially false tax credit certificates during its initial planning.

It could be argued that New Zealand and Australian tax inspectors should have been instantly suspicious about any tax certificates issued by a tax haven like the Cooks – after all, the whole point of using the Cooks was to avoid paying tax totally. Jones was understating the likelihood of detection – the IRD would have had to be braindead if it let a billion dollars worth of shonky tax certificates pass through unnoticed. Even now, I don't think the IRD was ever that gullible.

The importance of this memo, however, shouldn't be missed. It is the first blueprint for what later became the alleged Magnum and JIF frauds.

"*The structure,*" continued Jones, "*provides for the disbursion of Cook Islands tax credits into a number of countries who are net lenders. In these countries, there will not be an excessive amount of Cook Islands tax credits.*"

What Jones was saying here is that by using the tax certificates in countries with lots of money to invest and huge economies – like Japan or the US – the $1 billion volume of those tax credits is just one drop in an ocean of financial transactions. The memo went on to suggest that European Pacific set up its own "*special purpose*" domestic banking company to exclusively handle the fake tax certificate transactions.

"*It is suggested that rather than using EPBCL . . . a specific domestic banking company be established with a name like 'Pacific Islands Regional Development Bank'. Harcourt [HACL] could simply change its name!,*" Jones chirped enthusiastically. "*The payments to the foreign banks in – say Japan, the United Kingdom or the Low Countries [Holland, Belgium] – would be from an entity that purported to be a Pacific Rim Development Bank; that would give the Development Bank a reason for paying above the general bank bill rate for funds in those countries.*"*

I scratched my head a couple of times and tried to work out what Jones was up to. It was obvious he was looking to use banks in those countries for a Mitsubishi/JIF type deal, where the foreign banks would lend money to EP's "special" bank, and be taxed on the interest they earned on the deal. But why would world class banks want to lend huge amounts of money to a dubious little tax haven bank? The last line about paying "*above the general bank bill rate*" obviously meant that European Pacific needed to offer higher interest rates to lure the big banks down to the Cooks.

The beauty of calling yourself a "*Development Bank*" was that such entities normally indulge in high risk business and so are charged higher interest rates by the big banks that lend them funds. It was a perfect camouflage for European Pacific, which could hide behind a noble title as its reason for seeking the funding.

Not suspecting anything out of the ordinary, the big banks would pay tax and receive Cook Islands tax certificates in return, which they could then use to cut their tax bill back in their own countries. What they didn't realise, I thought as I read the memo, was that European Pacific was secretly and quietly planning to siphon the tax money they'd paid back out of the Cook Islands Treasury, making a mockery of the tax certificates the foreign banks had been issued with.

---

* A former European Pacific staffer, known only as "Witness A", told the Davison Commission that JIF schemes had been carried out in Belgium as well as Japan, and possibly also Malaysia and Indonesia.

"*The Cook Islands Government would refund the amount of the tax, less its cut,*" Jones continued in his blueprint.

This was great!, I thought, downing another gulp of coffee. If I'd had any doubts about the real intent of the tax credit schemes, they were dispelled in that sentence. Why would the Cook Islands Government give away tax money legitimately owned by the people of the Cook Islands? The only explanation I could come up with was that EP – as the biggest and toughest of the trust companies – effectively controlled the Cooks Government and could dictate policy. Reading on, I discovered that's exactly the sort of influence EP thought it had.

"*Implementation of this structure would involve: Consolidation of the Cook Islands Income Tax Act 1972, and in particular the re-establishment of the 35% withholding tax regime.*

"*This could be done and compiled by me,*" wrote Jones charitably, "*while I was in the Cooks (a simple renumbering of the legislation would suffice) or we could also* **concoct** *[author's emphasis] for the Government some other amendments to the non-resident income regime – perhaps the Harley Royal Commission on Taxation (Cook Islands) (etc) might be an idea.*

"*The Cook Islands should introduce new tax credit receipt forms as the present forms are rather crude (they provide for receipts from copra etc).*"

Whatever Mark Jones' job was with European Pacific, he seemed to be under no illusions about his power to rewrite Cook Islands domestic tax law to suit his plans. Certainly those early plans were ambitious. If the Japanese banks in the JIF deals had been paying 35% in withholding tax to the Cook Islands Government, then the yearly tax rort would have been US$45.5 million – close to quarter of a billion dollars over the five year JIF deals.

With the Mitsubishi/JIF document showing a withholding tax of only 15%, it's obvious that European Pacific didn't have the balls to attempt the scam on a larger scale. While the RIBUN memo was enlightening, it still didn't illustrate the exact mechanism for refunding the tax, and dated as it was a year before the Mitsubishi deal it didn't appear to have any forensic value in working out how JIF operated. The search continued, Deputy Director of News and Current Affairs Shaun Brown poking his nose in at one stage to see what I was up to.

"*What are those?,*" he quizzed, indicating the documents.

"*They're the European Pacific winebox documents,*" I replied innocently, enjoying the look of horror/surprise/lust that crossed his visage. "*Would you like to know where I got them?,*" I baited. Like Sergeant Shultz from the popular TV series *Hogan's Heroes,* Brown couldn't get out of the room fast enough, the words "*I don't want to know anything*" lingering briefly as he hightailed it out the door. You'd think the damn box was radioactive. Coming from a fly-by-the-seat-of-your-pants operator like TV3, I found that throughout TVNZ the technique of <u>protecting</u> the seat of one's pants had been raised to an art form.

It was quite sensible really, because it gave the journalist on the ground a certain leeway that we didn't have in the "refer upwards" regime at TV3.

By the same token, the message was clear: We don't ask questions that we don't want to know the answers to. If you get caught, you're on your own. On a noticeboard at both TV networks is a Hunter S. Thompson quotation:

"Television . . . a cruel and shallow money trench, a long plastic hallway where pimps and thieves run free and good men die like dogs."

It is an ongoing source of inspiration to all of us who work in the business, and it's essentially true. Television is Darwin's Theory of Evolution put to the ultimate test, where survival of the fittest often becomes a more entertaining watch for the insiders than the programming they're producing.

The petty squabbling in the industry can be both disheartening and amusing. An example of the latter in my case came from TV3 producer, Rennie Barrett. Barrett is a likeable guy, and I've whiled away many a quiet Saturday afternoon in the newsroom swapping yarns. His biggest claim to fame however was knowing *Day of the Jackal* author, Frederick Forsyth, before Freddie became a household name. Before, in fact, Freddie even wrote the book.

Barrett and Forsyth worked together as young reporters at the BBC in London, and Rennie remembers Forsyth being sent to cover the Biafran conflict in Nigeria in the late 1960's. As Barrett tells it, Forsyth went awol after four days – deciding to throw in his lot with one of the various factions in the conflict. When he finally returned to London sometime later, an eager and blooded young Forsyth caught up with his BBC pals at a pub, proudly informing them he'd just written a book that would make him a millionaire.

"Yeah, right," said Barrett among much raucous and supportive laughter from his equally sceptical colleagues, *"Pull the other one, it's got bells on! You can't write books. Come and see us if you want your old job back."*

Two decades later, Fred Forsyth was churning out multi-million dollar novels on a yearly basis, and Rennie Barrett was one of us – a hack journalist. It was with some considerable pleasure that I listened as the incredibly cynical Barrett told me, amid much raucous and supportive laughter from equally sceptical colleagues just before I left TV3, how the story I was working on was a load of hooey and would certainly never make a television documentary, let alone a book.

"You're pissing in the wind, Wishart. It's just another conspiracy theory, and you got sucked in by it. You don't seriously think TVNZ's going to do the story, do you? You're going to be working on ordinary daily news stories, boy."

If I could bottle up Rennie's curses I'd sell them on the side as a miracle recipe for success. On the other hand, I'd never hire him to bless a ship.

There was another memo in the box that caught my attention that morning. Dated February 11, 1988, it was another Mark Jones creation, addressed to David Lloyd, Rosemary Healy and Robert Hay. It was helpfully entitled *"STRUCTURES FOR THE ISSUE OF COOK ISLANDS TAX CREDIT PAPER"*.

Call me psychic, perhaps, but I couldn't help feeling that something dealing with the structures for issuing Cook Islands tax credits might just be something worth looking at.

"The purpose of this memorandum is to summarise the various structures for utilising Cook Islands tax credits. The memorandum contains an analysis of the structure of a variety of note issues by a Cook Islands domestic bank.

"This memorandum may be shown to other staff in order that they understand the transactions and elicit client interest. However under no circumstances can this memorandum or the detailed information it contains be given to other persons without my express permission."

Never wave a phrase like that under a journalist's nose and expect them not to react. Sorry Mark, first lesson in secret squirrel work is never use secret squirrel phrases. This memo was a "must" read. It outlined plans to use Pacific Rim Development Bank Ltd, formerly Harcourt Acceptance Corporation Ltd (HACL) to issue promissory notes with a value of $50 million. Don't get confused by phrases like *"issue promissory notes"*.

While banking terminology can sound difficult and is sometimes hard to get your ears around, it is essentially just another form of jargon. "Promissory Notes" are a product that banks sell, in much the same way as a jeweller might sell you a solid gold bar as an investment. The notes might carry a face value, with a promise to pay a certain amount of interest at a specified time.

In reality it's not much different from you depositing $50 million in your savings bank account and getting paid interest at the end of the year, but whereas you can't go around buying, selling or swapping your deposit book with other people, you <u>can</u> buy, sell or swap promissory notes – they're a bit like a portable savings account. In this case, the notes would then be sold to investors by European Pacific Banking Corporation.

"All monies used for purchase of the notes should be forwarded from offshore bank accounts," wrote Jones. In other words, the notes are being sold to companies and banks overseas. *"And notes themselves should also be purchased in the Cook Islands by an attorney of the non resident [overseas investor], so as to allow the interest income to have a Cook Islands source for income tax purposes."*

I had to admire Jones. The guy's plans may amount to prima facie criminal fraud, but he was as cunning as a snake. There was genius in the simplicity. I had come into the investigation expecting to find a myriad of hair-raising, complex and confusing transactions, shrouded in so much arcane financial wizardry that even Beelzebub and a horde of hefty hobgoblins couldn't undo their fiendish secrets.

Instead, I found myself facing a very easy-to-follow concept. By getting an investor to pay domestic Cook Islands withholding tax, European Pacific could conceivably be responsible for a huge increase in the tax revenue coming into the Cooks. Instead of putting that tax revenue into the Cooks' Treasury, however, imagine all of it being bundled in a huge bag and put to one side for a moment.

At this point, all these clients have paid tax in the Cooks, so they'll be wanting Cook Islands tax certificates to prove to their own Internal Revenues that they've "given" already.

But, by the same token, there'd be no point in these investors paying tax in the Cooks unless they were also getting some of their tax money back. I mean – why pay $100 tax in the Cook Islands instead of paying $100 tax to your own IRD? Unless you're motivated by a particularly nasty personality clash with one of your local tax inspectors, there doesn't seem much logic in choosing to pay the same amount of tax in a foreign country instead, not to mention the extra hassle.

No, the twist to these transactions would have to be a secret refund of the tax paid in the Cooks – *as well* as getting a tax certificate to wave in the tax inspector's face.

But who might the clients be? *"If a foreign branch of an international bank wishes to make a loan it will do so with the Pacific Rim Bank and claim the tax credit,"* suggested Jones in what was obviously a precursor to what later happened with JIF. The memo suggested the company do *"One-off deals in Australia for special clients"*, and mentioned one deal that had apparently already taken place with Euronational Australia.

OK, I deduced, instead of the huge bag of tax going through the normal channels – somewhere European Pacific was drilling a hole in the bag and whipping the tax back out as fast as their little hands could do it. But how did they keep such a raid hidden from the auditors of the Cooks' Government? We knew the New Zealand Audit Office did the Cooks' books, and if tens or hundreds of millions were being stolen from the Cooks' Treasury, surely they'd know! The answer to that was hidden in the next memo.

Dated April 10, 1989, it was addressed to Lloyd, Guy Jalland and Trevor Clarke and titled *"Cook Island Government Accounting"*. It was written by EP executive Peter Brannigan. I laughed out loud. These turkeys were making it far too easy.

"The present visit of the New Zealand Government Audit Office is to finalise their work on the accounts ended 31 March 1988. Consequently, it is believed that they will not be seeking access to transactions dated after this date.

"Pursuant to discussions held between Geoffrey Henry [Cooks' PM] and David Lange [NZ PM], a Cook Islands constitutional amendment will be promulgated when parliament next sits, estimated to be May 1989. That amendment will restrict the New Zealand Government Audit Office to an involvement with those areas wherein New Zealand aid to the Cook Islands is accounted for.

"The balance of their present duties will be reassigned by Parliament/Government to other auditors and should be effective for the 1989 year. Peat Marwick would be interested in undertaking all or part of this assignment provided that it could audit Government Department(s) in totality.

"Keith Rushbrook reports," continued Brannigan, referring to a senior Peat Marwick official, *"that two forms of accounting have been used to date. The first involves a gross receipt of taxes being accounted for throughout the system as a gross receipt with a corresponding expenditure item to the Property Corporation from the General Revenue Account."*

Yeah, I thought, that sounds normal. What was happening at the end of each day was that all taxes that came in were counted and noted in the book, along with any payments made to the Government Property Corporation each day from the Revenue Account. That made sense – an auditor could see the money coming in and see it going to the Property Corporation. No problem there, I would have thought. But Brannigan had more.

"*The second method has been adopted more recently whereby a gross tax receipt is issued and the taxes are paid to the General Revenue Account at EPBC (as before) but* **no consequent accounting entries take place** *[author's emphasis] at this stage. The General Revenue Account is then reduced by a payment to Property Corporation (as before) and again* **no accounting entries arise at this stage.**

"*The resulting balance in the General Revenue Account at EPBC is then transferred to the General Revenue Account at the BNZ Wellington (as before).*

"**It is only at this stage that the net amount so transferred gives rise to an accounting entry.** *That accounting entry is simply a revenue item of the net amount.*"

I knew from cursory reading of other documents in the box that Peat Marwick was already European Pacific's auditor, and was named in the winebox documents as an adviser in a number of the tax transactions.* From a previously open and fully accounted system of monitoring incoming tax money and following its disbursal to Government departments like the Property Corporation, this European Pacific document indicated payments to the latter were now being hidden, beyond the reach or scrutiny of the NZ Audit Office.

And just to make doubly sure, the Cook Islands Government was changing the Islands' constitution in order to boot out the NZ Audit Office. The Cook Islands people would never know how much money they were losing!

I popped my head in around Shaun Brown's door.

"*What do you want to do? That box is a mint – it's even got JIF!*"

"*I thought you said we'd never get any JIF documents?*" he responded, looking slightly taken aback at the turn of events.

"*Yeah, I know. Believe me, you aren't half as surprised as I was! I could have had this box a year ago, but I didn't bother actively pursuing it because everyone kept telling me JIF wasn't in it.*"

Of all the news directors I've met in my time, Shaun Brown had the greatest talent for permanently looking harassed. It wasn't an angry, harassed look – it was more the kind of bewildered look you can imagine a teddy bear might get as it's swung around in the air for the 14 millionth time by a toddler fiercely gripping its leg: a sort of "*What did I do to deserve this?*" type of harassed look. Shaun Brown was that teddy bear, and right now he was having one of those looks.

---

* In testimony to the Davison Commission in April 1995, KPMG Peat Marwick staff went on oath to deny giving European Pacific any advice on the tax rorts, much less signing off on them. Peat Marwick also quit as European Pacific's auditor on March 7, 1995, because of the "untenable" situation it had been placed in.

"I'll have a chat to Norris," he said, running a hand through his hair. *"The election is only weeks away. Logistically we don't have the resources to do the story at this point in time, and realistically we can't run a story that's as politically loaded as this one until after the election. We'd be crucified. Why don't you just keep digging away, write up another draft script based on what we now have, and we'll review it after the election."*

I couldn't argue with the logic in that, and returned to my treasure trove. In all, there were 78 pages of apparent final draft documentation relating to the Magnum transaction, and a few dozen more preliminary draft documents pertaining to it as well. Chief amongst all of them, however, were two signed agreements, both dated July 27, 1988.

In the first agreement, a European Pacific subsidiary named Dundee Investments was selling two promissory notes marked "A" and "B", to the Cook Islands Government Property Corporation.

"It is hereby agreed as follows:
"1. That DUNDEE agrees to sell the Promissory Notes and THE CORPORATION agrees to purchase the Promissory Notes for the amounts and on the settlement dates set out herein."

This first clause was important. Dundee was committing the Government Property Corp. to purchase the notes for a pre-arranged price, and on specific dates. Once Property Corp signed the agreement it had to go through with the transaction on Dundee's terms. The next clause set out the prices for the notes and the dates of sale to the Property Corp.

"2. That settlement and consideration for the sale and purchase of the Promissory Notes shall be as follows:
"(i) PROMISSORY NOTE 'A' – Consideration: <u>NEW ZEALAND DOLLARS TEN MILLION EIGHT HUNDRED AND EIGHTY-ONE THOUSAND FIVE HUNDRED AND EIGHTY-TWO</u>
(NZD 10,881,582.00)
Settlement Date: 27 July 1988

"(ii) PROMISSORY NOTE "B" – Consideration: <u>NEW ZEALAND DOLLARS ELEVEN MILLION ONE HUNDRED AND SIXTY-EIGHT THOUSAND SIX HUNDRED AND NINE</u> (NZD11,168,609.00)
Settlement Date: 27 July 1989

"3. That the respective considerations for the Promissory Notes to be paid by THE CORPORATION to DUNDEE shall be paid in cash on each of the respective settlement dates specified in clause 2(i) and (ii) above."

OK. Here we had an agreement in writing that forced the Government Property Corporation to buy two promissory notes for a combined total price of $22,050,191. The document had been signed by both Dundee and the Property Corp, and had been stamped with the Government Seal. That proved it had been executed. The next agreement, also dated July 27, 1988, was between European Pacific Merchant Finance Ltd (EPMF) and the Property Corporation.

> *"It is hereby agreed as follows:*
>
> *"1. That THE CORPORATION agrees to sell the Promissory Notes and EPMF agrees to purchase the Promissory Notes for the amounts and on the settlement dates set out herein.*
>
> *"2. That settlement and consideration for the sale and purchase of the Promissory Notes shall be as follows:*
>
> > *(i) PROMISSORY NOTE "A" – Consideration: <u>NEW ZEALAND DOLLARS TEN MILLION AND FIFTY THOUSAND</u> (NZD10,050,000.00)*
> > *Settlement Date: 27 July 1988*
>
> > *(ii) PROMISSORY NOTE "B"- Consideration: <u>NEW ZEALAND DOLLARS TEN MILLION</u> (NZD10,000,000.00)*
> > *Settlement Date: 27 July 1989*
>
> *"3. That the respective considerations for the Promissory Notes to be paid by EPMF to THE CORPORATION shall be paid in cash on each of the respective settlement dates specified in clause 2(i) and (ii) above."*

This then was the second agreement, an agreement where the Government Property Corporation is forced by prior arrangement to sell the Promissory Notes it has just bought from Dundee to another EP company called EPMF. But look at the sale price!

The Property Corporation had paid Dundee a combined total for both notes of $22,050,191. It was selling the notes on the same days to EPMF for only $20,050,000 – an instant loss to the Cook Islands Government of just over two million dollars.

The situation becomes even more transparent when you look at what a normal investor would have done. These promissory notes, like any investment, also carried an interest value over and above the $10 million face value of each note.

In the case of Promissory Note "A", that interest of $1.2 million was payable to the bearer of the note on January 27, 1989 – about six months away. Promissory Note "B" was paying a whopping $3.2 million in interest, payable on July 27, 1990.

OK, so the Cook Islands Government had purchased the notes at an inflated price, but the interest return would more than cover it and they could make an extra $2 million on the deal if they held onto the notes until the due dates. That's what you or I would have done.

But under the terms of the second agreement, the Cook Islands Government Property Corporation was being forced to sell the notes straight back to European Pacific at a price roughly $2 million **less** than it paid for them! It wasn't even allowed to hang onto the notes to get the benefit of the interest payments!

This did not look like a commercial arrangement! To me, it appeared to have more in common with money laundering – changing and disguising the nature of money. In this case, what could have been a simple refund of money from the Cook Islands Revenue to European Pacific was disguised as a loss on a supposedly separate transaction. The end result was the same.

Obviously if word of these sorts of loss-making deals got out in the Cook Islands the Government would get a roasting from its citizens, so the agreements contained another clause:

"The parties covenant with each other to maintain total confidentiality as to this Agreement and to the matters herein unless all parties agree to make public disclosure in an agreed format."

No one normally goes into a deal to deliberately lose money, but here was the Cook Islands Government agreeing in writing to take a bath in a promissory note deal with European Pacific. Our lawyers would later argue that it was an attempt by the two parties to hide the allegedly illegal repayment of Cook Islands tax money to European Pacific under the guise of a "commercial" transaction, except that this transaction was not commercial but pre-arranged.

We were heading into dangerous, uncharted waters. I sensed that all the hiss and spit surrounding the winebox could be condensed into these transactions, and now I knew we had some documentary evidence to back that scenario up.

All of the anger, all of the power struggles involving politicians and business leaders; all of it could go supernova as a result of the contents of this box. Guy Fawkes would have killed for a chance like this.

For more than a year, I had managed to stay out of the front lines – being bravely manned (or should that be womanned?) by Fran O'Sullivan and Jenni McManus – but the umpire was calling a new batter to the plate.

From here on in, it was no longer a case of **whether** a European Pacific flare gun would go off to bathe me like a journalistic possum in the headlights of doom: it was only a question of **when**.

CHAPTER 14

Popping the Magnum

"A little learning is a dangerous thing;
Drink deep, or taste not the Pierian spring:
These shallow draughts intoxicate the brain,
And drinking largely sobers us again."
– ALEXANDER POPE, 1688-1744

CONTACTING FORMER EMPLOYEES OF the merchant bank was always a nerve wracking exercise. I was acutely conscious of the possibility that each new contact might be the "tripwire" – the person who would set off the alarm bells at European Pacific. After a year of investigation, and calls to numerous former staff, David Lilly was the first to stand by his former employer. A former European Pacific Banking Corporation director, I discovered him working for the Tip Top icecream company in Auckland.

Most of the European Pacific employees I spoke to in the course of research have been given pseudonyms in this book to protect their identities. Not so Mr Lilly. As usual, I had taped the phone call on microcassette, but he had also requested that his comments to me be "off the record".

During the court action that later followed as European Pacific tried to stop the *Frontline* documentary from going to air, it became clear that Lilly had not maintained the confidence he had asked for, and instead had rung his former boss, David Lloyd, as soon as he'd hung up from talking to me, and recounted our conversation.

Lilly didn't deny that false tax certificates were being created but didn't accept that the transactions were illegal.

"One of the things that was suggested to us," I began, *"was that there was a particular scam going on whereby the Cook Islands Government would issue a tax certificate stating that a certain amount, of withholding tax on interest had been deducted, but in actual fact EP and others would split most of that tax revenue, and the Cook Islands Government would actually take in only five percent, whereas it issued a tax certificate stating it had taken 15 percent.*

"This money was funnelled back to the companies involved or, in some cases, the companies that had put the money on deposit didn't know they weren't paying the tax – the money was just kept by EP and associated companies."

"Mmm, OK," murmured Lilly. *"I don't discuss any of the transactions I'm involved in anywhere. It's a matter of principle with me."*

"I appreciate that," I continued to push, *"but what I'm saying is those transactions are illegal. As such they aren't covered by any confidentiality. I'm not suggesting for a moment you were involved in them."*

Boy, was I mistaken! I hadn't gone through all the Magnum and JIF documentation at this point, but I would soon find David Lilly's pawprints all over both deals.

"Oh no," Lilly responded politely, "I'm not taking it that you're suggesting I'm involved in them. So far you haven't described anything to me that says it's proven to be illegal. If that went on. It surprises me, from my knowledge of the company. God, when I was involved there, any transaction – you used to have QC's opinions!"

We agreed to keep the conversation confidential, but I was intrigued to see Lilly later tell the High Court that I had shown an extremely detailed knowledge of the company's deals – knowledge so thorough it could only have come from talking to former staff or seeing the documents.

Surprisingly, given European Pacific's normal haste to slap on injunctions or send threatening letters, there was no instant reaction from EP towards myself or Television New Zealand at this juncture. I continued my perusal of the documentation, unaware that – thousands of miles away in EP's Hong Kong headquarters – corporate gun turrets were rapidly swinging around in my direction. It was the first time a journalist had shown any knowledge of European Pacific's deepest secrets and, unexpectedly, it had not come from the already targeted members of the business press. Who the hell was Ian Wishart, and how on earth did he find out?

Wishart, meanwhile, was undergoing a teach-yourself crash course in taxation law, courtesy of the Magnum deal. The keen/masochistic reader may wish to follow the money trail of their own accord – if so, now would be a good time to grab pen, paper and calculator.

While reference is made throughout to "Magnum", Magnum Corporation had no knowledge of the allegedly criminal element of the deal it had been offered. EP's tax certificate scam was a closely guarded secret, and the bank would have been stark raving bonkers to inform customers that their good returns had come from illegal activities. It can be safely accepted that Magnum Corporation was as much in the dark about the sleight of hand as everyone else.

It's important to keep in mind a couple of other hard and fast rules in relation to this transaction. First, don't be bamboozled by the apparent complexity of the deal – that's only been done to fool investigators. Stripped of its embellishments, the Magnum deal is simply an investment of $34.4 million dollars in a European Pacific scheme. All European Pacific did was place that money on deposit in the BNZ Hong Kong for a year. It's that simple.

The insertion of a whole host of European Pacific subsidiaries in the deal was only an excuse to bill Magnum for extra fees.

Secondly, at the end of the day, the only real money in the loop is the $34.4 million paid in by Magnum, and the interest that is earnt on deposit in Hong Kong – a further $4.4 million.

When analysing tax haven deals, you find out how much is going in, and you find out how much is coming out – what happens in between tends to be financial trickery. Thus, in the Magnum deal, European Pacific has a maximum of $38.8 million dollars to play with in real money, but real expenses of more than $40 million.

It presents European Pacific with a problem – how to turn a $2 million tax bill in New Zealand into a nil tax bill, and still have enough money to pay back Magnum its $34.4 million, its $3.8 million dividend, and pay around $600,000 in fees to various parties. European Pacific had no choice but to pretend to pay tax without actually doing so, thereby, as our lawyers later argued in Court, committing an apparent criminal fraud in New Zealand.

The ingenious solution they came up with would have made Rumpelstiltskin proud – EP's answer to turning straw into gold. To understand Magnum, I knew, would provide a key with which to unlock the winebox. It began as an investment deal for the big Magnum Corporation, a Brierley Investments subsidiary and the owner of the DB Brewing group. In July 1988, European Pacific approached Magnum with a proposal.

EP could offer Magnum an above average rate of return if Magnum invested $34.4 million with European Pacific for a year. Instead of a straight loan, where the interest earned by Magnum would be taxable in New Zealand, EP chose to structure the deal using preference shares.

These are a type of share widely used in the late 1980's for tax deals because of their flexibility. They don't have to carry voting rights, and aren't bound by the same restrictions as other shares. The twist is that the return on a preference share investment is considered to be a share dividend, rather than an interest payment. Under New Zealand law at the time, investors weren't required to pay tax on their share dividends because the dividends had theoretically been paid out of the company's profits, which of course had already been taxed. As long as a company could show it had paid tax on its profits, the tax department didn't tax any subsequent dividend payouts to corporate shareholders.

Just to make this crystal clear – if XYZ Corporation makes a loss in the current financial year, it usually won't pay any dividend to its shareholders – it hasn't got any money with which to do so. On the other hand, if XYZ makes a $10 million profit, it might pay $3 million in tax and split the rest among its shareholders in the form of dividends. Because the dividends are, in effect, after-tax profits, they're not taxed again.

So instead of drawing up a normal lending contract and handing European Pacific $34.4 million in cash – receiving taxable interest in return, Magnum purchased $34.4 million worth of preference shares in a company called European Pacific Funds Management NZ Ltd – a company subject to New Zealand law and based in Auckland – and in return received a tax free share dividend.

All this means is that the responsibility for making sure tax is paid falls on the company paying the dividend, not the company receiving it. In other words, at the end of the tax year, EP Funds Management is going to have to show the IRD that it made profits, that it paid tax and then that it paid the rest as a dividend to Magnum.

As part of the deal, European Pacific guaranteed to pay Magnum a dividend of $3,807,500 on its $34.4 million investment – a return of 11.07%. While this seemed low in relation to commercial interest rates of around 14% at the time, you should remember that after paying tax on the interest you earnt, you might end up with only 10% net. So in fact the return on the pref share deal was a good one for Magnum.

Heavy going so far but, taking another swig of black coffee, I launched myself back into it. With $34.4 million sitting in its accounts, EP Funds put the cash out to work, firing $32,229,725 through on deposit to a Cook Islands domestic bank, HACL (Harcourt).

"On Day One," stated paragraph 19.7 of the August 8 memo, *"Harcourt will . . . pay 1,637,225 to [EP Funds Management NZ's] account in interest."* In a twist peculiar to this Magnum transaction, EP structured the deal so that most of the interest payments were "prepaid" on day one. I'll come back to this phenomenon shortly.

However, of that $32,229,725 now with Harcourt, $1,637,225 now goes whizzing straight back to EP Funds, which bounces that company's bank balance back up to the magical figure of $3,807,500, which it needs to pay Magnum's up-front dividend.

The mathematics is this:

	34,400,000	– Magnum's deposit into EP Funds
less	32,229,725	– EP Funds deposit into Harcourt
equals	**2,170,725**	– current EP Funds bank balance
plus	1,637,225	– first interest payment from Harcourt
equals	**3,807,500**	– tax-free dividend to Magnum

Harcourt meanwhile, is paying the tax due on that first interest payment, $881,582. *"On Day One, Harcourt will pay 881,582 to TD's [Tax Department] account."* Which is where the secret promissory note deal comes in to make sure most of that tax money comes back.

"PC [Property Corp] will . . . pay 10,881,582 to the account of [Dundee] for the purchase of the [Dundee] promissory note.

"[European Pacific Merchant Finance] will . . . pay 10,050,000 to the account of PC.

"[Dundee] will pay 881,582 to the account of [European Pacific Merchant Finance] to redeem the promissory note, so the 50,000 fee has been paid away. It balances the books of [European Pacific Merchant Finance]. (The PC/Dundee payment is balanced by way of a public account transfer to PC in order to effect certain Cook Islands public accounting issues.)

"On Day One [European Pacific Merchant Finance] will . . . pay 881,582 . . . to Harcourt's account."

Harcourt has been instantly reimbursed the $881,582 it paid in tax a few moments before – the $50,000 fee for the Cook Islands Government has been temporarily absorbed by European Pacific Merchant Finance, which at this moment is $50,000 in overdraft.

Harcourt's account looks like this:

	32,229,725	– deposit by EP Funds
less	1,637,225	– cash interest to EP Funds
less	881,582	– tax payment on interest
equals	**29,710,918**	– subtotal
plus	881,582	– refund on tax via EPMF
equals	**30,592,500**	– current bank balance

For the purposes of simplifying the reader's understanding of the money trail, I have consolidated some of the intricate "ping-ponging" of money between separate European Pacific group companies into single transactions. The "ping-pongs" were put in place to achieve certain chicken and egg legal and accounting issues, but have no bearing on the overall economics of the transaction. The net effect remains the same.

EP's ownership of the only retail bank in the Cook Islands was an added bonus – it meant that all the Government departments banked with European Pacific, and funds transfers could be done internally at the stroke of a pen. Now, on day one of the deal, Harcourt has paid EP Funds some of the interest up front. It's made up of $1,637,225 in cash, and a tax credit certificate to the value of $881,582.

You'll remember that EP Funds started the day with $34,400,000, and then deposited $32,229,725 with Harcourt Bank in the Cooks. That left EP Funds with only $2,170,275 in its New Zealand bank account.

Now, after getting $1,637,225 in prepaid interest from Harcourt, its account has risen to $3,807,500 – the exact amount it needs to pay Magnum's dividend. Here, on day one of the deal, EP Funds turned around and wrote Magnum a cheque for just over $3.8 million, in full and final payment of its dividend.

That left EP's only further commitment to Magnum being the return of the $34.4 million in 12 months time. From here on in, everything in the transaction was designed to square up EP's books and earn the almost $400,000 in fees that it was after.

It's in this area that EP's problems arise. In paying Magnum's $3.8 million dividend, European Pacific becomes liable for a New Zealand tax bill on top of that of just over $2 million. It doesn't have the money to pay that tax in reality, which is why it paid the tax in two apparent sham transactions in the Cook Islands and threw NZ tax inspectors off the scent with what appeared to be legitimate Cook Islands tax certificates.

It got away with it because nations generally agree to recognise the tax certificates of other nations so that people don't get taxed twice on their income. A big multinational may earn income in the United States for example and be taxed in the United States – it can legitimately avoid further taxation in New Zealand if it can prove – through the use of tax certificates – that it has already paid another sovereign government.

This business of "prepaid interest" was a device used in many tax-driven commercial deals. It gave the dealmakers enough flexibility to enjoy their profits straight away, if they wished – instead of waiting 12 months like the rest of us.

Magnum, for example, not only got an above-market return on its investment, but it got that payment on day one, July 27, 1988. That meant that the $3.8 million could be put towards profits in the financial year to March 31, 1989, whereas if Magnum had been forced to wait until July 27, 1989, the dividend wouldn't have shown up in the profit and loss accounts until March 31, 1990.

European Pacific, on the other hand, utilised another advantage of prepaid interest: the ability to spread interest earnings over two financial years. As I mentioned earlier, EP Funds was earning more than $5.8 million in total interest from its deposit with Harcourt, but only part of that interest was prepaid – just enough to allow EP Funds to meet its obligations to Magnum. The accompanying certificate for $881,582 of Cook Islands withholding tax was used to offset EP Funds' New Zealand tax liability in the December 1988 financial year (EP Funds had a calendar year balance date). EP Funds was liable for tax because it was earning income (interest from Harcourt).

It just so happened that its NZ tax liability was around $881,582 but, because it could prove it had paid the same amount of tax in the Cook Islands, it didn't have to pay any tax in New Zealand. This is where the Magnum transaction became, on the face of the documents, criminal not just in concept but also in practice.

Here, on Day One of the deal, Harcourt's account is currently holding $30,592,500. Out of this must come European Pacific's fees for the entire deal, $370,500. Also deducted is the BNZ's fee of $172,000 (although there are indications that fee may later have been reduced.

The mathematics of Harcourt's bank account looks like this:

	30,592,500	– balance after tax refund
less	370,500	– EP Group's fees
less	172,000	– BNZ's fees
equals	**30,050,000**	– current account balance

To return European Pacific Merchant Finance's $50,000 overdraft back to zero, that last fifty grand drops out as the money flows past, leaving $30 million to go, via EPBC, on deposit at the BNZ in Hong Kong for 12 months.

It's important to remember, at this point, that EP Funds' after-tax dividend payment to Magnum of $3,807,500 meant EP Funds had to show the New Zealand Inland Revenue Department that it had earnt $5,857,691 in profits from which to pay that dividend.

The difference between the two figures, $2,050,191, was the amount of tax due in New Zealand on that part of the deal. Of course, EP Funds didn't have that extra money, but it now had a Cook Islands tax certificate worth $881,582, which it could use to offset that tax liability. But that still left a tax bill of $1,168,609.

Remember also, EP Funds is legally committed to paying Magnum back its $34,400,000 at the end of the 12 months, but it currently has a bank balance of zero. EP Funds knows it is due to receive back the $32,229,725 it deposited with Harcourt, but that leaves the company still $2,170,275 short of its target.

Ideally, EP Funds needs a Cook Islands tax certificate for $1,168,609 to present to the NZ IRD and wipe out its NZ tax liability, and also a cash payment of $2,170,275 to square away its books: a total of $3,338,884.

Just "co-incidentally", the terms of EP Funds original deposit agreement with Harcourt required it to pay the second interest instalment on the day the Magnum deal was wound up. The size of that interest payment from Harcourt to EP Funds? Just "co-incidentally" it was $3,338,884 – the exact amount EP Funds needed. Of course, that sum was subject to a 35% withholding tax in the Cook Islands, so Harcourt went into overdraft to pay that tax, of $1,168,609, to the Cook Islands IRD, while the balance, $2,170,275, was paid in cash to EP Funds.

Harcourt, of course, couldn't be left with a million dollar tax bill, so the money was promptly reclaimed from the Cook Islands Government Property Corporation using the second of the two promissory notes. That meant that EP Funds received at that time $2,170,275 in cash, and a Cook Islands tax certificate to the value of $1,168,609. Again, its New Zealand tax liability just happened to be around the same figure, but that was offset by the foreign tax credit.

When the deal was to be unwound, all the loans along the chain would be repaid, until finally Harcourt repaid EP Funds the $32,229,725 that had been deposited a year earlier. That $32,229,725, together with the $2,170,275, would leave EP Funds with cash in hand of $34,400,000, exactly the amount it needed to buy back its preference shares from Magnum. Effectively, this was the repaying of Magnum's principal. It was this part of the deal – the repayment of Magnum's money, that had attracted initial attention from both Winston Peters in Parliament and *NBR's* Fran O'Sullivan back in October 1992.

The repayment would be done by taking the money deposited with the BNZ in Hong Kong and using it to buy out the preference shares that Magnum had purchased the previous year. As European Pacific itself noted: *"This money 'run around' from The Issuer [of the pref shares – EP Funds] to BNZ is likely to be a breach of s.62 of the Companies Act 1955 (New Zealand), as The Issuer will have financially assisted BNZ to purchase The Issuer's preference shares.*

"The result is a $200 fine for the offence and possible ancillary contractual illegality. It is doubtful however if this illegality would affect EPBC's rights against BNZ under the buy out/deposit arrangement. We do not consider this issue to be a serious legal or commercial problem."

Both O'Sullivan and Peters had taken a whack at the Magnum transaction at the time, and in particular this acknowledged "likely breach" of the Companies Act. Neither had even been vaguely aware of the fake tax certificates, although it now seems certain that this was the reason O'Sullivan was attacked in a lift and her hotel room ransacked. She had just been sent the Magnum papers.

Pushing aside the documents, the calculator and my doodlings as I'd attempted to draw my own "wiring diagrams", I felt quiet confidence welling up within. I felt then that the decision to approach it as a crime story had been the right one. Sure, they used bank accounts and tax certificates instead of knives or guns, but the effect was the same, and the amount they got away with in the Magnum transaction alone was seven times more than New Zealand's largest-ever bank robbery. The victims were the taxpayers of an entire country.

After the November 1993 General Election, events picked up pace. Shaun Brown and Paul Norris had fired off a copy of my latest draft to TVNZ's hired legal advisers, Willie Akel and Helen Wild of the big lawfirm Simpson Grierson Butler White.

Co-incidentally, I'd been advised by taxation QC Dr Tony Molloy to take the Magnum transaction to one of the Simpson Grierson team who'd been assisting him on another tax matter. Molloy was working with Chris Dickie on the alleged bloodstock frauds, and didn't want to get too heavily involved with another big project like EP.

"There's a guy at Simpson Grierson, his name's Gary Muir. He's bloody clever, and he's got the advantage of working for a firm that had no taxation section until recently, so he's got clean hands as far as these dirty little schemes go," Molloy assured me.

When I met Akel, I remembered Molloy's advice and dropped both his and Muir's names into the conversation in the hope of boosting the credibility of what I was saying. Unfortunately, Gary Muir's name didn't appear to ring instant bells with Willie or, if it did, Willie wasn't giving anything away this early in the game. Somewhat on the back foot, I moved onto stage 2 of trying to promote my conspiracy theory.

The draft in Akel's possession still lacked what they call "focus" in the television business – tacked on to it were some other ancillary matters pertaining to the BNZ which we proceeded to dump from the script* in favour of staying locked in on the alleged tax fraud.

It was my first meeting with Akel, and it took me an hour of going through the evidence before I convinced him it wasn't a fantasy. Akel, like Julian Miles, is a very astute operator. His expertise is defamation and, in front of him, he saw a potentially very defamatory piece of television, naming some of the most powerful people and companies in New Zealand.

He had however, long ago, taken a course in taxation law and, somewhere deep within the recesses of long forgotten memory, something stirred. *"Look,"* he said as he rose to leave, *"I'll take these to – Gary Muir did you say? Yeah, I'll take them up to Gary and see what he's got to say about it all."*

---

* See Chapter 27, *The Piggy Bank*.

Three days later, it was a much more excited Akel that spoke to Paul Norris. *"We think Wishart's onto something,"* the message had come back.

"I've been going through it with Gary Muir, one of our taxation partners. I understand it now but I'm not sure I can explain it. I'd like to bring Gary over to show you how it works."

I cracked open a bottle of cheap plonk that night to celebrate. Finally, after more than a year, I had the legal beagles on side, and I had a story. I had only just managed to keep a family.

"Darling, I promise it'll be over soon," I told my wife, after a couple of glasses of bubbly. *"It's scheduled to go before Christmas. The kids won't have to ask 'What's a daddy?' anymore."*

I had virtually missed the first year of our daughter Melissa's life, and three year old Matthew was showing resentment at the long hours I spent at work or on research. He had a long memory too. Towards the end of 1994, five months after the programme had gone to air, Matthew saw me packing an overnight bag for another trip down country for the current affairs show *Eyewitness*.

"Please daddy," he begged, taking my hand and trying to pull me back inside the house as I left, *"Please don't go to the Cook Islands again."* I would have laughed, but there were tears in the little fellow's eyes.

It's hard to know what kind of strain my family was under as I in turn shouldered the burden of the European Pacific and Citibank investigations. It's hard to know because I was never there.

The following Monday morning, November 15, 1993, was our first full production meeting on the story. It would be fair to say that *Frontline* staff still had serious doubts about the outsider from TV3 and his bizarre allegations – and rightly so. In their position, I too would have been highly suspicious, especially after the last group to peddle a conspiracy theory even close to this had been frogmarched out of the building never to be seen within its hallowed halls again.

Watching *Frontline's* Carol Hirschfeld, Michael Wilson and producer Mark Champion lined up on the couch opposite me in Norris' office, I was reminded of Larry Johnson's quip about the way Iraq had paraded shot down US fliers in the Gulf War. Yep, like ducks in a shooting gallery they sat there, and I felt bad inside for dragging them into it.

Paul Norris, on the other hand, was the perfect caricature of a General marshalling his forces for battle. Norris, a quietly spoken, urbane fellow with a private school education and a long stint in the BBC behind him, moves his various journalists and current affairs teams like chess pieces across life's chequerboard. This, both he and I knew, had the potential to be the biggest set-piece manoeuvre either of us had attempted, and yet the stakes were incredibly high. We could all lose our jobs if we got it wrong – me first.

Sensing the disquiet among my *Frontline* colleagues in earlier weeks, I had asked Norris to leave them in peace and let me continue largely unassisted if necessary. The General had dismissed that suggestion with a wave of his hand. While I had been puzzled at the time, history showed Norris had made the correct call – the investigation became so massive and resource-consuming that it would have been impossible to do without the extremely valuable input of Hirschfeld, Wilson and Champion.

The incredible energy and commitment they threw in was all the more impressive when one knew that they had all been called off other projects they'd been planning for months including – in Carol's case – a trip to Africa to film a series of current affairs reports. The production team was joined by Shaun Brown, who would become executive producer of the project, with Akel, Wild and Muir consulted on an almost daily basis and present at script meetings. One of the first hurdles to be crossed – whether we could get Witness 7 to go public on camera with his claims.

"Sorry guys," I responded quickly, "but this witness will not talk on the record. He's got a career at stake, not to mention the potential legal ramifications. If we can't do the story based on what's in the documentation, then we don't do the story. Finish."

There was a moment's silence. Television, by its very nature, relies on having interviewees – "talent" – front up to tell their stories. It adds to the credibility of a report by giving it a first hand feel, and it saves a whole heap of extra effort in finding pictures to fill the holes. Not only was I asking Frontline to take on a very complex financial story, I was asking them to do it without any of the key players in European Pacific explaining what was going on.

"How did you get hold of the documents?," someone piped up in an attempt to change the subject. Before I could answer, Paul Norris had already intervened. "I don't think any of us need to know that. Suffice to say that they came from someone who's not under any injunction."

That too, was a conversation killer for a moment, but the silence didn't last long. Still to be defined were the roles of the team members, and a deadline for screening the programme.

Carol Hirschfeld, best known to New Zealanders for her anchoring of the monthly police liaison show Crimewatch and presenter of Air New Zealand's in flight video programme Blue Pacific, would be the field producer – the eyes and ears for the story. Hirschfeld's expertise would be drawn on to find ways of illustrating the programme, working out what shots to use, defining the on air "look" of the investigation. It wasn't hard to see how difficult that was going to be.

Here was a draft script with no interview talent, based on documents – which don't make gripping visual fodder – and requiring huge amounts of graphics to bring to life the complex web of transactions. In addition we were dealing with a company that didn't have a high public profile, and consequently there was very little library footage to draw on.

Michael Wilson's speciality was business and finance. He would act as a "check" on my research, summoning his own skills in business storytelling to help make the complexities easier to understand in the script. He would also assist Carol in field direction.

Willie Akel was heading off to the Privy Council in London to represent investors in the collapsed Goldcorp company in a claim against the BNZ. His associate, Helen Wild, would oversee the script for defamation issues, while Simpson Grierson tax partner Gary Muir would work with us on defining the allegedly fraudulent nature of the transactions in a way the public could understand, without sacrificing accuracy.

Above all else, this investigation had to be 100 percent accurate. Everything we said or alleged had to be provable in a Court of Law. We were taking no prisoners.

While Hirschfeld, Wilson and I reported to Brown on a daily basis, there would also be meetings with Paul Norris and the legals on a regular basis to oversee progress. Our on-air date: Sunday, December 5, 1993, just under three weeks away. It would be a race against time.

What we didn't realise was that the ticking of the clock was really the ticking of a timebomb, and it was set to go off underneath us.

CHAPTER 15

The X-Files

"Thus Freedom now so seldom wakes,
The only throb she gives,
Is when some heart indignant breaks,
To show that still she lives."
– THOMAS MOORE 1779-1852

SCRIPT WORK BEGAN THAT morning. My initial draft had, for security reasons, been compiled on my home computer, not one of the TVNZ news computers. We took draft one to pieces, and began re-assembling from ground-zero on the TVNZ system.

To throw interested parties off the scent, we divided the script into four parts, with exotic titles like Palm Trees, Hula Skirts, Coconut Shells and Tropical Heat. These segments were "locked" with the codeword "laundry", so that our colleagues couldn't access them. The locking mechanism, naturally, would not be effective against senior managers, but it provided a modicum of protection against random access.

Rather than work in the general news or *Frontline* production area, we were assigned an office close to Norris' with a lockable door. There was to be no discussion of sensitive material on cellphones, and no unnecessary discussion of the project with anyone not working on it. To all intents and purposes, it became "Project X".

In later months the legend surrounding Project X would become much bigger than the reality. I remember listening to talkback on a national radio network soon after the documentary finally went to air, and hearing the announcer explain to the listeners how the project had been so secret, that not only did we work in a different office, but that we used a new, experimental kind of videotape not available anywhere else in New Zealand and not available to anyone else in Television New Zealand! We may have been secretive, but not quite that much.

While Michael and I had been working feverishly to rewrite part one – Palm Trees – Carol had been searching through TVNZ's vast library of archival footage and stumbled across some early material on the setting up of the Cook Islands tax haven. We also found that Australia's *Four Corners* programme had done a big investigation of former billionaire Alan Bond in 1989 – an item that touched on Bond's use of European Pacific's tax haven operation.

Suddenly, the visual prospects for part one weren't looking so horrific. It needed to be an introduction to European Pacific, a scene setter. We could touch on the creation of the tax haven, the launch of European Pacific amid the hype surrounding Fay's America's Cup challenge, Winston Peters' campaign targeting EP and a hint of what would be revealed in parts two to four.

Hirschfeld had a visual brainwave for the opening paragraphs of the item. We would see shots of someone rifling through a filing cabinet in a darkened room, pausing and retrieving a folder marked "European Pacific".

We would see this anonymous individual photocopying documents in the twilight of this office – a veiled reference to the company's claims that its documents had been stolen. This, as a visual device, would be easy on the eye and lead the viewer symbolically into the complex story. It was an effective concept and, when they filmed the sequence that weekend, it looked stunning. A blue spotlight filtering through stylish venetian blinds created the impression of a dusky moonlight, a shadowy figure emerged from the gloom and flicked on a small desk lamp, its incandescent glow bouncing balefully off the office wall but failing to pierce the darkness enough to identify the intruder.

"No company likes the idea of its most sensitive commercial documents being leaked," began the voice over. *"For a company running a tax haven operation, such a breach of security is more than damaging . . . it spells ultimate destruction. For once the veil of secrecy is blown, the company and its clients' most intimate financial dealings are exposed for all to see.*

"The disclosure of a number of documents belonging to tax haven specialist European Pacific Investments has dragged them and their owners into the spotlight." As the intruder began photocopying, the script went straight for the corporate jugular.

"Contained in documents Frontline has obtained is evidence that European Pacific broke New Zealand law and defrauded the Cook Islands people." Within 30 seconds of the programme beginning, viewers would be aware that this was to be an extremely hard-hitting piece of journalism. We were essentially alleging that crimes had been committed – a very rare thing to see on television, and not something done lightly.

Both lawyers – Helen Wild and Gary Muir – were confident we had the facts and the documents we needed to back up such serious claims. If we were sued for defamation, we would win. And this was just the opening sequence. After a brief description of European Pacific's commercial pedigree – its ownership by the BNZ, Brierleys and Capital Markets, we launched into a history of the controversy surrounding it.

"In the past 18 months some European Pacific documents have become public property courtesy of Winston Peters and parliamentary privilege. He told the House in November last year . . .

"European Pacific is a secret and covert group of companies operating beyond the scrutiny of the Inland Revenue Department and the Serious Fraud Office in New Zealand. Such companies have been used to defraud the New Zealand revenue and New Zealanders."

The inclusion of Winston Peters was only natural. The man had been at the forefront of the campaign to investigate European Pacific – everyone in the country knew of his involvement. To ignore Peters' parliamentary allegations would not only be churlish, it would be biased and it would be comparable to writing a book about Watergate without mentioning Woodward and Bernstein – the journalists who discovered the conspiracy that led to President Nixon's resignation.

This was a particularly significant bridge for Television New Zealand News and Current Affairs to cross. The network had done its fair share of "potting" Peters during the year and, I later learned, a senior TVNZ corporate executive had been suggesting what editorial line to take on Peters on at least one occasion prior to the 1993 General Election.

"For God's sake don't lionise him!," came one order from on high. The apparent interference in what should have been independent editorial decision-making by the news team was something I found disturbing. Especially on a matter as sensitive as politics.

I kept those reservations to myself for the time being, preferring to watch and wait. As a rule, the programmes that appear on *Frontline* or *60 Minutes* each week are not vetted by people at corporate level – those decisions are correctly made at news management level – Paul Norris and below.

It was a major turnaround that the two men heading Television New Zealand's newsgathering operation recognised, on the face of the documents, not only that Peters had possibly been right but also that he deserved some recognition of that fact as well. It was a mark of the calibre of both Norris and Deputy News Director Shaun Brown that each accepted this.

The remainder of "Palm Trees" was mostly innocuous, a trip through the history of the tax haven and what its role was. We then came to the listing of European Pacific on the NZ Stock Exchange in January 1987.

"At the same time, two of EP's owners – Capital Markets and the BNZ – were sponsoring a boat race that had us all pre-occupied [the America's Cup]. Having seen Capital Markets' share price soar, small investors climbed aboard the merchant bank's new investment vehicle – European Pacific.

"Within days of EP's listing, its shareprice soared to $40, one of the highest prices ever paid for a New Zealand stock. So with European Pacific floated on a wave of high expectations, in a summer when business leaders were feted as public heroes, it was up to EP staff to get down to the hard business of doing deals."

This last paragraph had been scripted over vision of Michael Fay's triumphant parade up Auckland's Queen Street after being defeated in the Cup Challenge – a parade in front of 200,000 cheering people waving flags and throwing ticker tape in celebration of Fay's challengers even making it as far as they did. It was a valid postscript to the launch of European Pacific, a piece of history that helped describe the mood surrounding the company's launch in New Zealand and the sort of hype that accumulated around anything to do with Fay Richwhite back in those days.

Part Two, "Hula Skirts", was solely confined to the Magnum deal. We began by raising questions about the legality of the *"money-run-around"* referred to in the documents concerning the buy-back of the Magnum preference shares.

"Remember, 34.4 million dollars started off on this money trail. As it moved

along the trail there were various deductions – the dividend for Magnum was taken out and so were certain fees. In the end, 30 million dollars remains. It is then deposited with the BNZ in Hong Kong.

"*The BNZ in turn agrees to use this 30 million dollar deposit, plus the interest it earns, to buy back off Magnum the original EP shares for exactly the price it first paid. Our documents show that, in itself, is likely to be illegal. EP's advisers had expressed doubts as to whether this leg of the deal, which completed the money loop, was in accordance with New Zealand law.*"

We then quoted the documents again. "*This 'money-run-around' from The Issuer (EPFM) to BNZ is likely to be a breach of Section 62 of the Companies Act 1955 (NZ), as The Issuer will have financially assisted BNZ to purchase The Issuer's preference shares.*"

Just to ram home the point, we added a comment from Professor of Tax Law, Dr John Prebble, confirming the apparent breach. Normally Section 62 offences carry a small fine, but if a Section 62 breach leads to a loss of money by another party, then those involved in a deliberate breach of S 62 can be jailed for fraud. It was a point that Prebble touched on only briefly in our documentary, but we were not looking at the S 62 implications, we had our sights set on bigger game, and our script reflected it.

"*So here's one apparent illegality. Let's return to the original transaction where even more serious legal concerns arise.*

"*Remember, EP Funds Management paid Magnum 3.8 million dollars tax-free. To make such a payment tax-free to Magnum, EP had become liable for any tax due. In short, EP had to accept liability for a two million dollars tax bill in order to leave Magnum with its tax-free dividend.*

"*But paying this two million dollar tax bill would leave EP with a major loss on the whole deal. We're now going to focus on that part of the deal – on how EP got away with paying no tax at all.*"

We used the word "remember!" quite frequently in the script. It was a type of signposting, a way of refreshing people's memories about what they had just seen, a way of recapping.

After going through the promissory note deal where the Cook Islands Government Property Corporation was guaranteed to make a loss and EP was guaranteed to get its tax back, we explained to viewers what they had just seen. "*To recap, by doing this EP achieved two goals. It recovered by prior arrangement the withholding tax paid to the Cooks Government and, at the same time, created the illusion that tax had been paid in the Cooks, and so obtained a tax certificate. That then was the Magnum deal: elaborate, complex and, on the face of it, fraudulent.*"

We were pulling no punches. EP staff members had been involved in a deal that was arguably a prima facie criminal fraud. We named, for the record, those whose names were attached to the deals: Group managing director David Lloyd; two Auckland accountants – Peter Brannigan and Anthony McCullagh; Cook Island lawyer Trevor Clarke; corporate accountant David Lilly; lawyer George Couttie; and merchant bankers Robert Hay, Mark Jones and Geoff Barry.

Rosemary Healy and Guy Jalland had worked on the JIF deals but not on Magnum – at least, their names weren't on the Magnum documentation in a significant capacity.

Part Three, "Coconut Shells", was aimed squarely at JIF. In the preceding weeks I had trolled through the winebox yet again for any more hints about JIF transactions. We had, at that point, only discovered JIF/Mitsubishi – and even then only half the deal. Somewhere, there had to be more, and the documentation on Magnum had shown me what to look for. On this third attempt we hit paydirt.

One of the Mitsubishi documents had been dated November 9, 1988. We matched it to a document titled "DUNDEE NO. 3". I remember wondering where Dundee's One and Two had got to. Dundee 3 was also dated November 9, and other similarities soon emerged. Both deals had been approved the previous April 20th; in both cases the client was European Pacific; in both cases the transactions were denominated in US dollars; in both cases the deals were to last five years and, even more telling, the dates that Mitsubishi Bank paid tax to the Cook Islands Government in the JIF deal coincided exactly with the dates of the Dundee 3 transactions.

And just what were the Dundee 3 transactions? They were promissory note sale and re-purchase agreements with the Cook Islands Government Property Corporation and European Pacific Merchant Finance – the same players that featured in the Magnum scam.

It was patently obvious we had discovered the hidden side to the Mitsubishi JIF deal – the allegedly criminal side that Witness Seven had warned us about. Just in case I had any doubts, European Pacific executive Geoff Barry had set out in great detail just how the apparent fraud would work.

"EPMF [European Pacific Merchant Finance] is to issue the Notes with a par value of USD10m to PC [Property Corporation] on the date and for the amounts listed in Annexure 3."

I couldn't immediately find Annex 3 – it turned up on the fourth attempt, but I could make a very educated guess about what was happening. EPMF was selling promissory notes with a face value of US$10 million to the Government Property Corporation, but obviously for a price over and above face value – a price listed in Annexure 3. I read on.

"PC will sell the Notes to Dundee on the dates and for the amounts listed in Annexure 3. EPMF will redeem the Notes from Dundee for the price at which Dundee acquired the Notes from PC.

"Out of the transaction, EPMF will initially make a profit on the issue of the Notes at a premium, PC will loose [sic] on the transaction, Dundee will break even as it will receive redemption proceeds equivalent to the purchase price for the Notes, and finally EPMF will redeem the Notes at par.

"This redemption will crystallize EPMF's profit on the transaction. The above transactions will all occur on the same day. The same series of events will occur on each date scheduled in Annexure 3."

If you needed any evidence of pre-arranged theft from the Cook Islands

Revenue, this was it. A deal where Property Corporation is guaranteed to *"lose on the transaction"*, where EP will *"make a profit"* – not just once but on a whole string of transactions over a five year period. This, I knew, was how European Pacific was laundering tax money paid by the Japanese banks back into its own accounts.

I looked again at the Mitsubishi deal. The crucial dates, dates when Mitsubishi was paying tax to the Cooks Government, began in November 1988, then again *"on 28 February, and six monthly thereafter until 31 August 1993, presuming the facility continues for the full term."*

When Dundee's Annex 3 surfaced it provided the vital link with Mitsubishi/JIF. Geoff Barry had left gaps for the promissory note sale prices to be filled in, but the dates had been clearly typed. The Dundee transactions would begin in November 1988, and continue on:

28 February 1989	31 August 1989
28 February 1990	31 August 1990
28 February 1991	31 August 1991
28 February 1992	31 August 1992
28 February 1993	31 August 1993

Annex 3 was headed *"DATES, ISSUE AND REDEMPTION PRICES OF PROMISSORY NOTES (PAR VALUE OF USD10,000,000 EACH).*
After the column marked *"Payment Dates"* was a column headed *"Amount CIGPC is to pay EPMF (USD)"*, a column headed *"Amount Dundee is to pay PC (USD)"* and a final column headed *"EPMF profit on note issue"*.

European Pacific obviously wasn't intending to lose money on any of its promissory note deals with the Cook Island Government Property Corporation. It appeared to be an attempt to secretly defraud the citizens of the Cook Islands by stealing their tax money, not to mention an attempt to defraud the Japanese Government by allowing Mitsubishi Bank to present essentially false tax certificates and thereby reduce the amount of tax it paid in Japan. European Pacific claimed it wasn't in on its own, either.

"Peat Marwick* , Auckland, will be signing off in respect of the transaction in the next month. They have previously given oral advice as to the accounting treatment." And just what was the advice from one of the biggest accounting firms around? Apparently EP had been advised it wouldn't have to include the profits on its published balance sheet, because of financial trickery.

"The transaction involves EPMF having an **option** *to issue promissory notes ("the Notes") to PC, and Dundee having* **a potential liability** *to purchase such notes from PC* **if** *they are issued.* **If** *this occurs EPMF would crystallize a profit, hence no balance sheet consequence exists."* [author's emphasis]

---

* KPMG Peat Marwick staff gave sworn testimony to the Davison Commission in 1995 that they had never given European Pacific advice on the tax transactions as claimed in the documents, and were not involved. The declaration, on oath, raises further questions about whether European Pacific's documents gave a true picture of the transactions.

In other words, because it's legally phrased as "ifs, buts and maybes" they don't have to declare it in their accounts. As can be seen from the contractual documentation however, there were no ifs or buts about it: European Pacific was **guaranteed** to make a profit on a series of transactions set down for the next five years!

There was other JIF documentation too. A letter dated December 6, 1988 from Trevor Clarke was addressed to the giant Sanwa Bank.

"The existing facility is to stand, but the facility amount is to be extended from USD200 million to USD400 million by way of a second tranche," wrote Clarke.

It confirmed for us that a Mitsubishi-style deal had definitely been done with Sanwa, and was being doubled in size. European Pacific was offering to pay an up front fee of US$200,000, with an annual fee of US$750,000 payable to Sanwa. The Sanwa letter also provided us with our only hard evidence of the interest rate the Japanese banks were being paid – in this case 11.925%. This was extremely important for us to find out, because it allowed us to work out how much the Japanese banks would be earning and therefore how much tax they were paying.

Further documents came to light indicating a similar deal worth US$100 million with Fuji bank. The Fuji deal appeared to be set down to last until December 1994. Adding the deposits together gave us US$700 million in total, earning interest at, say, 11.925% – nearly US$83.5 million a year, or US$417 million over the full five years.

With a 15% withholding tax, nearly US$63 million had been deducted over that period in tax and presumably funnelled back to European Pacific under the table – and this was involving just three banks! How many more of these apparently criminal deals were out there? How many foreign governments had been defrauded by a company part owned by the New Zealand Government through its state bank?

My extreme elation at locating the hidden side of JIF was now beginning to be tinged by disillusionment. Here we had evidence which, on the face of it at least, indicated criminal dealings were contained in the winebox.

I turned away from the box, momentarily disgusted. Even if the deals somehow managed to squeak through on this side of the law – and I personally doubted the chances of that happening – did we really want a country where the rich could only increase their fortunes by cheating other people of their tax money? Was this what deregulation was all about – was this the so-called "level playing field" the Government had been rabbiting on about?

If they were innocent of a crime, they were still guilty of immorality, and the public had a right to know about that and about any attempt by the establishment to cover it up.

This would become our motivation in the months that followed; a story that must be told, versus an alliance of scumbags desperate to stop us from telling it. We had European Pacific's nuts nailed to the wall and we knew it. Escape was never an option.

"Coconut Shells" would deal with European Pacific's most closely held secret, the proposed JIF frauds. This, I knew, was what could cost EP dearly. The Magnum transaction could potentially put the staff in jail in New Zealand, but having to repay US$63 million in apparently stolen tax money – if the deals did indeed go ahead – to the Japanese revenue, with possibly up to three times that much in penalty taxes, would financially cripple European Pacific and possibly seriously damage its owners – whoever they now were.

Again, we pulled no punches. With the approval of the Simpson Grierson legal team we called the Mitsubishi deal *"a proposed tax fraud similar to the Magnum deal"* before going back over the secret promissory note deal in Magnum.

Remember, TVNZ was not making these allegations from the protected sanctuary of parliamentary privilege. These extremely serious allegations were being made in the certain knowledge that "truth" and "honest opinion" would be our defence in any court case. And we fully expected to be sued – if only to intimidate us into cancelling any follow-up stories.

For good measure, just so viewers would be left under no false impressions about what we were alleging, we hit them again.

"That's a brief description of the apparent fraud at the heart of the Magnum deal. The Dundee 3 documents involving the Japanese bank describe transactions almost identical.

"Did the Mitsubishi deal go ahead? We can't be certain. But we do know that Mitsubishi had already consented to take part in the structure and it was due to begin less than a week after the date of the final proposal.

"The losers on the deal would have been the Japanese Government, pumping money into the loop every six months in the form of tax refunds to Mitsubishi based on misleading tax certificates from the Cook Islands.

"So just to recap, what hard facts do we know about the Japanese bank deals? We know that all three of the banks had agreed to lend EP a total of 700 million dollars. We know in fact that Sanwa did lend 200 million US dollars to EP Bank. We know EP had drawn up plans to recover the tax money paid by one of the banks.

"We know that some of the deals did in fact go ahead, because a report to EP directors the following April notes fees earnt by one EP subsidiary for its role in the Japanese bank transactions. The report, from EP chief executive Trevor Clarke, discussing the role of the Cook Islands Government, concludes with the line:

"We received extraordinary co-operation from the Prime Minister and other Government officials with regard to EPBC Jap Banks transactions."

We also added the same rider that we had to the Magnum deal.

"Frontline has no evidence to show Mitsubishi or any other Japanese Bank was involved in or even aware of the special tax deal EP had set up in the Cook Islands."

Part Four, "Tropical Heat", was our grand finale.

"The documents we've disclosed tonight provide evidence that this company lay at the very heart of the Magnum and JIF deals.

"Firstly, we identified an apparent illegality that EP executives themselves

acknowledged – a Section 62 breach of the New Zealand Companies Act. Then we told you about the creation of misleading tax certificates in the Magnum deal – certificates that when presented in this country could give rise to fraud charges.

"And finally, we showed you how EP proposed a much larger deal along the same lines as Magnum – this one designed to involve major Japanese banks and a potential investment in excess of a billion New Zealand dollars.

"We've already identified the EP executives involved in planning these transactions. The question that inevitably arises is whether the executives operated alone, or whether they referred these deals to the directors of the company."

This was where we ran into the most difficulty. Just prior to the Magnum and JIF deals being carried out, the ownership of the EP group became cloudy.

The parent company, EPI, sold 51% of its Cook Island based subsidiary European Pacific Trust and Banking Group Limited to what was essentially a secret trust, whose ownership was unknown. That meant that the Cook Island operation was technically no longer under EPI's direct control.

"Who owned that trust and who consequently controlled those subsidiaries are questions only the beneficiaries of the secret trust can answer."

We discovered some more documentation about the identity of the secret trust – a statutory declaration to British authorities filed by European Pacific during one of its deals for Alan Bond. It revealed the owner of 51% of the Cook Islands group was a company called Laverton Securities, which in turn was owned by Palmerston Securities, which in turn was the trustee for a hidden trust, the Laverton Trust. This was the level of smoke and mirrors that EP was prepared to throw up to mask its true ownership.*

The reason for the secrecy was simple. In 1988 the New Zealand Government moved to close some tax haven loopholes, declaring that all New Zealand-controlled foreign companies – CFC's – offshore would be deemed to fall within NZ tax jurisdiction.

The definition of control referred in part to whether the offshore company had a New Zealand shareholding of 50% or higher, or whether board business was carried out in New Zealand.

---

* In August 1995, the Davison Commission heard new evidence about the restructuring of European Pacific. A document discovered by Sir Ronald Davison's investigators managed to crack the veil of Cook Islands tax haven secrecy. It showed that on March 19, 1993, Fay Richwhite still owned nearly 33% of European Pacific Group, while Brierley Investments owned a similar-sized parcel. Although the reality appeared to be that NZ interests held 66% of the group, in a legal sense the structure meant European Pacific was not a CFC as defined by legislation. While the Project X team had tried to dig behind the Laverton company, it's now clear how deep we would have needed to dig. Laverton was owned by three tax haven companies, one of which was owned by another tax haven company, which in turn was owned by Aldgate Holdings Ltd. – a New Zealand based company in the Fay Richwhite group. David Richwhite and Brierley's Paul Collins were on the Board of European Pacific. The document was an agreement to sell European Pacific to new owners. The ownership transfer was to be completed by May 1, 1995. See ownership chain in Appendix.

By shrinking NZ listed company EPI's holding down to 49%, the Cook Islands entities were not subject to NZ tax. Unless of course, the beneficial owners of the Laverton Trust were New Zealanders or New Zealand companies. Unfortunately, the tough secrecy laws in the Cook Islands prevented us from penetrating that particular corporate veil.

If the secret trust did represent New Zealand interests, then European Pacific should have paid tax on all its Cook Islands profits. Failure to do so could amount to tax evasion.

"The question that remains unanswered is: What direct involvement, if any, did the three major New Zealand corporates – BNZ, Brierleys and Capital Markets – or their director representatives, have in setting up or approving the Magnum and JIF deals?," we wrote in "Tropical Heat".

"Our documents show two of those companies had specific and instrumental roles in the JIF proposal. The BNZ is named as the Bank which primed the pump for the JIF deal, lending $200 million US for just a few hours to get the money go round working. Capital Markets is named as the owner of two tax haven companies, Halcome and Credence Investments, that were to be involved in the Mitsubishi JIF deal."

The ending of the programme was something we were particularly proud of. Apart from another comment from Peters confirming his view on the need for an inquiry based on the evidence we uncovered, there were also very strong opinions from Dr Prebble and also New Zealand's former Auditor General, Brian Tyler. Tyler in fact had the last word.

"I was concerned on a number of fronts. I was concerned at the artificiality of the agreements: the papers describe those schemes as a money run around – I thought that was descriptive.

"I was concerned at the scale of the schemes. The papers again said that they were likely to have a major impact on the tax base of New Zealand. Big money involved. I was concerned at the steps that were being contemplated at that time to conceal the arrangements from the NZ Revenue authorities, from the Tax Department.

"I was intrigued at the assurance apparently being sought that the NZ Audit Office wouldn't be looking at these arrangements. The NZ Audit Office at that stage was the auditor of the Cook Islands Government. I noted with some concern that the schemes were said to be in breach of the NZ Companies Act, but they proceeded nevertheless."

"Is there evidence here," I asked, *"that would justify further enquiries?"*

Tyler didn't bat an eyelid. *"From the evidence I've seen, I believe further inquiry is definitely required!"*

Finally, on Sunday November 28th, we had a final draft of the script. In fact it was version 14 of the script by that stage, but it had been fully discussed by the various production committees, endorsed by the lawyers and given the green light for production. None of us had taken a day off since the project began.

Carol Hirschfeld would go straight into an editing suite on Monday with vision editor Will Kong, while Michael Wilson, myself and cameraman Peter

Day were to fly to the Cook Islands on Tuesday to film everything we could of European Pacific and relevant Cook Island companies, as well as doing "pieces to camera" in front of locations like the Cook Islands Parliament.

Pieces to camera, or PTCs, are the shots you sometimes see in television stories showing the reporter on location. They're normally used for only two reasons. One is to boost the ego of the journalist – the more PTCs the bigger the ego. The other reason is to cover holes in a programme that you don't have any vision for.

Television reports on court cases often have pieces to camera, for example, because TV cameras are not allowed in all court hearings. The journalist must stand outside and explain what happened inside the courtroom. In our case, we had some major holes in our programme and no pictures to fill them with. The only solution was to film 13 PTCs up in Rarotonga.

Faced with the prospect of two days on a hot tropical paradise, set in an azure sea far, far away, sipping daiquiris as the sun descends over a golden horizon with palm trees silhouetted against the sky and waving gently in the breeze – faced with that prospect we groaned inwardly. Like hell.

CHAPTER 16

Tropical Heat

"Fauntleroy, the banker, was hanged at the Old Bailey on the 30th of November, 1824, for forging orders for the transfer of stock."
– WEEKLY DISPATCH, 1856

THE FIRST THING THAT hits you in Rarotonga is the landing. It's a short runway, requiring maximum braking from the Boeing 747's when they touch down. Our appreciation of this had been somewhat heightened as, the night before, our Air New Zealand flight on this very same jumbo jet had been cancelled because of a minor brake failure. Cheerfully, Air New Zealand had informed passengers in its first class lounge at Auckland that normally the plane would continue on with a fault like that, but because of the extraordinarily short runway in the Cook Islands, discretion was the better part of valour. We were therefore 18 hours late, and needed to squeeze all our filming in to a window of opportunity now only 22 hours wide on the ground.

The second thing that hits you is the moist tropical air, gently spiced with fragrances like frangipani and quickly all-enveloping. Standing at the top of the boarding steps, you soak all of this up in an instant, while your eyes take in the glittering Pacific Ocean beating incessantly on the coral shore beside the airport, and your ears are bombarded with the cacophony of a minstrel with a guitar and a public address system singing welcome songs in the local dialect, Cook Islands Maori. God, it was good to be here, I reflected, taking a lungful of what passed for a tropical breeze as we made for the terminal.

It was 3:00pm by the time we hit the street in a taxi, exclusively ours for the rest of the afternoon. Motorbikes and scooters buzzed around us as we made our way into town – the main form of transport in the islands' capital, Avarua. Even most of the taxi vans and jeeps appear to run on clapped-out, two-stroke motorcycle engines.

The road from the airport is guarded by an ageing World War II anti-aircraft gun, once pointed toward the Land of the Rising Sun, now presumably a lone sentinel against hordes of invading tax inspectors. The other thing you notice – and it has absolutely no relevance to the story – is that every house has its own graveyard, usually on the front lawn. The requirements of local custom through the generations have demanded that relatives are buried close to their surviving families.

Some houses ran out of space eons ago, or so it appeared, the tombstones and sarcophagi crumbling back to dust, in some cases open to the monsoons and the sticky heat. Elsewhere, the houses themselves were crumbling – long since abandoned – the tombs in front overgrown with lush vegetation, their inmates forgotten.

The European Pacific Centre in Avarua, Rarotonga. Deep in the interior,
a huge concrete vault was allegedly used to store documents hidden
from foreign revenue agencies at the behest of corporate clients.

26 year old computer dealer Paul White. In the space of 12 hours he was paid $15,000, robbed of it, and killed in a car crash.

COURTESY PETER AND MAUREEN WHITE.

The motorway support pillar Paul White's car collided with at 5:00am on September 5, 1992. The vehicle ended up straddling both lanes.

The Fanshawe Street motorway onramp. White was continuing straight ahead through the lights; the road curves around to the right.

Another perspective of the Fanshawe Street onramp. Note that there is one overbridge support pillar that can obscure the view of the impact point as a motorist rounds that corner. This photo was taken on a telephoto lens, so the distances appear compressed exaggerating the curves.

The last five photographs show Paul White's damaged vehicle a couple of weeks after the crash. The author can be seen in the top right corner of image one, examining scratch marks on the wraparound bumper (images four and five). The scratches maintain a consistent level along the length of the rear quarter bumper, on the side of the car that hit nothing. In addition they appear deeper in some parts of the bumper than others, consistent with two objects not maintaining constant contact. There is no vertical scoring, only horizontal. Could it be the result of another vehicle pushing Paul White's car off the road by nudging the rear passenger side in the driver's blind spot? If another vehicle did shunt White's car off the road, it would have to have done so on this side of the car.

Image One.

Image Two.

Image Three.

Image Four.

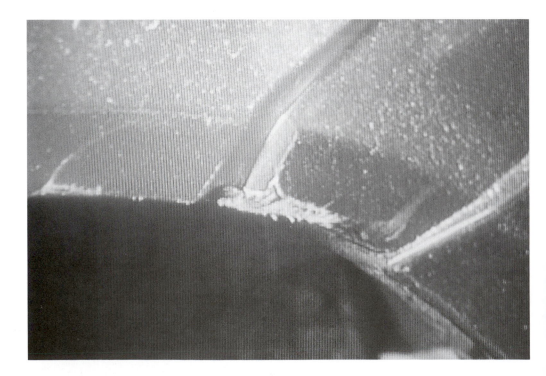

Image Five.

We had three hours before sunset to film as much as possible, and it quickly became a race to complete the PTCs. Standing outside the Cook Islands Monetary Board offices for one particularly long shoot, I could see the faces of the curious – noses pressed to the windows as this foreign television crew seemed to take over the main street outside.

It was going to be extremely difficult to be inconspicuous in a place this small. As an indicator of size, rush hour takes place at 4:00pm each day and generally lasts two and a half minutes. Despite the fact that more money can go through here than the entire GNP of some fairly sizeable countries, Wall Street this was not.

Conscious of the fact that I needed to get more than a dozen reports down on videotape by sunset if possible, on different sides of the island, we tried to rattle them off quickly, and the strain was showing in the speed of my speech. It wasn't helped by the fact that each PTC was up to 45 seconds long, and all had to be memorised word for word. The lawyers back in Auckland had carefully vetted exactly what we would say – one deviation could be the difference between success and a multi-million dollar lawsuit.

While Michael Wilson and cameraman Peter Day had the luxury of wearing sunglasses, I was in double jeopardy – not only no eye protection but, for reasons of lighting, I also had to stand facing directly into the intense glare from a tropical sun. All of this whilst repeatedly walking up and down the middle of the main street trying to dodge mopeds and the occasional four wheeled vehicle.

This also added to the "troppo" atmosphere that quickly overtook all of us – every time a scooter went past it sounded like a buzzsaw on the video tape. We marked out 19 "takes" on the first PTC alone.

Terrified of alerting European Pacific to our presence and setting off a Court injunction, we were also trying not to broadcast the contents of our PTCs too loudly. In some situations this was achieved by suddenly mumbling at the crucial point as a nosy local walked past, but occasionally it degenerated into farce. A group of Cook Islanders walking along a beach we were filming at saw us in the distance pointing a stick into the sand, talking into the camera and then suddenly dancing furiously on the spot before shifting to a new point on the beach and starting the ritual again.

After five or six of these little dances they could have been forgiven for thinking we might be filming some bizarre new kind of rock video, but instead each time they got close we were having to rub out the words "tax fraud" which we'd carved in the sand with a stick, and move further away to film it again before they got too close.

The astute reader may ask why we didn't let them go past, instead of trying to "outrun" them on the beach? We had another problem, in that the sun was dropping like a stone on the horizon and very soon there would not be enough light for the shot to work. We were trying to outrun the encroaching shadows.

By the time night fell, we'd filmed nine of the 13 required PTCs, far more than we expected to complete. We checked into the Edgewater Resort Hotel, and looked for somewhere to eat. We found it in the form of PJ's Bar, a tavern and restaurant a short distance from the hotel. The place was rocking, helped along by a singer with a keyboard who could cover anything from Meatloaf to the Beatles and everything in between.

Forcing our way through the crowd we found a table in the restaurant section. Three beers, two wines and three Glenfiddich whiskies later, we really started to feel mellow. So mellow in fact that when a tiny lizard – no longer than my thumbnail – dropped onto Mike Wilson's forkful of food just as he was about to take a mouthful, I nearly didn't tell him. In fact the fork got halfway to his chops before I let out a strangled squawk and pointed to the extra morsel happily perched on a piece of fish. It proceeded to jump onto his beer glass rim before scurrying off into the gloom.

It was also a good state of mind in which to observe the clientele. In one corner, two tables from us, were a group who looked like wild young merchant bankers. Loud and brash, yet totally at ease with the locals. These had to be boys from one of the trust companies, I reasoned. We later found out they were from European Pacific.

Over at the bar, a tall sunbleached American dressed in combat fatigues and looking for all the world like a mercenary who'd just stopped in for a drink. Peter Day was adamant the guy was a CIA agent – an idea that appealed to my sense of mystery and intrigue. It was easy to envision. Rarotonga was one of the stopovers on the old trans-Pacific "coral route" – the series of island hops made by the flying boats en route from the United States to Asia and Australasia back in the 1930's, '40's and '50's.

Although no longer an essential stopover for the traveller, Rarotonga had lost none of its "tradewinds" aura. Rambo the American was one example, but PJ's bar had an extremely full flavoured range of nationalities represented. Sifting through the chatter you could hear British, German, Italian and Asian accents: all of them people going places, thrown together for a moment in time before continuing in their inexorable quest to explore the world. And here we were, a team of investigative journalists, nestled deep within the midst of the enemy, enjoying our own moment of anonymity. Cast adrift on a sea of fine wine and conviviality, the pressures and dramas of the past weeks faded from our consciousness as we absorbed the here and now.

"*Hey look,*" Peter piped, looking particularly pickled after glancing up momentarily from the interior of his glass, "*It's Miss Rarotonga at the bar*".

"*Yeah,*" said Mike, who'd noticed her sometime earlier, "*but she's with Mr Rarotonga*". Fred and Ginger, Charles and Di, Nixon and Watergate – all of them great couples we have come to know and love. Now we were looking at Rarotonga's own Ken and Barbie, two stunning looking individuals. We wondered who else was going to appear at the already crammed PJ's when the islands' former Solicitor-General, Mike Mitchell, stood up to take part in a duet on the keyboard. Would there be no end to the entertainment laid on for us, we wondered?

The merchant bankers were up and dancing – sadly, Billy-Ray Cyrus'

Achy Breaky Heart had even been a hit here. We didn't leave until they closed the bar at midnight.

Breakfast the next morning was a treat to behold. We'd been up since dawn trying to film pieces to camera as the sun rose – the lighting is particularly soft and friendly at dawn and dusk – and by 8:00am we'd taken our bag of PTCs up to 11.

Arriving back at the hotel, we plotted our next moves over tropical fruit salad and sizzling bacon, eggs, toast and coffee, ensconced under a cloudless blue sky with the ocean lapping at the white coral sand just metres away.

"I think we should get the local market scenes as soon as they open this morning," said Mike, dragging his attention back to the task at hand. *"And Ian if you can go to the Companies Office and get what you can on European Pacific, we'll meet up in town after that and knock off the other PTCs outside European Pacific's building at lunchtime."*

The previous afternoon we had also slipped in visits to the local newspaper and television companies to check on some information and get video footage of the fire that had burnt down the Cook Islands Company Office in 1992. The tape was due to be uplifted this morning.

As expected, our visit was beginning to cause ripples. Just as we got ready to abandon breakfast the hotel manager pulled up a chair at our table.

"So tell me. Exactly what are you all doing here,?" he quizzed. We shuffled uncomfortably in our chairs.

"Ah, we're up here getting some library footage of the Cook Islands," I ventured lamely. Wilson picked up the ball and ran with it.

"Yeah, and we're also doing a story on the Sheraton Hotel project while we're here."

The hotel project was something of a national scandal in the Cook Islands. One of the financial advisers was found murdered, and the project itself had been abandoned halfway through construction the year before, after a big anti-corruption drive in Italy. It seems the Italian partners in the joint venture turned out to have organised crime connections and had been arrested back in Italy, along with hundreds of other business leaders. How come this didn't surprise me?

The arrests brought a complete halt to the joint venture, and the Cook Islands Government was now carrying a national debt of some $200 million – a large portion of it due to the unfinished hotel.

Our answer to the inquisitive manager of the Edgewater wasn't exactly a lie, but we could tell from the sceptical look on his face he didn't buy it. European Pacific, in its heyday, had practically owned the Cook Islands. The last thing we needed was for the merchant bank's many friends to get wind of our real intentions and blow the whistle.

We were paranoid for another reason too. What we were doing in the Cook Islands was illegal. The tiny nation has very tough laws safeguarding its tax haven operators, and the idea of being stopped at the airport with videotapes and documents clearly discussing not only tax haven business but allegedly criminal deals involving the Cook Islands Government – it wouldn't have looked good, although admittedly it was momentarily amusing to think of being sentenced to hard labour breaking coconuts whilst on a penal diet of breadfruit and water.

We were in fact lucky enough to escape the long arm of the Cook Islands law on this occasion: another TVNZ camera team following in our footsteps a few months later wouldn't be so fortunate. In addition, the programme was due to go to air in just three days – our detention would put the kybosh on any hopes of putting it to air before Christmas.

My sojourn at the Companies Office proved a waste of time. Staff confirmed that European Pacific's files had been destroyed in a suspicious fire in 1992, soon after Peters' revelations began. A local drunk had been arrested and charged with arson. Despite repeated requests, European Pacific had not replaced any of the missing files by the time of my inquiry at the Companies Office public counter.

If European Pacific's alarm bells didn't start ringing when we began filming their building, I'd be very surprised. The EP Centre was now going under the name Standard Chartered Equitor House – but we knew EP still maintained some kind of presence in the building.

We'd left the EP PTCs until last so as to avoid setting off the tripwire until we were almost ready to board the plane and fly out again. Standing right in front of the EP building, talking about alleged tax fraud, I may as well have been wearing a rhinestone-clad Elvis costume and waving a placard screaming "PICK ME". It was then that we realised the merchant bankers we'd seen at PJ's the previous night were EP staff – the faces at the window looked very familiar.

By the time we hit the air terminal later that afternoon, it felt like we'd been there a week. Adrenalin levels rose as we checked out through Customs, but there was no attempt to interfere.

Watching the island vanish out the window as we took off, I had no idea that we would return within a fortnight. I really believed that by Sunday night, the whole story would finally be out in the open. More fool me. Arriving back at work on Friday morning, video cassettes in hand, we were greeted by Norris at our daily planning meeting with an ominous new twist.

"I've given the script to Brent Harman while you were away. He's very positive, very supportive, says it's a great story. However, he's had to leave the country on business, and he's asked me not to run the programme until he gets back. He feels, and I tend to agree, that it's going to attract a lot of flak and he wants to be around to go in to bat on our behalf when it goes to air."

Brent Harman was Television New Zealand's Chief Executive. A former station manager of Wellington rock station 2ZM in the early 1980's, he'd moved to a provincial station after one of those many creative-type conflicts that arise in the radio business. His revenge had been to guide that provincial station to become the country's number one in its market. It was enough to bring him back in from the cold, and in 1987 he was given a metropolitan position again – turning Auckland's top rating middle-of-the-road Radio New Zealand flagship, 1ZB, into a newstalk station.

While I'd never worked for Harman, who arrived at TVNZ shortly after I joined TV3, I had some grudging respect for what he'd been able to achieve. I had no reason to doubt Harman's sincerity on the European Pacific issue, but nevertheless, something didn't feel quite right. We quickly established he wouldn't be back for a week and a half, putting off our broadcast date until December 19th at the earliest. A quiet chat to one of the production team in the corridor soon gave us a more in depth analysis of the sequence of events.

"Norris and Brown gave Harman the script at the last minute, and we were kind of hoping he wouldn't open it until he was halfway to Hawaii with no access to a phone. The guy bloody well pounced on it and started going through it with a fine-toothed comb! I don't like the sound of it."

My disquiet worsened considerably with a phone call that came in half an hour later. It was a detective who'd cut his teeth in the Police Criminal Intelligence Section, CIS. He'd recently lent me a file on another matter, I assumed he was wanting it returned.

"No, it's not about that bloody file," he muttered down the line, *"it's about your bloody European Pacific story. Someone's given a copy of your script to the enemy. You've got a leak and you need to find it. How the hell am I supposed to feel secure giving you highly sensitive files if you can't keep your secret project secret?"*

"Look," I sighed, *"why don't we meet at the duck pond tonight. Seven OK for you?"*

"Yeah. I'll be there." He hung up.

Seven pm came and found me wandering around the Auckland domain duck pond trying hard to look inconspicuous. It was a blinding failure.

"Hello Ian," came a woman's voice from behind me. I jumped out of my skin. Last time I looked my detective mate hadn't been a female. Spinning around I recognised *One Network News* reporter April Greenlaw, a colleague of mine who'd also chosen tonight for a walk by the duck pond. Damn, I cursed to myself, if Dave sees me here talking to someone he'll probably take off. After exchanging pleasantries I managed to disengage and continue my circuit. No sign of Dave, and it's already quarter past.

"Hello Ian." I jumped again — another woman, this time *60 Minutes* reporter Pauline Hudson. What the hell is this?, I cursed — Grand Central Station for TV reporters or something?

"What are you doing?," she asked in her naturally interrogative tone of voice. For a moment I toyed with the idea of saying *"would you believe feeding the ducks?"*, but I knew she wouldn't believe it so I didn't bother.

"Not much," I lied, *"just thought I'd take a walk."*

When I had worked at TV3 Hudson had been my arch-rival. She was then the crime reporter for *One Network News*, and was noted for her incredible tenacity. We'd once had a helicopter race to the scene of a siege that had an entire town cordoned off — ignoring police airspace restrictions we both touched down in the middle of the town to file reports. There was such intense competition it resulted in another helicopter race back to the nearest Telecom video transmission point – the TV equivalent of a whole bunch of journo's all fighting to be first into the phone booth.

Later that night we were both waiting in our rental cars outside the police siege headquarters – an old farm building in the middle of a paddock just outside the town. It was just after 2:00am, midwinter, and we'd both left our engines running to maintain heat to the passenger compartments.

Nearly all of the police were out combing the countryside with guns and heat-seeking infrared binoculars, looking for one of the country's most notorious escapees.

My cameraman, Peter Stones, had gone to sleep in the passenger seat beside me, and in the rear vision mirror I could see Polly Hudson and Alan Silvester were also dozing. When a cop came screaming out of the farm building at a sprint with a rifle in his hand and jumped into his patrol vehicle, I was ready to drop our car into gear and wheelspin off after him.

Hearing the commotion and seeing our taillights vanish down the track at high speed, Pauline Hudson was panicked into action and stamped on the accelerator of her car as hard as she could.

"Why aren't we moving?" she screamed in Silvester's ear as their car revved its guts out on the spot. *"Because,"* he replied calmly, *"You're still in neutral."*

On another hunt for armed gunmen, Peter Stones and I ended up in motel rooms next to Hudson and her crew, ready for a dawn start. As a precaution, we had placed a carton of milk under Hudson's back tyre, so that if she tried to sneak out early we'd hear it explode. As it was, Stones and I were first to wake, and we pushed our own camera vehicle 100 metres back up the motel driveway before we started the engine and drove to find the police searchers.

Oh yes, if anyone was going to get suspicious about seeing me at a duck pond, it was Pauline Hudson. Fortunately, Pauline was with her fiance looking for wedding photography venues. She didn't stick around for too long. There was still no sign of Dave. I decided to try his mobile.

"Where the hell are you?" he answered.

"I'm at the duck pond, where are you?"

"I'm at the bloody duck pond too, but I can't see you," he retorted.

I looked around, confused, but there was definitely no one around fitting Dave's description. And then the penny dropped.

"And just which duck pond are you at, my friend?"

"Western Springs. No, don't tell me – you're at the Domain duck pond, aren't you, you dumb-assed bastard!"

You had to laugh. Inspector Clouseau would have been proud. Dave was still chortling quietly when he pulled up beside me 15 minutes later, but the conversation quickly took a more serious tone.

"Like I was saying, about a week ago the shit hit the fan, they even know about it in Wellington. The talk is they got a script out of TVNZ over to TV3 and someone there has given it to Fay Richwhite."

My heart stopped beating. *"What do you mean TV3 got hold of one of our scripts – why the hell would they want it?"*

"How the hell would I know? All I know is a TV3 guy was on a plane sitting next to a Fay Richwhite boy last week, and he apparently gave him the script. They were talking about it and were overheard by some of the other passengers."

My mind was spinning. Trying to figure out what had happened was like tossing a jigsaw into the air and expecting to catch it again in its original formation – damn near impossible.

"They couldn't have got one of our current scripts," I reasoned. *"They're locked in the computers."*

"What about a traitor at your end?"

I considered the possibilities and rapidly ruled that option out. It was possible that someone might have picked up an old draft out of the rubbish, but we'd been shredding most of those. Even if they had, the likelihood of a TVNZ staffer passing it to TV3 was pretty slim.

"The only other thing I can think of," I ventured after a moment, *"is a synopsis that I left behind at TV3 when I came to TVNZ. There were only two copies of that document, and Keith Davies and I had one each. But I can't see him giving it to that crowd. Maybe someone else at 3 got hold of it and took a copy."*

I'd already had bitter experience of that. The more I thought about it the more likely it seemed.

"It's your problem," replied Dave. *"I suggest you clean it up."*

Which left me with a dilemma. How to approach Keith Davies without approaching Keith Davies. I decided to make a two-pronged attack, utilising Spook and Brian Henry, independently of each other. Both, I knew, had talked to Davies from time to time.

I was actually sitting in Henry's office listening on the speakerphone when Brian made the call. He played it softly, suggesting a rumour was sweeping the traps that a named TV3 individual had somehow gotten hold of a synopsis and passed it to a Fay Richwhite employee on a plane. Question was, said Brian, if there is a copy floating around of what Wishart's up to, it would be really good to see it.

Davies knew of the individual named, but ventured that the item in question was not in fact a Wishart synopsis on European Pacific, but instead a script from an upcoming mini-series on the 1984 election crisis involving former PM Sir Robert Muldoon and David Lange.

So the story went, the TV3 staffer had found the script in a rubbish bin at the Wellington courthouse where, apparently, part of the miniseries had been filmed. Keith was genuine in his explanation of cause and effect but, sitting in the background listening, I couldn't help but feel that perhaps two stories were getting mixed up here. Why would a cop warn about a European Pacific script being purloined, and why would Fay Richwhite want a copy of a miniseries script dealing with events 9 years earlier?

Spook gave Davies a ring later the same day, leaving the poor guy even more perplexed, but still I couldn't manage to square the circle. My people were adamant it was an EP script, even describing it themselves as a synopsis or early draft.

The waters were later muddied even further when I discovered the

Independent's Berryman and McManus had been gloating about knowing what I was up to and knowing about JIF. Through the traps, the word came back that they too had access to a synopsis left behind at TV3.

When I confronted Jenni McManus she conceded she had seen the synopsis, but claimed she'd been told that I OK'd its release to her. Fat chance. Still, it was too late to undo the damage – all I could do was rely on the fact that there was nothing in the document referring to Magnum, and nothing which explained the promissory note mechanism. The intrigue didn't stop there, however.

As a crime beat reporter, you quickly build up a network of contacts and sources from all walks of life. Drug dealers, bank robbers, hired guns, police and private investigators can all be useful additions to a journalist's news antennae. At a loose end, I dialled up a couple of mates at private investigation companies to see if they'd heard the buzz about the script leak. One of them had, but both had something even more significant to report.

Both agencies had been approached by a business executive asking them to *"Put Winston Peters out of politics, permanently."* The request came with an assurance that, no matter what the cost, the people the businessman represented wanted Peters utterly and completely disgraced, and they didn't care what tactics were used – including trick photography. Despite the promise of as much money as they wanted, both agencies had turned down the job. It immediately rang a warning bell within me, as a respected Radio New Zealand journalist had recently boasted to his colleagues that he'd seen a photo of Peters doing an unnatural act.

The latest computer programmes make such composite photos a breeze to create, and the dirty tricks potential is enormous. The photo never surfaced, probably because newspaper editors – well aware of computerised tricks of the trade – would smell a rat.

It illustrated the existence however of an orchestrated conspiracy to discredit the MP for Tauranga, at the same time as many media commentators were ridiculing him as a wacky conspiracy theorist. Someone, with a lot of money, was pulling the strings.

Spook, meanwhile, had been doing some digging of his own into the script affair. What he came up with sent a chill down my spine.

"I can't find any evidence that a script actually left TVNZ, so I think you're right in the assumption that it's an old TV3 one, but I do have some bad news for you."

He told me that the jungle drums were already throbbing with rumours of our secret documentary. *"You won't be allowed to put it to air. Apparently some guy named Wilson is going to veto it."*

Wilson, I figured, had to be TVNZ General Manager Graeme Wilson, a former journalist who'd given up the pen to take up a managerial sword some years back. I couldn't see how Wilson would even be involved in something that was between Paul Norris and Chief Executive Brent Harman, so I put little emphasis on Spook's warning.

Brent Harman arrived back a week later but there was no move to put the programme to air that Sunday. Instead we were using the interregnum to fine tune the post-production on the programme. The graphics showing bouncing money bags had cost the best part of $70,000, and there were other little things that needed tweaking as well.

By chance, Michael Wilson and I bumped into Keith Davies at Auckland airport the following week.

"*I hear Graeme Wilson is trying to stop your programme from screening,*" he divulged conspiratorially over a coffee. I still had no proof that Graeme Wilson had in any way been called in, so keeping a straight face I told Davies that as far as we knew, Wilson wasn't involved in the story and had no power to stop it.

"*As far as I'm aware, it's between Norris and Harman.*"

Returning from Wellington later that day, our worst fears were confirmed. Graeme Wilson was involved, and was demanding changes to the programme. What changes? For a start, Winston Peters' comments had to come out. The production meeting was stormy.

"*What right has that jumped up prat got to order us to remove Peters?,*" demanded one of the team.

"*I know what you're saying,*" came the response, "*but they don't want our programme to be seen endorsing or glorifying Peters in any way.*"

What the hell did that mean? Just because Peters happened to be right didn't mean we were glorifying him. The inclusion of a couple of small comments where he called European Pacific a secret and covert series of companies that defrauded the New Zealand revenue hardly made our documentary "Peters-driven". Another senior journalist was equally shocked.

"*I can't really believe we're having this discussion. The man's the leader of a political party, for God's sake! If we were talking about taking the Prime Minister out of this piece for political reasons there would be hell to pay!*"

Everyone present agreed with the sentiment, but the reality was that the programme would not be allowed to go to air with Winston Peters in it. It was a case of compromise or lose the story – end of story. There were to be other changes too. The opening sequence was to be erased – goodbye to Carol's carefully crafted shadowy figure rifling through a filing cabinet. Too sinister, might give us some legal problems, came the explanation.

"*You can't be serious,*" Mike, Carol, myself and *Frontline* producer Mark Champion yelped, almost in unison. But there was more. Our documentary did not allege Sir Michael Fay was guilty of anything. His company, of course, was involved in what our lawyers believed was a proposed fraud against the Japanese Government, but we weren't sure at what level within Capital Markets approval would have been required for such participation.

We had included a shot of Sir Michael Fay in the 1987 America's Cup parade in Auckland – now we were being told to take it out as well. Graeme Wilson did not want us casting aspersions on Sir Michael Fay. Fay's 1987 America's Cup challenge had caught the public mood, a mood that EPI capitalised on. His photo had been included for no other reason – his success in the Cup was integral to the skyrocketing share prices of his companies, and integral to the public float of EPI. There was no reason to drop Fay from the story in that context, and to do so would actually detract from public understanding of that segment in the programme.

"This script has been approved for broadcast by our lawyers, on what grounds are they doing this?"

"Well," came the response, *"they feel that we can't be sure of the facts, that we're taking on some very respectable businessmen, and that we don't want to leave ourselves open to lawsuits."*

Bollocks!, I thought. Not only were we being ordered by TVNZ management to remove Winston Peters from the programme because *"they don't like him or his politics"*, but they were expressly bucking the recommendations of our extremely highly qualified legal team from Simpson Grierson.

To have the executives suggest we couldn't be sure of the facts was an insult to Gary Muir – a doctorate in tax law – and Professor John Prebble, also a doctor in tax law, not to mention the former Auditor-General, Assistant Treasury Secretary and IRD tax investigator Brian Tyler.

By Friday, December 17, we'd finally finished most of the surgery on the programme, changing some of the vision and excising Peters*. We all felt unclean and sick to the stomach. Just as we announced the programme was ready for airing, the dynamic duo, Brent Harman and Graeme Wilson, found a new way to make our lives hell.

They ordered us to ring European Pacific and seek comment on our investigation. Not only EP, but we were also to ring David Richwhite, Paul Collins and Peter Travers. Without their responses, the programme would not screen on Sunday. To those of us on the Project X team, it was patently obvious that there was now no chance of the programme going to air on Sunday – the moment we tipped off European Pacific we'd be caught up in the injunction battle.

As I dialled European Pacific in the Cook Islands and asked for David Lloyd, I knew that this might just be "goodnight nurse" to Project X. Somehow, there had to be a way out – a way of saving the project. If such an escape route existed, then come hell or high water we would find it.

"That much I promise you," I muttered under my breath as I listened to ringing tone on the line to European Pacific.

---

* We'd obtained a stay of execution on removing the Fay sequence, however it was subsequently excised in an early 1994 recut. We'd managed to keep a brief parliamentary quote of Peters whilst ditching a more in depth interview clip. Again, in early 1994, Peters was dropped completely but, like Lazarus, featured in the broadcast version in May 1994 as a result of his tabling the winebox.

CHAPTER 17

Brinkmanship

"INCOME TAX: You may think that you have played a clever trick by making a return at your place of business, that you were assessed at your place of abode, but it will probably turn out an awkward affair. Your return will be passed on to the assessor of the district where you live, and when he reports thereon that you have made a false return, the commissioners will either direct you to be sued for the 20 pound penalty, or that you will be assessed on treble the sum that you attempted to evade the payment of, and in default of not finding sufficient goods they will arrest your body."
– WEEKLY DISPATCH, 1856

THROUGHOUT THE PREVIOUS 12 months I had done everything possible to avoid tipping off European Pacific about my investigation, and it was an approach endorsed by TVNZ when Project X began. It really, really galled me to turn myself in to the enemy at the last minute. It felt as though we were being made to surrender. Although the Director of News and Current Affairs, Paul Norris would later tell *Metro* magazine that we decided to approach European Pacific for *"sound journalistic reasons,"* the truth is that we had our backs to the wall. There was no "sound journalistic reason" for us to give European Pacific a right to comment.

Our case was not a "he says/she says" mudslinging that required equal input from either side – it was a very carefully crafted story alleging that a company had either planned or committed a prima facie fraud against New Zealand and Japanese taxpayers, based on a fully documented trail examined by a number of experts. A story that would have to stand up in any court of law without the need for European Pacific's explanations. European Pacific's predictable response would add diddly-squat to the substance of our investigation – it was almost irrelevant.

By now, those of us working on Project X had lost any illusions that corporate management held dear the same things that we journalists treasured. To us, this was a documentary of major public importance, a story that must be told. To them, it wasn't. This came as no huge surprise to me – I had been aware for months that corporate and political New Zealand wanted to squash any investigation into these matters. But for those I was working with, Carol Hirschfeld and Michael Wilson in particular – it was an experience that would change their outlook on life forever. Lost innocence would be one way of describing it, shattered illusions – another.

The realisation that they, like most other New Zealand journalists, were just unwitting puppets, being used in a game to divert public attention from the real issues, was a very traumatic experience.

As one current affairs staffer privately noted, *"it was one of those things that I didn't really want to discover first hand. I was sort of happy in my ignorance – until this came along and we couldn't avoid it. It makes you feel like you've been swimming in excrement."*

Up in European Pacific's Rarotonga office, meanwhile, the alarm bell on David Lloyd's desk was ringing. He picked up the receiver.

"I think you're barking up the wrong tree, Ian," he ventured as soon as I'd explained we were doing a story on the creation of misleading tax certificates.

"We were thinking perhaps of the Magnum deal of 1988," I continued.

"I think someone's trying to put a connotation on something that is different from what it is."

"Alright, help me out here – What's the connotation that it should be?," I asked.

"Um, look, I'm quite happy to sit down and have a talk to you about this at some stage, but I don't think trying to deal with it over the phone is the most appropriate. Are you under any time urgency on this?"

I wasn't, at this stage, prepared to tell Lloyd we were going to air on Sunday, so I just got more specific in the questioning. *"What I'm thinking about is the transactions between European Pacific – particularly Dundee and EPMF and the Cook Islands Government Property Corporation, which was a pre-arranged loss for the Cook Islands Government."*

"Ian, look, as I say, I'll sit down and talk to you. I don't want to talk about it on the phone – I don't think it's appropriate. I'm sure you realise that there's a number of issues as far as we, as an organisation, in terms of what we're permitted to say by law or what we're prepared to say ourselves. I'll be in New Zealand next week. I can see you on Wednesday."

Everyone, including Norris and Brown, gathered around in the Project X editing suite to hear the conversation replayed. Norris' gut feeling – and one that I concurred with – was that we should fly back up to Rarotonga to speak to David Lloyd mano a mano – face to face. He and Shaun exited at this point, leaving us to discuss logistics. Just as we were doing so, a fax hit the desk from European Pacific's lawyers, Rudd Watts and Stone. It was addressed to Brent Harman but had been cc'd to me as well.*

"Dear Sir," it began, *"We are aware that there have been recent discussions between yourself, Mr Geary and others concerning a proposed current affairs television programme on, inter alia, the European Pacific Group and some of its business activities."*

The others in the room must have sensed my utter disbelief.

"What's wrong?"

"It's this letter from EP's lawyers. It says they are aware of – get this – recent discussions between Harman, Norman Geary and others about a quote 'proposed current affairs television programme' unquote on European Pacific.

---

* See Appendix.

"I never mentioned anything to David Lloyd about Brent Harman or Norman Geary – hell, I didn't even know Geary was involved!"

The implications were serious. Not only had the programme been discussed by TVNZ's Chairman of the Board, Norm Geary, but European Pacific and its lawyers appeared to be aware of the content of those *"recent"* discussions. And this was before we even told EP we were doing the story.

Exactly what gave the Chairman of the Board the right to interfere in a news story, I wasn't sure. Perhaps Geary's involvement was entirely proper – maybe he'd been rung by EP or a politician asking him what the hell was going on, and he'd referred the matter down to Brent Harman.

But who were the "others" that were briefed, and how did EP come to know about all this? What had been said? The letter went on to remind us of the injunction already in place, and that we were bound by it.

"OK," said Norris later, mulling it all over but adding nothing further on the latest development, *"Ring back Lloyd and tell him we plan to go to air this Sunday, offer him a right of reply."*

Predictably, Lloyd's response was negative.

"I understand your position Ian, but I'm not prepared to do things out of context. I've offered to sit down and go through it with you but I'd like to do that in a balanced way where I've got an idea of what you're doing."

"Essentially there appears to be a secret transaction with the Cook Islands Government, was there not?"

"I've already told you my views on that. People are trying to put connotations on something and misunderstanding it."

"Alright, I'll diverge from that briefly. The directors of European Pacific Trust and Banking Group Ltd, during 88/89, did they include David Richwhite and Paul Collins?"

"Ian, I'm not going to discuss it on the phone, alright?"

"We've got to go to air on Sunday – "

"Well, Ian, I should point out to you that in relation to the transaction you discussed with me earlier, that transaction is specifically covered by the present, interim injunction."

"Yeah, I'm merely asking you the question as a journalist," I explained cautiously, not wanting to make any concessions that could weaken our position. *"I'm not discussing the legal aspects of it one way or the other."*

Nervous laughter broke out at Lloyd's end of the phone.

"The legal aspect of it is that there's a court order preventing publication or discussion of any material in relation to that."

Lloyd would later misquote me in his affidavit to the High Court, saying *"I reminded him of the injunctions in place, and he indicated to me that that had nothing to do with him, he was just a journalist."* As will be noted from my careful answer to his question, I didn't say the injunction had nothing to do with me, I simply was not going to be drawn into a legal argument on the phone – dangerous territory when talking to a lawyer. Lloyd's later testimony is an example of how one's comments can be twisted to put one in a bad light in the eyes of the Court. Judges are not particularly fond of the media, they're even less fond of journalists who say the law has nothing to do with them.

"*Did the Japanese Bank transactions go ahead?*" I pressed on.

"*Ian, I'm not going to go into that on the phone. If you wanted to have a talk to me in a proper way about your programme, you could have done it before today.*"

"*Yeah, but the injunction – I note that we had a fax straight away after our conversation this morning – *"

"*Of course, and I'm happy to sit down and discuss that with you. If you'd wanted to have appropriate comments from me, you could have contacted me in plenty of time for it to be done in the normal manner.*"

"*So you would deny that any misleading tax certificates have been created?*"

"*Of course! Obviously I deny it.*" We parted company at this point, Lloyd reminding me that if we tried to race ahead and do our own thing it would end up being debated in "*a different forum*" – a reference to court.

Of course, I knew damn well that approaching Lloyd earlier in the piece would have been fatal to the story. There was never going to be any negotiation by EP on the central point – the use of the company's confidential documents. Asking Lloyd for input would inevitably have led to an injunction or, worse, the cancellation of the project in its infancy by TVNZ corporate management. I had already seen that happen at TV3. The extreme secrecy surrounding our work at TVNZ had been beneficial not only in keeping EP at bay, but also making the programme a fait accompli by the time the General Manager, Graeme Wilson, saw the script. We had already spent probably $200,000 on production and legal costs by that point.

The second conversation with Lloyd had changed nothing – we still had the invitation to discuss it in person, so we decided to exercise that option. Up on the 7th Floor of the TVNZ building, however, other plans were afoot. EP's lawyers were seeking, and gained, assurances that the programme would not run until we had met David Lloyd to discuss it. Unlike the *NBR* and the *Independent*, which had been injuncted without prior notice, EP's lawyers seemed more than happy to accept TVNZ's assurances. The tax haven bank made no move to injunct us.

Given the already strenuous efforts being made to castrate the programme, it wasn't hard to imagine further attempts to sink it without trace before an injunction was even laid.

Twenty-four hours before our flight, I took out a journalistic insurance policy. Figuring that the European Pacific programme was in danger of being permanently iced by the corporates on the 7th Floor, I tipped off the *Sunday Star*'s television columnist, Toni McRae.

"*Look Toni, I can't tell you why, but it's absolutely imperative that you get a story up in tomorrow's paper about this investigative documentary we're working on – but it can't look like the information came from me.*"

"*I'll do my best,*" she answered, sounding confused, "*why – what's this all about?*"

"OK, we've been doing an investigation into that company Winston Peters has been rabbiting on about in Parliament. It's called European Pacific, and it was owned by some major bananas like Fay Richwhite, Brierleys and the BNZ. I can't tell you what's in it but it's a major investigation.

"The problem is, we've been so secretive about this programme that no one knows we've done it, and now there's a danger it could be stopped. We'd be really grateful if you could write a line saying it's expected to screen next Sunday."

McRae asked a few more basic questions, before adding one final request. *"By the way, what's it called?"*

"It doesn't have a name, but its nickname is Project X."

It was with a huge sense of relief that I opened up the paper the next morning and found Toni's report on page 3.

"Frontline will screen a documentary next Sunday which has been dubbed inside TVNZ 'Project X'. Financial sources say the film probes European Pacific (EPI), the Cook Islands tax haven company which first came to the fore when Winston Peters made allegations about the BNZ in Parliament last year.

"European Pacific was listed in 1987 on the stock exchange and was owned by the BNZ, Brierleys and Capital Markets. A number of injunctions have been served on print media attempting to investigate the company."

It was only two paragraphs, but it sent a ripple of fear through certain circles. More importantly, for the first time it was acknowledged publicly that a documentary existed. If it didn't screen, people might start asking questions. It was also a throwing down of the gauntlet to the corporates: *"Mess this up boys, and there'll be blood on the floor publicly. We won't be taking prisoners."*

It was, in effect, a declaration of war. I didn't stick around to monitor the aftermath internally – we had a plane to catch. Michael Wilson, Peter Day and myself flew back up on that afternoon's flight. With luck we could fax back Lloyd's responses to our questions and incorporate them at the end of the programme. By meeting him face to face, we would have fulfilled our commitment to sit down and talk about it – the programme could run on Monday night.

We had discovered during the second call that Lloyd was staying at the Edgewater Hotel, so we booked ourselves in there again. No one was more surprised to see us return than the hotel manager who'd been so inquisitive the first time around.

"What are you guys really doing? Is this about our tax haven?"

Politely declining to comment, we began to feel we were fast wearing out our welcome in the Cooks. David Lloyd had a lot of friends there.

When we rang David Lloyd at 8:30am the next morning and told him we were in town, you could almost hear the thump as he fell out of bed. This was one trick he hadn't expected us to pull.

"We thought rather than wait until Wednesday we'd come and see you up here, when can we call around?"

He consented to see me at 10:00am, no cameras – but it would be an on-the-record interview. *"Gotcha!,"* I gloated as I hung up the phone, before dialling TVNZ for any last minute orders. *"I've got the microcassette recorder with me,"* I told Shaun Brown, *"do you want me to go in wired?"*

"No, not this time. Play it by the book. Take your recorder along, ask him if you can record it, but leave it off if he insists."

It was a decision that even today Brown cannot believe he made. He spent the next few months mentally kicking himself, because it turned out to be a crucial conversation and it would have been handy to have a transcript for the court case. Instead, I went in alone, and the tape recorder remained turned off.

Lloyd was staying in one of the hotel's full size apartments with his wife, Kay. It was the first time I'd actually met the guy – we had tried and failed on the earlier visit to find a picture of him at either the TV station or the newspaper. We talked for an hour – Lloyd opening up with surprising candour.

"I've never actually been interviewed before," he confided, *"you're the first journalist who's ever come to see me about this matter."*

Lloyd's innocence in dealing with the media became painfully transparent as the interview progressed. *"I'm happy to answer any questions you have, but don't expect me to give you any information you don't already have,"* he warned.

OK, I thought, let's try an easy bluff first up. Exactly who controlled the Cook Islands group during the time it was owned by the secret trust – it was a question that had been gnawing at me for weeks. I wanted to know whether Richwhite, Collins and Travers were effectively in control, despite the ownership sleight of hand.

"Alright," I began, *"The European Pacific Trust and Banking Group Ltd: I've got the directors listed as yourself, David Richwhite, Paddy Marra - "*

"No, no," Lloyd quickly corrected me, *"Paddy was just an alternate for Paul Collins. Paul was the appointed director for Brierleys. I was Managing Director, David was Chairman, and we had Peter Travers* on board as well."*

For a man who wasn't going to tell me anything, David Lloyd had just been incredibly helpful. I felt I was pushing my luck when I asked if they'd all remained on the board from March 1988 through to December 1989 – the crucial period when the Magnum and JIF deals were initiated. David Lloyd didn't see the trap and fell straight into it.

"Yes, we all stayed in the same position," and then the penny clanged to the floor. *"Ah. I see now where this might be leading. If you're implying that my fellow directors were somehow responsible for individual transactions, I can assure you that's not the case. David Richwhite and Paul Collins certainly did not know about the Magnum transaction."*

---

* "Witness A" told the Davison Commission in August 1995 that Peter Travers may not have been aware of much of what was going on. He also stated that Brierleys had not been involved in the JIF deals in any way, although I presume as part owners of EP they would have indirectly benefitted from any profits.

Lloyd explained that directors were generally not consulted about the specifics of a particular deal, unless the transaction exceeded internal credit or prudential guidelines. On all other occasions, he said, the deals were crafted and approved by *"an executive committee of the bank, comprised entirely of employees."* He did concede that *"there may well have been discussions about the general principles"* of a deal structure at board level, but not specifics.

Asked about the JIF deals, Lloyd became evasive, saying that because they had no revenue impact on New Zealand, he would prefer not to comment further on them. He didn't deny that the documentation showed EP was clawing back the tax money paid by the Japanese Banks, but when I asked him if the Japanese banks knew EP was doing this he again refused to comment.

I tried another approach, asking him if the directors had been informed of the structure of the Japanese deals, given the large amount of money involved.

"They are large amounts of money," he agreed, *"large to anyone, but you must remember the criteria is the risk being taken by EP. You shouldn't be blinded by the huge amounts of money involved. If there was no risk to the group, the directors would not have to be involved. Just because there's big money doesn't mean they [the directors] were a party to devising them [the schemes]."*

In fact, in the Mitsubishi deal at least, the documentation on the deal acknowledged that European Pacific was indeed taking a credit "risk" and that prudential limits were being exceeded. If Lloyd's definition was strictly adhered to, the directors should have been informed, although we have no evidence that they were alerted.

As the interview drew to a close, David Lloyd explained that European Pacific could not be wound down until mid-1995 at the earliest, because of a number of deals that had set times still to run. When I asked if this included JIF deals, he again refused to comment.

Almost wistfully, he added that he didn't want his company's corporate behaviour in the 1980's judged by the new morality of the 1990's, and he was insistent that the Magnum transaction didn't break New Zealand law.

"There was no requirement on us to tell the New Zealand Revenue that we got the tax money back. That deal was not illegal."

Perhaps realising that his honesty with me might cost him later, Lloyd added a warning.

"You must realise, I am going to try and stop you using this."

We needed him to do more than just try. A discussion with my *Frontline* colleagues had confirmed they too had serious concerns that we were being set up to take a fall. I quickly formed the view that we were going to have to force European Pacific to injunct us – that way the whole issue would go before a court and be taken out of the hands of the state television network.

Once it was before a judge they would be very hardpressed to kill the project. The only way to achieve that was to undermine whatever assurances had been given to EP, and the only way to do **that** was to terrify David Lloyd with the prospect of imminent publication. Yet even then our Machiavellian scheming had a downside – we didn't want Lloyd taking court action today, because that would rule out any chance of screening the documentary tonight – our last "window of opportunity" before next Sunday.

"And you must realise," I told Lloyd, *"that we fully intend to broadcast this programme as soon as we've completed our filming requirements here in the Cook Islands."*

We both knew the next plane out was the next day, and we both knew we were all booked on that flight. I guess David Lloyd figured he had 24 hours to work with. I wasn't content, however, to leave him stewing solely over our interview. As soon as we'd faxed details of the conversation to Auckland, I whistled up the camera crew, and we proceeded to stake out his apartment.

It was the rainy season in Rarotonga, I lost count of the drenchings after six warmish tropical downpours. We lurked around his unit for six hours until he finally returned. Spotting his car making its way down the drive in the rain, I called Peter Day away from his monotony-relieving attempt to smash open a coconut.

Day leapt to attention, grabbing his camera in a fluid motion and whisking it up to his shoulder. Michael Wilson stood there in his sunglasses in the rain – looking for all the world like some kind of tropical hood.

It was then that we realised David Lloyd wasn't driving, and was instead in the passenger seat. It was then that Lloyd realised we were trying to take his picture, and asked his wife to turn around without stopping and drive back out.

Too late, Peter Day twigged to the fact that he hadn't been filming the right person and tried to leap around the other side of the car, but he couldn't get there in time. It vanished at a reasonable clip back down the drive. If that didn't spook him, nothing would.

Back in Auckland, things were looking promising for the programme to go to air. It was a weird kind of feeling. The production that had overtaken our lives was finally due to be broadcast, and here we were, stranded in paradise with no television set to watch it on.

While the Cook Islands took a satellite feed of TVNZ news each night, *Frontline* was sent up on videotape, and generally screened in Rarotonga about two weeks behind the New Zealand schedule. We'd had no time for dinner so, settling down with beers and bags of potato chips, we dialled up Mark Champion. The news was all bad.

Project X was being slotted in at 9:30pm, Monday night New Zealand time, in place of the *Primetime* mid evening news bulletin and subsequent comedy show. However, Wilson and Harman had been locked in the conference room with Paul Norris and Shaun Brown, demanding yet more changes to the programme. Carol Hirschfeld and Mark Champion were not permitted to take part in *those* discussions.

Wilson and Harman had first appeared in the newsroom around 7:00pm that night, ostensibly to approve the final mix of the programme that had just been completed, ready for transmission. As they watched in the edit suite, the first item to fall foul was the "mood music" in the opening sequence. Get rid of it came the order.

"Oh Paul, you haven't!," Brent Harman had said to Norris despairingly when he heard the music, burying his face in his hands for a moment. Harman had been involved in the internal inquiry into *For The Public Good*, and one of the main recommendations from that inquiry had been to avoid the use of sinister music.

It was a farcical recommendation, of course. If we were factually correct the 'sinister music' would have no impact on a defamation lawsuit. If we were factually incorrect, we would have bigger things to worry about than whether the music was appropriate.

A few minutes later – probably faster than expected – the music in that opening sequence had been removed, but instead of giving the go ahead, Wilson and Harman summoned Norris and Brown back to the newsroom's conference area for a private pow-wow. Journalists and producers watched in awe through the floor-to-ceiling glass as an at-times heated exchange took place.

When they all trooped out, a new problem had surfaced. There was more music further down the programme. It too had to go. At 8:30 pm, the *Primetime* staff had been sent home, including anchor Maggie Barry. It looked as though *Frontline* was definitely going to run its special investigation. Forty minutes later, only 20 minutes before they were due on air, the *Primetime* team were called back. Standby they were told, it looks like *Frontline* won't fly.

Right up to the final minute Carol and editor Nic Craig had been furiously hacking the programme and reassembling, each time going back to the conference room to announce it was ready for screening. I could see why Harman might have been feeling overwhelmed and panicked. It wouldn't have been helped by Graeme Wilson's subtle needling of him.

"It's your decision Brent," Wilson would say with a shrug of the shoulders. *"Are you sure you want to run it Brent? It's on your shoulders, Brent."*

At 9:25 Harman and Wilson discovered a new problem – Wishart's voice in one of the pieces to camera sounded too rushed, it couldn't go to air like that. To us on the production team it was another utterly asinine excuse for pulling the plug, given that the changes already demanded had made the programme much harder for viewers to follow and understand. A slightly fast voiceover for 10 seconds was nothing compared with the workover the programme had already received, but it was enough to stop the countdown.

The abiding impression left with staff working that night was that management had simply been stretching out the recuts: rather than coming to the meeting with a list of everything they wanted changed, and getting it done at once, everything was instead drawn out to the point where it was too late to run the programme. It was also the first time that tape editing staff could remember the Chief Executive and his 2nd-in-command coming down to personally vet a news and current affairs programme.

Launch was abandoned – at 9:30pm it was *Primetime*, not *Frontline*, that screened, and the rest of New Zealand didn't have an inkling of the battle-royal behind the scenes.

Television New Zealand's two most senior executives had pre-empted the screening of a programme cleared by the best lawyers and tax experts in the country, a programme clearly of major public interest. Simultaneously – separated as they were by thousands of miles of ocean – members of the Project X production team were dumbfounded.

With nothing left to lose we would throw everything the next morning at scaring European Pacific out of the water – if we couldn't drive them into court we could kiss goodbye to any hope of ever breaking the story.

The unspoken thought in all our minds: if we couldn't salvage something from this "Valley of Death", we'd end up in our own "Charge of the journalistic bantamweight brigade", not a mantle any of us were keen to wear.

CHAPTER 18

The Empire Strikes Back

"They are slaves who fear to speak
For the fallen and the weak;
They are slaves who will not choose
Hatred, scoffing, and abuse,
Rather than in silence shrink
From the truth they needs must think;
They are slaves who dare not be
In the right with two or three"
— JAMES LOWELL, 1819-1891

ANOTHER EXQUISITE TROPICAL SUNRISE, and suddenly life didn't feel so bad. The angst of the previous evening gave way to more plotting as we made our way to the airport. Please God, let David Lloyd be on this flight. We were among the first to go through Immigration, and quickly made our way to a good vantage spot for filming. Lloyd had to emerge through the same door as everyone else — if he was travelling this morning he'd get a TV crew up his nose.

Michael Wilson opted to cool himself off in the air conditioned comfort of Air New Zealand's first class lounge, not that TV crews travel first class — the lounge is also open to the airline's Koru Club members. Koru cards were standard issue for TVNZ current affairs crews, forced as they often were to trot the globe in search of stories.

Peter and I remained in the heat. Waiting. And waiting. By 10:00am it was 31 degrees Celsius in the shade. Finally, 20 minutes before takeoff, David and Kay Lloyd emerged. He spotted the camera instantly, but too late; there was no where to run, no where to hide. Like a sheep to the drenching pond Lloyd could only grit his teeth as he went through the metal detector under the gaze of our lens and continue through the only exit available. Too dignified to break into a trot, David merely smiled weakly and headed for the first class lounge.

"I don't know what the world's coming to!," his wife muttered in an annoyed tone of voice as they closed the door, leaving the camera crew outside in the heat. *"What on earth is all this about?"*

Neither she nor Lloyd realised the man sitting in the seat behind them was Mike Wilson, but the look on their faces was priceless when Peter and I calmly entered the lounge as well, camera in tow. After forking out for a first class ticket, his despair at seeing the barbarians passing through the gates was almost palpable.

"When are you planning to run this, anyway?" he asked, trying to disguise his eagerness to hear the answer and failing badly. Inside I was grinning

from ear to ear, outside I was a picture of respectability and restraint.

"I should think we'll have all this in place within a few hours. Where will you be staying if we have to get hold of you for reaction tonight?"

Lloyd went white.

"By the way," I added, *"please understand that this is nothing personal. We simply had to get pictures of you because we don't have any."*

It was true, about it not being personal that is. Lloyd had been a very polite and affable interviewee. The fact that we were poles apart in our view of the schemes' legality was neither here nor there — I actually felt sorry for the guy. It's always harder to hunt the friendly and reasonable ones — it's much easier being an investigative journalist if your targets are ogres.

We lost sight of Lloyd after boarding the jet, but we'd arranged for Carol Hirschfeld and a camera operator to be at Auckland airport and film anyone meeting Lloyd's description who got off the flight.

It turned out we'd scared him good! He was so fast off the plane that Hirschfeld thought he must have been a straggler from the previous aircraft to arrive. She didn't have any idea who he was, but he literally sprinted out of the Customs Hall and straight to the nearest phone. This, she decided, was "suspicious" behaviour.

As a result we got some great shots of the silver-haired fox dialling furiously, and then turning around to see another camera pointed at him. His jaw dropped for the second time that morning.

Our own return to work was somewhat anticlimactic, although it coincided with media inquiries about the events of the night before. When *Primetime* had been cancelled to make way for the *Frontline* investigation, a frisson of excitement had rippled through TVNZ staff, some of whom had apparently contacted friends in other media companies to suggest they watch it.

When it didn't show, those journalists wanted to know why. By mid-morning Winston Peters had apparently got in on the act, issuing a news release accusing TVNZ bosses of censoring the programme and pulling it off air. Someone had posted the Peters release on a number of noticeboards around the huge office and angry TVNZ staff were secretly delighted that the corporate chiefs were being publicly humiliated for their actions. I too, was cheering from the sidelines. Crowds gathered to read it.

"The Hon Winston Peters, Leader of New Zealand First today accused TVNZ's management of canning release of a programme on certain New Zealand business practices.

" 'I have been aware for some time that production of the story was underway, and because of that withheld releasing further information on this story in Parliament believing that television could more comprehensively deal with a number of the elements behind big business operations. The programme has been completed and TVNZ Lawyers cleared it for public showing. I am gravely concerned to have found out that Management of TVNZ is now refusing to show the programme.'

"Mr Peters said that the evidence behind the programme would be released by

him shortly. 'Television New Zealand can do it or be exposed as an organisation that censors news – the choice is theirs', said Mr Peters."

I later discovered the MP had been rung by one of my concerned colleagues from TV3 after the *Primetime* debacle. His comments were picked up by national radio networks and newspapers, the *Herald* of December 22nd carrying a brief denial from TVNZ that the programme had been scrapped.

"The programme is not yet completed and until I am satisfied with the piece it will not be broadcast," Brent Harman told the newspaper between clenched teeth. You could almost hear the snarls of rage from the 7th Floor, although it was Paul Norris whose ear was chewed by the big boys. Paul was piggy-in-the-middle, torn between his requirement to show loyalty to his superiors and his determination to somehow get the story to air. He also faced an almost mutinous staff, some of whom were ready to quit over the interference, all of whom felt betrayed.

The scrap to get the programme to air on the Monday night had taken a terrible toll on all of us, and our immediate bosses could sense the journalistic posse wanted to go a-lynchin'. Wisely, the Deputy Director of News and Current Affairs, Shaun Brown, stepped in with cautionary words.

"It's getting to the stage where we decide whether we resign on principle, or whether we go on. I for one would prefer not to have to walk the plank on this story, and I say that because I feel we can still get it to air.

"I know how demoralised you all are, but don't be tempted to fight this through the papers unless you are prepared to put your jobs on the line for what you believe."

It was a sobering comment. If I had to quit to get the story out I would, but I was running out of bolt holes. *National Business Review* editor Fran O'Sullivan offered me a job if I needed it – an olive branch I was grateful for. I didn't have long to consider it – at precisely 4:43 pm on the day we arrived back from Rarotonga, European Pacific filed suit against Television New Zealand and myself as second defendant.

Citing possible imminent broadcast of the programme, the tax haven company had gone to the High Court seeking an injunction. The matter would be fought out in Court the following morning. The documents also showed something curious. European Pacific had sent a fax to Brent Harman the previous evening requesting his assurance by 10:00am this morning that the programme would not be shown prior to a meeting on Wednesday with Lloyd. Brent Harman had not replied, despite the deadline.

Was it an oversight by the Chief Executive, I wondered, or had I been too harsh in my first assessments of his role? Had Harman deliberately let the deadline pass in the secret hope that EP would injunct – taking it out of his hands? Was Harman really a serious threat to the project, or was he trying to tread the middle ground between his News Director, Paul Norris, and his General Manager, Graeme Wilson – the latter being vehemently opposed to the screening of the programme in any form? It is perhaps significant that when the programme did finally air in mid-1994, Wilson was overseas and Harman did not interfere in its broadcast.

The rest of the afternoon was spent in a strategy session for the court hearing in the morning. I almost keeled over in fits of laughter when Julian Miles QC was wheeled in to act on TVNZ's behalf.

"I assume you know Julian," said Helen Wild by way of introduction.

"You could assume that," I grinned back. It was as if Julian was my own personal Jiminy Cricket, accompanying me along the tortuous path of the investigation, almost from day one. But where I had failed to convince him over the Citibank case, European Pacific was entirely different. He took one look at our script, listened to the briefing from Helen and tax expert Gary Muir, and knew straight away he was dealing with an arguable criminal fraud. Co-incidentally, Miles had just been brought in to act for Chris Dickie and the investors in the Russell McVeagh bloodstock case.

The hearing itself was short. European Pacific could obviously argue from a position of strength – the documents were clearly theirs and clearly confidential, therefore they had a prima facie right to an injunction. The onus was on TVNZ to prove the documents contained evidence of "iniquity" or, alternatively, to show that they had already been published and were no longer confidential.

EP's thrust was that the information I had discussed with David Lloyd and, three months earlier, David Lilly, was so detailed it could only have come from an in-depth knowledge of the documents or discussions with former employees who knew about the transactions.

This was good news for us. It meant European Pacific was not challenging the authenticity of the documentation, nor was the company challenging our thesis that it had been given its tax money back. The company was, however, arguing that no one had a right to interview its staff or see its documentation. The programme should not go ahead, ever. Miles sprang to his feet, informing the judge the programme must go ahead.

"Given the importance of the programme and given the defence of TVNZ, which is that it will seek to justify every allegation that it makes . . . it is a programme of great public interest. It will suggest that there are strong indications of fraud by the plaintiffs [EP Group]. It will suggest fraud on the IRD both in New Zealand, the Cook Islands, and possibly Japan."

Miles probably didn't realise at the time just how important his comments were. Our biggest fear in the preceding 12 hours had been that the 7th Floor would lose the stomach for an expensive court fight. As a result we made every effort before the hearing to get Julian up to speed and set him loose, hoping that his submissions would be picked up by other media who'd gathered to hear the case.

I knew the claims of fraud would get them going, and once those comments hit the front pages of the country's newspapers, it would be even harder to justify canning the programme. It would also give TVNZ bosses some comfort if the ball was picked up by others. Miles had made the allegations for the benefit of the judge, but I knew their real power lay in the hands of the media.

Justice Henry was on the bench, the same judge who'd granted the previous injunctions against the business press. As claim and counterclaim ricocheted back and forth across the courtroom like bullets, he realised it was going to take a lot longer to sort out than the hour of free time available.

"Christmas is three days away," he said plaintively to the feuding lawyers, adding that it would be preferable if both parties could reach some sort of understanding until the case could come back before the Court at the end of January. Clearly Justice Henry wasn't going to be able to rule one way or the other before Christmas; clearly we would have to strike some sort of deal not to publish in the interim.

The issue was, how tight would the restriction be? We had a programme that had been designed to go to air as a pre-emptive strike against European Pacific. The element of surprise had been lost, and the programme had been gutted by the hatchet team. It was going to need a lot of corrective surgery, and we wanted to be ready to broadcast again at the end of January.

To achieve that, we'd need to re-interview our experts like Dr Prebble, re-shoot the pieces to camera in the Cook Islands that Harman and Wilson didn't like, and offer rights of reply to people named in the documentary.

We felt that approaching these people would not be further breaching EP's confidentiality – these people had been intimately involved! How could my interviewing them tell them anything about the transactions that they didn't already know?

While the issue seemed clear to us, European Pacific didn't like it. There was to be no contact with anyone else, including our own experts. Despite our pleas to the Court, we had no choice but to accept European Pacific's list of demands. We couldn't even talk to other TVNZ staff about the case.

"Can't say too much," I snapped irritably as I got back to the newsroom after the hearing, *"If I tell you, they'll have to shoot me."*

Christmas didn't last long enough. By December 27 I was back in the office furiously compiling an affidavit for the January 25 hearing. As affidavits go, it was a monster – some 170 pages long!

"We've got to be careful writing this," warned Helen Wild, *"because it's supposed to be your own words. You may have to get up in Court and recite this. Please make it look like you understand it."*

Yeah, right Helen. Next time I write a paragraph like *"Both New Zealand and Japan provide some measure of unilateral relief for taxation paid in an offshore jurisdiction where income so taxed would also suffer further taxation upon receipt in the country of residence of the investor"*, I'll let you know. And that was one of the easier-to-understand sentences. I don't think the judge was taken in by our little charade for one minute.

One thing the affidavit did spell out very clearly, however, was the law that was broken by European Pacific's misleading tax certificate scam.

"It is alleged that the presentation of the certificates would be a fraud on the country from which tax relief was sought. The relevant New Zealand provision in 1988 and 1989 was section 301 Income Tax Act 1976. This provided:

"A credit for foreign tax shall not be allowed unless, within four years

after the end of the income year in which the taxpayer derived the income against the New Zealand tax on which the credit is claimed, or within such further period, not exceeding two years, as the Commissioner in his discretion allows any case or class of cases, the taxpayer claiming the credit:

"(a) makes application in writing to the Commissioner for the credit; and

(b) furnishes to the Commissioner all information (including information in relation to any amount to which the taxpayer is entitled in respect of <u>any relief or repayment of the foreign tax</u>) [author's emphasis]necessary for determining the amount of the credit."

In other words, leaving out the gobbledegook, anyone who wanted to claim a tax credit using a foreign tax certificate had, at the same time, to provide in writing any information about whether they had been given any or all of their tax back in the foreign country. In essence this law was to stop companies or individuals from earning money in a foreign jurisdiction – perhaps getting all their tax back because they were non-residents there – but using the tax certificates they'd gained to reduce New Zealand tax, without disclosing the refund. The law was crystal clear – how European Pacific thought they could get away with non-disclosure to the New Zealand Revenue will remain a mystery to me.

Similar affidavits were requested from retired Auditor-General Brian Tyler, and Dr Prebble. The latter was firmly ensconced at a remote bush campsite for the holiday period, but had taken with him a laptop computer and home office equipment in order to meet our legal deadlines.

Graeme Wilson seemed to be always hanging around the newsroom, keeping an eye on what we were doing. At one point he wandered uninvited into a meeting I was having with Shaun Brown.

"I don't know why we're doing this story," he began. "It's not illegal, it's just tax minimisation. I mean to say," Wilson continued, "there's a lot more people out there committing GST frauds, and we don't do stories about them."

"We do actually," Brown interjected. "I can think of several we've covered."

"Yes, but I mean – how much was this? $800,000?"

"More than two million, actually," I corrected Wilson.

"Eight hundred thousand," he said, ignoring me, "it's nothing."

"Actually Graeme," said Shaun, "it's fraud. That's what our experts say, and that's why we're doing the story. It's the same law for everyone in this country."

How dare he come down here and describe what our lawyers were calling an apparently criminal enterprise as harmless "tax minimisation"? I seethed. Occasionally Wilson would pull me aside in the corridor to make similar sarcastic comments about how wrong we were.

There were other diversions as well. Approaches were made by people claiming to represent one of the world's largest movie studios, offering air tickets and accommodation in Australia for a meeting to discuss whether I would be prepared to sell them the rights to Project X and its follow-ups.

One of the studio's executives – so I was told – a regular traveller to

Australia, had happened to see the *Four Corners* documentary on Fay Richwhite, the BNZ and the America's Cup challenge. He'd caught up with the international gossip over Christmas about our court case and the fraud allegations, and felt it had the makings of something bigger.

Despite my pointing out that TVNZ had the rights to the already-completed Project X, the studio was insistent on at least having preliminary discussions with me to see if there was any common ground. Recognising my inability to speak in New Zealand because of the injunction, they felt Australia would be a suitable mid-point to rendezvous.

I was also made aware that they had obtained a bootleg copy of the documentary that had been pulled off air on December 20, 1993. Somehow that didn't surprise me. The video had become an underground cult classic within TVNZ and its immediate circle of interest, despite the injunction.

The studio's representatives got as far as setting travel dates and ordering tickets, but due to a combination of logistical hassles and my feeling that the story could still be told on TVNZ, I pulled out with two days to spare.

The cynical paranoid within me half felt it might be a bizarre plot to knock me off out of the country or perhaps even a ploy by European Pacific to get me to breach the injunction, my quintessentially optimistic side told me I was overreacting and missing a shot at a major opportunity. The realist told me there was no great hurry – Project X would be around for some time to come.

Instead, for myself and the project team, it was once more back to the beach – to Rarotonga again to re-shoot the pieces to camera. This time we would stay for the leisurely period of nearly a week, and instead of Michael Wilson, Carol Hirschfeld would accompany us to the azure tropical location.

Climbing on an aircraft with Hirschfeld is a challenging experience at any time, let alone when it's an Air New Zealand jet. Not only is she one of the most well recognised faces on NZ television, she also presents Air New Zealand's inflight video programme, *Blue Pacific*. On both previous trips to Rarotonga we'd failed to escape Carol's presence as she lectured us from the jumbo's video screen.

Now we were travelling with the star herself, and it didn't take long for passengers and flight crew to twig that the woman on the screen was the same as the woman in the seat beside us. While it provoked the occasional stare, the upside was extra attention from the flight crew and free bubbly for the TVNZ contingent.

"Keep this up and we'll bring you along more often," joked Day.

"Not you again?," the Edgewater's genial manager, Albert Numanga, gasped in disbelief as we checked in for the third time. Just as I expected, it was quickly followed by the inevitable question.

"Just what are you really doing here?"

I smiled enigmatically. *"You know, one of these days I might even tell you. Maybe."*

While we were in the Cooks, another storm broke over the heads of Graeme Wilson and Brent Harman, in the form of an article by Jenni

McManus in the *Independent* revealing some of the behind-the-scenes drama from the previous month.

"The programme had been due to run on Sunday 19 December, but was rescheduled for the following night's Primetime slot. About 20 minutes before it was due to go to air it was pulled – apparently on the orders of TVNZ Chief Executive Brent Harman.

"Sources outside TVNZ this week told the Independent the production team working on the programme had made a conscious decision not to approach European Pacific for comment before the programme went to air, thinking EPI would seek – and most likely obtain – a High Court injunction.

"But they were overridden by the TVNZ hierarchy, which insisted EPI associates David Richwhite, Peter Travers, Paul Collins, and David Lloyd be contacted. This provoked the not-unexpected move by EPI on 21/22 December to muzzle TVNZ.

"Nobody connected with the programme or TVNZ was prepared to comment yesterday on any matter connected with so-called 'Project X'."

The newspaper also reported being threatened by EP's lawyers if it reported the fraud allegations made by Julian Miles QC in the December hearing. Despite the fact the allegations were made in open court and protected by privilege, solicitor David Hurd from Rudd Watts and Stone warned the paper the claims were "grossly defamatory".

"Our clients will not hesitate to exercise their legal remedies in respect of any repetition of these defamatory allegations," he thundered.

Empty threats. There was nothing EP could do to stop the *Independent* from reporting claims made in court, and no legal remedies that could change the situation. It was clear however that European Pacific realised the extremely dangerous significance of Miles' comments, and was trying to limit that damage by threatening the media.

At TVNZ meanwhile, the report of the censoring of the programme went down like a bucket of manure with management. Nobody for a moment bought the clumsy phrase "sources outside TVNZ". The heat was on to stop the leaks and stop the bosses' embarrassment. While I would have liked to claim credit for the latest instalment it wasn't actually my doing, although I had a fair idea who might have been responsible.

Thankfully I wasn't around to endure the inquisition. Instead we were sipping cocktails by the pool, watching native spear fishermen stalk the coral reef in the distance, striking out every so often as a glint of silver appeared in the boiling surf. As the sun crept lower they became dark silhouettes on a golden sea.

We completed all our filming requirements with a day and a half to spare, the only delay had come half way through when we were supposed to be doing some dawn shooting. The previous night we'd dined at one of the island's many restaurants and, arriving back at the hotel around midnight, sat outside Carol's unit in the balmy tropical night air for a quick drink before turning in.

Unfortunately Carol, who loved gin, had not had a lot of experience at actually mixing gin and tonics herself. A little heavy handed, three quarters of my tall glass turned out to be gin and one quarter tonic. On top of everything else we'd drunk that night, it was a killer.

When the alarm on my watch went off at 4:00am, the first step out of bed saw me practically collapse on the floor. This did not feel good. After being violently ill a couple of times, I felt sufficiently better to proceed out to the car where the others were waiting. Walking past the sickly pong of the hotel's sewage tanks did not help however, nor did the harsh judder of the Suzuki jeep as it discovered every pothole and every tight corner on the road to our location.

By the time we got there, the sun was just rising – perfect light to film in. Unfortunately, even the gentle dawn rays couldn't enhance my decidedly green appearance. We could have been there all morning trying to get it right, but thankfully God smiled on me: the clouds opened and it bucketed down.

Filming for the day was abandoned, we all retreated to our rooms to recover. Never again, I swore as I sat under a palm tree during the rain later on, never again will I let Hirschfeld mix so much as a glass of water for me.

I could pretend that we spent our time off like coiled springs, staking out known European Pacific associates, but I'd be lying. Instead we sunbathed, shopped, snorkelled and windsurfed.

We also had the opportunity to attend the Cook Islands gala premiere of *The Firm*, the movie of the book by John Grisham. There was something comically ironical about hearing people in the crowd talking in hushed tones about a *Frontline* team on the island apparently investigating European Pacific – a tax haven bank with more lawyers on staff than bankers – and comparing it to the movie. Chuckling quietly to myself I remembered the approach from the movie studio. Yep, truth can definitely sometimes be stranger than fiction.

CHAPTER 19

Blood and Feathers

*"Mitch, we've had trouble with the FBI, as well as the IRS. It's been
going on for a number of years. Some of our clients are high rollers –
wealthy individuals who make millions, spend millions and expect to
pay little or no taxes. They pay us thousands of dollars to legally
avoid taxes. We have a reputation for being very aggressive, and
we don't mind taking chances if our clients instruct us to."*
– JOHN GRISHAM, THE FIRM, 1991

THE TRICKIEST THING ABOUT the whole European Pacific investigation was
working out which party was the organ grinder and which were his
monkeys. Of one thing we could certainly be sure – the lawfirm Rudd Watts
and Stone was a definite contender for the simian category.

While RWS was officially EP's legal agent in all of the injunction
proceedings, it appeared they were not pulling the strings. In fact it became
clear that not even European Pacific could be said to be pulling the strings
totally; someone else was in the background winding up EP and Rudd Watts
staff and setting them loose like the battery powered toys in a Duracell
commercial. Rudd Watts had sent our own lawyers at Simpson Grierson a
draft document that they probably hadn't intended to disclose. It showed
that after months of inaction, European Pacific had contacted Rudd Watts
on November 26, 1993. The faxes flew almost daily for a couple of weeks
and then, on December 7, Rudd Watts began liaising with big lawfirm
Russell McVeagh McKenzie Bartleet and Co. It was the first of many faxes
between both firms on the case.

This correspondence was in relation to European Pacific's legal action
against TVNZ, so the flow-on was obviously that Russell McVeagh had more
than a passing interest in the case. The same document also disclosed
correspondence between Rudd Watts and Fay Richwhite.

It was probably no co-incidence that a senior Russell McVeagh lawyer,
Mark Gavin, soon to be made a partner in the firm, sat in on the EP/TVNZ
hearings from the back of the courtroom. * So closely involved was Mark in
the legal discussions each day that I mistakenly assumed he was a European
Pacific staff member advising the company's lawyers.

Our arrival back from the third foray up to the Cooks coincided with the

---

* In testimony to the Commission of Inquiry, IRD's Chief Audit Adviser, John Nash,
recounted a discussion he'd had with former European Pacific executive, Anthony
McCullagh, about EP's tax and banking transactions. *"Mr McCullagh also emphasised the
point that actions were taken with the benefit of advice – both legal and accounting advice –
whether it be Russell McVeagh or Peat Marwick was regularly sought."*

re-opening of the injunction hearings on January 25th, followed by two more days in court the following week on the 2nd and 3rd of February. Dropping my suitcase at work, I drove down to the High Court at breakneck speed. This was something I didn't intend to miss in any way, shape or form.

After the fraud allegations made during December's hearing, we'd attracted a full press gallery this time. European Pacific had wheeled in their own hired legal gun, Richard Craddock QC, to contend with the firepower from Miles and the Simpson Grierson team.

Craddock and Miles promptly unsheathed their claws – Craddock demanding that the Court order TVNZ and Wishart – as second defendant – to cough up not only the documents, but also to disclose where we got them and who we'd spoken to in the course of the investigation.

These are the kinds of submissions that strike a chill into the heart of any investigative journalist. The rule about not disclosing sources is drummed into every reporter, even on pain of going to jail for contempt of court. I had told our lawyers as much.

"You realise," I explained, *"that if this judge orders me to come up with that information I will refuse?"* Helen Wild had looked at me nervously. To lawyers, such thoughts – let alone actions – are anathema. They too have a code of ethics drummed into them – the cynical might suggest drummed out of them – at an early stage of their careers, and the rule is that you always obey the judge, obey the rule of law.

Many legal beagles ignore this of course, which is one of the reasons that lawyers and accountants are the most well represented professions in New Zealand prisons. For all of the attempts by politicians and other professional groups to deride the media in the public estimation, I know of no journalists jailed in recent New Zealand history for any criminal offences. That's not to say there haven't been any, but I am certainly not aware of them. On the other hand, even Doctors come higher on the criminal or unethical conduct scale than journalists.

For all of the public bleating about the media, these are points people should ponder before putting mouth into gear. The downside to this altruistic and noble calling of mine (now I really am being sarcastic) is this need to protect one's sources of information, even if it means being imprisoned.

One or two nights, even a couple of weeks, I could handle, but when it's contempt of court the judge can place you there as long as he or she likes. Worse, they can also impose fines, sometimes up to a thousand dollars a day for non-compliance with a court order.

What really worried me was the knowledge that I definitely was not flavour of the month on the seventh floor. Not only would Wilson and Harman probably crack open a magnum of champagne to celebrate my incarceration, but they'd be highly unlikely to fork out dollars in support of my ethical wish to hold my tongue.

Hell, for all I knew they'd probably dock my pay for failing to turn up to work each morning!

"Don't be so despondent Mr Wishart," Director of News Paul Norris had chortled, *"A few days in the clink never did any journalist's career any harm. I might even join you in the cells."*

"Wouldn't that be classed as cruel and unusual punishment in terms of United Nations conventions?," one of the X-file team had joked in the corridor outside later, *"having to do time with Norris?"*

It was a rare moment of mirth, but Helen Wild thankfully didn't bring such hilarity into the legal process. *"If that's how you want to play it,"* she reassured, *"then obviously we're going to have to do our best to stop you from ever having to cross that bridge."*

In a cold courtroom, the dungeons dating back to the 1860's only a few metres below me, her words no longer had quite the zing of confidence about them that they'd had a few days earlier. Craddock was making what to me seemed a powerful case to Justice Robertson to have me hanged, drawn, quartered and fed to a herd of carnivorous piglets. Hell, after Craddock's pleadings, even I wanted myself punished for being such a despicable, devious, horrible little television reporter. And then Craddock QC tripped up, a victim of his own eloquence.

"You're not suggesting this hearsay stuff has any evidential value?," Justice Robertson interjected at one point as Craddock was trying to paint a particularly large conspiracy theory with me in the middle of it. Describing some of the QC's submissions as *"conjecture"* and *"innuendo"*, Justice Robertson then began attacking Craddock over the standard of the affidavits presented by European Pacific to support its claims.

"I'm very surprised about the tone and attitude in these documents . . . These things may be lawyers' submissions at most, but they are not affidavits."

In developing his argument against our investigations, Craddock went so far as to suggest that no one, not even the Courts and certainly not the media, could call into question taxation matters because of the strong secrecy provisions contained in tax law and Craddock's belief that only the Commissioner of Inland Revenue was empowered to investigate.

"The news media is not an appropriate place for determining tax liability." Such apparent arrogance did not go down well with the Court.

"Is that really a sustainable argument, Mr Craddock?" Justice Robertson interrupted, before drawing comparisons with the effect on taxpayers' money of recent controversial overspending at an air force base.

"It's clearly a public affair."

Sensing an opportunity, Julian Miles stirred the pot some more – pointing out how European Pacific's carefully designed schemes had been set up to *"defraud"* taxpayers in New Zealand and Japan, and that such information must be broadcast in the *"public interest"*.

"It's public interest because we're dealing with New Zealand companies, the European Pacific group, the shareholders were three major public institutions, the directors included three prominent New Zealand directors, the Cook Islands are linked closely to New Zealand constitutionally and were set up as a tax haven where companies – New Zealand, Australian or Japanese – can make massive

profits by not paying tax to the proper authorities.

"*Every New Zealand tax payer has an interest because they have been defrauded,*" he added sternly, just in case anyone in the courtroom had missed the point. "*If we can establish evasion of this extent took place, that destroys confidentiality. If the JIF transactions went ahead, and from the documents it seems they did, then they were still going up to February this year.*"

The Judge was also far from impressed at the 15-month delay in bringing to a conclusion the interim injunctions against the business press, pointing out Justice Henry's earlier recommendation for a speedy resolution of the problem. "*You are gagging the world,*" he opined from the bench, describing the case as a "*running sore*". Yeah, sock it to 'em Judge, I was mouthing from my position in the rear of the Courtroom.

One of the other factors in Craddock's submissions that annoyed me – and it was a claim that kept coming up over the months, even from politicians – was that we were talking about events that had happened back in 1988/89, water under the bridge.

In fact the JIF deals in particular had been set down to last at least five years, one of them, the Fuji deal, may have lasted right up to the start of 1995.* Miles seized on the opening to push our case for an urgent resolution of the injunction.

"*There's a great deal more immediacy to these transactions than my friend [Craddock] has suggested.*"

As *NBR* journalist David McEwen later noted, "*He [Miles] also disagreed with Mr Craddock's suggestion that this hearing was similar to the one in which an interim injunction was awarded.*

"*The difference was that TVNZ had presented documents which allowed the court to determine the likelihood of wrong doing having been committed. He was confident they did and said it was 'distinctly probable' TVNZ would succeed if the dispute went to trial. It was also likely that European Pacific had been involved in 'a massive number of similar transactions'.*"

One of the curious factors about the case was European Pacific's desperate wish to prevent any details emerging at all of the alleged frauds at the heart of Magnum and JIF.

Craddock tried to get the judge to ban publication not just of actual evidence, but also of Miles' submissions to the bench. The TVNZ QC argued forcefully against such draconian secrecy measures, reminding that even at the height of attempts by the British Government to ban publication of *Spycatcher* by former MI5 agent Peter Wright – even then, in matters involving national security, no one had suggested that lawyers' submissions be kept secret as well.

"*There is already the perception, rightly or wrongly, that there have been cover-*

---

* Subsequently confirmed at the Commission of Inquiry, the JIF deals did go ahead and were still going when our documentary finally went to air. European Pacific's share, in the 1993 year, was nearly US$6 million – making up 94% of EPBC's total annual income.

ups. *The court's protection of privacy covers only legitimate transactions. Going beyond that would mean the court almost becoming an accessory to the wrongdoing till it's finally brought to the light of day,"* he warned.

In truth, neither Julian nor I had any wish to see the actual evidence published at this early stage. It was bad enough alerting the extremely competitive business papers to exactly what had taken place in the winebox, without giving them free rein to publish as well and make our story redundant. Yet we had a small dilemma. We didn't want to be seen arguing publicly for suppression of the evidence – such a stance would be seen as hypocritical when we were also arguing that such evidence should not be suppressed because of its immense public interest.

."Don't fret," I remember saying at one strategy session, *"I think we can safely rely on European Pacific to go for blanket suppression on that score. If we put up a token resistance we'll be OK."* So, whilst keeping the exact fraud mechanism out of the papers, we would use Miles' submissions to publicise the fact that fraud had definitely taken place.

Carefully treading the middle ground, Justice Robertson accepted that the injunction would be pointless if full details of the evidence were published in reports of the court proceedings, but he also took on board Julian's comments and refused to suppress general submissions from the lawyers.

Julian also took a whack at the mysterious owners of European Pacific. We'd been unable through our inquiries to find out who owned the secret trust behind the group now, and we'd asked the court to order European Pacific to come clean on its ownership. After all, we had a right to know who was really taking action against us.

Miles referred in court to the *"shadowy nature"* of the plaintiffs.

"I don't think I've ever been involved with a case where the plaintiffs have been as anonymous. We don't know their shareholders, their capital, directors or assets and liabilities. We don't even know their registered office."

All of this was lapped up by an eager press contingent.

As Miles would later tell *Metro* magazine, that he never during the course of six months of legal hearings discovered the true ownership of EP was *"unique, in my experience"*.

Not everything was going our way, however. Late in the piece Craddock scored a direct hit on TVNZ, in Robertson's eyes at least. Craddock, whose style of delivery on this particular day could have been bottled and sold as a cure for insomnia, had been meandering through his case for what seemed like hours on the final afternoon. It was one of those scorching February days where events in the courtroom recede in the consciousness as one thinks what one would rather be doing.

I was jolted out of my summery complacency by the words *"contempt of court"* being cast in my general direction by Craddock, who'd turned to look at me as he said it. The thrust of his argument was that by daring to investigate at all, Television New Zealand and I had deliberately acted in breach of the November 1992 injunction against *NBR* and the *Independent*.

To my mind his claim had little merit. For a start, that injunction applied specifically to the winebox, and my inquiries had been centred on JIF, a series of transactions I'd been led to believe weren't in the winebox. I was as surprised as anyone else to find out they were in there.

I knew that my document source had not been injuncted, so had felt unrestrained in taking delivery of a set and quietly working on them. From a legal point of view, discussing my findings with the European Pacific staff involved could hardly be said to be publishing or further disseminating the information – after all, what could I as a mere journalist add to the knowledge of someone who'd actually worked on the schemes?

Even so, contempt of court or otherwise, I could not believe that the intention of the original injunction was to stifle all investigation of what was possibly a criminal matter. If that was the intention, how could the two papers have ever broken free of the injunction, prevented from ever contacting experts who could show them where the deals were illegal?

If it was good enough for the police to ignore the injunction in the Citibank case, it was good enough for us to keep digging on European Pacific. Justice Robertson, however, didn't see it in the same way. The contempt issue could become crucial to the entire case, he warned. Even if TVNZ could show the documents were *"iniquitous"*, our case could be thrown out if our evidence was illegally obtained – ie via a breach of the first injunction. It would be equivalent to the police case against a drug dealer or murderer being thrown out because of an illegal wire-tap or some other procedural glitch.

Saving his criticisms for his interim decision, however, he made no final ruling on the contempt issue, saying it should be resolved only after the more substantive issue of iniquity had been decided. Turning then to my own *bête noire* – disclosure of source – the Judge stated that while he had no doubt he could make such an order, compelling me to cough up the names of all my "deepthroats", the free and unimpeded flow of information between journalists and the public was an *"important and desirable attribute"* in a democracy. Interference in that relationship should come only if it is essential and crucial to the case.

It all came down to this moment. My entire career could be destroyed by this moment. Depending on how Justice Robertson structured his next deliberation, I could be wearing striped pyjamas to bed tonight.

The essence of the present case, the Judge continued, was a claim by European Pacific that its documents were confidential, and a counter-claim by TVNZ that they contained evidence of fraud, thereby removing the right to confidentiality. In that context, he posed, was European Pacific's desire to know my sources crucial to determining the heart of the matter? The present proceedings, he concluded, came *"nowhere near it"*.

Elation, not blood, flowed through my veins for the next few seconds. That moment had been make or break for me. The look of disgust on the faces of the bank's representatives was worth at least a million dollars. I just grinned happily back.

It wasn't over yet, however. Still to come was the big one. We'd placed the documentation and expert testimony before the judge. Would he be willing to throw off the injunction and let us publish on the basis of iniquity? In short, no. Preferring the more cautious route, Justice Robertson decided the issues should be thoroughly thrashed out at a full trial, where both sides would have plenty of time to assemble expert witnesses and build their cases. He did however put European Pacific on notice. He would grant them an injunction today, but it would expire on April 30, and would probably not be renewed. It was up to the merchant bank to bring the matter to trial within that time, or risk losing the injunction altogether. Disappointed but not surprised, we slowly filed out of the court complex.

In an office across town, Serious Fraud Office director Charles Sturt was quietly considering his next action. The injunction had given him an opening that he'd been waiting for. The first we knew of it was the *National Business Review* the following morning, February 4th.

"SFO POISED TO SEIZE TAX FRAUD FILE," bawled the front page headline. *"The Serious Fraud Office is poised to swoop on Television New Zealand demanding it hand over confidential European Pacific Group documents detailing an alleged Japanese withholding tax fraud.*

"SFO director Charles Sturt yesterday made clear his office was carrying out a 'watching brief' as two European Pacific companies tried to get an interim injunction preventing TVNZ from showing a special Frontline programme detailing the alleged fraud."

Throwing the paper down on Norris' office coffee table with a satisfying thud, I felt that old familiar distrust welling up within me again.

"This is ridiculous. When these turkeys last had the winebox they didn't want to investigate it, they kept trying to give it back to European Pacific. I'll bet you the SFO will give the documents a clean bill of health again and be subpoenaed on EP's behalf at the April trial. With the SFO testifying, there's no way we'll kick the injunction over."

Paul Norris had foreseen a similar scenario, but wanted clarification on the SFO's role in the saga to date. Specifically, its part in the winebox affair had begun in the latter half of 1991, when entrepreneur Stephen Lunn bumped into an old colleague now working for the SFO, John Hicks. The upshot was that Lunn went back with Hicks to meet Sturt, and the item on the agenda, Lunn later told *Metro*, was the BNZ.

"This was six months before it all blew up. He asked whether I'd seen any documents regarding the BNZ and I replied that I had. He asked if I could get hold of them and I said he could only get them if he paid, that the people who had them were in the business of buying and selling."

Chas Sturt, on the other hand, told *Metro* that Lunn was trying to sell the documents. In a statement to the magazine the SFO director said he wanted to meet Lunn after hearing claims that Lunn was *"endeavouring to sell documents alleging fraud by people involved in the BNZ."*

According to Sturt, the asking price had started at $100,000 and dropped to $10,000.

"*If he says that,*" Lunn snarled to *Metro*, "*I'll sue him.*"

The dapper financier claims he never tried to sell the documents to the SFO, merely pointed the office in the direction of people who were trying to sell them, in the United States. The SFO's influence didn't extend to the US, and if Sturt wanted the papers he'd need to fork out the bikkies. There was a later meeting between the two men, but again nothing eventuated.

The next development had been the one I was partially responsible for, the October 1992 meeting with Lunn and Dickie that was followed the next day by the first injunction papers, delivered by helicopter, and a telephoned death threat, and Lunn and Dickie the next morning dropping the winebox in Sturt's lap. Sturt, by all accounts, was furious.

"*He took real exception,*" Lunn revealed to the magazine. "*He thought I'd had them when he interviewed me. Within two days he was on the phone trying to give them back. His sidekick rang to say that after assessing the documents the SFO considered that they were of no interest and asked for consent to give them back to EPI. My lawyer doubted whether it had been possible to have examined the documents so quickly.*"

Both Lunn and Dickie had been stunned at the request for permission to give the documents to European Pacific – in Lunn's words "*to the accused*" – and instead they wrote a letter to Sturt.

"*I confirm that I will not authorise you to deliver these documents to the plaintiffs or their solicitors. In my view they are documents which require careful consideration by law enforcement agencies and the Inland Revenue Department.*"

The letter was faxed to Sturt on November 5th, seven days after the documents had been dropped off.

"*Sturt threw a tantrum at that,*" *Metro* later quoted Lunn. "*He seems to be upset that the press got it [the winebox] before he did. He then tried to discredit me by telling journalists that I'd offered to sell him the documents.*"

For his part, a clearly "*irked*" Serious Fraud Office director replied that if Lunn "*had any sincere intention of having these documents examined by the Serious Fraud Office, IRD or other statutory body, he wouldn't have waited more than 18 months before producing them.*"

"*Lunn is right,*" wrote journalist Jan Corbett, "*that the SFO sought his permission to return the documents to EPI the day after it had received them. What Lunn didn't know was that each page had been photocopied. Sturt had issued specific instructions that Lunn wasn't to be told that, a move he 'considered necessary given that he had not been completely forthright with me.'* "

What was driving Sturt? It had, after all, been the SFO that had been asking Lunn for the documents for 18 months. If Sturt was so keen to get hold of them why didn't he simply swallow his pride and get on with it?

European Pacific had asked the High Court to order the business papers to hand over their boxes, and the court had refused to make that order. Why on earth would Sturt seek to give them to EPI, especially in the face of an ongoing court hearing to determine who had the rights to the box? Sturt's claims to *Metro* make even less sense when placed alongside the correspondence between his office and Lunn in November 1992.

"Notwithstanding our earlier communication to you seeking your authority to deliver the documents to the plaintiffs," wrote John Hicks, *"the director is of the view that as these documents are said to be copies of what are alleged to be stolen documents, they will be retained by this office meantime.*

"For your information, we are in the interim still evaluating the documents and the director will no doubt deal with them as he deems appropriate."

Forbidden from physically giving the documents to EPI's lawyers, the SFO took the next best option, letting them go through them in the SFO office, just to see what was there. It was the first time European Pacific had gained access to the winebox in the form it had been given to the media. It was a priceless opportunity for the merchant bank, handed to them on a silver plate by a Government law enforcement agency.

Once again, I had visions of the Citibank episode before it. In both cases, law enforcement agencies had given plaintiffs in civil litigation access to documents that the High Court had refused to give them access to in the interim.

Lunn's lawyer, Gary Judd, fired off another letter to Sturt the next day, November 6, 1992.

"Mr Hicks twice told Mr Lunn that he should assume that the SFO had no further interest in the documents and requested Mr Lunn's authority to give the letters to the plaintiffs or their solicitors.

"Because Mr Lunn would be most concerned if that were to happen without them first being made available to the Inland Revenue Department, he directed you to deliver them to the Inland Revenue Department.

"Mr Lunn is aware that you have allowed the plaintiffs' representatives to inspect the documents. If the documents are not to be delivered to the Inland Revenue Department then, in Mr Lunn's view, they must at the very least be made available for inspection by Inland Revenue Department officers, and he invites you to adopt that course."

It was only a few days later, on November 9, 1992, that Justice Henry formalised the existing interim injunction against Lunn and the business papers, and Charles Sturt seized on it as a chance to throw another punch at Lunn.

In a letter to Judd, Sturt claimed the injunction might make it impossible for him to give copies of the documents to Inland Revenue. It seemed the only place the Serious Fraud Office wanted to put the winebox was back in European Pacific's clutches. Gary Judd, not to be outdone, got hold of Justice Henry for clarification on the terms of the injunction. Could the SFO provide copies to other investigating agencies? Yes, replied Justice Henry, the injunction applies only to the named parties.

Inland Revenue did, eventually, get a box. The SFO and European Pacific continued to jointly pressure Lunn into giving the box back to EP which, co-incidentally, they finally achieved on December 22, 1993.

The SFO managed to hand the winebox over to European Pacific on the very same day the company was trying to injunct Television New Zealand in the High Court. I said as much to Norris.

"They've blown their chips as far as I'm concerned. The SFO didn't even bother turning up to our court hearings to listen to the evidence.* It's only been all over the papers for a month! The entire bloody media was there, even Winston Peters had someone there, but not the SFO. Why now, all of a sudden, are they interested?"

The SFO, I felt, had as much likelihood of effectively investigating our winebox as I had of going home and digging up the back garden in search of elephant bones. It wasn't going to happen.

Still, this was only a newspaper report that the SFO was planning to act. It hadn't happened yet. I spent the next two days photocopying files furiously and shifting them to safe locations. My worst nightmare was having the SFO raid home or office and taking away all of our research material. If they had wanted to stop the investigation dead in its tracks, that would have been the way to do it. The raid, when it came, was low key. Serious Fraud Office investigator Gib Beattie and an associate turned up on TVNZ's doorstep on the afternoon of February 9, 1994.

"There's two policemen here from the fraud squad wanting to speak to you, Mr Wishart," came the phone call from TVNZ security at Level 3.

I must admit, this threw me slightly. For a moment I wondered what on earth I'd done to attract the attention of the police fraud squad. Somehow I didn't think failing to display a current Warrant of Fitness certificate on my car qualified as a criminal matter. On reaching the reception desk, however, all became clear. Serious Fraud Office, not police.

"We require your attendance at the Serious Fraud Office tomorrow afternoon at 4:30, and bring with you the documents we're asking for," said Beattie.

He then, very pleasantly, directed my attention to the serious penalties for seriously pissing off the SFO. These included a 12-month jail term or $15,000 fine for "giving an answer to any question or producing any document knowing that it is false or misleading in a material particular or being reckless as to whether it is so false or misleading."

For serious offenders, a 2-year jail term or $50,000 fine applies if one destroys, alters or conceals any document or sends it out of New Zealand. It was like a visit from the mortician. On reading the warrant, however, a wave of relief washed over me.

"This isn't so bad," I told Norris, "they only want my High Court affidavit and attached exhibits. They're not seeking all our documentation and notes at all."

"I wouldn't speak too soon if I were you. They've served a warrant on Brent Harman as well, and in that one they specify everything – winebox, notes, videotapes – the works," warned Paul.

---

* Witness A testified to the Davison Commission in August 1995 that because of his own high profile in the case, he had been expecting an interrogation from New Zealand authorities. "I have never been approached by the Inland Revenue Department or the Serious Fraud Office. After the publicity I thought the Serious Fraud Office would interview me, but they did not."

Willie Akel, the Simpson Grierson partner in charge of our case, was equally fired up about it, and decided to call the SFO's bluff. The injunction awarded against us prevented us from disseminating, copying, publishing or in any way making use of the information contained in the European Pacific documents. That meant if we gave them to the SFO we'd be in breach of a High Court injunction. He sent a letter to the SFO advising of the impasse. Sturt's public response was cold.

"Some of the parties have resisted producing the documents on the Court file including affidavits and exhibits which I sought under my powers . . . I believe that in the interests of justice my powers outweigh the injunction."

In another statement Sturt talked of TVNZ and myself relying on the injunction in a bid *"to refuse to obey the Notices"* issued. "Refuse to obey" I took as a slightly "loaded" comment.

To add to this public slap in the face to the SFO's authority from TVNZ, Winston Peters took the opportunity to drop a load of documents, including Magnum and JIF, in the SFO's lap. In a covering letter he noted that Sturt had had the documents in his possession nearly 18 months earlier, and the MP feigned surprise that the SFO should want them again. It was already a matter of public record that the SFO had been trying to pass the winebox to European Pacific within a day of receiving it from Stephen Lunn.

The *National Business Review* noted the box had been given a clean bill of health by the SFO at the time. Which begs the question, why go through the same laborious process again?

As the weeks unfolded with still no resolution to the TVNZ/SFO impasse, Sturt approached the New Zealand Solicitor-General, John McGrath, seeking clarification of his powers.* The SFO had been reportedly under the impression that it could seize the files despite the injunction.

The Solicitor-General, however, reportedly told the SFO it would need a declaratory judgement from the High Court. For the time being at least, the Serious Fraud Office couldn't place itself above the court-imposed injunction.

At TVNZ we were under no misconceptions: we knew the SFO would eventually get the documents, because the Court would approve their release. For us it was much more important to make sure the proper protocols and procedures were followed.

Sure enough, the Court agreed, although Sturt accepted the legal to-ings and fro-ings with bad grace. He had stated that his deference to the High Court was only a *"courtesy"* as he continued to believe his powers under statute were superior.

---

* The Serious Fraud Office Director raised hackles later in 1994 when called before a Parliamentary Select Committee investigating irregularities at an Air Force base. Charles Sturt refused to provide the Committee with an SFO report on the matter, citing the secrecy provisions of his Act. Senior politicians and lawyers noted that Parliament's powers overrode those of any Government agency.

In testimony to the Commission of Inquiry, Charles Sturt acknowledged that his office had never formally investigated the winebox. Upon its delivery by Lunn it was passed to John Hicks for an initial examination. Hicks went through the box cataloguing the transactions as best he could, but not re-ordering the documents to see if any of the transactions linked. His initial report to Sturt noted no serious or complex fraud.

With the Court's permission, it was over to Simpson Grierson to deliver the documents to the SFO on TVNZ's behalf. The SFO swiftly reported it had found *"nothing new"* in our documents or affidavits.

CHAPTER 20

Fanning the Flames

"Them Injuns ain't that tough!"
– Lt Col George Custer, 1876

February 4, 1994 wasn't notable just because of the sudden appearance of the SFO on the horizon: someone who'd sat in on the court hearings had written an article for *The Australian* newspaper, containing everything that had been barred from publication in New Zealand.

The first I knew of it was when a copy was faxed through to me by a contact at a major public relations company. He told me that faxes were running hot around the country with the document – the first article to go into any detail of how the alleged frauds worked. Skimming through, it wasn't hard to see why it was sought after.

"A Cook Islands-based company owned by the Bank of New Zealand, Brierley Investments and merchant bank Fay Richwhite was used by corporations to defraud the tax departments of Australia, New Zealand and Japan of hundreds of millions of dollars, the High Court in Auckland heard yesterday.

"It is alleged that EPI [European Pacific Investments] conspired with the Cook Islands Government to produce false tax credit certificates which corporate clients in Australia, New Zealand and Japan used to convince their tax departments that withholding tax had been paid in the Cook Islands. It is claimed the Cook Islands Government then returned this withholding tax to EPI, after taking its own cut."

All of this information, barring the opening paragraph, had been suppressed by Justice Robertson, but the article went further still. It named Magnum Corporation, and it named the three Japanese banks – Mitsubishi, Fuji and Sanwa. If European Pacific was worried about the financial implications of JIF being publicly exposed, this story would be its worst nightmare.

"Documents produced in court claim that BNZ lent the money to the Japanese banks by channelling it through EPI and hence through two Bermuda-based buffer companies.

"From there the money was loaned to the Japanese banks, and from there back to EPI and the BNZ. At the end of the chain, withholding tax was paid, thus enabling the Cook Islands Government to issue the allegedly bogus tax credit certificates – but this money was then split between EPI and Cook Islands officials, the court heard."

The article contained some minor factual errors, but the essence of the deals was correct. It was obviously written by one of the journalists who'd attended the hearing but, instead of a name, the byline read *"By a New Zealand correspondent"*. European Pacific staff subsequently attempted to find out who wrote it, but without immediate success.

The cat was not only out of the bag, it was scampering rapidly around the South Pacific. An election was pending in the Cook Islands and, just co-incidentally, one of the candidates was former domestic auditor Richard McDonald – a man whose name had appeared on some of the confidential cable traffic contained in the box shown to me by former EP staff member John a year earlier.

On March 2nd, McDonald addressed an election meeting in Rarotonga and read out sections of *The Australian* article to the crowd. This in itself is illegal under tough Cook Islands laws which prevent discussion of tax haven business in public. Being an election candidate, however, McDonald probably thought he would get away with it.

The former Director of Government Auditing highlighted the portions of the article dealing with the issue of false tax certificates, then revealed he'd tried to investigate a similar scam in 1987, and lost his job because of it. This tallied with our own investigation: former New Zealand Auditor-General Brian Tyler had recalled meeting a Cook Islands official *"some years ago"* who had tried to alert New Zealand about a tax certificate dodge but, without being able to discover further information, the warning was passed to the NZ IRD and filed away.

McDonald had been caught in 1987 making allegations of tax fraud – a no-no in a tax haven country. The Cook Islands Government had set up an "Inquiry" to examine some of the allegations, specifically *"to inquire and report on the collection, payment of, assessment of and any other matters relating to withholding tax that is payable to the Inland Revenue Department,"* according to the Notice of Inquiry published in Rarotonga on July 29, 1987.

The three member inquiry panel included Michael Fleming, the head of the Cook Islands Treasury Department. Our own research had shown that an "M Fleming" was later a signatory to documentation used in the fake tax certificate deals, documentation that allowed his Government to make a loss in all its dealings with European Pacific.* McDonald had been suspended pending investigation, and was himself the victim of foul play.

"I wish to inform you of a burglary," he wrote to Inquiry head Richard Chapman on October 12 1987, *"which involved documents of a highly confidential nature that do involve Government. I hold at my home a box file containing all documents relating to a Commission of Inquiry that involved myself."*

---

* Fleming testified to the Davison Commission in August 1995 that he had indeed signed the documents, but didn't realise what they were. He had been summoned to the Crown Law Office in Rarotonga to sign them – unprecedented, he said – and he acknowledged under cross examination that Cook Islands law may not have been followed in the procedure. The Cook Islands Government Property Corporation's transactional activities require an appropriation from the Cook Islands Parliament. Fleming admitted that in the Magnum deal, no appropriation had been made that would allow the paying out of two million dollars to European Pacific. He testified that the Solicitor-General, Tony Manarangi, told him verbally that an appropriation was not necessary.

It transpired that McDonald had just finished arranging his documents on the tax fraud allegations when a Mr Pomani Tangata had turned up and invited him to an impromptu barbecue. Tangata was another whose signature appeared on the European Pacific documents we were using, listed as Secretary to Cabinet and signing on behalf of the Cook Islands Government Property Corporation. When McDonald returned from the barbecue, he found some of his key documents were missing.

"The matter has been reported to the Police and my solicitors," he told Chapman, "I consider this serious as these documents, in the wrong hands, could gravely embarrass the Government. You are informed accordingly."

McDonald's problems had begun in a conversation with his Governmental colleagues. "The then Solicitor-General . . . Tony Manarangi, boasted to the then Financial Secretary and I that he had cooked up this tax certificate deal. The whole thing stank of fraud."

The auditor flew to New Zealand to meet Brian Tyler and then on to Canberra to discuss the matter directly with Australian revenue authorities. According to McDonald, the Australians knew the fake certificates were in circulation but hadn't seen any.*

In a letter later released to the New Zealand Commission of Inquiry into the winebox, McDonald alleged that the 1987 fake tax certificates had been prepared for Aussie billionaire Alan Bond's companies, the man who wrested the America's Cup yachting trophy from the US in 1983. When McDonald arrived back in the Cook Islands word leaked out, and the establishment took its revenge. He was lambasted in the Cook Islands Parliament by Minister of Police Norman George. George accused him of selling the country's secrets.

"What kind of person would do this so the poor people of the country will miss out on millions of dollars of withholding tax?"

This was the same Norman George who, after questioning what kind of man would let the "poor people of the country miss out on millions of dollars in withholding tax," was a signatory to documents that in 1988 allowed the Cook Islands Government Property Corporation to make a loss in its dealings with European Pacific, roughly equivalent to the amount of tax paid earlier in the day by EP.

As a result of those schemes, millions of dollars due to the people of the Cook Islands appeared to have been illegally handed out to big business by Cook Islands politicians and civil servants.

Of course, the 1987 "inquiry" in the Cook Islands found no evidence of

---

* Michael Fleming testified to the Davison Commission that Australia had been a major victim of a direct covert attack by the Cook Islands Government. The Cooks administration was earning a million dollars a month in a withholding tax rort on the Australian Revenue. The scam would have provided about a third of the Cooks annual $35 million budget, so when Australia cracked down on it in July 1987, the Cooks found its finances were sorely stretched. Fleming said he believed this is what Richard McDonald may have been referring to.

wrongdoing, and unfortunately citizens in Westminster-style democracies tend to have blinding faith in the outcomes of Inquiries of any kind.

My own experience working as a Cabinet press secretary had shown me that many politicians and their staff will have no qualms about either lying or sweeping something under the carpet, and the best way of doing that is to have some kind of tame investigation. What never fails to amaze me is how the New Zealand media falls for it. Radio news is among the worst offenders – while there are some notable exceptions, many radio journalists have forgotten that they're there to find the truth, and have simply atrophied to the point where they are stenographers with microphones, taking dictation from whoever shouts the loudest. Reporting it might be, journalism it certainly is not. If all we do is accept at face value, without genuine attempt to verify or inquire into, the glib statements of politicians, business leaders or officials, then we're play-acting and even more stupid than the PR companies and political spin doctors already think we are.

Every time a Minister of the Crown announces he or she's personally ordered an inquiry into something that they've been getting a roasting over, you can usually bet next year's salary that the outcome is a foregone conclusion. It's the favourite method of deflecting attention or taking the heat out of a situation, and it's a trusty weapon in the arsenal of the Ministerial press secretary when it comes to advice.

There's a civil service maxim on "inquiries" adhered to fervently by Governments everywhere: Never ask a question that you don't already know the answer to. The New Zealand Government had been hoping the winebox inquiry would be a tame one as well, but proponents of a real investigation outsmarted them and hijacked it. I am, perhaps, getting ahead of myself however. In March 1994 the New Zealand authorities were steadfastly resisting any inquiry of any kind into the alleged frauds outlined in *Frontline*'s court case.

Richard McDonald's observations were being carried around the world on the *Agence France Presse* wire network. *"I can't understand how it [the tax certificate scam] succeeded, because after my investigation the tax authorities should have been thoroughly aware in Australia and New Zealand of the dubious nature of tax certificates from here."*

After all these years, and despite all the evidence, Cook Islands authorities were still playing dumb. Collector of Inland Revenue, Jim Ditchburn, told the daily *Cook Islands News* he was unaware of the latest allegations until he read about them in the Australian papers.

"I would not know, but I am pretty sure false certificates were not issued from my office," he claimed. Any tax money that came in was received in a *"normal fashion"* and, he reassured Cook Islanders, his department did not repay money back out, unless a citizen's tax return showed they had overpaid their tax for the year. Jim Ditchburn didn't know that we had his name on one of the allegedly false certificates.

The Cook Islands Government would, in March 1995, table a report it had commissioned from Deloittes which cleared it of any wrongdoing in the

Magnum transaction. Deloittes' Sydney office said that as the tax certificates were genuine, not forgeries, no crimes had been committed in the Cooks.

The *Agence France Presse* report was carried in a number of countries, including New Zealand, where the New Zealand *Herald* ran the story in its first edition on Saturday March 5. Mysteriously, and without explanation, the report vanished from subsequent editions and, like the article from *The Australian* a month earlier, became a cult "collectors' classic".

Editorially, the *Herald* is a conservative paper whose establishment owners mix in similar social circles to many of those we were accusing. The paper would later lambast the allegations of tax fraud made by *Frontline* and Winston Peters as misrepresentation of legitimate, legal, tax avoidance; our claims the result of *"envy"*. Ironically, faced in late-1994 with a hostile buy-in by Brierley Investments, the paper's owners made a number of stinging public attacks on the would be suitor, including a snide dig at its lack of ethics in the taxpaying arena. I guess it all depends on where you're standing at the time.

Back in court, meanwhile, the main combatants were squaring off again. European Pacific gave notice it was going to the Court of Appeal to force both the TV network and myself to reveal our sources. The April 30 deadline set down in February had already been extended to May 23rd – the first opportunity in the Court's diary for a two week trial.

On Wednesday March 16, Winston Peters let loose in Parliament. European Pacific – already under fire from both the *Independent* and the *NBR* in articles almost weekly on EP's battle against TVNZ, and starting to bleed profusely from the many wounds inflicted by the network's lawyers – now found itself under attack once again from the sanctuary of parliamentary privilege, not to mention the various bushfires raging in Australia and the Cook Islands. It was the opening skirmish in what would become the Battle of the Little Bighorn, the beginning of the end for European Pacific and the Knights of the Roundtable associated with the company. EP Managing Director David Lloyd would find himself cast in the role of Custer, and the "Injuns" were circling.

It wasn't the first time Winston Peters had spoken of European Pacific in Parliament, but it was the first speech since *Frontline* had been injuncted. This was a moment I was both looking forward to and afraid of – afraid because it was a fair bet Peters would see fit to fastrack the legal process by blowing it wide open in the House.

"*Mr Speaker,*" he began, "*I want to raise a matter that the Government of this country knows about but, despite its own international commitments, is refusing to act on.*

"*It was a concerted and planned effort on the part of high-powered tax lawyers and merchants of greed in this country, and crooked officials and politicians in the Cook Islands, to use the tax laws of both countries to enrich themselves with countless millions of dollars by raiding the tax revenues of both countries.*

"*It is done through the issue of millions of dollars of false tax certificates, secret accounts and banking secrecy laws. Put simply, the Government of the Cook*

Islands collects tax but gives it back to the favoured and malevolent few. Documents exist that show that, in just one example, a tax deal raided the New Zealand revenue for a sum in the order of $2,050,000.

"Before the tax was paid a deal was entered into, to buy and sell promissory notes, incurring a loss of $2 million. Who signed the deal? A Mr Norman George . . . and a Pomani Tangata, Secretary to the Cabinet. For a mere $50,000 they gave away $2 million in taxes due, on the face of the documents, to the Cook Islands Revenue. They allowed people who should be labelled criminals in this country to steal from the revenue of New Zealand."

Peters was enjoying himself now, teasing and toying with the tax haven operators. *"They have allowed the sort of people in this country that in another great time a former President of the United States called 'malefactors of great wealth' to raid foreign revenues under the protection of the tax and banking laws of the Cook Islands. That means that those corrupt and evil 'malefactors of great wealth' here in New Zealand can hide behind a facade of legality created by the conspiracy of silence in this Parliament and outside it. Our Government, by its persistent refusal to honour its own pledge to hold a public inquiry, is helping them to get away with it.*

"The full story of what is happening here is going to be told. The international news media have published parts of the story. The New Zealand news media, due to those malevolent few who use our court procedures to prevent publication, cannot. But I promise this country that the truth will be told. I know the names, and the names will be known to every New Zealander."

Peters ran into troubled waters when he alleged that the people responsible for the frauds might have New Zealand politicians *"in their pockets"*. Deputy Prime Minister Don McKinnon took offence, a complaint upheld by the acting Speaker of the House.

"I apologise," taunted Peters, *"but I say to the Deputy Prime Minister who found offence, that there will come a time when we will know who funded the National Party. We will know why there has been a coven of silence in this country and why there has been a conspiracy to stop full disclosure, and those days will come very soon.*

"They have sought to shut down disclosure by Television New Zealand by a series of injunctions, and that case will be heard on 23 May. Why do they want to shut it down? Because it is a one hour pictorial of criminality by big business-people.

"They are the political friends of the National Party. They have used their power and have abused it in their personal interests, for their personal greed."

The biggest sting came in the tail, however. On 16 previous occasions, going back two years, Winston Peters had been refused permission to table the winebox documents in the House. "Tabling" allows documents to be published by Parliament, cloaking them with the protection of parliamentary privilege and allowing the media to report on them without fear of being sued.

All it takes, however, to prevent documents being tabled, is an objection from just one MP. Often the objections came from a junior Government MP like Tony Ryall, a former BNZ staff member and a supporter of Prime Minister Bolger.

But on this one occasion, a strange set of circumstances intervened that would blow apart efforts to protect European Pacific. National MP Bill English questioned whether Peters had the courage to name names, instead of *"resorting to the politics of insinuation"*. Deputy Prime Minister Don McKinnon evidently chipped in with some kind of put-up-or-shut-up challenge as well, because Peters was on his feet in an instant.

"I seek leave now to table the documents supporting my speech today. They are the documents that I have sought to table 16 times in the House, and I ask for leave now because I have been challenged by the Deputy Prime Minister to do so and name them."

There was a stunned silence. Normally Deputy Prime Minister Don McKinnon, acting PM in Bolger's absence, would have been able to object. Indeed, all eyes were on him. But, perhaps because it was he himself who'd challenged Peters to show the proof, McKinnon didn't act to stop the tabling. No one was more startled than the Member for Tauranga, who'd been expecting the routine objections.

Winston Peters gulped, suddenly realising the predicament he found himself in. He was finally allowed to table his beloved winebox but, because of 16 failed prior attempts, he didn't actually have it with him.

By now the Government benches were in uproar. Sensing that the documents were not immediately accessible, Government strategists sought to set a deadline for their tabling by the end of the afternoon session, only 20 minutes away.

Peters' staff were meanwhile locked in consultation with the Clerk of the House, the official who oversees the rules of Parliament's debating chamber. How much time did they have to retrieve the documents from Auckland, 700 kilometres away, and get them tabled? The advice was reassuring. Peters had until the end of the parliamentary day to table the winebox – 10:30pm.

On advice from Brian Henry, his Auckland barrister, Peters arranged for two wineboxes to be flown to Wellington via different routes and on different airlines. It was an insurance policy, in case something happened. TV3's evening news programme actually captured a shot of the second, backup, winebox being delivered, describing the process as *"unprecedented security"*. Under the glare of television cameras from both national networks, the box was tracked from Wellington airport to Parliament by the news media.

Aladdin's Genie was now well and truly on the loose, a point both the Government and those in the European Pacific camp were acutely aware of. But he was still a young and inexperienced Genie. Perhaps there was a way to confine the creature before he discovered the enormity of his powers.
It was an issue that Wogistani authorities would devote their entire attention to over the next 24 hours.

Within hours of the tabling, European Pacific's lawyers were in contact with parliamentary officials, reportedly advising that the documents were subject to a High Court injunction and shouldn't be published. It was a brazen move, but not out of character for the merchant bank. European Pacific also issued a news release the following day.

"*Company representative, Mr David Lloyd, said that European Pacific believes that it has at all times acted within the laws of New Zealand and of any other country in which it has conducted business.*

"*Documents tabled in Parliament yesterday by Mr Peters are confidential documents stolen from European Pacific. These documents have already been the subject of close scrutiny by various investigative and regulatory bodies. The documents are also subject to existing High Court injunctions preventing their distribution, of which Mr Peters is aware.*"

But Thursday March 17 also brought with it a constitutional crisis unprecedented, according to the record keepers, in the history of Westminster democracy. Once tabled, the Speaker, Peter Tapsell, refused to allow them to be published.

On the grounds that "*some*" of the 2500 pages of documents "*may*" be subject to High Court injunctions banning distribution, copying or publication, Parliament was required to protect itself from potential legal liability by not releasing the winebox to the media.

"*It is a convention that the House and the courts respect each others' role and procedures as far as possible,*" Tapsell claimed, and "*for this reason the Clerk [of the House, David McGee] will not allow his office to be used as a means to transmit material contrary to an order of the court.*"

Among the numerous experts unimpressed by the curious position taken was Dr Bill Hodge, a constitutional law expert and Deputy-Dean of the Auckland University Law School.

"*If what's going on in the courts is not a criminal trial which determines the guilt or innocence of someone, but rather what is going on in the courts is a suppression order or gagging writ, it seems to me the original purpose of the self-inflicted rule is frustrated if Parliament is gagging itself by this bootstrap operation of doing the work of the plaintiffs, or those who seek to gag Parliament, by simply echoing the court action.*"

Dr Hodge told *The Dominion*'s Catriona MacLennan that in a **criminal** trial it may be appropriate for Parliament to defer debate until a verdict is reached. "*It's a totally different matter for Parliament to be supine and deliberately turn its eyes away from material which may be in the public interest . . . simply because someone has enjoined its publication.*"

The convention that Parliament does not cut across the courts, he reminded, developed purely as a "*courtesy*", not as a rule of law.

The *Independent* interpreted events as the Government going to "*unprecedented lengths to suppress details of alleged multi million dollar tax frauds masterminded by Cook Islands-based tax dodge designer European Pacific — at the time owned by the Bank of New Zealand, Fay Richwhite and Brierley Investments.*"

The newspaper also reported that Richard McDonald in the Cooks was facing a possible $10,000 fine "*and/or a year in jail if he opens his mouth. His* lawyer, former Cook Islands Attorney-General Mike Mitchell, has advised him to shut up, for a number of reasons.

" 'You're meddling in something you don't understand,' he told the Independent this week. 'There's enough corruption in New Zealand. You keep out of Cook Islands business. Concentrate on the arseholes in the Beehive and leave us alone . . . I gave him [McDonald] the best advice I could and I advised him in the national interest.' "

So in two countries, gags remained in place on politicians trying to release European Pacific documents. Peters described the Tapsell ruling as *"bizarre and extraordinary"*, while former Labour Prime Minister David Lange also fought unsuccessfully against what he saw as a very dangerous precedent. Lange's campaign was long and vociferous. At one point, after European Pacific eventually lifted the injunction against *Frontline* on the grounds that we return the winebox, he demanded that Parliament publish the winebox documents and re-establish its supremacy.

Parliament, he argued, should not find itself beholden to a deal struck between *"shady bankers and shonky broadcasters."* A master, as always, of the great one-liner. Parliament, of course, is not subject to any action of the courts and can, if it so chooses, breach any court order. This is a privilege dating back to the 1688 Bill of Rights that enshrined the ultimate supremacy of Parliament above the King and Courts. The issue had been tested in 1703, and ended with the imprisonment of Court supporters for contempt of Parliament. It should be remembered that in those times, Courts of Justice were essentially carried out by members of the Sovereign's Court, a carryover from medieval times when the Lord of the Manor adjudicated in peasant squabbles. As such, the Courts – still known in England today as the "Queen's Bench" – were fundamentally a direct extension of the Monarch's power, which brought them into conflict with Parliament.

The question of ultimate authority had already been partially answered in the beheading of King Charles I at the hands of Parliament's Oliver Cromwell. The demarcation lines between the three branches of state – the executive, parliament and the judiciary – were much less clearly defined then, than they are today.

Three centuries later, in one of Britain's far-flung former dominions, the constitutional checks and balances would be placed under threat yet again, this time by the Kings of Commerce and Law. As Peters hammered at their right to do business unfettered by laws or morals, the two groups were in turn lobbying hard to castrate the powers of Parliament. They lobbied even harder after Peters gave his second contentious speech a week later.

The first one had, to some extent, caught TVNZ on the hop. Peters, whilst spilling the beans on the fraud mechanism, had not named names, and that meant we couldn't use our alternative defence to the injunction – whereby if a document or information is already public knowledge it can no longer be described as "confidential". Logical really.

Peters had instead left us in limbo, leaving enough of the detail secret to prevent *Frontline* from going back to court and getting the injunction lifted.

"*Bloody hell,*" muttered one X-File team member, "*the least he could have done was shoot us down cleanly and put us out of our misery*".

I knew Peters' advisers had been keeping tabs on the evidence we presented in the injunction hearings. I knew also, from gossip around the traps, that the two business papers and Brian Henry had been working furiously in the wake of our case to identify the crucial documents in their own care, dust them off and figure out how we'd managed to make two and two equal four. Henry, of course, already had a head start by virtue of knowing about JIF before we did.

As one journalist was quoted in the *NBR* on March 25th, "*writing a story from confidential financial source documents is like reconstructing a spider's web with some of the individual threads, without any guarantee that it will catch flies.*"

The paper's media commentator, Tom Frewen, noted that the wineboxful of financial gobbledygook would need a lot of analysis by the media.

"*While dubious deals may be buried in the detail, it will be the headline that determines whether Winston Peters' papers will have the consequences of Daniel Ellsberg's Pentagon Papers.*

"*If it ever appears, that headline will contain the amount of tax that big businesses avoided, possibly legitimately but probably immorally. If it's tens of millions, it will be the story of the year. If it's hundreds of millions, it will be the story of the decade.*"

The Serious Fraud Office, meanwhile, was continuing to state that it had fully examined all the winebox documents, including the TVNZ files, and found nothing new nor any evidence of criminal fraud.

The SFO appears to have been mistaken. At the Commission of Inquiry in late-1994, director Charles Sturt repeated his claim that the TVNZ documents added nothing to the equation. However, the SFO document index released to the Inquiry did not contain any reference to the Dundee 3 transaction – the hidden side of the JIF deals. And yet Dundee 3 was contained in the TVNZ affidavits seized by Sturt under the SFO Section 5 notices.

SFO investigator John Hicks joined Sturt in testifying that they couldn't really figure out what the Mitsubishi JIF deal was all about – again, neither of the men mentioned seeing the Dundee 3 documents, which complete the JIF money-go-round.

The Inquiry later discovered that when the SFO issued its clean bill of health about the winebox, including the Magnum transaction, in March, it hadn't taken a really detailed look at Magnum, despite the High Court action centred on it.

In fact, it wasn't until June 1994 that Sturt and forensic accountant Gib Beattie dusted off the Magnum deal for a more thorough analysis. In my opinion, all they ended up doing was effectively rubber stamping their earlier claim that it did not "*evidence serious or complex fraud.*"

A clear case, perhaps, of shooting first and asking the questions afterward. I would have thought the Serious Fraud Office would have completely investigated the transaction in the first place.

CHAPTER 21

The Coup D'etat

*"A Brave man struggling in the storms of fate,
And greatly falling, with a falling State."*
— ALEXANDER POPE 1688-1744

BY THE TIME WINSTON Peters opened his mouth to begin the second of three major speeches on European Pacific, it had already been a week of high drama and intrigue. After the first speech on March 16, 1994, Cook Islands politicians and officials came out swinging. Norman George, now the leader of the opposition Alliance party in Rarotonga, claimed he couldn't remember signing any documents in a withholding tax scam, and then revealed just how much control EP really did have over the Cooks Government.

As the *Cook Islands News* reported on March 17 local time, *"Speaking of his time in Cabinet, Mr George said* **anything he signed was on the advice of offshore banking representative Trevor Clarke** *and the solicitor-general at the time, Tony Manarangi. [author's emphasis]"*

Here was a Minister of the Crown acknowledging he was getting advice from European Pacific employee Trevor Clarke on which documents to sign!*

Despite claiming there had been no dirty dealing and therefore no need for an inquiry, Cook Islands Premier Sir Geoffrey Henry couldn't resist a chance to put the boot into his main rival during the election campaign.

"Norman was chairman of Cabinet, therefore chairman of Cook Islands Government Property Corporation at the time these products were being approved, and they were the ones whom Winston has been accusing as corrupt politicians."

The article also revealed just how deeply the Cook Islands Government would have had to be involved.

"In the 1991/92 Audit Report by Peat Marwick it was noted that the accounting and auditing requirements for several government entities, including CIGPC, 'appear inconsistent and in several cases non-existent'.

"The corporation itself is made up of the members of cabinet who are the directors and the chairman of cabinet who is the chairman of the corporation."

If the secret agreements were not forgeries, then the entire Cook Islands

---

* In a subsequent interview with the author, Norman George repeated his claim that he had not signed the promissory note deals. He believes legitimate documentation carrying his and Pomani Tangata's signatures and the Government seal may have been misappropriated and altered without his knowledge. *"I have seen what I signed: there are some hairy documents around that I did not sign."*

cabinet should have been aware of the massive losses they were taking in deals with European Pacific, deals where European Pacific got tax money back as well as – to all intents and purposes – a false tax certificate to use overseas in what appeared to be fraudulent double-dipping.

Among those to seize on the latest Peters revelations were the tiny Democratic Party, whose members included former Premier Sir Tom Davis and former auditor Richard McDonald. They told the *Cook Islands News* that they might distribute the European Pacific documents at the centre of the storm during a political rally that evening.

Within hours of that boast, European Pacific had added both men to its grab-bag of gagged individuals and media outlets – obtaining an ex parte injunction over the telephone after contacting a New Zealand judge – New Zealand still supplies the judges who administer Cook Islands law.

One Network News and *3 National News* had both flown reporters and TV crews up to the Cooks after the parliamentary allegations, as had media organisations from Australia and Japan. TV3's Steve Christensen had managed to get inside the European Pacific office for a quick shot of EPBC manager Mark Dowd.

However, sensing they had filmed "hot property", he and cameraman Amos Ngaia decided not to return to their hotel until after they had sent the tape out of the Cooks on a flight to New Zealand that afternoon. For six hours, the TV3 crew languished on a beach, fearing arrest at any moment. Their tactic worked – the interview with Mark Dowd played the following evening on *3 National News*.

In the eternal battle for supremacy that is television, TVNZ's John Stewart tried the same trick the next day, Saturday March 19. Sweet-talking one of EP's own security guards, Stewart and his crew were given a guided tour of the interior of the EP offices. By the time they arrived back at their motel rooms, Cook Islands police officers were waiting for them.

The four officers seized all the camera gear, the tapes and even the TV crew's car, claiming Cook Islands secrecy laws had been breached. It was only after hours of negotiation lasting into the night that Stewart and his crew escaped imprisonment, and then only after agreeing to allow the destruction of the footage taken inside the EP office.

Just to make doubly sure, European Pacific obtained another court injunction preventing any of the footage from ever being used. The injunction also prevented *One Network News* from even using videotape of the outside of the EP/Standard Chartered building.

There but for the grace of God, I breathed a silent prayer of thanksgiving. It could easily have been myself and the *Frontline* crew clapped in irons if European Pacific staff had cottoned on to our earlier filming expeditions.

Monday the 21st brought with it more heat, political rather than tropical. Peters had signalled that he planned another keynote speech the following day, Tuesday, but European Pacific opted for its most novel and daring gagging attempt yet.

Fresh from the successful attempt to get Parliament to forbid publication of the winebox because the case was before the courts, EP Group figured it could take out Peters in the same fashion. If the maverick MP could be injuncted as well, Parliament's Speaker might take the even more extraordinary step of preventing Peters from speaking.

At least, that's how Peters was reading it. A few months later under parliamentary privilege he would accuse Deputy Prime Minister Don McKinnon of "colluding" with European Pacific to shut down his speaking rights via legal action.

"Liars and cheats and fraudsters raiding the revenue but with mates in Parliament who were not going to see them attacked and pursued under the law," Peters raged. He claimed McKinnon knew about EP's plans to injunct him with a writ designed to stop him from producing EP's documents in Parliament.

"He arranged it. That is called collusion." The MP then claimed McKinnon would have told the House that Peters had been served with a writ, making the matter sub-judice, *"and it would all be over,"* Peters snarled. Don McKinnon later remarked that he had no idea what Peters was on about.

Certainly, European Pacific tried to serve Peters with a writ. A series of anonymous phone calls were made to Peters' various offices, seeking his fax number. Suspecting that European Pacific was trying to put the MP on written notice of the injunctions, his staff declined to reveal the fax number. Winston stayed in hiding, on the move, for most of the day, avoiding his home and other areas that European Pacific could be staking out.

From the safety of his bolt-hole that Monday night, Peters wore a Cheshire-cat grin as TV3's *20/20* entered the fray with a Keith Davies-engineered item on the fracas to date. Davies and producer Chris Harrington had been careful not to exceed the strict terms of the injunction, relying in the most part on Peters' parliamentary revelations. The pair neatly circumnavigated the legal restriction in fact and went straight to the heart of the matter – the involvement of New Zealand's government-owned bank in an alleged fraud on the Japanese Government.

I too was cheering from the sidelines. Sure, TV3 was the enemy now, but in this particular investigation any publicity was good publicity, especially when so many influential powerbrokers were doing their utmost to stop it from ever screening at all.

Against that backdrop, Winston Peters MP set out the next day to make the second in what would become a trilogy of major addresses to Parliament.

Waiting for him at the entrance to the halls of Government were legal process servers, sent there by European Pacific in a last ditch bid to injunct him before he made the speech. Anticipating just such a scenario, the MP's minders had hired a limousine with darkened windows to drive Winston right up to the doors of Parliament, where security guards would smuggle him up to the debating chamber in an express elevator, safely out of reach of the writs. And then he opened fire.

"The evil day cannot be delayed any longer, Mr Speaker," he began, but it was

shortlived. Don McKinnon interrupted with a question to Parliament's "referee", the Speaker.

"I raise a point of order, Mr Speaker. The Member for Tauranga has advertised the fact that he wishes to read documents that have been tabled . . . Obviously you have ruled that those papers which have been tabled are for the privilege of Members only and cannot be published and therefore cannot go beyond the House."

The Deputy Prime Minister, still smarting from his slip-up the previous week that allowed Peters to table the winebox in the first place, was now attempting to stop the New Zealand First party leader from quoting from the suppressed documents. It came across as another last ditch effort from the establishment to shut Peters up, and it failed.

"Yes," replied the Speaker, Peter Tapsell, *"They may not be published outside the House without infringing the Court injunction. That does not apply to a Member speaking in the House who may refer to the papers and, indeed, quote from them with absolute privilege. Mr Peters?"*

"Mr Speaker . . . In the past week we have witnessed the most telling example of political and big business corruption ever to rear its vile head in this country. I am talking about the activities of European Pacific Group, and people in positions of power, to aid and abet international money-laundering criminals in a massive cover-up of crimes."

Peters knew that the alleged crimes had been given the all-clear by the Inland Revenue office and the Serious Fraud Office. Indeed, in an attempt to defuse the upcoming Peters speech, Revenue Minister Wyatt Creech had earlier released a report from Inland Revenue Commissioner David Henry, which revealed 93 investigations had taken place into Cook Islands tax dodges, resulting in $55.7 million in extra tax. The investigations, claimed Henry, showed legal tax avoidance, rather than illegal tax evasion.

"Tax avoidance is not an offence or a crime, but can be struck down by provisions in the tax laws when the transactions are tax driven and have no commercial reality," David Henry opined. Unfortunately, the small print in Henry's report revealed nearly all of his investigations related to the period pre-1988, when the loopholes had been closed. The Magnum transaction took place in 1988/89, which meant Henry's statement was irrelevant in that context.

Even more damning, the Commission of Inquiry was told in 1994 that the investigations showing *"legal tax avoidance, rather than illegal tax evasion"* didn't relate to the winebox at all; instead it was an earlier series of investigations into other Cook Islands deals. That this point wasn't made clear, when Revenue Minister Wyatt Creech was using the figures to reassure the public that the winebox contained no evasion, was, in my opinion, misleading.

Peters, however, knew that the Government would rely on those clearances to try and blast him out of the water in the war of public opinion. In a country where the average New Zealander didn't believe that its law enforcement agencies could be corrupt or incompetent, it would be easy for the Government to pour scorn on the Tauranga MP. His solution was a dangerous one.

By demolishing the credibility of the Government's advisers, he could simultaneously demolish the credibility of the Government itself. In doing so he was calling into question public confidence in the integrity of the entire democratic institution but, in the balance, Peters felt the evidence justified it. If the SFO's Chas Sturt and IRD's David Henry were going to spring to the defence of European Pacific, then they should realise they did so at their peril. Winston Peters paused to glance at his notes and then let fly in Parliament with every gun he could muster.

"Today I am calling for the resignation of Mr Charles Sturt [Serious Fraud Office Director] for the most serious reasons. Mr Sturt issued a press release on Friday last, saying not only that he could not find, that he could find nothing criminal in those documents, but also that he could not investigate tax fraud allegations because they were outside his jurisdiction.

"Mr Sturt lied to the news media and he lied to the people of New Zealand. Section 37 of the Serious Fraud Office Act 1990 states: 'Any member of the Serious Fraud Office may disclose any revenue information to any other member of the Serious Fraud Office for the purpose of investigating or prosecuting any Inland Revenue offence'.

"There is his power, yet he put out a press release saying that he was without power. That was a demonstrable, palpable lie or he is totally incompetent. Under his own Act – the only Act that he need know – Mr Sturt's claim that he cannot investigate tax fraud, if made in a Court of Law, would warrant a charge of perjury.

"Mr Charles Sturt is prepared to turn a blind eye to corporate criminals, when they are the same men who donate money to political parties. Was Mr Sturt's pursuit of the Equiticorp boss, Allan Hawkins, really motivated by a desire for justice, or had Mr Hawkins simply failed to pay his political dues on time?

"If the Director of the Serious Fraud Office is so incompetent that he does not realise his powers to investigate tax fraud, he should resign immediately or be dismissed forthwith."

They were telling, vicious, body-blows against the man heading the country's most prestigious crime-fighting unit. It was a clear indication that this was a fight to the political death. There would be no prisoners, only winners and losers – and the losers would be stripped entirely of their reputations and careers. Sturt's reputation was being mangled and shredded by a senior politician, an almost unprecedented attack on a senior civil servant from the sanctity of Parliament.

If Peters was wrong, his own career hopes would be finished, his public credibility ruined. This was ground zero, and Winnie Peters was the one megaton nuclear teddy bear from hell. Having publicly raked his claws into the SFO's soft underbelly, Peters turned momentarily from the SFO carcass to feast in detail on the Magnum transaction.

"Not only were the Cook Islands robbed of $2,050,000 in tax earnings, but European Pacific had a double bite of the apple by using the fraudulent certificates

to gain a $2 million tax credit in New Zealand as well," he noted after going over the promissory note deal again.

"The evidence of this comes not just from the transaction documents and the promissory note agreement, but also from the tabled internal bank instructions that show how the money flowed. These tabled banking instructions are signed and dated, and they clearly show criminal intent.

"To those in the Cook Islands who suggest that I have misinterpreted the facts, I quote from a tabled memorandum of 25 November 1987 – tabled here – which is headed 'Cook Islands Withholding Tax'. Paragraph 8.5 of that memorandum states: 'The Cook Islands Government would refund the amount of the tax, less its cut.' What is to misunderstand? What is to misinterpret? The intent was to manufacture fake tax certificates and then use them to defraud unsuspecting foreign governments. The cut for the Cook Islands Government was the fee paid to corrupt politicians for their help in engineering the scheme.

"The victims include New Zealand . . . Australia, Japan, the United States, Britain and Belgium to name a few. I name the guilty in this transaction as the following: David Lloyd, Managing Director, European Pacific; David Richwhite, Chairman, European Pacific and Managing Director of Fay Richwhite; Paul Collins, director, European Pacific and Managing Director of Brierley Investments; and Peter Travers, director, European Pacific and formerly of the Bank of New Zealand."

After another round where he named the European Pacific staff involved, Peters lashed out at "the following lawyers and outside accounting firms who gave approval to this criminal fraud on the New Zealand and Cook Islands revenues: Russell Florence, KPMG Peat Marwick, Auckland, and Jonathan Flaws of the legal firm of Bell Gully Buddle Weir.

"Apart from the tax evasion charges that arise from the Magnum Corporation transaction, there is also clear prima facie evidence of conspiracy to defraud and of using a document to gain pecuniary advantage, knowing the document to be false. These are criminal charges punishable by long jail terms.

"If the Serious Fraud Office cannot find enough evidence in the Magnum Corporation transaction alone to put a number of these men behind bars, then the Serious Fraud Office should be immediately suspended from operating, pending an inquiry into possible corruption of that office.

"If the Inland Revenue Commissioner David Henry can find no evidence of tax fraud in the Magnum Corporation transaction alone," he barked angrily, "he should resign or be sacked! If the Commissioner of Inland Revenue stands by his press statement of last Friday and today and continues to claim that all of this, including the use of fake tax certificates, is legal, he should be fired immediately and charged with conspiracy to pervert the course of justice in New Zealand."

It was vintage Winston Peters, with all the venom, outrage and anger he could muster. The National Government could sense that its SFO and IRD crutches were being knocked out, but it could do nothing.

"Decisions by the Serious Fraud Office and the Inland Revenue Department not to prosecute have been made behind closed doors and I ask what right have they to be judge and jury away from the scrutiny of justifiably suspicious New

Zealand people? Who knows what favours are being called in, or bribes are being paid, even as we speak, to save the reputations of some of New Zealand's so called leading business figures and top political campaign donors. It is time for charges to be laid and the evidence to speak for itself."

Of all of the points in the speech, this was perhaps the most damaging to the Government in the long term. By suggesting that deals had been done behind closed doors Peters was casting doubt on the decisions reached by the law enforcement agencies. Having already provided detailed evidence of the alleged Magnum fraud and the relevant criminal charges that could be laid, Peters was now suggesting that if the Government wanted to continue claiming he was wrong, why not throw all the evidence before a judge and let a court decide? The MP knew that this would appeal to the average New Zealander's sense of "fair-mindedness".

But so far he still hadn't completely rescued the *Frontline* documentary. While the Magnum transaction was now fully in the open in New Zealand, we couldn't get the injunction lifted unless Peters touched on JIF as well. I needn't have worried.

With a few minutes left up his sleeve, the Tauranga Terminator turned to the Japanese deals, naming Mitsubishi, Sanwa and Fuji banks as the players. Again, the importance of this cannot be overstated: This was the first most New Zealanders had heard of the intricacies of both Magnum and the JIF deals. Peters was attempting to do what he'd failed to a week earlier – blow the confidentiality applying to our documents so we could go back to the court and get the injunction lifted.

"These Japanese deals detailed in the documents provide clear evidence of a conspiracy to defraud. Could it be that the National Government's unprecedented efforts to stop me from revealing this are because the then Government-owned Bank of New Zealand was a key perpetrator in this crime? Also involved were Fay Richwhite, Michael Fay and David Richwhite of Capital Markets."

The media went wild. The speech was the lead story on both television networks that evening, and in the next morning's papers.

"Peters wants top bankers 'behind bars' ", was emblazoned across the front page of the *New Zealand Herald*, while the *Dominion* opted for a more sober **"Top officials under fire in tax row"**.

All the media carried the main allegations, of course, but importantly they also carried the rebuttals from those alleged players willing to poke their heads up into the firing line.

David Richwhite *"categorically denied"* all of the Peters' allegations.

"At no time has Fay, Richwhite, Sir Michael Fay or myself been involved in any transaction that contravenes the laws of New Zealand or any other country."

Attorney-General Paul East came out in support of Chas Sturt and David Henry, saying the Government had *"complete confidence in the integrity and independence"* of both men.

Magnum, now renamed DB Group, was also quick to distance itself from the allegations, with DB company secretary John Shaw explaining to the *Herald* that Peters was not levelling any accusations at Magnum itself.

"He refers to Magnum to identify a transaction made by others. The company has not been involved in any tax fraud or unlawful contract."

Serious Fraud Office Director, Charles Sturt, was scathing in his criticism of the MP. *"I do take issue with the democratic system which allows parliamentary privilege to be prostituted in such a manner. I cannot help but feel the whole episode had distinct overtones of McCarthyism and as such raises in me feelings of revulsion at this part of our democratic process."*

In a 16-page statement, Sturt again stated he did not have the power to investigate tax fraud. Section 37, he said, could be invoked only after the IRD had first asked the SFO to become involved. The SFO, he stated, had examined the winebox and found no evidence of criminal fraud.

Winston Peters, meanwhile, was staying anything but quiet. On the evening of Thursday, March 24, he told Parliament of another *"straight-out fraud"* in a new transaction – a wiring diagram entitled *"JAP Bank"*. The document covered a plan to borrow $200 million from the Bank of New Zealand at an interest rate of 11.2 percent, and deposit it in a Japanese bank at an interest rate of 12.8 percent. The margin, 1.6 percent, would be the profit on the deal.

"But the document shows that along the chain European Pacific paid 15.45 percent interest, and the question is 'why?'," argued Peters. *"Everybody knows that it is bad business to borrow at 15.45 percent and lend that money at 12.8 percent, which on $200 million is a huge loss."*

European Pacific's problem was that the total interest earned in Japan would be taxable as profit in New Zealand, the resulting tax liability would be somewhere in the region of $7 million. They scratched their heads and looked hard at the deal. The 1.6 percent margin would only provide $3.2 million, less than half the tax liability on the deal. Clearly, European Pacific would have to find a way to get rid of that tax liability.

The document showed that instead of depositing the money directly in Japan, the $200 million would first go through a couple of Cook Islands companies, including European Pacific Bank. The interest rate was artificially inflated on paper to 15.45%, so that after tax had been "deducted" EP would still be left with 11.2% to pay the Bank of New Zealand. This enabled withholding tax to be "paid" in the Cook Islands and, of course, European Pacific would be given a Cook Islands tax certificate for its troubles.

Naturally, argued Peters, the tax would not really be paid in the Cooks, but instead EP would get the money back, and an $8.5 million dollar false tax certificate to be used to defraud the New Zealand Inland Revenue.*

The tax payment taken care of, European Pacific was free to take its $3 million profit from the margin. In fact, the document showed that the profit would be split three ways. Fay Richwhite would get 60%, European Pacific

---

* All numerical values and equations are based on Peters' speech and the figures contained in the tabled document.

would get 30% and the *"CIG"* – presumably Cook Islands Government – would get 10%, apparently for agreeing to manufacture a fake $8.5 million tax certificate.

"Everyone knows that businesses do not borrow money at 15.45 percent, then lend it at 12.8 percent," questioned Peters.

"How can such an arrangement have an innocent explanation? To be tax avoidance it must have an innocent explanation. These people know what they are doing. They are qualified tax lawyers and accountants. They intended to do what they are doing.

"They intended to take money out of the New Zealand Revenue by the presentation of a tax receipt. They knew the tax receipt was false. They knew that the tax was not paid because the money was in their pockets. The money was in their pockets before the sent the receipt to the Inland Revenue Department in New Zealand.

"That is a conspiracy to defraud the revenue under section 257 of the Crimes Act 1961," he barked.

"The courts have defined an intention to defraud the revenue as an intention to 'get out of the Revenue something that was already in it, or prevent something from getting into the Revenue which the Revenue was entitled to get.' "

Easy money if you could get it, although there was no evidence in the winebox that that particular deal actually proceeded past the planning stages. But even the planning may be a criminal offence. Just as police may arrest someone for conspiring to rob a bank or conspiring to commit a murder, conspiracy charges can also be laid for planning to defraud, if authorities can identify any of the conspirators.

"The Cook Islands Government gets $300,000 for providing a monopoly money tax certificate for presentation in New Zealand," lectured Peters to an increasingly nervous National Government. Indeed, several cabinet ministers had asked the Speaker to stop Peters from repeatedly accusing MP's of acting to cover up the huge frauds.

"On at least four occasions," wrote Bernard Orsman in the *Herald*, *"Mr Peters was made to withdraw allegations he made about other MP's and Government departments. The Minister of Tourism, Mr Banks, said he was concerned about the compounding effect, even after Mr Peters had withdrawn his accusations, which implied that 'we are all crooks'."*

Peters maintained the broadside.

"For the average New Zealander, cheating the Revenue is cheating the Revenue . . . If Mary Bloggs went down to the Department of Social Welfare and made out a false set of accounts to get an additional benefit, it would be deemed to be fraud, and she would be put in jail.

"However, if a person has a Mercedes, a corporate jet, owns a few islands, and wines and dines the National party, that is called 'an aggressive incomes policy'."

Revenue Minister Wyatt Creech attempted to justify the decision to call the Magnum transaction "avoidance", rather than criminal evasion. In a television interview he stated: *"If anyone paid tax overseas, they would get a certificate for it. If they actually go around the back door and get it paid back to*

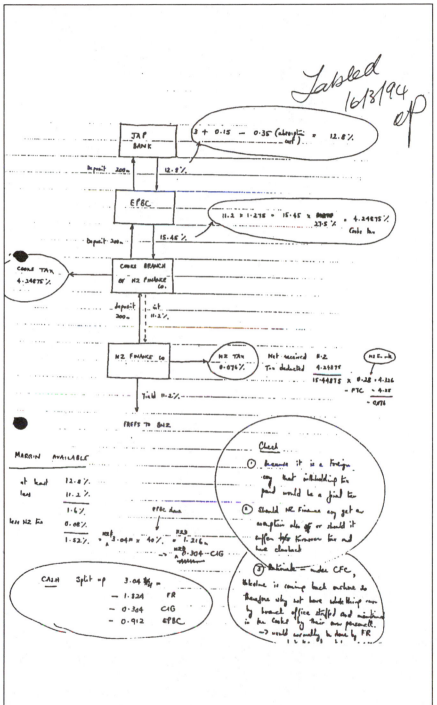

them, that is clearly a sham transaction, so even though it is avoidance if the Commissioner was aware of it he would be able to charge them tax as if that tax credit did not exist."

"I call on the Minister," thundered Peters from his parliamentary pulpit, "to go and look at the Magnum transaction and to get his facts right!

"Every document, including the [tax] receipt, is dated 27 July 1988. The transaction – the 'money go round' – took place that day. They had the money back in their pockets – and those documents prove it – before they had the receipt posted to them.

"That is the critical issue. That is the critical date, time, place and point. But it is worse. In paragraphs 18.12 to 18.15 we see that they planned a year in advance the second same sham.

"The Minister is playing with words. He knows that these people entered agreements with the intention of taking revenue from New Zealand based on a tax certificate that falsely represented to the New Zealand commissioner [of Inland Revenue] that tax had been paid in the Cook Islands."

Peters left another serious allegation until last.

"Fay Richwhite gave the National Party $1 million, NZ First leader Winston Peters said last night as he continued to use parliamentary privilege to make claims of a tax sham involving the Cook Islands," wrote the *Dominion's* Simon Kilroy the next morning.

"Prime Minister Jim Bolger denied the donation claim.

"Mr Peters said Mr Bolger wanted to associate himself with crime prevention but did not want an investigation into the 'real crimes' that he had outlined using documents he had tabled in Parliament.

" 'Why not? I'll tell you why,' Mr Peters said. 'Because the coffers of the National Party are stuffed full of money coming from the purses of the people who appear all over these documents. That's the reason. Millions of dollars.'

"Mr Peters said merchant banker Fay Richwhite alone had given $1 million, a statement which Mr Bolger denied immediately.

"Mr Peters said: 'In terms of political parties you know what that is? That's protection.'

"Speaker Peter Tapsell ruled Mr Peters had to withdraw that remark, and Mr Peters responded by saying: 'I withdraw, and let me say this then, that's looking after your mates.' "

Fay Richwhite also denied making a million dollar donation to any political party.

* * *

IN FAR OFF WOGISTAN, Aladdin *gazed into the distance, eyes squinting from the sun's late afternoon glare. He could just make out the huge sandstorm lashing the desert kingdom's capital, scattering camels and the occasional peasant.*

Setting his fingers to his mouth he whistled three times, on the third a ripple appeared in the swirling sand and took form as it sped over the harsh landscape toward him.

"Have we beaten them yet, Genie?", he asked dubiously as the ripple suddenly

materialised into his familiar lamp-bound sidekick. The Genie grinned from ear to ear.

"Not yet my fortunate fellow, but we're sure having fun trying."

Aladdin looked relieved. "By the way, Genie, We still haven't been properly introduced. What should I call you?"

"Just call me Winston." And with a flash of his gleaming white teeth and a wave of his carefully coiffed hair, he was off.

CHAPTER 22

Unleashing the Genie

*"When a young man obtains a sum of money from a young lady,
for the purpose of furnishing a home previous to their marriage,
and absconds with it, he is guilty of obtaining money under false
pretences, and may be prosecuted for felony."*
– LONDON JOURNAL, 1851

NO SOONER HAD THE ink dried on Peters' March 22 speech than our Project X team had swung back into operation. We would go back to the High Court seeking to get the injunction lifted on the grounds that the whole matter was now public anyway. To prove that the contents of our programme were the same as the transactions disclosed under parliamentary privilege, we were required to submit a copy of the script to the High Court. Once that script was submitted, lawyer Willie Akel warned, the court would not look kindly on further changes. To all intents and purposes, this had to be the definitive, final version of Project X.

Once again, there was direct interference from management. Graeme Wilson ordered that every reference to *"fraud"* or *"apparent fraud"* in the script be erased. The only references to alleged criminality that we could keep were those made by tax expert John Prebble.

There was no valid legal reason for removing those phrases – the programme had been cleared by the legal team already. It appeared to be a case of damage minimisation, a forlorn hope by someone that perhaps if we didn't allege it was fraud, viewers wouldn't realise that it was either.

Once again, the *Independent's* Jenni McManus got wind of it.

"It is believed the documentary at the centre of the row," she wrote, *"was sanitised by TVNZ on Wednesday on the orders of general manager, Graeme Wilson, with all references to 'apparent fraud' being expunged.*

"The programme has been edited several times since December on management's instructions. Prior to the initial injunction hearing just before Christmas, screening was delayed at least twice – once so the 'mood music' could be changed and a second time because it was considered the reporter was speaking too quickly."

Wilson was extremely angry at the leak, and Paul Norris and Shaun Brown were asked to find the culprit. I was questioned, and I, correctly, denied involvement. The only leak I could take the credit for was the original one to the *Sunday Star* back on December 19, 1993.

I had a fair idea where the leaks to McManus were coming from, but I wasn't about to blow the whistle on a colleague. McManus had in fact rung me earlier in the week and reeled off what she knew of the sanitisation attempts. She asked me to comment.

"C'mon Jenni, do you think I'm nuts? It would be worth more than my job to spill the beans to you. You've obviously got good sources though, ask them some more."

I have to admit, and I'm sure others within TVNZ would as well, that getting phone calls from people like Jenni McManus or Frances O'Sullivan was akin to having the Grim Reaper pop around every Friday morning for tea and scones! My stomach used to sink every time I heard them on the line. Invariably they already knew exactly what the story was, and could relate so much detail I half expected them to describe the boxer shorts I was wearing. They are the "great white sharks" of the journalism business in this country, voracious feeders who appear to thrive solely on a diet of jetfuel and matches – when they knock on your door you just *know* an explosion is bound to follow.

McManus and I did have differing opinions on the effect of the "cleansing" attempts. While Jenni quickly came to believe that the entire programme had been castrated and would end up a weak brew with no punch, I still felt the essence to the story was so strong that it would overcome anything that was chucked at it.

It is a credit to the calibre of the TVNZ news and current affairs team that the documentary – when it eventually aired a few months later – still contained enough "bite" as to totally overshadow the interference with it. Whatever the bitching that goes on in the media or in public about the quality of TV news, New Zealanders should be thankful that the people behind *One Network News* and, for that matter, *3 National News*, are honest and bloody hard-working.

They take their independence and integrity seriously and they take their responsibilities to inform the public seriously. Subtle attempts to influence, once identified, are resisted. Having said that, it's often hard for news organisations to accept that they are being toyed with.

The Simpson Grierson legal team had long since ceased to be shocked at the forces arraigning themselves against us – when they put it in context with the bigger picture emerging.

The concerted efforts to shut down Peters, shut down the documents in Parliament, shut down the business papers and shut down Project X – it was a raging battle for the right of the public to know, and most New Zealanders never realised it was happening. Anyone watching *One Network News* or *3 National News* up to this time would have seen routine stories about unemployment or bank robberies – legitimate stories but nevertheless diversions from the real struggle seething just under the surface of public consciousness.

Likewise, in most daily newspapers, little coverage had been given to the EP-TVNZ court fight. Indeed, staff at one major newspaper were ordered not to write any stories on European Pacific without clearing them first with the editor, and some journalists talked privately of having their stories gutted of the major developments and allegations, or of their stories being "re-slanted" in a different light – less harmful to European Pacific.

I found it disturbing to see legitimate news stories being tampered with – the influence on public opinion through such subtle behind-the-scenes activity is impossible to measure. Still, the tide appeared to be turning.

It had begun when a full press gallery turned out to hear the actual evidence in the injunction hearings back in January. For most who attended, it was the first dim realisation that maybe there was something to the allegations about European Pacific after all. By the end of that hearing, many of those journalists had become convinced that the transactions were indeed fraudulent, at least on the documentary evidence available.

This in turn created a second wave. Close to burnout, Fran O'Sullivan, Jenni McManus, Warren Berryman and myself were beginning to find it difficult to keep hammering away while the rest of the media had been turning a largely blind eye. Now, new recruits were seeing for themselves what we were on about, and began to look for ways to climb on board.

The articles in the daily media became more frequent, more daring. No longer did they pour as much scorn on Winston Peters or the rest of us, now there was a sense of anticipation developing. It became in essence a loose alliance of the news media starting to push against European Pacific, to test the boundaries.

Journalists like the *Sunday Star-Times'* Bob Dey, the *Herald's* Graham Skellern and Andrew Stone, and the *Dominion's* Catriona MacLennan began to see the light. Whereas a year earlier Peters' speeches may have been generally dismissed by the news media as more wolf-crying, now there was a core of mainstream press journalists who knew the background, and were not prepared to write it all off as fantasy any more.

Couple that with the equally aggressive reporting of TV3's Steve Christensen, already well aware, through our earlier work together, of the situation, and European Pacific could be forgiven for thinking the media was hunting as a pack. Indeed, it was one of the first accusations levelled by EP when TVNZ went back to Court after the March 22 speech to get the injunction lifted. More specifically, I was one of the accused.

"*Acting for EP,*" wrote Warren Berryman in the Independent, "*Richard Craddock QC suggested that TVNZ reporter Ian Wishart and Win Peters were in cahoots – that there existed a suspicious co-incidence between the case presented in the House and the case presented in TVNZ's programme.*"

In the *National Business Review,* Alastair Thompson made a similar point. "*Craddock indicated allegations of collusion between TVNZ reporter Ian Wishart and Mr Peters would become an issue at the trial scheduled for May 23.*"

"*The winebox,*" droned Craddock, "*is said to contain 43 transactions. Mr Peters and TVNZ deal with just two, and the same two. Evidence points to Peters being the distributor of documents to Wishart,*" he threatened.

It didn't exactly take an Einstein to work out why we were both dealing with the same transactions. The details had all been read out in open court during earlier hearings, and one of Peters' assistants had been sitting in from time to time.

As I had pointed out many times before, once you find the key to the winebox documents the rest is easy, and the key was simply fake tax certificates and promissory note deals with the Cook Islands Government. A five year old could have figured it out.

Peters worked it out the same way as the *Independent* and *NBR* did: they listened to our testimony in court, went back through their own documents and realised what they'd missed the first time around. There was another reason for Peters' knowledge being more detailed than most – we had interviewed him on videotape for his reaction to our investigation, in the same way as we had interviewed Professor Prebble and former Auditor-General Brian Tyler.

Although the project team had essentially been banned from using Peters soon after this, the MP would have known from our questions which transactions we were dealing with and what the general thrust of the allegations was. Craddock was going to need better evidence than this half-baked bleating if he wanted to attack me for collusion.

European Pacific knew it, too. They allegedly began interrogating former staff and associates with the preface: *"We've been monitoring all of Wishart's phone calls, we know you've been in contact with him so why don't you make it easy on yourself and tell us what was discussed."*

It was a good bluff, sufficiently so that I received a call from the United States, warning me that European Pacific was boasting about bugging our phones.

"Just a warning, old boy," cautioned my informant, *"They dragged one poor soul through this last week and tried to psychologically beat it out of him. He denied talking to you, of course, but it was a close shave.*

"If I were you, I'd get your home and office swept for bugs."

We did. Unpacking a box about the size of a phone book, the security firm's technician explained how it operated. The concept was similar to "feedback" when a microphone is placed too close to a loudspeaker at a public rally or concert or similar event.

This device would scan radio frequencies rapidly while at the same time transmitting a tone through its speaker. If a bug was operating in the room, it would begin "feeding back" into the scanner, creating a screaming effect.

The downside to sweeping for bugs is that those on the other end are immediately aware, through the noise created, of what's going on and, more importantly, when they've been sprung. Depending on the sophistication of the surveillance, the bugs can sometimes be remotely shut down to minimise detection.

While the home search turned up nothing, my office in the combined space shared by *Eyewitness* and *60 Minutes* did turn up a "hit". One of the two phones I use was broadcasting conversations on it into the ether.

"That," stated the de-bugging technician, *"is definitely suspicious."* It was the only telephone out of some 16 in the office that was actually transmitting on radio frequencies as well as down normal phone lines, and it just happened to be the phone I used for some of the more sensitive conversations with sources.

If a conversation was *extremely* sensitive I would normally use a phone in another part of the building, on the off chance that my line may be tapped, but still, this was not a welcome development.

The technician explained that, in very rare cases, it was possible for signals travelling down a phone line to be picked up harmonically by adjacent mains-supply electrical wiring and broadcast as radio waves. But he emphasised again – this is extremely rare.

It was possible that this was the case with my phone, a pure co-incidence, but a bugging device of some kind could not be ruled out without an entire stripping down of the office walls and a thorough visual check of the wiring. Obviously this was not an option within TVNZ.

What were the chances, I pondered cynically, of such a "rare" event happening to me, the only person in TVNZ likely to be under surveillance. It had been impossible to keep the sweep totally secret from others in the office that evening, and news that we may have detected a bug spread like wildfire throughout the TVNZ building within 24 hours, causing a frisson of excitement and intrigue.

The security technician came back two days later to see if the phone was still transmitting conversations. This time the sweep turned up nothing. The fault, or bug, had gone.

Unbeknown to me, TVNZ management also called in their own security consultants to sweep possibly affected offices. The first I knew of it was a summons to see Director of News and Current Affairs, Paul Norris.

"Ian, you may be aware that after the bugging scare the other night we got our own security people in to do a sweep. They didn't find any external surveillance, but they did find a bug in your office. What do you know about this?"

He was holding up an old cigarette packet containing a tiny transmitter. I burst out laughing.

"I'm sorry to burst the bubble of intrigue, Paul, but that's a bug we made here at TVNZ, to use as a stage prop in an Eyewitness piece about prostitutes bugging their clients. I'm not even sure that the silly thing works."

Norris looked kind of sheepish and relieved at the same time. *"Well that would explain why the security people couldn't make it work either,"* he murmured, before continuing, *"You mean to say you haven't been eavesdropping on people yourself, which you know, of course, is illegal?"*

"No," I smiled, *"we haven't been listening in to anyone. That bug has been sitting in my drawer for six months since we did the story, we actually filmed me holding it in my hand. There's nothing secret about it."*

It was a humorous interlude, but it didn't explain why the security company had been going through the drawers of my desk. Word of the two sweeps soon hit the rest of the media.

"Television New Zealand was told its news offices were being bugged during production of its documentary on the secret tax schemes of European Pacific," wrote Toni McRae in the *Sunday Star Times*.

"TVNZ had 'very real concerns about the potential of the bugging' of their offices, said spokesman Roger Beaumont yesterday. 'I can confirm we took

appropriate measures to protect ourselves after we were tipped off by a credible overseas source'."

Bugging devices, however, were the least of our worries. It was in the High Court that the real battle was being fought, and TVNZ was consistently losing. Nearly every day I was swearing new affidavits containing press clippings and radio and TV transcripts, to show the Court just how much the Magnum and JIF transactions were now in the public domain.

It seemed impossible that Judge Bruce Robertson wouldn't see it our way and agree that the confidence of the documents was well and truly blown. Craddock, however, was employing one of those crafty "chicken and egg" arguments that always tie judges up in knots. To any ordinary citizen, it was obvious that Magnum had been well and truly canvassed in Parliament, down to the exact amounts and nature of the transactions.

Craddock, though, was arguing that even if all the **information** was public knowledge, that did not make the **physical documents** themselves public. In other words, Peters could have read the documents verbatim, and Craddock would argue that the documents themselves were still confidential because the public hadn't physically seen them. To me, it was an utterly ridiculous and facile argument, but Justice Robertson couldn't see his way past it legally.

Julian Miles QC, our lawyer, tried in vain to point out that all that was left after the information was publicised was a physical piece of paper, surely the Court wasn't suggesting that protection apply to the paper, not its contents? Borrowing a quote from Justice McGechan, Miles told the Court "*Justice, as the famous statue, should appear blind but should not appear stupid.*"

Going further, Miles pointed out that Peters had already read out all the significant information contained in the documents, and that our TV programme would go no further and do no more damage than had already been done.

The Judge didn't accept that argument either, saying that from his reading of the documents, there were still pockets of information that hadn't been read out by Peters. He didn't say whether the information was significant or not, but added this wasn't important. What mattered was that parts of the documents were still confidential, therefore European Pacific was entitled to keep the injunction on.

Why didn't TVNZ source its programme to Peters' comments and forget about the documents, suggested the Judge?

"*The credibility of our programme depends on being based on documents,*" Miles responded. Allegations of fraud would be hard enough for the public to accept, without taking away the added credibility of seeing signatures and actual documents used in the allegedly criminal transactions.

Justice Robertson erred on the side of caution. A few more weeks wait for TVNZ would not hurt, whereas European Pacific ran the risk of losing confidence forever if the injunction were lifted now.

To be fair, Justice Robertson was treading a knife edge with this case. Whichever way he turned, his judgements were likely to be scrutinised in the Court of Appeal or perhaps even the Privy Council in Britain. It's the judicial equivalent of having the boss standing over your shoulder making sure you do it right.

Such fears manifested themselves in humourous ways. It had been a regular routine for Justice Robertson to purchase a wine carton from a vineyard owned by eminent tax QC Tony Molloy. It was Molloy himself who usually dropped off the carton to Bruce Robertson.

The winebox was often swapped in the carpark beside the Auckland High Court. Molloy, of course, was well known in legal circles for his probe into the alleged bloodstock and film frauds, and some people joked that Tony Molloy voodoo dolls would be appearing in the Christmas stockings of more than a few legal beagles and merchant bankers.

It just so happened that one of these wine cartons was due to be hand delivered to Justice Robertson by Molloy on the same day as one of the EP/TVNZ winebox hearings that the good judge was presiding over. Rather than be spotted by European Pacific's lawyers furtively accepting a wine carton from Dr Molloy behind the High Court, and risk all the suspicion that was bound to follow, Justice Robertson opted to drive several blocks away for a more discreet rendezvous with the plonk.

But while we lost the big one – the injunction staying on – we did score some other victories against European Pacific. Justice John Henry, in a separate hearing, ordered the European Pacific Group to comply with a TVNZ request to disclose its true ownership, and also to hand over under "discovery" all further documents held by EP relating to the Magnum and JIF deals.

Discovery is a legal process that allows parties in litigation to obtain, before trial, all of the evidence each side has that may be relevant to the case. TVNZ, for example, had to provide European Pacific with a full list of all the winebox documents we had. In turn, we were asking EP to cough up any documents on Magnum and JIF that we didn't have.

European Pacific was on the ropes and, with nothing left to lose, filed an appeal against those orders with the Court of Appeal. European Pacific attached a third request to its legal wish-list – a demand that the Court of Appeal force Ian Wishart and TVNZ to reveal the names of all the sources. Clang, went the psychological prison doors in my mind. The Court of Appeal heard the case in the second week of May.

Craddock, who gives the impression, at best, of disliking the media and, at worst, of hating them, stridently talked of an *"unrelenting campaign"* by the news media to *"undermine"* the existing High Court injunction, and demanded that I be forced, by order of the Court, to immediately squeal on everyone who'd supplied me with information.

This, he argued, was necessary so that European Pacific could decide whether those sources needed to be injuncted and, if EP eventually won its case, whether those sources should be sued for damages.

Julian Miles used the flip side of the same coin to argue against it, saying that if TVNZ eventually won the trial, disclosure of source now would have been unwarranted and unfair to the sources whose confidentiality had been blown.

European Pacific wheeled in its advisers from Russell McVeagh McKenzie Bartleet and Co to take up the cudgels on the "discovery" and revelation of true ownership issues. Tax expert Richard Green, a Russell McVeagh partner, argued that the Income Tax Act prevented third parties from questioning any decision made by the Commissioner of Inland Revenue. Green argued that because both the Commissioner and the SFO had declared that no fraud or tax evasion existed, those judgements couldn't be legally questioned and Television New Zealand's case should be thrown out on that basis. The argument that no one could question the authority of the IRD did not wash with the country's top judges – the Court of Appeal burst out laughing.

The following Monday, May 16, they dealt a fatal blow to European Pacific Group. In a 10-page ruling handed down by Appeal Court President Sir Robin Cooke, Justice Sir Maurice Casey and Justice McKay, European Pacific was blown out of the water, in a very civilised way.

The Appeal Court, of course, was not in a position to make binding "findings" on the substantial issue of the case – ie, whether there was fraud or not. This was an issue that would be determined at trial, and the Appeal Court could not openly prejudge it. However, the Court was required to take into account the likelihood that fraud could be proven in assessing whether TVNZ's case was strong enough to survive EP's move to strike it out.

"From the affidavit evidence before the High Court judges, the reasons given for their rulings, and the arguments of counsel in this Court, we consider that the appeals can be determined on the basis that the facts are probably substantially as follows.

"Of course we make no findings. But the probabilities appear to be that, within the European Pacific Group, there were devised schemes of business, attractive to investor clients, having among their elements the payment of withholding tax to the Cook Islands Government on behalf of a company in the Group and the immediate payment out of almost the whole amount of that tax by another agency of the Cook Islands Government, which payment out was received to the benefit of the Group, although not necessarily by the member on whose behalf the tax payment was made.

"That member, however, would claim a tax credit in its own country (for example New Zealand or Japan) against income tax there payable, which claim would be supported by a certificate of the tax payment in the Cook Islands.

"The immediate contra payment would not be disclosed to the taxation authorities, with the result that the credit would be allowed. By these means, the defendants [TVNZ] allege, the New Zealand Government was deprived of tax of the order of more than $2 million (the Magnum transaction) and the Japanese Government of tax of the order of more than $100 million (the JIF transactions)."

Any fears I might have held that their honours might not grasp the nature of the transactions had been swiftly dispelled. These judges clearly knew exactly what we were getting at.

They went on to note the effect of s.301(1)(b) of the NZ Income Tax Act, which states that a credit for foreign tax will not be allowed unless the taxpayer claiming the credit also provides detail of any repayment or relief of the foreign tax – information necessary so the Commissioner can decide on the amount of the credit, if any.

The Appeal Court noted EP's claim that the group member receiving the payback, EP Merchant Finance, was not the same group member that applied for the NZ tax credit, EP Funds Management.

"And they [EP] apparently suggest that information as to the existence and elements of the schemes is not necessary for determining the amount of the credit. On the other hand, the defendants contend that the virtually contemporaneous payments out should have been disclosed under s.301 and that the elaborate schemes (of their remarkable international elaboration there is ample evidence in the documents) were designed to conceal the truth from taxation authorities.

"Fraud in the form of tax evasion, not mere avoidance, is alleged. Among other matters attention is drawn to what is alleged to be a blueprint of the schemes, an internal memorandum of the Group, dated 25 November 1987, which refers to the desirability of not making 'detection an easier task for the authorities'.

"On the evidence as it now stands we do not attempt to make any pronouncement on the issue just outlined. It is enough for us to say two things.

"First, the Magnum scheme apparently resulted in the allowance of a tax credit in New Zealand. Secondly, since the Commissioner's public statement records that he has been advised by an independent barrister that 'it is clearly a tax avoidance scheme which is void for income tax purposes in terms of section 99 of the Income Tax Act 1976', the inference is open that when initially allowing the credit the Commissioner was not aware of material facts."

Minds like steel traps, these Appeal Court judges. While being very careful not to *"make any findings"*, they were clearly gunning for European Pacific, almost to the point of opening up lines of further inquiry for us to pursue. In legal realms, subtlety is the order of the day. These judges were subtly beating the crap out of Craddock, Green and the EP Group.

"It may be that the promissory note transactions were not disclosed when a tax credit was claimed in New Zealand. There may also be room for the inference that those transactions were conceived and documented as they were in order to conceal any connection with the contemporaneous payment of tax in the Cook Islands."

This was a crucial point of the judgement. While making no "findings", the Appeal Court was signalling the likelihood that the NZ IRD had not been *"aware of material facts"* when it initially allowed $2 million of tax credits for EP in the Magnum deal. Such concealment could amount to fraud by evasion. At the very least, the Court was casting a major doubt on the IRD's claim that the transaction was legitimate avoidance.

To be avoidance, the IRD generally has to be given all the facts at the time of the tax claim. The admission that a barrister had only recently decided it was avoidance indicated the Commissioner had not seen the whole deal originally.

"At this interlocutory stage it is enough for us to say that on the evidence now

before the Court the defendants have a seriously arguable case for their defence of iniquity. It is not a defence that could be struck out."

The Court turned its attention to tax expert Richard Green's claim that, under s297 of the Act, the decisions of the IRD could not be questioned and that all such decisions are final and deemed to be correct.

"If well-founded, this contention would have entitled the plaintiffs [European Pacific] to apply successfully for a striking out of the defence of iniquity. We fully share Henry J.'s doubts of its soundness. On their face provisions such as s.297 are not directed at curtailing freedom of speech. There is no authority for the view that they shut out a defendant, to an action for defamation or for breach of confidence, from proving the truth of a statement by him that the revenue authorities have been deliberately misled.

"Such proof by way of defence to such an action does not question the conclusiveness of the assessment. Indeed, the conclusive deeming of the assessment to be correct may be **part of the very advantages which a fraudulent scheme is designed to secure** *[author's emphasis]."*

Now that was a slap in the face, a really hard one. The judges were saying, in essence, that European Pacific may have known it was away scot-free forever, if it got a clean bill of health from the IRD, knowing that that assessment could not be challenged afterwards.

European Pacific, in fact, were left with nothing. On the issue of ownership and further discovery of Magnum and JIF documents, the Court of Appeal rejected claims that they were simply "fishing expeditions", and ordered European Pacific to comply immediately with TVNZ's demands.

On the issue of disclosure of source, the issue that I felt particularly close to, EP also received a hammering. The three judges decreed that European Pacific's desire to know the names of my informants was irrelevant to the central issue: did the documents disclose fraud? As all the relevant documentation and evidence was already before the Court, that issue could be determined without finding out who leaked the documents in the first place. That, said the Court, was a secondary issue.

If TVNZ could prove at the trial that an iniquity had indeed taken place, then European Pacific would probably be denied the right to know who the source was. If, on the other hand, European Pacific won, the issue of source was something they could pursue at that point.

"The courts nevertheless recognise that there is a legitimate public interest in protecting media sources from unnecessary revelation," the Appeal Court ruled. Thank you, Jesus, I prayed silently. Wishart escapes jail for contempt of court yet again.

It was an incredibly important ruling for all New Zealand media organisations and, indeed, all New Zealanders who may find themselves wishing to blow the whistle on something in the future. This was the first time that protection of source had been pushed so far or so high up the legal ladder in a breach of confidence action.

The Appeal Court had essentially decided that disclosure should properly be decided only after the Court has determined whether the original complaint from the whistleblower was justified.

From European Pacific there was a deafening silence. By Wednesday May 18 the company was clearly in contempt of the Court of Appeal, having still failed to deliver up the remaining Magnum or JIF documents and failed also to reveal its true ownership.

The trial was due to begin on Monday – if European Pacific entered the High Court on Monday while still in contempt of the Appeal Court it could expect to lose its case against us pretty swiftly. By Thursday we knew something was up. European Pacific had approached TVNZ offering to settle out of court. It was crucial, warned Willie Akel, that no one in the news media discovered we were negotiating.

Those negotiations continued all weekend and even into Monday morning, the day the trial was to start. I'd been phoned during the weekend by our lawyers informing that the basis of a deal had been reached – the remaining discussions were centred on a few fine points.

The basic deal would be that European Pacific drop its legal action against Project X, thereby paving the way for the programme to be broadcast and, in addition, one of the parties was to make a contribution to the other's costs – the terms of which remain confidential.

In return, TVNZ would agree to hand back the remaining winebox documents not already used in the programme's production. This was OK by me – there was more than enough evidence in the documents we were using to indicate possible criminal fraud, and I had no particular deep dark urge to keep trawling through the winebox in search of stories.

On Monday morning, the media contingent and Winston Peters, who'd gathered for the start of what they expected to be a two week trial, were staggered to find the case had been settled.

Craddock QC told the Court that European Pacific had decided to end the legal action because the Magnum and JIF deals were now *"in the public domain"* courtesy of Peters' parliamentary speeches and media coverage.

This was a facile argument as well, but it went over the heads of most journalists who blindly took it at face value. If Craddock's reasons were correct, then European Pacific should have ended its legal action back in March when the speeches were actually made, instead of fighting for eight weeks – arguing that the documents were still confidential because Peters hadn't said enough.

No, the real reason EP quit was the "horror judgement" from the Appeal Court. Faced with two evils, EP chose the lesser – letting *Frontline's* investigation take wing. The alternative was to go into Court and be forced to reveal whether Fay Richwhite and Brierley Investments, or any individuals associated with those companies, still have a financial interest in the ownership of EP, and also be forced to hand over more possibly incriminating documentation. That was the bogey hanging over EP, and that alone was probably the reason they caved in.

Emerging from the High Court on a blustery and damp winter Monday, the sense of exhilaration was palpable. Finally, two years after first beginning the investigation, it was going to air. It would be grossly unfair and churlish to suggest that I gloatingly danced in maniacal circles around EP's lawyers as they came out, whilst chanting *"Yah, sucks, boo, hiss, gotcha!"*. On the other hand, it would be accurate to admit that the thought crossed my mind. Smug was an understatement.

After such a bitter and bloody struggle, the victory was personal as well as business. A number of my sources had been effectively expelled from New Zealand, some had been threatened with massive lawsuits if they ever so much as thought about opening their mouths.

Families had been torn asunder. One six-year old boy wrote poems at school wishing that his father was dead – his father was one of those whistleblowers forced to flee the country. The little boy didn't understand, all he knew was that his dad wasn't there anymore; that his dad had abandoned him.

How many careers had been sacrificed or destroyed as people struggled and failed to tell their stories to a disbelieving media? Why had the law enforcement agencies not lifted a finger to carry out a thorough, painstaking investigation?

My own marriage had come perilously close to the rocks on more than one occasion, my career at TV3 had not survived.

All of this flooded over me in ferocious waves of emotion as I tried to make a more cautious and neutral statement to the waiting media outside the Court. Yes, this was a victory for press freedom, I told them.

"If you can measure the significance of this programme by the extraordinary efforts to stop it from ever screening, then that should be a message to all New Zealanders that this is about something very, very important."

If it sounded trite, it was probably because I was far too acutely aware of the intricacies involved.

The High Court settlement gave us the rest of the week to get the programme ready for broadcast. At the end of the day, Graeme Wilson's censoring efforts would have little real impact. While the cosmetics and labels had been changed, the heart of the story revealed a prima facie fraud had taken place. In addition, we'd been able to incorporate the new information from the David Lloyd interview which enabled us to zoom in a lot closer to whatever responsibility existed within EP for the deals. The extra months had allowed more of the jigsaw to take shape.

That Sunday evening, May 29, 1994, at precisely 6:30pm, a switch was thrown in the TVNZ transmission centre and Project X began broadcasting, six months after it was first scheduled.

The Genie was unstoppable.

CHAPTER 23

An Asian Cockfight

*"What! from his helpless Creature be repaid
Pure Gold for what He lent him dross-allay'd:
Sue for a Debt he never did contract,
And cannot answer — Oh the sorry Trade!"*
— FROM THE RUBAIYAT OF OMAR KHAYYAM, C 1100AD

IT WAS AS IF the enchantment holding the whole shebang together had been broken; the hastily cobbled-together forces aligned against us began disintegrating, crumbling away, slowly at first and then with increasing force and fury as the splits became more obvious.

The first brick to fall from the wall came even before Project X was aired. During the preceding week the documents used in the programme's production had been unshackled by the court, and Parliament was forced to follow, allowing copies of those documents to be distributed to an eager media.

It resulted in what seemed at the time to be a maelstrom of adverse publicity for European Pacific on newspaper front pages nationwide for a few days but, with hindsight, was in reality only a momentary eddy in comparison with the tempest that would rage after the Sunday May 29 broadcast — a broadcast that became a one, two punch with the addition of a studio debate hosted by Ian Fraser immediately afterward.

Public reaction to **that** was swift, unanimous and ice-cold deadly for the Government. Veteran media commentator Alex Veysey summed up the views of many in an editorial in Wellington's *Evening Post*.

"The Frontline investigation was finely crafted television," he observed. *"It was one of the peculiar triumphs of two hours of the Cook Islands-European Pacific tax avoidance investigation last night that no one shouted at anyone.*

"I don't know that I have ever seen or heard a more civilised debate on a matter justifying outrage. There was outrage of course, but quite superbly controlled, a towering tribute to the people of known passion and of sometimes intemperately-expressed principle who contributed.

"Here was restraint taken dangerously close to the edge of refinement, courteous disagreement, deferential debate, soft thunder. Yet the Fraser-commanded segment, thus presented, was an even more complementary adjunct to Frontline's compelling investigation, long cellared from public scrutiny through the processes of legal restraint, than if Winston Peters had beaten Wyatt Creech vigorously over the head with a loaded wine-carton.

"It is not sufficient to say the Cooks-European Pacific shenanigans has captured the imagination of New Zealanders. There is something much earthier than healthy curiosity here. Like indignation."

Others, like the *Dominion's* Simon Kilroy, also recognised the power of television, when harnessed properly, to fuel rebellion within the masses.

"The problem for the Government, and the reason an issue that looked to have gone dormant is back on the front pages, is the big difference in public impact between the at-times tortuous explanations fogged with detail Mr Peters gave in Parliament, and a two hour slot on primetime television.

"Frontline turned a labyrinthine series of deals into a slick video game of tax invaders, inviting its audience to follow the bouncing bag of money around various European Pacific subsidiaries in the Cook Islands.

"Regardless of whether the audience fully took in the complexities, the abiding impression left was that something was not right and that the Government seemed to have little interest in finding out about it."

The ultimate irony, revealed in Kilroy's column, was that the Masters in the Beehive, New Zealand's Government offices, were spitting with fury at the decision by TVNZ management to run the programme.

"At the end of the week at least one senior minister was still blaming the whole thing on Television New Zealand and privately questioning the motives behind TVNZ's decision to devote two hours of prime time television to allegations about events six years ago."

This was rich, a political hiding was being dished out in newsprint, if not reality, for allowing the programme to air when, in fact, there had been considerable behind the scenes activity to delay its broadcast.

The simplistic argument that the alleged crimes were six years old and therefore not deserving of investigation was correctly ridiculed by most observers, on the basis that those responsible for such crimes could theoretically continue committing them unless brought to justice. Where do you draw the line? Six years? Six months? Six minutes?

That senior members of the New Zealand Government were advocating such an approach to investigating white-collar crime is staggering but, in view of the circumstances, not surprising. I must say it conflicted just a tad with the prosecution in 1992 of former millionaire Allan Hawkins on charges arising from the 1987 collapse of his company, Equiticorp.

It was on talkback radio, however, that the public delivered their verdict with a ferocity not seen in years. For days on end the message was the same from both caller and host: rage at being the victims of a corporate raid on the treasury chest, disgust at the morality of so-called pillars of society, and a growing suspicion that the politicians attempting to quash the prospect of an inquiry might have something to hide.

It was a national outpouring of savage emotion on a scale unimagined even in the Government's worst nightmares. Sensing the need to quench the flames, parliamentarians agreed to send the still-banned winebox to Parliament's powerful Privileges Committee for a ruling on whether it could be released to the public.

Of course, there was only ever one possible outcome to that issue. To my mind, the decision in the first place by the Speaker, Peter Tapsell, to restrict publication had been a flawed one. The argument that Parliament should not cut across the Courts while a case was being deliberated had some small merit: in doing so Parliament was essentially respecting the possibility that European Pacific might win the right to eternal confidentiality of its documents.

But what would Parliament then have done if the High Court had finally ruled that EP's documents should remain forever hidden? Logic would dictate that Parliament would have to also permanently ban publication of the papers tabled in the House, otherwise there would have been no point in imposing a temporary ban in the first place.

Putting it another way, Parliament was in a Catch 22 situation. The Speaker had inadvertently set a trap for himself. Parliament should only ever have banned publication of the documents back in March if it was prepared to make that ban permanent in the face of a Court decision in EP's favour.

Constitutionally, Parliament's legal advisers – Solicitor-General John McGrath and Clerk of the House David McGee – should have fully appreciated the conundrum when they advised the Speaker that the interim injunction should be respected.

The documents themselves had already been tabled by Peters, they couldn't be "un-tabled". Much as European Pacific and Rudd Watts Stone might have dreamed that Parliament would permanently suppress the tabled documents, constitutionally such a move would always have been a total non-starter.

The whole idea of tabling documents in Parliament is that they are made available to every citizen by virtue of that move – it is a cornerstone of Westminster democracy.

If EP <u>had</u> won its case, Parliament would have found itself forced to publish the winebox, regardless. A decision not to publish would have placed the rights of Parliament, and therefore the rights of the nation, below those of a tinpot taxhaven company that had just won a minor court action in a civil, not criminal, dispute.

Does anyone, outside the Business Roundtable, seriously believe, even for a moment, that Parliament would – for the first time in its 300 year history – make itself subservient to a permanent Court injunction, let alone on a matter as sleazy and piddly as this one?

It was not as if the winebox contained blueprints for the military defence of the Western World in a nuclear confrontation. The box didn't even contain any official New Zealand Government documentation. It was simply a box of tax rorts already admitted by the IRD as *casting little credit on the business ethics of the designers*".

So I raise the question again – why didn't the National Government and the Parliamentary authorities face up to the inevitable back in March and just allow the documentation to be published? Constitutionally, the cat was out of the bag – but our rulers were trying frantically to stuff it back in and pretend that everything was under control.

It was analogous to Guy Fawkes lighting a fuse under Parliament, with no means of extinguishing it available, and watching pretentious politicians preach and pontificate – finally passing legislation ordering the barrels of gunpowder not to explode. A complete and utter farce.

There was no way this winebox was not going to detonate underneath them: it was always going to go bang, we knew that from the moment Peters tabled it. It was simply a question of when. Peters, of course, was continuing to fan the flame on the end of the fuse. On Wednesday June 1st, four days after the screening of Project X, he marched into the Parliamentary debating chamber determined to finish the job once and for all.

"This story was never about tax avoidance or clever accounting," growled Peters. *"It is about criminal fraud on New Zealand, the Cook Islands and Japan. This is bank robbery without guns. Richwhite, Collins, Travers and Lloyd should be in jail."*

But whereas the directors and staff of European Pacific had been the main targets in the March 22 speech, this time Peters' guns were turned almost exclusively on Serious Fraud Office director, Chas Sturt; Inland Revenue Commissioner David Henry and the Government.

"This Government, the Inland Revenue Department and the Serious Fraud Office claim that everyone else has got it wrong and that the National Party's chief campaign donors acted within the law.

"Charles Sturt . . . is supposed to be the Government's hired gun to combat fraud. He could not hit a barn at 10 paces! Today I am calling for the immediate suspension of the director of the Serious Fraud Office and the Commissioner of Inland Revenue."

Peters talked of *"secret, non-prosecution agreements"* which let the culprits off the hook, and warned that he'd had calls from staff in both offices who said *"their bosses are plainly wrong"*. As to the transactions themselves, roared Peters from centrestage in the debating chamber, not only tax experts but even the Court of Appeal had tumbled to the fact that Magnum *"is a fraud"*.

"If it looks like a duck, if it waddles like a duck, and if it quacks like a duck, then I suggest to the House that it is a duck."

And still the Government steadfastly refused to duck, National MP's telling journalists the Government could take *"a lot more political heat"* before caving in to calls for an inquiry. Coming as it did on the eve of the 50th anniversary of the D-Day invasion, some commentators couldn't resist drawing analogies.

"Prime Minister Jim Bolger," wrote Ian Templeton in the *Sunday Star-Times*, *"as he stands on Omaha Beach in Normandy tomorrow, may reflect on the enormous casualties suffered when an irresistible force meets an immovable object.*

"Back home, it is the Government's own reputation that is taking the pounding – and Mr Bolger, after another week under fire from Winston Peters, is still counting the cost."

But it was even more serious than that. The multi-pronged Peters attack may have washed off the Government, but it was rapidly eroding public confidence in the tax system and the Serious Fraud Office. Both agencies were haemorrhaging gravely, prompting Templeton to note the words of a retired National MP, Rob Munro.

"Public confidence in democracy is a fragile flower. It needs to be nurtured."

Against that backdrop, the Privileges Committee opted to pull Parliament's finger out of the dyke. Resistance, they figured, was useless.

Peters had earlier managed to "take out" Attorney-General Paul East, who would normally sit on the powerful Committee, when he named senior Russell McVeagh partner John Lusk in Parliament as part of an alleged criminal conspiracy linked to European Pacific. Lusk was the Attorney-General's cousin.

Peters had been harping on in Parliament about Russell McVeagh's alleged crimes for two years, and one of his opponents on the issue was East. Now, however, with the direct naming of Lusk, the Attorney-General chose to declare a conflict of interest.*

East's position on the Privileges Committee was taken by Bill Birch, another trusted Bolger lieutenant. He was joined by Justice Minister Doug Graham and acting Prime Minister Don McKinnon on the Government side, while the Labour contingent included former PM and shadow Attorney-General David Lange, and a split-shift comprising shadow finance minister David Caygill, whose place was taken on the final day of deliberation by Jonathon Hunt, another senior Labour figure. Doug Graham was acting chairman. Both Lange and Hunt had been outspoken in support of publishing the tabled winebox – if only to reassert Parliament's supremacy over the courts.

Also assisting: legal opinions from the Solicitor-General, John McGrath; Clerk of the House, David McGee; and the President of the Law Commission, Sir Kenneth Keith. McGee's main concern in recommending suppression of the winebox back in March was his desire not to be used by Peters as a means of beating a High Court injunction.

Sensitive to the fine balance that exists between Court and State, and earbashed no doubt by his staff lawyers after the tabling, McGee recognised that before he could release the winebox to the news media, parliamentarians would first have to vote to "print" the documents.

This technical problem arose because in 1839 someone tried to sue Parliament's official stenography service, Hansard, on the grounds that privilege did not extend to documents published by Hansard.

The British Parliament fought back, enacting in law, later adopted in New Zealand, a clause protecting absolutely any papers published by Parliament. But to gain that absolute protection, the House had to go through the motions of publishing, by making an express order to *"print the papers"*.

Normally this technicality is not an issue. The tabling of the document

---

* In a conversation with the author in May 1995, East said he felt it was *"inappropriate"* for him to chair the Privileges Committee in a decision-making role, given Lusk's name being dropped into the debate. He added, however, that Lusk's role was only peripheral and, with New Zealand being a small country, it was impossible to avoid perceived conflicts of interest in some cases. *"Where do you draw the line?,"* he asked.

itself often confers enough protection on the media to escape court action, without the express "publication" by the House. In this case, however, McGee perhaps felt the extremely litigious European Pacific Group and its business and legal allies would not hesitate to challenge Parliament's authority – contempt of court being just one avenue.

From the Clerk's point of view, absolute protection from legal action would be conferred on winebox documents only if the House specifically ordered that they be printed. *"Whether or not this is a desirable step to take is a matter for the committee and, ultimately, the House to determine,"* McGee concluded in his report to the Committee.

In his report, the Solicitor-General immediately recognised the obvious:

"As a matter of constitutional law, no Court has jurisdiction to impeach or call into question any proceeding of the House of Representatives. This is the principle arising from Article 9 of the Bill of Rights 1688. It has force in New Zealand.

"It follows from Article 9 that as a matter of law no injunction is enforceable in the Courts in respect of actions taken by the House of Representatives. The answer . . . is therefore that the House is not constrained by any legal obligation to comply with injunctions against parties to Court proceedings."

This, of course, reinforced earlier misgivings about the wisdom of Parliament's earlier refusal to publish the documents. John McGrath did point out that in his view the Speaker had acted correctly back in March, because the central issue of confidentiality versus disclosure of iniquity was still before the Court and scheduled for trial on May 23rd. On that basis it was reasonable, he argued, for Parliament to give the Court a chance to rule on the matter.

Others of us, of course, saw it differently. The end result was inevitable from the moment the winebox was tabled. It would have saved everyone a lot of money and heartache if Parliament had published the papers then and there – ending the expensive legal action without further wasting court time.

The subsequent consensual settlement between TVNZ and EP had, McGrath said, removed the likelihood of an early ruling on the central issue. Interestingly, although the matter was still before the Courts in the case of European Pacific Banking Corporation vs Fourth Estate Publications Ltd., McGrath didn't consider that it merited the same need for sensitivity from Parliament.

"If the House, including the Privileges Committee, chooses to address the question of publication of the suppressed papers, they would not be trespassing to the same extent into the area of the Court's jurisdiction. Arguably it would not be entering into the Court's province at all."

In essence then, the Solicitor-General was happy on two fronts. Firstly, that Parliament was under no legal obligation to abide by the Court's injunction orders in the first place and, secondly, that in terms of sensitivity the chessboard had altered since the March 17 Speaker's ruling. At that time, the Court had been only weeks away from a full trial on the issue. Now, while it was still before the Courts, the likelihood of a full trial had receded. Parliament was free to do what it wished with the winebox.

Law Commission President, Sir Kenneth Keith, echoed McGrath's legal opinion, but added an extra flavour to the debate. Not only was Parliament not beholden to the Courts in this matter – the Courts also took a particularly generous view of the powers of Parliament, he added.

"The Court of Appeal . . . referred to an established principle of non-interference by the Courts in parliamentary proceedings. It stated its opinion 'that public policy requires that the representative chamber of Parliament should be free to determine what it will or will not allow to be put before it'."

The Privileges Committee met twice, on June 2 and June 8, delivering its verdict to Parliament on the evening of June 8.

"There seemed to be general agreement between all of the witnesses," reported Doug Graham to Parliament, *"that the House is not restricted in ordering the documents tabled be printed. Although there was no direct evidence before the Committee, it is common knowledge that the plaintiff in the actions has alleged that the relevant documents were stolen from it.*

"Without determining that issue, for the purposes of this inquiry, the Committee is prepared to accept that the documents may have been stolen and that accordingly the plaintiff would, if asked, object to their publication.

"Having taken those matters into account, the Committee has concluded that the public interest in this case justifies a recommendation to the House that the documents referred to should now be printed, and recommends accordingly."

It was with a great deal of uncharitable glee that I watched as the winebox papers went on sale at bookshops around the country the next day for the princely sum of $41.85 a set. They rapidly sold out.

The screams of anguish from named corporate entities could be heard reverberating around the country's glass office towers for days. Loudest was Brierley Investments.

"All those named in Parliament," he hissed in a sizzling news release, *"and in the documents released [yesterday] stand publicly accused, with no entitlement to defend their reputations and standing through the established court system."*

This wasn't entirely true. European Pacific had been given the chance to have a full Court trial and defend itself and its staff from TVNZ's fraud allegations. Instead of having its day, or in this case fortnight, in Court, European Pacific and its allies turned tail and ran. I, for one, would have been more than happy to take the case right through trial.

But Bob Matthew continued his bleating about the actions of Parliament, which by now had also decided to open an investigation of the winebox documents by Parliament's Finance and Expenditure Select Committee.

"These abuses of the rights of individuals and the firms they represent have brought the standard of New Zealand's Parliament down to that of an Asian cockfight. No one should be comfortable with the current political circus appointing itself prosecutor, judge and jury as it plans to do via the select committee process."

Intemperate language from a man whose company had owned Magnum Corporation, and which itself was named in, and linked to, transactions referred to in the winebox. Brierley Investments had also been a 28 percent shareholder in European Pacific with representatives on the board.

At the date this is written, Brierleys* is yet to testify before the Commission of Inquiry about its role. To my mind, Matthew's statement also came close to bordering on contempt of Parliament.

The decision to fire the matter off to the Finance and Expenditure Committee was an attempt by the Government to take some of the heat out of Peters claims of a cover-up. The Committee had a majority of Government MP's, and was chaired by former Finance Minister Ruth Richardson – an arch-opponent of Peters and his inquiry campaign.

Peters, and others, naturally lashed out at the prospect of a select committee inquiry, saying it wouldn't be independent enough from behind the scenes Government manoeuvring, and questioning the role of Richardson. At the same time, Peters had been doing some backroom dealing of his own. In a secret meeting with Opposition Labour leader, Helen Clark, he pointed out the advantages to Labour of supporting his calls for a full enquiry.

For a start, most of the Ministers in the last Labour Government who should have been responsible for policing the tax frauds were no longer part of the Labour Party, and instead had formed a new, right-wing political organisation. The only Labour MP who could be linked with any failure to detect the rorts was deputy leader David Caygill – a man totally opposed to the need for an inquiry. Peters pointed out to Clark that an inquiry would provide a way for Labour to exorcise its right wing "ghosts" from the deregulated '80's.

An equally astute Simon Kilroy in the *Dominion* gave the Bolger administration a serious case of speed wobbles with his analysis of the options.

"After a week of continual misstepping on the Cook Islands tax schemes the Government's image impresarios were left contemplating a nightmare scenario:

"NZ First leader Winston Peters continues to denounce the select committee examination of the Cook Islands schemes as a sham and announces he will be proposing a private member's bill to establish a royal commission inquiry into the whole issue.

"The Government, which has continually and vehemently denied there is anything worthy of further investigation in the winebox of documents that have already been examined by the Inland Revenue Department and the Serious Fraud

---

* Brierley Investments initially played a major role in attempting to stop winebox transactions being publicised at the Inquiry. When that failed, it took a different tack, arguing that the deals involved subsidiaries either no longer owned, or which were overseas-based with their own independent boards of directors. BIL, it said, was not a party, in itself, to any winebox transactions. In July 1995, the IRD revealed at the Inquiry that it had ordered Brierleys to pay tax on an extra $156 million, as a result of discovering an alleged tax avoidance scheme in the winebox. Brierleys is legally challenging the re-assessment.

Office, feels it cannot endure a humiliating backdown and opposes the move.

"Labour, which showed last week that it has belatedly woken up to the fact that it can only lose political capital by backing the Government on the issue, supports the Peters' proposal."

Kilroy gambled that enough disgruntled Government MP's would cross the floor to support a Commission of Inquiry as well, handing the Government a humiliating defeat.

"By the end of last week, even the mention of a private members bill to set up a Commission was enough to make Beehive strategists visibly pale."

The immediate constitutional crisis out of the way, attention now focussed on the select committee inquiry. Labour, privy now to a legal opinion from Dr John Prebble on the criminality of the Magnum deal, moved closer to the Peters' position, offering to give up one of its slots on the committee to the maverick NZ First leader. He accepted.

Max Bradford, one of the Government MP's on the committee, threw his weight behind Peters also, announcing after reading the winebox documents that *"there were some very sophisticated machinations to avoid, if not evade, paying tax in a variety of jurisdictions around the world."*

Max Bradford had previously been a chief executive of the NZ Bankers' Association – a man well qualified to follow the arcane and complex financial wiring diagrams and transaction details. He had long called for an inquiry into the Bank of New Zealand issue and, in fact, had been offered the winebox of documents before Winston Peters was, but turned it down. He had many opportunities since that day in 1992 to indulge in political self flagellation over the issue.

It was also probably no coincidence that Bradford's attitude was shaped, if only in part, by the fact that his own electorate was side by side with Peters' stronghold in Tauranga, and Bradford would benefit from Peters' popularity in the region by backing the right horse.

His "defection" to the side of those favouring a full and open inquiry left the Government without a clear majority on the committee. It added to the jitters of those corporate players who began to fear that a real inquiry might have inadvertently been created. They began to plot, their scheming intensifying after the resignation of Ruth Richardson from the committee and Parliament. That left the chairman's seat vacant, and Bradford was the obvious candidate. It was a prospect that terrified the Government, as well.

One of the first public examples of the fracas was later described in the *Herald* as a *"fairytale meeting"* of Parliament's powerful Finance and Expenditure Committee.

Unable to reach a decision on a new chairman to replace the outgoing Richardson, the Government had asked Ruth to cancel that week's committee hearings. Richardson didn't bother notifying the Labour MPs or Winston Peters, who duly turned up at the appointed time and found themselves staring at a gift horse – no sign of any National MPs and enough of their own ilk to create a quorum.

Declaring the meeting open, Labour's Michael Cullen was voted to the chair by Peters and Labour's Trevor Mallard, and for an hour they reigned supreme in the hearing room.

To embarrass the Government, the trio released to the news media copies of confidential submissions made by the absent Government MPs on the committee – Tony Ryall, Max Bradford and John Robertson. Robertson, a junior MP, was the Bolger administration's pick to replace Richardson as chairman of the committee. His "leaked" submission revealed he favoured a very narrow inquiry by the committee into the winebox allegations, preferring not to put anyone on trial – a perfect Government handmaiden.

Naturally enough, Robertson was irked at the *"disgraceful"* behaviour of the trio, and Bolger waded in as well.

"I am just astonished a senior Labour frontbencher like Michael Cullen should engage in such antics. Winston Peters? Sure, we expect it. Michael Cullen? We expect a little better," complained the Prime Minister to reporters.

None of this solved the core power struggle over who was going to take over the *"potentially explosive"* Cook Islands tax scandal inquiry. Finance Minister Bill Birch summoned the four Government members on the Committee to a private meeting to try and push Robertson as the candidate.

"Prime Minister Jim Bolger and Finance Minister Bill Birch were last night closeted in talks aimed at shutting Tarawera MP Max Bradford out of chairing the Cook Islands tax inquiry," trumpeted the *Dominion* in a front page lead.

"Mr Bradford is a firm supporter of an inquiry, including examination of the role of the BNZ, and Beehive sources said his strong views might make him unsuitable. John Robertson has been suggested as an alternative. He favours a very limited inquiry, and questions whether those who do not wish to appear before the committee should be required to attend."

It was *NBR's* Fran O'Sullivan who got behind the headlines however, and discovered just what lengths the Government was prepared to go to to rein in Bradford.

"He was called to a meeting at Bolger's Wellington home, Premier House, on Sunday July 17," she wrote. *"Present were the PM, Birch and Creech. Creech led the charge. Discussion is said to have been 'robust'. But Bradford held his ground. It was made clear to the troika that the MP and former Bankers' Association executive director would not step out of the running to allow a more junior MP . . . to be elected chairman.*

"When he left the Tinakori St address the troika would have been in no doubt that they would have to risk a severe political backlash if he was pushed into a corner. The plain fact is the executive [wing of Government] does not want the inquiry to take place. At the highest Cabinet level, Ministers are being advised to think again – to consider the option of shelving the committee's inquiry in favour of a limited formal inquiry. One the political cynics are saying should preferably be headed by a less-than-rigorous person, hearing evidence in confidence with its report timetabled for after next year's expected general election."

Certainly an indicator of the Government's commitment to a real investigation was shown in the Committee's actions under Ruth Richardson's leadership. Richardson imposed an incredibly short deadline for submissions on the issue and, even more notably, submissions had already closed before the Committee even announced its terms of reference for the inquiry or what immunities from prosecution might be offered. In other words, by the time interested parties finally found out what the terms of reference were, the deadline had passed for them to make submissions.

Despite the powerful opposition to Max Bradford, he was given the chairmanship, although some National Government sources were still floating the possibility that the inquiry could be shunted sideways to a sub-committee headed by someone other than Bradford.

Peters, meanwhile, attacked the involvement of Bolger and Birch in the discussions over the chairmanship as an *"outrage constitutionally"*. The problems didn't end there, however. After his appointment, Bradford tried to get ministerial approval for the committee to give immunity from prosecution to witnesses if needed. One senior Minister reportedly asked him why any witness would need immunity? No one had done anything wrong. Attorney-General Paul East was also involved in decisions on whether to grant immunity from prosecution to key witnesses.

But big business and legal sources were working furiously behind the scenes to sink the select committee inquiry. The jungle drums of the "old boys network" began to throb with "rumours" of a planned legal challenge to the authority of Parliament's Finance and Expenditure Committee by interests linked to Fay Richwhite, European Pacific, Brierleys and some of the legal and accounting firms associated with them.

At the same time, a public attack was mounted in the form of submissions by the Law Society's Mai Chen and former Attorney-General Sir Geoffrey Palmer. Their submissions, which were similar in thrust, claimed the select committee inquiry could become "McCarthyist" a reference to the US senator Joe McCarthy whose anti-communism crusade in the 1950's turned into a witch hunt.

Palmer, in particular, described the committee as *"a political and media circus in which peoples' rights are trampled on without proper protection being afforded to them."* He noted that legislative committees could cause *"irreparable damage to innocent people"*, which to my mind was making a premature assumption about the innocence of some of the named players.

The proper place for such accusations, claimed Palmer, was in a court of law – a claim later described as *"failsafe"* by Peters, because none of the regulatory authorities was willing to prosecute to test the case, and therefore the matter would never *get* to court.

The whole point of the select committee process, countered Peters, was to establish the evidence and then refer any matters needing further inquiry to the police or other relevant authority.

Peters, and others, also noted Palmer's "Ronald Reagan-like" selective memory – reminding the retired Attorney-General that he had once turned down the call for an independent Commission of Inquiry when he was in power, where witnesses would have had full legal representation and immunity, opting instead for a select committee.

Palmer's ability to do incredible U-turns on matters of principle was well known, however. Prior to becoming Deputy Prime Minister when the Labour Government of David Lange swept to power in 1984, Palmer – a constitutional law professor – had written a book called *Unbridled Power* which criticised the excesses of bureaucrats and politicians. The Lange/Palmer led Government then went on to break many of the cherished principles that a younger Geoffrey Palmer had held up as sacrosanct.

Another example, highlighted in the *New Zealand Law Journal* of July 4, 1972, was Palmer's attitude to the defamation laws.

"We need uninhibited, robust and wide open debate on public issues in New Zealand. We are not getting it and we will not get it unless the libel laws are altered. To this end I propose an amendment to the Defamation Act 1954:

"No action for defamation shall lie in respect to a statement on an issue of public concern unless the plaintiff can prove that the defendant made the statement with knowledge that it was false or with reckless disregard as to whether it was true or false."

Contrast that position with Palmer's current foray into parliamentary privilege, and you'd think they'd been written by different people. In my own time working alongside Palmer in 1986 whilst working as press secretary to Labour's No. 3, Mike Moore, I quickly formed the opinion that Palmer was incredibly ambitious, incredibly arrogant, and far too removed from the ebb and flow of daily working life as experienced by average New Zealanders as to be totally out of touch.

None of this is to suggest that Palmer had done anything untoward, but to my mind the man had a conflict of interest in now jumping to the defence of those involved – if only because cynics would argue his stance was political, a move to save the former Labour administration from embarrassment should an inquiry decide that Labour had failed to close the relevant loopholes.

There was some evidence that Labour had indeed been warned but failed to act – a letter dated 19 December 1986, and addressed to then Finance Minister Roger Douglas, from Treasury officials.* Names on the document had been twinked out, but whoever wrote it was recommending to Douglas *"that you make a statement as soon as possible aimed at halting blatant tax avoidance schemes which channel money to and from tax haven entities."*

Treasury, after consultation with the Inland Revenue Department, called on the Government to introduce tough new penalties for tax avoidance to provide a deterrence to those using tax havens. It noted that IRD didn't have enough staff to detect non-disclosure of information, but also pointed out *"that the Commissioner **has authority under existing legislation to require taxpayers to furnish the necessary disclosures of tax haven transactions."** [author's emphasis]*

---

* The irony here was that only weeks earlier, Douglas had given approval to a BNZ request to become involved in the EPI tax haven business.

The Treasury/IRD penalty requests were never put into place by the Labour Government, which instead set up a consultative committee to advise on tax haven problems. The loopholes remained open until 1988.

The Palmer attack on the Parliamentary select committee inquiry resurfaced in an even more sinister guise – legislation introduced to Parliament by Labour's David Caygill which would have repealed Article 9 of the Bill of Rights 1688 – the law that guarantees Members of Parliament freedom of speech in the House and absolute privilege from any legal action resulting from what they say there.

Palmer had actually helped Caygill draft the Parliamentary Privilege Bill – a law that, if passed, would prevent someone like Peters from ever speaking out on matters like European Pacific again. How two elected representatives of the New Zealand Parliament could try to write a law taking away a freedom enjoyed by other Western democracies for 300 years, shows just how degenerated New Zealand democracy had become by 1994.

While Caygill was at pains to point out that the bill wasn't aimed at Winston Peters, I viewed it – uncharitably perhaps – as an attempt to protect the reputations of a few business executives. Allegations surfaced during a parliamentary debate on the matter that certain "major lawfirms" had been involved in the proposal, and in fact had lobbied MPs to support the Bill.

Under the Palmer/Caygill "Trojan Horse", MPs wanting to speak on controversial matters such as *"impropriety, breach of duty, dishonesty or criminal conduct"* by people outside Parliament would first have to seek the permission of the Speaker, and satisfy that official that they had full proof to back up their claims. If they went ahead and spoke out regardless, they could face criminal charges.

At a time when the introduction of proportional representation in the electoral system looked set to remove the powers of big business to buy influence with entire political parties, this Bill opened the door for big business to potentially corrupt just one elected representative – the Speaker of the House.

As former Prime Minister David Lange noted, *"If parliamentary democracy depended on the Speaker, it would have withered about 400 years ago."*

In a future Parliament, if the Speaker had been bribed by a lobby group, he or she could not only prevent MPs raising allegations that reflected badly on that lobby group – the Speaker could also veto the raising of any allegations that came close to revealing his or her role in the corruption. The latter example, of course, would only delay the inevitable, but it is a thoroughly undesirable scenario.

It was, to my mind, the most dangerous piece of legislation to ever come before the New Zealand Parliament, bar none. If passed, this Bill would take away the rights of citizens to an unfettered Parliament – the last bastion of free speech in a world where the mega-millionaires can buy an expensive lawyer and secure an injunction with a snap of the fingers.

Thankfully, Caygill and Palmer have found little support for their position. Paul Rishworth and Grant Huscroft, of the Auckland University

Law Faculty, argued that, whatever the rationale behind it, the Bill was a non-starter.

"Regardless of how the system would operate, the consequences of this proposal are apparent: The Speaker would become the gatekeeper to the sanctuary of parliamentary privilege and exercise a power of veto over what could safely be said in the House.

"Thus, the proposal is a restraint on freedom of speech in the place where that freedom is of fundamental constitutional importance. Why should MP's not be subject to the law of defamation for statements made in the House? The rationale for the free speech privilege is that it is undesirable that the threat of defamation proceedings should restrain members of Parliament from speaking out when they consider it necessary in the public interest.

"It is not a right to defame members of the public, or to abuse freedom of speech. MPs are responsible to the House, as well as the electorate, and there is a political price to be paid if privilege is abused.

"But speech which can only safely be uttered with the prior approval of a public official is not free speech. There should be no room in a democracy for restrictions of this sort."

National's Max Bradford also waded in against the draconian attempt to gag MPs, in an article for the *National Business Review*.

"I have put the word 'privilege' in quotes throughout this article, because it is not a privilege in the normal sense of the word. It is not a privilege for members of Parliament, but a protection for the public.

"If parliamentarians are not able to speak out freely in the House, then many matters which should be revealed in the public interest would be swept under the proverbial carpet.

"Nor is the fact that 'privilege' attaches to any member of the public who appears before a select committee well understood. They enjoy the same rights and protections from legal action for speaking their minds as do members of Parliament. Would the public want its own rights circumscribed?"

They were valid questions. It was a fight for control of a country swirling behind the scenes, with most citizens unaware that the battle was even being fought, with most media outlets barely even covering the debate. Those in the daily press that did often highlighted the emotive criticisms of parliamentary privilege made by people in business and the legal professions, without recognising that such proposals would take away a cornerstone of democracy – the right to put the greater public interest above that of a few select and well placed individuals.

Supporters of the Caygill/Palmer gagging bill had argued that the original Bill of Rights had been drawn up to protect MPs from the power of kings and queens, and as such had outlived its usefulness in a modern age where the throne could no longer pose a threat. Instead, they claimed, the pendulum had swung to the point where ordinary citizens needed to be protected from the ravages of Parliament.

Rishworth and Huscroft blew that red herring out of the water as well. *"This argument is misleading. Free speech has always been the need to allow*

members of the House to voice matters of public concern without the stifling effect
that fear of retribution brings.

"That rationale is no different now that 'retribution' principally comes in the
form of litigation brought by citizens and corporations rather than retaliation from
kings and queens.

"In England, parliamentary free speech remains absolute. In Canada, the
Supreme Court has recently confirmed that parliamentary privilege enjoys
constitutional protection. The United States Supreme Court has long recognised
that all Americans must be free to discuss the activities of public figures, and
accordingly has fashioned extensive protection from defamation proceedings even
for private citizens."

That one cardboard box could cause so much division, fear and intrigue, speaks volumes for what it contained and what it represented.

I believe it personified what, by the early 1990's, had become an orthodox way of doing business in New Zealand; a kind of "there but for the grace of God . . . " icon to the greed and sleaze of the 1980's. Why do I believe this? Because of the fury that whipped through corporate New Zealand at the way the media and Peters were portraying the winebox transactions, because of the persistent and, in my view, misguided efforts of a number of accountants to ignore the blatant illegalities and publicly give the transactions a clean bill of health.

I say accountants, because it was mostly only accountants who were daft enough to stick their heads up into the crossfire. Senior tax lawyers chose not to enter the debate publicly.

The ludicrous sight of seeing junior and mid-grade accountants telling three men with doctorates in tax law that they'd got it wrong was almost too galling to swallow. It was almost akin to letting some 19-year-old, spotty-faced, snotty-nosed kid in Treasury write the Budget.

Methinks they doth protest too much.

CHAPTER 24

Dances with Wolves

"Yet much remains to conquer still; Peace hath her victories
No less renowned than war, new foes arise
Threatening to bind our souls with secular chains:
Help us to save free conscience from the paw
Of hireling wolves whose gospel is their maw."
— JOHN MILTON, 1608-1674

IN THE IMMENSE GLASS corporate totem poles that pass for office blocks these days, the "hireling wolves" paced and plotted, sniffing and scratching at any chink in the armour they could find. All the way through, they whined, their best-laid plans had become unmitigated disasters. If only Don McKinnon, the Deputy Prime Minister, could have stopped Peters from tabling the winebox.

If only. It had turned into something of a familiar refrain around the office towers lately. If only the blasted news media hadn't obtained the documents. The wolves looked skyward – even God wasn't smiling on them as He used to. Hell, some of the damned journalists had even *understood* the complex transactions.

And now this select committee inquiry. It was supposed to have been a Claytons inquiry, controlled by dependable Government politicians who could be relied on not to rock the boat. The kind of Inquiry you have when you're not really having an Inquiry. Now Peters was on board, and it was being run by a loose cannon like Max Bradford. One or two of the wolves snarled rather loudly at this point: they were taking quite a number of direct hits, and more than a few had resulted from "friendly fire".

Not that Winston Peters was running short of ammunition. On June 8, 1994, he had his parliamentary colleagues in the crosshairs.

"The Member for Selwyn, [Ruth Richardson] though, knows more about this than anyone else except the Prime Minister. She wanted an inquiry, initially. She said so in Cabinet papers of 1991. She said there were 'fertile grounds for investigation'. She was the Minister of Finance. She knows the truth.

"Why is she so silent – not a syllable, not a murmur? But by her own Cabinet documents she is condemned. The Minister of Housing [Murray McCully] does not want an inquiry. I wonder why. He headed the National Government's damage control campaign on this issue. His company owed the BNZ a fortune, now part of the Adbro debt that all New Zealanders have had to pay off.

"The Prime Minister boasts of five corporate donors to the National Party. Their parent bodies include Fay Richwhite, Brierleys, and Lion Nathan. Collins, Fay, Richwhite, Congreve, and Ricketts are all directors of those companies. Are these the people the Minister of Tourism [John Banks] calls 'big boys'?

"All the same faces in all the same places – key names in European Pacific. These four men do not want an inquiry into the BNZ and European Pacific because they will be discovered."

Peters paused only briefly to reload his gun.

"On 27 August 1982, David Lloyd, a European Pacific director – and here is the pertinent point – came to New Zealand, extolling the virtues of tax havens. He was supported by the International Tax Planning Association, which advocated captive insurance schemes – BNZ-type scams.

"On 'Morning Report' this morning the Minister of Justice said he and other members were concerned about the use of parliamentary privilege. I bet he is! Remember that in 1980 he challenged Allan Highet in an expensive nomination campaign that the media reported as having been 'money no object'.

"His nomination committee included then and later Geoff Ricketts – the same name again.*

"An Auckland lawyer, according to the Christchurch Star report of 27 August 1982, was the spokesperson for the International Tax Planning Association, and he spoke in favour of European Pacific and captive insurance scams.

"He said: 'The Cook Islands is quite an interesting experiment' . . . that member is the Minister of Justice today. That is what is behind this scam."

An outraged Justice Minister, Doug Graham, savagely denounced Peters in Parliament for what he called *"disgraceful"* behaviour.

"I believe that you have acted totally without responsibility. I think that you have acted improperly. I think that your behaviour in this House is disgraceful and you bring this House into disrepute."

Graham added that it was improper of Peters to use Parliament as a forum to accuse people of criminal behaviour, when those people can't defend themselves. Although he didn't say it, I interpreted "defend themselves" as a euphemism for using the defamation laws in their defence.

It was of some small comfort to the hireling wolves, dejected as they were over McKinnon's failure to stop the tabling, and the Government's failure to knock Bradford out of contention. Still, as some of the younger and brighter wolves had pointed out, their strength lay in the cohesion of the pack, and there was still time to hunt. By June 24, the pack was well and truly on the move.

That day's edition of the *National Business Review* suggested that lawyers acting for European Pacific and its associates were weighing up a legal challenge to the Parliamentary Inquiry. Among the options being considered was a direct confrontation with Parliament through the Courts, using the 1990 Bill of Rights Act [not to be confused in any way with the 1688 Bill of Rights which guarantees absolute parliamentary privilege] as a weapon.

Because of Parliament's considerable powers – witnesses subpoenaed would have had no right to counsel, to silence or a right to respond to

---

* Doug Graham told Parliament on September 6, 1994, that Ricketts was his fund-raising chairman.

allegations – it was felt those powers breached a citizen's rights under the 1990 Act.

Senior Russell McVeagh partner, John King, told *NBR* that testing Parliament's powers in the Courts was *"certainly an interesting idea"*, while Rudd Watts partner, Chris Allan, remarked that *"obviously anyone for whom I am acting would be looking at every available avenue"*.

Legal opinion on the mechanics of a challenge differed somewhat. One expert felt a challenge couldn't be mounted until an individual had first been subpoenaed, but Otago University's Grant Liddell, in a colourful turn of phrase, suggested a *"pre-emptive strike"* was possible, if the lawyers could successfully argue that *"a kangaroo court was still a kangaroo court before it jumped on you."*

Even so, there was considerable disagreement on whether any challenge under the Bill of Rights to Parliament's supremacy would be successful. A similar constitutional impasse arrived in the Canadian Supreme Court in 1992; the result was that the equivalent to NZ's Bill of Rights was found to be subordinate to the Canadian Constitution Act, which enshrined Parliamentary Privilege.

Auckland law lecturer Paul Rishworth considered it was unlikely that any New Zealand court would assume it had the jurisdiction to apply the Bill of Rights to Parliament. *"It is quite possible a court would say that the Bill of Rights applies to the House, but that the House is its own arbiter as to how it applies and to what extent,"* he told the *NBR*.

As events transpired, European Pacific didn't need to mount a legal challenge to the Finance and Expenditure Committee Inquiry. Parliament's legal adviser, the Solicitor-General, pulled the plug on the Inquiry. On August 23rd, John McGrath QC, wrote to Prime Minister Bolger to *"confirm the concerns I have expressed to you about the role of the Finance and Expenditure Select Committee in inquiring into matters surrounding the so-called 'winebox' papers.*

"I have little confidence that the Select Committee can comply with the requirements of natural justice given the type of issues that are likely to arise. The Committee is a political forum. It is simply not sufficiently free from political bias to give the appearance of conducting an impartial and objective investigation into what are highly charged issues.

"It is likely that Committee procedures will provoke litigation from parties affected by the inquiry. Such litigation has the potential to derail the inquiry."

The opening paragraphs of the letter, also addressed to the Attorney-General and the Ministers of Finance, Revenue and Justice, immediately raised a number of major points, not lost on some of the Select Committee members. How did he know it was *"likely"*, they wondered, that the Committee would be targeted for a legal challenge?

The statement from the Solicitor-General that he has *"little confidence"* in the parliamentary select committee process was something I found staggering.

"I have also advised the Clerk of the House," continued McGrath in his

letter, "*that the New Zealand Bill of Rights Act 1990 applies to the workings of the Select Committee.*

"*While I do not consider the Committee's proceedings to be amenable to judicial review, there is a significant risk of such a challenge through the Courts given the potential for public embarrassment and/or harassment of business leaders and senior public servants.*

"*Such litigation would raise novel constitutional issues and it is highly likely that my view will be strongly opposed. It is desirable to avoid putting the Courts in the position of having to address such matters in this particular context. Sir Geoffrey Palmer has recently added his views to the debate on these matters.*

"*I agree with his view that the situation in the Select Committee might get out of control, and that 'titillation of the public taste for sensation must not outweigh fundamental legal safeguards, individual rights and the rule of law'.*"

I had long since learnt to detest attempts by lawyers to dismiss legitimate public interest on serious matters as mere "*titillation*" or "*sensation*".

As Jenni McManus later wrote in the *Independent* on a related matter, it's the sort of piss-weak muckraking by the legal profession that is guaranteed to set off a television reporter's "*bullshit detectors*".*

In an all-out ethical scrap between lawyers and the media, the media would win hands down! Even SFO boss Chas Sturt, a man with whom I do not normally see eye to eye, couldn't resist referring to the large number of "*defalcating solicitors we have charged*" when he testified to the Commission of Inquiry later in 1994.

Instead of a Select Committee investigation into the winebox deals, the Solicitor-General was recommending a Commission of Inquiry, using a retired senior judge, which would not focus on the winebox deals themselves, but instead would look at the side issue of whether the IRD and SFO had investigated lawfully, properly and competently. It was a neat sidestepping of the real question: Had the winebox deals been criminally fraudulent? It was a question that wouldn't necessarily be answered within the terms of reference of the new Commission of Inquiry.

Prime Minister Bolger took McGrath's advice and announced the judicial inquiry two days later, on August 25. It would be headed by former Chief Justice Sir Ronald Davison.

Peters, Bradford and the Opposition members on the Finance and Expenditure Select Committee were enraged. Once again the Wogistani "Vasirs" had managed to pull the magic rug out from under them. Peters publicly questioned "*the political manoeuvrings*" behind the Solicitor-

---

* Similar legal argument was advanced by lawyers acting for European Pacific, Fay Richwhite and Brierley Investments in the Court of Appeal in December 1994. At that point they were trying to prevent secret tax deals from being publicly discussed at the Commission of Inquiry. They argued that commercial confidence, and the public interest in maintaining IRD secrecy, far outweighed the public's right to know the detail of the transactions or the Inquiry's right to publicise that detail. Their argument was fatally flawed – it was unanimously rejected by the Appellate Judges.

General's actions, asking why the Crown Law Office had, only a few days earlier, been helping draft natural justice guidelines for the Committee to follow.

"On 18 August Crown Law supplied the Finance and Expenditure Committee with a preliminary opinion on protecting the rights of witnesses appearing before it, with the clear commitment that a more substantive opinion would be provided the following day.

"Prior to that, the Crown Law Office had also been involved in providing legal opinion, at the Committee's request, on the question of extending immunity to witnesses. But then, instead of the Crown Counsel involved providing the follow up opinion on 19 August as indicated, he rang the Clerk's Office on 22 August to say he now had nothing further to add."

It was the following day, August 23rd, that McGrath wrote to Bolger and the other Ministers referring to his *"earlier"* concerns about the Committee Inquiry. Winston Peters seized on it. *"One of the questions I will be raising is what happened between Thursday 18 August and Monday 22 August that saw the Crown Law Office move from a position of supporting the Select Committee to one of stressing its inability to do the job.*

"What is quite clear from the opinion tabled yesterday by the Prime Minister, is that there had already been significant contact between the Government and the Solicitor-General, before that opinion was formally provided, at the same time as the Solicitor-General's staff had been providing very different and supportive advice to the Clerk of the House and the Select Committee."

The NZ First leader concluded by taking a swipe at the shifting sands approach of Crown Law depending on which party it was giving legal advice to. It will, said Peters, give the public *"little confidence in its ability to provide competent advice of the highest quality free from any suggestion of political bias."*

None of which is to suggest that the guidelines being drawn up by Crown Law for the Select Committee were designed to uncover the full story. Paragraph 6.1 of the draft guidelines suggests that *"any written submissions which are received by a Committee and which impute unlawful conduct to any person may be returned, in whole or in part, where the Committee considers that the making of such a submission creates a risk of harm to that person which exceeds the benefit of the submission."*

A similar clause covered oral evidence where a witness suggested foul play. On a Committee with a majority of Government MPs, it was easy to see how the Committee could ignore all the evidence if it so chose. The select committee however, took a more robust view of its powers of inquiry, despite the Solicitor-General's view that natural justice issues were paramount.

"The Committee . . . considers that every principle of natural justice must be balanced against the responsibility of Parliament to 'get to the bottom' of sometimes controversial issues.

"Natural justice should not mean the right to stifle or hide matters which need to be vigorously and robustly explored because of the wider public interest issues that may be involved."

The Solicitor-General came under fire himself when he was twice summonsed before the Select Committee to explain why he'd taken a course of action that effectively scuttled their own inquiry.

Grilled for two hours on September 13, and again on September 27, he told the Committee that he initially believed that the inquiry would look at the need to tighten tax legislation, not examine the affairs of the corporate taxpayers in the winebox. Back then, of course, the Select Committee had still been headed by Ruth Richardson, a staunch opponent of any kind of inquiry.

It was the moving of the goalposts in the aftermath of Ruth Richardson's resignation that caused corporate and legal consternation. Rumours began to permeate the old boys' circuit of plans to mount a challenge to the Select Committee inquiry, and those rumours eventually reached the ears of John McGrath. Sensing that any legal challenge would be *"destructive"*, the Solicitor-General went to the Government. On no less than five occasions – June 13, June 14, July 19, August 17 and August 24 – McGrath met senior National Government ministers to discuss the issue. According to Prime Minister Jim Bolger the meetings followed the allegations made by Peters against SFO boss Chas Sturt and IRD Commissioner David Henry.

Bolger told Parliament that the Government wanted to *"see how we could set up a procedure so those two gentlemen could clear their names of serious allegations which were made under the privilege of Parliament by the member for Tauranga."*

The Solicitor-General told the Finance and Expenditure Select Committee that indications of a planned legal challenge to the Committee's investigation helped convince him it wasn't the right forum for an inquiry.

"Even on social occasions lawyers were hinting to me something was going to happen."

Needless to say, Committee members were unimpressed at McGrath's reasons. Labour's Dr Michael Cullen said McGrath had apparently succumbed to an *"effective pre-emptive strike by rumour, by the legal profession, on Parliament's power. We have substituted the rule of lawyers for the rule of law."* Committee Chairman, Max Bradford, agreed.

"It does worry me that you seem to be taking the view that if these guys are all girding their loins up to have a whack at Parliament, rather than let that happen your advice to the Government was effectively to say 'Look, we really ought not to allow this challenge to take place' – and get it out into some other forum.

"Do you think that's a proper basis on which Parliament should . . . roll over – when it's a challenge from outside, from people who are clearly implicated in the very things the Committee was charged to look at?"

Bradford went on to ask how it was that a senior partner in one of the law firms named in the winebox knew about the Government's plans to shut down the investigation – *a week before it was publicly announced!?*

The man, said Bradford, had openly discussed the decision to cancel the inquiry at a social function on August 18, even though Bolger didn't announce it until the 25th.

In a later report to Parliament, the Committee noted that on August 17, 1994 – the previous evening – the Solicitor-General had met *"the Prime Minister, Deputy Prime Minister, Attorney-General, [and] Ministers of Revenue and Finance."*

"The Solicitor-General . . . noted that the Ministers were now ready to move on the matter. He confirmed that he was requested to put his views in writing. He had assumed that the discussion and the presumed decision were confidential and only those who needed to know about it in his Office were informed. Mr McGrath assured the committee that his Office did not leak the decision to a senior partner of a legal practice."

The question of the leak was never solved.

The Committee also took issue with the Solicitor-General's decision to brief the previous Committee chairwoman, Ruth Richardson, about his concerns in a meeting on June 21, 1994.

As legal adviser to the Executive wing of Government, McGrath's meeting with Richardson – without the knowledge of the Committee, was described as *"a departure from normal practice."*

Michael Cullen went further, telling Parliament *"the fact that the Solicitor-General approached Ruth Richardson independently was peculiar and was in conflict with his evidence that his sole direct responsibility was as chief legal adviser to the Executive, and that his lines of communication were with the Executive.*

"It is my view that if that were true, then the Solicitor-General had no role to play and no responsibility to approach the previous member for Selwyn independently."

McGrath said his reasons for taking up the matter with Richardson were simply because she was the chairwoman and he felt it unnecessary to brief the whole committee. He acknowledged that his actions were unusual. Max Bradford was far from pleased at the end result of the Solicitor-General's actions.

"The awful, nasty feeling I have at the pit of my stomach as a result of all this is that . . . if the legal fraternity so chooses, it can in fact mount a challenge against the powers of Parliament and derail what would otherwise be the only redress available to citizens of this country when the legal system either can't deal with it, or alternatively is too expensive to deal with it.

"I think Parliament is in great danger of being circumscribed by powerful vested-interest groups out in the community.

"At least in part, [McGrath's] advice was given in order to shy away from what could have been a major constitutional challenge by some members of the legal profession. I think it's a matter of profound regret if that is even 20 percent of the reason why it happened. It's clear it is."

When the Finance and Expenditure Committee reported back to Parliament toward the end of November, 1994, it rebuked the Government for attempting to usurp Parliament's authority.

The Committee warned that it would not cancel its winebox investigation – it would merely defer it until the Commission of Inquiry headed by Sir Ronald Davison had reported back. Parliament would be master of its own destiny, not a Government lap-dog.

As the *Independent* noted, the Committee fired a diplomatic warning shot across the Government's bows, saying it wished *"to make the point that the fact that the Executive has taken certain action outside Parliament does not necessarily mean that a select committee must discontinue any inquiry into a related matter."*

"Considerable reservations" were also expressed about Solicitor-General John McGrath's role. *"In my view,"* stated former Labour cabinet minister Michael Cullen at the tabling of the committee's report, *"the body language of the Solicitor-General conveyed, at all times, an indication to me that there were still material facts that did not emerge in the evidence that was given.*

"At all times I felt that the whole truth had not been given to the select committee – and perhaps would never be known – such as the nature of advice of officials to ministers."

McGrath had told the Committee that his reason for folding in the face of a challenge was because he preferred to be on solid ground when staking out a defence: he didn't consider that the select committee had a sufficiently strong legal position from which to mount such a defence. Michael Cullen disagreed.

"I could not imagine that Fay Richwhite, Brierleys, or European Pacific, to name but three bodies, when faced with the same advice, would immediately conclude that they should surrender in advance of anybody firing a shot in anger in terms of the legal procedures.

"What has happened, therefore, is that we have established a dreadful precedent. We have established the precedent that this Parliament may fold in the face of legal threat from the rich and powerful. That is an awful thing for this Parliament to have done."

The stage, however, was set. On November 7, 1994, the Commission of Inquiry into Certain Matters Related to Taxation began in an Auckland office tower, ironically overlooking what used to be European Pacific's New Zealand branch.

In the weeks leading up to the hearing I had been fighting for the chance to cover the Inquiry on TVNZ's behalf. Surprisingly, it was not an easy task or a foregone conclusion. Because I was no longer a *One Network News* journalist, preference had been given to one of that show's staff, reporter John Stewart, to be assigned to the Commission hearings.

I suggested to the newly-promoted Director of News and Current Affairs, Shaun Brown, that I should be there as well to maintain an overview for any current affairs follow-ups we may require during the coming months, not to mention being able to keep John Stewart appraised of developments as he rushed off to meet his production deadlines. My arguments finally succeeded.

Stewart and I made an interesting combination. I had long known he was a personal friend of Russell McVeagh consultant Robin Congreve – a man with strong links to European Pacific, a former director of the Bank of New Zealand and a director of Fay Richwhite. Congreve had also been named in

Parliament in relation to alleged fraud in the financing of the movie *Merry Christmas Mr Lawrence*.

What I didn't know was that John Stewart's partner was Susan Pilgrim, a senior investigator with the Serious Fraud Office. John, of course, had been hearing conspiracy theories about my role in the whole case and my alleged links to Peters, while I, conversely, was fully versed on the other side of the coin. We joked that we'd actually been assigned to spy on each other, to keep each other honest.

Day One of the Inquiry wasn't without its teething troubles for the TVNZ contingent. We'd arranged for the Live Eye broadcast truck to beam out a live insert into the 6:00pm *One Network News* programme. Unbeknownst to us, however, the elevators in the office tower were locked off at 5:30pm. Stewart had arrived back at the building at 5:40pm to prepare for his 6:00pm broadcast from the Commission rooms.

He climbed into the lift and spent 20 minutes riding up, riding down, riding up and so on – unable to get out on the ninth floor or anywhere near it. They finally managed to exit the elevator at the top of the building, and sprinted down several flights of stairs on the fire escape before finding a back way into the Commission office.

Panting and exhausted, John Stewart lumbered into the Inquiry room just in time to hear the cameraman say "*10 seconds to air*", and begin the final countdown. Out of breath, with no script, he adlibbed his way through the intro to his item, silently vowing never again to get trapped in a lift.

The Inquiry itself turned out to be a lot more pro-active than the Government or the business community had been expecting. Far from getting a tame retired judge to rubber-stamp the actions of the IRD and SFO before laying the winebox to rest, anxious parties found themselves facing a retired former Chief Justice determined to do the job the public expected him to do: conduct a full, independent inquiry into the whole affair.

As the *New Zealand Herald's* political commentator, Andrew Stone, noted: "*The risk is that the Government might have a tiger by the tail. While ministers expect vindication, more cautious advisers recall the Fitzgerald Inquiry in Queensland. That, too, was established with comparatively narrow terms of reference. It went on to reveal institutional corruption remarkable even in Australian history.*

"*No one, besides Mr Peters, has suggested that an Inquiry on this side of the Tasman could lift the lid on what in Parliament he has called criminal schemes and tax frauds. But inquiries, once initiated, can take on lives of their own. Further, the Davison Commission will work under an intense public and political spotlight.*"

And a "tiger" it turned out to be. One of the first signals that Sir Ronald Davison meant business was the appointment of eminent tax QC, Dr Tony Molloy, as an expert adviser/investigator to the legal counsel assisting the Commission.

His role would be to assess the winebox schemes himself, gather evidence relating to the transactions and then present his findings in open court where he could be cross-examined and challenged by all parties.

Molloy is regarded as one of New Zealand's, indeed the world's, foremost tax experts, and an authority on tax crime. His book, *Molloy on Tax Disputes, Investigations and Crimes*, is regarded as a Commonwealth "bible" on the investigation of tax evasion and fraud. He had been hired to investigate the Russell McVeagh film and bloodstock partnerships, and he had taken part in a televised debate following the *Frontline* programme on European Pacific where he described the transactions he'd just witnessed as prima facie tax evasion.

European Pacific, Fay Richwhite and Brierleys immediately lobbied to have Molloy removed from the Inquiry, arguing that he was biased. This of course is akin to accusing a police officer of bias simply because he or she suspects someone has committed a crime and is gathering evidence to establish the facts.

If everyone was automatically presumed innocent, nothing would ever get investigated, now, would it? In both cases, any evidence uncovered by the investigator will be placed before the Court for consideration. It is the job of the Judge/Commissioner to assess whether it proves guilt or innocence, and therefore Dr Molloy's personal views were irrelevant to the issue – he was never going to be in the position of deciding the verdict.

Sir Ronald Davison began by defending Molloy's position publicly. Instead, the corporates turned to dirty tricks. Somehow, they stole a copy of an article Molloy had written for the *NBR* some months earlier, but which hadn't been published because of his appointment to the Commission. The article took a look at the Magnum transaction in the light of the laws that existed at the time.

The corporates threatened to use the article to prove Molloy had pre-judged the issue, if the Commission didn't dump him. They told the Commission they'd obtained their copy of the article from Parliament. Molloy's article had, however, only been circulated to a select few, and all copies were accounted for. The only copy in Parliament had been under lock in key in the office of Max Bradford, the Chairman of the Finance and Expenditure Select Committee. He was adamant that anyone who had copied the article there, had done so illegally.

If unauthorised burglars are able to break into Parliamentary offices and steal sensitive documentation, it raises questions about the security of Parliament. It also raises questions about the origin of the copy used by the corporates to blackmail the Commission into dropping Molloy.

While the Commission felt it would win any court challenge to Molloy's position, it knew that legal challenges would delay the Inquiry for up to 18 months. Faced with those options, Tony Molloy walked the plank.

He would cease actively investigating the winebox, but would be allowed to make submissions to the Commission as an expert witness. In effect this removed his ability to investigate under the Commission's aegis.

First blood had been drawn, and the Inquiry hadn't even begun.

CHAPTER 25

Crash, Boom, Bang

"I spent in excess of 40 hours considering the papers."
– SFO Director Charles Sturt, 1994

On Monday, November 7, 1994, the whole House of Cards came crashing down. In a building right next door to the headquarters of the Russell McVeagh lawfirm, former Chief Justice Sir Ronald Davison began the Commission of Inquiry Into Certain Matters Related To Taxation. Alright, so it wasn't the most scintillating title in the world – it didn't exactly grip the ear and make you want to listen, but hey!, it was all we had.

Sir Ronald had already set out his agenda for the Inquiry. It would begin with the Inland Revenue Department and Serious Fraud Office detailing exactly how they had investigated the winebox documents. After IRD and SFO staff had given their testimony, then the Commissioner would decide whether he needed to delve further into the matter.

IRD boss David Henry was first to take the stand, eager to clear his name and his department's reputation *"because of the attacks that have been made under parliamentary privilege on the integrity of the tax administration and on my own integrity by the Hon. Winston Peters MP."*

The allegations, as listed by Henry, included incompetence, gross negligence, evidence of a criminal conspiracy involving the IRD and secret agreements not to prosecute European Pacific. *"If the department responsible for collecting 80% of total Government revenue is indeed headed by a crook, as Mr Peters claims, then the consequences for the country are grave.*

"Let me say right now that I emphatically and unequivocally reject those allegations. The evidence which I and my officers intend to present to you will, in my view, show that we have at all times acted in a lawful, proper and competent manner in dealing with the transactions referred to in the 'tabled papers'.

"Our evidence will demonstrate that no matter what view one takes of the transactions, the allegations made by Mr Peters are groundless, are wrong and are false."

The sequence of events in the IRD's investigation of the winebox was this: Apart from a general awareness, through the media, of the Peters campaign against European Pacific in 1992, it wasn't until November 5 that year that the IRD became directly involved in the Winebox affair. It came in a phone call to IRD Deputy Commissioner Robin Adair, from Auckland lawyer Chris Dickie. Adair took a note of the phone conversation.

"Mr Molloy and Mr Dickie have evidence of extremely serious tax evasion in relation to the New Zealand Revenue. They are in possession of documentation which shows these are the New Zealand Revenue 'highly criminal tax evasion' one of the alleged transactions is for $500m and another $200m [sic]."

Dickie and Adair arranged to meet the following day, Friday November 6, 1992. Also present at the meeting was Director of Taxpayer Audit, Tony Bouzaid.

"Mr Dickie raised at the meeting . . . that he was in possession of various papers that showed very serious tax offences, with offshore schemes far bigger than anything IRD had ever seen before," Bouzaid testified to the Inquiry.

"My notes refer to him mentioning journalists talk in the pub, EPI, Steven Lunn who he said was a blackmailer ex Challenge Corporate Services, knows of offshore tax structures, a death threat, 5000 pages, a bond wash involving Lion Nathan, IRD being referred to in the documents as the enemy, delivery of the documents to the SFO and a gagging order and 20 sets of the documents.

"He referred to the documents being ex Tony Molloy from 6 weeks ago, who described them as the largest tax frauds ever in New Zealand, and he also made comments on Tony Molloy's thoughts on SFO. He also referred to Russell McVeagh and a Wellington forestry deal."

At the end of the meeting, Dickie gave the IRD 21 pages of documentation. Wary of breaching the High Court injunction imposed on the NBR and the Independent, the IRD moved slowly in its attempts to access a full set of the winebox documents. It wasn't until February 17, 1993, that the IRD obtained a copy of the documents held by the SFO.

A project team was established under the leadership of senior adviser John Nash, and they commenced investigating with the best of intentions.

"My view was that the papers contained valuable information and, in particular, it was a rare occurrence for papers detailing the inner workings of a tax haven operation to fall into the hands of Revenue Authorities – the IRD had to make the most of this opportunity, but we should proceed cautiously as we did not want to compromise IRD's position by acting unfairly or illegally," Nash told the Commission of Inquiry.

The team beavered away over the next 12 months, identifying 59 winebox transactions. By February 1994, when the TVNZ/European Pacific legal stoush was in full cry, IRD boss David Henry was poking his nose in to see how the project team was getting along. Because of the internal structure of the IRD, it's very unlikely that David Henry had really been aware of the ongoing European Pacific investigation prior to this point.

His role as chief executive was to manage his team, rather than personally manage investigations.

On February 21st, 1994, John Nash signed off on the last of the 59 analyses the project team had undertaken. There is no evidence, in his testimony to the Commission, that he or his colleagues were aware, up to this point, of the substance of the TVNZ/EP legal battle. The first "alarm" about Cook Islands tax credits was raised by Nash in a memo only five days earlier, on February 16.

The IRD investigators had missed the hidden twist in the Magnum deal.

"Initially," said Nash, "the focus of enquiries was on the tax consequences of Magnum Corporation's participation, as the European Pacific New Zealand Ltd Group had closed its operations in this country."

In other words, the project team was looking at the "public" face of the Magnum deal, the preference share dividend payment of $3.8 million made tax-free to Magnum. This was not surprising. As we ourselves had discovered at *Frontline*, to understand the hidden side of Magnum and JIF you first had to know that a hidden side existed.

OK, the IRD **had** been warned about shonky Cook Islands tax credit certificates by former Cook Islands official Richard McDonald, and ample evidence existed in the winebox of plans to use shonky tax credit certificates but, unless you were paying really close attention, it was a detail easily missed. It would be petulant to point out that IRD tax experts are supposed to be **the** experts.

IRD worksheets show that on February 16, John Nash had ordered his staff to *"review all tax credit claims made by EPNZ Group companies."* The following day the IRD discovered that EP Funds Management Ltd. had been struck off the company register, making recovery of any tax owed extremely difficult.

A brief flurry continued for a few days, but on February 21st, John Nash decided not to pursue EP Funds Management Ltd. any further. Just five days passed between the time the IRD worked out it had been rorted, and the time it decided to quit, apparently on the basis that it was all too hard.

This is where we had a philosophical difference of opinion with the IRD. The department took the pragmatic view that the cost of taking action wasn't warranted. Others of us believed that if an arguable case existed, it should be pursued so as to test the limits and, if necessary, set an example.

The analogy, under the criminal law, is this: If a person robs a bank of two million dollars, but blows all the loot before they get caught, would police drop the prosecution on the basis that there was no money left to recover? Would they drop it on the basis that the trial was going to cost tens of thousands of dollars?

On 21st March, the review of the Magnum deal, already undertaken, was hastily sent off, along with IRD internal legal opinion that no offence had been committed, to Wellington barrister Grant Pearson, a man with some taxation experience but not as highly qualified as the specialist tax QC's used by the department – like Molloy or Peter Jenkin QC.

Pearson effectively had only a couple of days to assess Magnum "out of the blue", compared to the several weeks TVNZ's tax advisers had taken before delivering their opinions.

Pearson's assessment that Magnum, *"on the evidence received so far, did not constitute evasion"*, was made without the benefit of accessing the TVNZ legal affidavits prepared by Dr John Prebble, Dr Gary Muir and former Auditor-General Brian Tyler.

Pearson had, if you like, been somewhat "ambushed" by the IRD – a department which had missed the tax certificate swiz the first time around and which now faced real public ridicule if it had to back down and admit it had cocked-up.

Clutching at straws, the IRD project team and its legal advisers justified their own decision not to lodge tax evasion charges by setting out European Pacific's likely defence to any criminal proceedings.

"In concluding that the claiming of Cook Islands' tax credits by EPFML [European Pacific Funds Management Ltd – an NZ company] did not amount to tax evasion, the project team was mindful of the following key aspects:

"1. there was no evidence of any sham or false documentation,* but rather slavish adherence to the form of the arrangement detailed in the planning documents,

"2. tax had been paid to the Cook Islands Inland Revenue by or on behalf of EPFML,

"3. the tax paid had not been refunded to EPFML, although an offsetting benefit (but for $50,000) had been derived from another branch of the Cook Islands Government by a non-resident member of the same group as EPFML.

"Aside from section 99 [combating tax avoidance as opposed to evasion] or a finding of sham," wrote Nash in his brief of evidence to the Inquiry, "it is not legitimate for IRD to disregard separate corporate entities, or the nature of the contracts made, and impose tax on the basis of economic equivalence."

In other words, despite the reality that EP had in fact been given its tax money back *and* a shonky tax certificate as well, the IRD was arguing that it couldn't legally challenge the setup as criminal because the transaction was not a "sham". A sham is a transaction where the documentation sets out one course of events but the parties actually do something different. Other experts we'd been talking to, however, ripped the argument that it wasn't a sham to pieces.

Tony Molloy QC seized on a point that we at TVNZ had missed – the Magnum deal was definitely a sham. The thrust of his argument was simple: Follow the money trail! The only way European Pacific could be liable for tax in the Cook Islands was if the money actually passed through the Cook Islands jurisdiction. While the elaborate paper trail created by European Pacific suggested that this was the case, Molloy had taken a closer look.

He discovered the $34.4 million paid in by Magnum on day one of the deal never ever made it to the Cook Islands. Hidden in the transaction documentation was the revelation that the money was shuffled between a couple of Bank of New Zealand accounts in Wellington, and then deposited straight into a Hong Kong BNZ account where it stayed for a year.

---

* As I have already noted, the Cook Islands Cabinet Minister who allegedly signed the documents denies doing so. In addition, the former Cooks Treasury head, Michael Fleming, admitted under cross-examination at the Inquiry that Cook Islands law may have been broken, in that the money paid to European Pacific by the Cook Islands Government Property Corporation had not been appropriated for the purpose by Parliament, as required under the Act governing the Corporation.

European Pacific had broken its Magnum transaction into two parts: internal funds flow and external funds flow. In doing the documentary, and not being tax haven banking experts, we had taken the documentation at face value. Molloy, however, highlighted the external funds flow, as quoted in the Magnum memo of 8 August 1988.

"EXTERNAL FUNDS FLOW:
SETTLEMENT: DAY ONE: 28 JULY 1988
19.1 *On Day One, The Issuer [European Pacific Funds Management] will receive NZD 34,400,000 from Magnum into its account with EPBC at BNZ Wellington (International Division).*
19.2 *On Day One EPBC will deposit $30 million into the charged deposit account with BNZ (Hong Kong).*
19.3 *The Issuer will pay $3,807,500 to Magnum.*
19.4 *EPBC will pay $137,600 to the account of BNZ."*

What did all this mean? It meant that Magnum's money arrived at the BNZ Wellington, then went immediately to BNZ Hong Kong where it stayed for a year as per a legal agreement, less about four million in the form of Magnum's pre-paid dividend and the BNZ's fee.

European Pacific certainly, according to Molloy, did not have $32 million odd with which to lend to its subsidiaries in the Cook Islands. If you looked at the internal funds flow in the documents, it would have you believe that the money went from the BNZ Wellington, then via the Cooks and eventually into Hong Kong, creating a tax liability along the way. As the external funds flow or, he argued, **real** funds flow shows, that never happened.*

All the embellishments that *Frontline* and Peters had focussed on were just "paper entries" in EP and the Cook Islands Government's ledger books. On the face of the documents, the money physically never went to the Cooks, explained Molloy, therefore European Pacific could not be liable for Cook Islands tax, therefore the on-paper creation of a tax liability and

---

* The IRD's lawyer, Grant Pearson, continued to attack the Molloy analysis, saying it ignored accepted banking practice. However, it is possible that people are reading too much into the Cook Islands' tax haven status. The Cooks are not a banking haven. Even Witness A acknowledged as much to the Inquiry: *"Some clients prefer to have the money actually go to the Cook Islands for such transactions, but banking in the Cook Islands was not particularly good, and this took time to do. It took a lot of effort to achieve this and it was not uncommon for the banks to lose track of the money in the system or have delays in receipt of the funds."* Unlike the Caribbean havens, where major banks all had full branches and money could be electronically transferred at the punch of a button, the Cook Islands did not have the same streamlined capability. To give the Cook Islands the same status as Bermuda or the Bahamas is to ignore the reality. If tax haven banking was legally as simple as scrawling transfers in a ledger book without ever seeing a money flow – and while your money remains in another country – every tax haven would be doing it and none of the big banks would bother to have full branches there.

subsequent tax certificate appeared to be even more criminally fraudulent than any of us had first thought.

As Molloy put it, *"When you have got $30 million in the Bank of New Zealand for 12 months earning interest, you can't lend any other company $32,229,725 'of it' at the same time!"*

Forget all the earnest debate about a fine line between avoidance/evasion, about how the tax credit scam just *"squeaked in"* on the right side of the law because of a loophole that regarded all the EP subsidiary companies as separate legal entities – all of that goes out the window if you accept the argument that tax never had to be paid in the Cooks.*

"There arises a case that those persons may have committed, or been accessory to, the crime of conspiracy to defraud the Crown, an offence against Crimes Act 1961 s 257, punishable with 5 years' imprisonment," wrote Molloy in a later legal opinion.

If the money never came within a thousand miles of the Cook Islands, European Pacific was never in its wildest dreams legally liable to pay tax there. The whole deal, from that point on, becomes a financial farce. By the IRD's own definition, the transaction could be classed as a *"sham"* and attacked as a fraud.

As the Serious Fraud Office took the witness stand, we were curious to find out on what grounds the SFO had ruled out investigating the winebox. It quickly became apparent that, like the IRD before them, the SFO had invented a new definition of criminality – it had to be *"conscious fraud"*. Chief Forensic Accountant, Gib Beattie, told the Inquiry that it wasn't enough for a transaction to be criminal, the participants had to **consciously know** it was criminal before the SFO could mount a prosecution.

OK, most of us would call that a measure of criminal intent. What, I wondered, was the SFO expecting to find in the winebox – a piece of paper with the words "CRIMINAL TRANSACTION DETAILS" emblazoned across the top, and a "TOP SECRET" stamp in the corner for good measure?

Maybe those are the sort of clues they're taught to look for in the Mickey Mouse School of Serious Fraud Detection, but they're not the kind of pawprints that a seasoned player will leave behind.

Beattie acknowledged that he had read the arguments of Professor John Prebble that the Magnum transaction was a sham and that no tax was, in reality, required to be paid in the Cooks, therefore the tax certificates issued by the Cooks were false. The SFO accountant also acknowledged Prebble's *"sophisticated analysis"* of what actually constitutes "tax" under the terms of the law. *"Perhaps the Magnum scheme may not have been effective for tax purposes,"* Beattie conceded, *"I do not know. But a criminal prosecution would*

---

* As an interesting comparison, the BNZ's international transaction auditor, George Scott, gave expert testimony to the Inquiry on money flows in EP transactions. On the JIF deals, for example, BNZ records showed European Pacific had money wired up to the Cooks by telegraphic transfer, in other words a real money flow. For the Magnum transaction, Scott confirmed that no money had been wired up to the Cooks.

not turn on the tax efficacy of the scheme but rather whether the parties knew that the scheme was ineffective."

SFO Director Charles Sturt made another surprising claim: *"I wish to emphasise that my view that the documents do not disclose evidence of fraud is not based on a sophisticated analysis of their fiscal effectiveness."*

Hold the line! Go back three spaces. Here is the Director of the SFO saying he didn't look at the financial reality of the transactions before deciding they weren't fraudulent? It's no wonder I'd found it impossible to take the SFO seriously all these years!

"I was looking at the documents," continued Sturt, *"in a way quite different from that of the TVNZ witnesses in the EPI case but, at the same time, more relevant to my role as an investigator and prosecutor. What I was looking for was evidence of conscious dishonesty."*

There goes that phrase again. A distinction between the actual criminality of a deal, and whether the participants realised it was criminal.* We, at TVNZ, had approached the transaction in what we regarded as a logical way: we looked at its substance, at what the real effect of the money-go-round was. This is how fraud is supposed to be investigated, or so we thought. Evidently the Court of Appeal had agreed with us, otherwise it wouldn't have stated that TVNZ had a *"seriously arguable"* case of fraud against European Pacific.

But by its own admission, the Serious Fraud Office had never even investigated the European Pacific winebox. The SFO has a series of steps that are set in place during its enquiries. The winebox underwent "step one", an initial examination. In February 1993, after an initial assessment, Chas Sturt decided *"that there was nothing in the 'wine box' which then justified investigation under the Serious Fraud Office Act."* Instead, the box was reclassified as an *"intelligence"* file, meaning it would remain with the office for general background information, nothing more.

It wasn't until the TVNZ legal fight against European Pacific that Sturt dusted the winebox off and re-activated it to *"assessment"* level.

"In early 1994 we issued Section 5 notices against TVNZ, with a view to

---

* In a 1995 decision on the Cook Islands "Letters of Guarantee" scam, the Serious Fraud Office ruled that the documents were intended for *"illegitimate purposes associated with . . . fraud"*, and the SFO also decided that some of the overseas principals in the scam *"are fraudsters"*. The documents, said SFO boss Charles Sturt, were to be traded on a so-called secret market for such bank instruments. The SFO said no such market existed, described it as *"mythical"*, with *"Alice in Wonderland"* qualities, but then went on to conclude that it couldn't prosecute NZ lawyer Derek Firth for his *"pivotal"* role in the attempted scams, because *"Mr Firth did believe, and indeed continues to believe, in the existence of [such a] market. The fact that such belief was held is inconsistent with fraud."* Sturt decided Firth had abandoned the rules of commonsense. In my view, the ruling is proof that if you are galactically stupid, and can convince the SFO that you believe in the Tooth Fairy, then no matter what you've done you can't be prosecuted! I'm sure many of those jailed by the SFO despite protestations of innocence would appreciate the inconsistencies.

obtaining all material documents. I became aware that particular allegations of fraud were being made by TVNZ by way of answer to the injunction proceedings brought by European Pacific.

"I wanted to know the basis of those allegations and, if necessary, to activate assessment of the 'wine box' documents should that be appropriate. The matter, however, remained in assessment rather than investigation phase."

In his own words, SFO Director Charles Sturt admitted to the Commission of Inquiry that he'd never carried out a formal investigation of the winebox, despite all the allegations. Sturt even admitted that he found evidence of "criminality" in one of the European Pacific transactions carried out for Aussie billionaire Alan Bond. Because the offence was carried out in Australia, Sturt couldn't prosecute obviously – but it should have been a clear signal that more criminality might exist in the winebox.

Instead, the Serious Fraud Office witnesses appeared to give European Pacific every benefit of the doubt they could find. The RIBUN memo, for example, where EP's Mark Jones wrote: "Antipodean tax authorities will experience a huge increase in the volume of tax credits remitted from the Cook Islands. That apparent increase may make detection an easier task for the authorities."

"The reference to 'detection' attracts the eye," Gib Beattie told the Inquiry. "So too does the reference in para 5 to payments from an entity 'that purported to be a Pacific Rim Development Bank'. Also of interest is the apparent ability of European Pacific to rewrite the laws of the Cook Islands and a proposal to do so in a way which appears to have been intended to be, at the least, confusing."

Beattie had just outlined three clear hints in the winebox documentation that pointed toward sham transactions. What does he do next?

"They refer to existing legislation and reveal efforts to comply with that legislation. As an example, I refer again to the risks ascribed to the Magnum transaction in the 28 July 1988 document as 'change in tax laws'.

"It is possible that the statement 'change in tax laws' is merely a reference to any move by the authorities to close loopholes. The same applies to the word 'detection'."

I, and others, would have argued that the "detection" line was clear evidence that EP staff knew they were doing something dodgy, but still the SFO was finding reasons not to prosecute.

The RIBUN memo goes on to inform that "The Cook Islands Government would refund the amount of the tax, less its cut, by way of a loan, relief from EPBCL of domestic tax payable, purchase of equipment for EPBCL, defraying of expenses (etc); or some other investment incentive.

"The benefits of the scheme are . . . because the taxes that are raised are general in nature and the money that the Cook Islands Government plows back by way of incentive allowance is for a 'public purpose' there are no legal difficulties that there is any intent to defraud any persons revenue of monies owing."

"I would also comment," stated Beattie, "on the sentence which states 'no legal difficulties that there is any intent to defraud persons revenue of monies owing'."

To the TVNZ team and its lawyers, that phrase was a clear indication that

EP was well aware that its tax credit scheme could be criminal, and they were trying to find ways to "window dress" it to give it an air of legitimacy. Gib Beattie, however, saw it differently.

"This is the sort of odd phrase that would normally attract our attention in an assessment of documents. But in viewing this statement in the general context of the documents, it is reasonable to infer that the author appears to have satisfied himself that the proposed structure met the requirements of existing (presumably NZ and Cook Islands) tax legislation."

Give me a break!

Beattie was extremely generous with his next extrapolation and misuse of the facts. *"The references to 'investment incentives and allowances' suggest that the promissory note structure is designed with the specific purpose of taking advantage of allowances made available by the Cook Islands Government, and that it is the benefits afforded EPBC under these incentives which allow the overall structure to work and make a profit."*

This, of course, assumes that the investment incentives and allowances are legitimate. The SFO seemed to think they were.

"The documents reviewed do not give explicit details of the background to any incentive schemes for investment or how a party such as EPBC may qualify. They do however suggest that such schemes exist or are being formulated."

There was a good reason the documents didn't contain explicit detail about the incentive schemes. Despite all our digging in the Cook Islands, we could find no proof that such incentive schemes actually existed. Indeed, when I had asked EP Managing Director David Lloyd up in the Cooks about the secrecy surrounding the promissory note deals with the Cook Islands Government, he claimed the secrecy was to ensure that EP's competitors in the Cooks didn't find out.

If an "incentive scheme" for "public purpose" had existed, there would have been no need for European Pacific to keep the deal quiet from competitors, because they would have been eligible for the "incentives" as well.

I was aware, and I knew Gib Beattie was as well, of Dr Prebble's analysis that the tax refund had actually broken the criminal law in the Cook Islands as well as New Zealand.

Article 70 of the Cook Islands Constitution imposes strict conditions on how the Government utilises tax money, and giving it away in pre-arranged losses wasn't one of the criteria. Prebble believed the refund was theft, and broke the Cook Islands Crimes Act in three places.

Gib Beattie had already testified to being aware of Prebble's *"sophisticated analysis"*, so should have taken a more robust view of criminal intent when examining this deal. In addition, the Magnum transaction documentation contained specific clauses forcing all parties to absolute secrecy about the handing back of the tax money in the promissory note deals. Why did the SFO overlook those specific provisions?

One indication of intent is the way something is structured. If somebody is going to a hell of a lot of trouble to keep something secret, to the extent of disguising the tax refund as a profit from a promissory note deal, it's pretty clear that someone doesn't want someone else to know what's going on.

If European Pacific's refund was an honest incentive from the Cook Islands Government, why wasn't it handed directly to European Pacific in the form of a public grant? Or does every Cook Islands citizen who's entitled to a tax refund enter into promissory note transactions with the tax department? Somehow I don't think so.

If the SFO had bothered to dig – and it didn't – it might have located a document later discovered by the Inland Revenue Department, a legal opinion on the use of Cook Islands tax credits in Australia.

Dated January 28, 1988, the document revealed that an EP executive, Alex Adamovich, *"expressed concern about the relationship of EP with the Cook Islands Government,"* and he also questioned the *"legality"* of using the Cook Islands tax certificates in Australia. European Pacific decided to seek legal advice.

"A criminal barrister, Mr [Brian] Oslington QC was approached and his response focused upon one critical issue. One element of a 'tax' is that the money raised by the taxing authority is used for 'public purposes'.

"In the structure devised, the Cook Islands Government Property Corporation pays to an EPBC subsidiary a premium that is calculated in direct proportion to the tax that has been levied. In Mr Oslington's view as the premium paid for purchase of the note by the Property Corporation is essentially for a smart business dealing by the Government, it is not for public purposes.

"Therefore, the Cook Islands withholding tax is not a 'tax', promotion of the note constitutes a criminal offence by company officers and those knowingly involved in a conspiracy to defraud the Australian revenue."

Understandably not happy at this legal advice, European Pacific's Sydney agents, Mallesons Stephen Jaques, sought two other opinions from leading QC's, who argued that because the actions of a sovereign government couldn't be called into question, Australia would have to accept that 'tax' really had been paid and the transaction would not be criminal.

"None the less," the opinion warned, *"there remains the chance that if the matter ever went to court it may well be that a judge could side with the view taken by Mr Oslington."*

European Pacific executives could hardly argue that they were not fully aware that their tax credit deals may be criminal. There is another point I should add here. The two subsequent legal opinions suggesting that a sovereign Government could not be questioned overlooked an important point. Under international case law, sovereign immunity – as it's known – does not apply in cases where the Government is involved in a commercial transaction. By entering into the trading of promissory notes with European Pacific, the Cook Islands Government had waived its right to claim sovereign immunity.

If the SFO had made one phone call, maybe called in one former executive for questioning, they might have found this memo themselves. Certainly it was further ammunition for a possible prosecution.

So far, the scorecard for the SFO was not looking good. First, they had failed to actually investigate the winebox. Secondly, they had decided that even if the Magnum transaction itself was criminal, they couldn't prosecute because the documentation contained no evidence that those involved realised they were breaking the law. Thirdly, they had failed to call in for questioning even one EP employee who could have told them what the deal really meant.

Fourthly, the SFO had taken at face value an assurance that laws existed in the Cook Islands that would make the schemes legal, without ever once lifting a finger to find out whether these supposed "incentives" really did exist, and the office was now charitably giving EP the benefit of the doubt on some extremely dubious points.

One of Professor John Prebble's particularly telling arguments went along these lines: European Pacific's tax schemes drew on the best legal and accounting wizardry available. These people clearly knew that the Magnum transaction wouldn't stand up to full IRD scrutiny, so they hid the deal in a tax haven – away from the Revenue's prying eyes. By filing tax returns that they knew they would otherwise never get away with, they were committing deliberate fraud.

"It is not a view which occurred to me at the time of my first assessment of the documents," testified Sturt. "I understand the argument and acknowledge that, at least at a theoretical level, it has some force. But a prosecution based on such a stance or view could only expect to succeed if it stood alone, in the sense that the scheme was so outrageous that it necessarily crossed the boundary from avoidance to evasion.

"In my view that simply can not be said about a scheme where the evidence as to the minds of the proponents does not demonstrate an appreciation of dishonesty but rather a reasoned approach, flawed as it may have been for tax purposes."

If the deliberate use of a foreign tax certificate to gain a credit – knowing that you've already been paid back the money under the table – is not "outrageous" in that context, then I'm not quite sure what is.

Leave aside for a moment the clear inference from the SFO that the transaction may have been illegal, and examine another aspect of the law enforcement agency's behaviour.

In March, the SFO issued a statement claiming there was nothing new in the TVNZ documents or affidavits, and no criminal fraud in the Magnum transaction. By the SFO's own testimony to the Inquiry, however, it's clear that the SFO had not fully investigated Magnum at that stage. In fact, it wasn't until June 1994 – after the *Frontline* programme went to air – that Gib Beattie was asked by Sturt to take a good look at Magnum.

Three months **after** they had cleared the transaction publicly, the SFO finally got around to taking a very close look at Magnum. What faith can the public have in a law enforcement agency that clears a party of wrongdoing **before** it's done a thorough investigation?

The refusal by IRD or SFO to prosecute – because of a lack of **obvious** criminal intent – also flies in the face of overseas experience. The US Internal

Revenue Service has an entire Criminal Investigation Division, specifically set up to track money laundering and tax fraud. Agent Dave Burdick says criminal intent is obviously a factor in determining whether an offence has taken place, but the IRS has drawn a line in the sand. In the United States, at least, tax professionals and lawyers are expected to get it right every time.

"If we're investigating a firm of tax advisers for fraud or evasion, criminal intent is almost never a problem for us," says Burdick.

"Under our law, they are expected to know what the law is and where the line is. If they don't know, they have a legal duty to find out. If they cross that line, they've committed a crime."

Unlike Joe Public, who may be able to convince a Court that he didn't realise he was committing tax fraud, US tax lawyers and tax advisers cannot legally fall back on the excuse that they didn't know. Criminal intent is virtually a given.

It is unlikely that a New Zealand Court, faced with the full facts, would decide that New Zealand legal, accounting and taxation advisers had a lesser responsibility to know the law inside and out.

Criminal intent is something that must be proven, beyond reasonable doubt, to a jury. It is interwoven with issues like motive and opportunity. It is certainly something that cannot be judged on its own, but as part of the entire package.

The SFO's Gib Beattie stated that a prosecution would not turn on the tax efficacy of a scheme, but rather on whether the participants knew it was ineffective. This is akin to placing the cart before the horse. First, the transaction itself has to be illegal for any prosecution to succeed. If the law has been broken, it is then the duty of prosecuting agencies to formally investigate and assess all the available evidence, including that relating to intent.

One could argue that, following the principle of justice being seen to be done, all cases where the criminal law has been broken should automatically come before a Court, unless it is so blindingly obvious that no criminal intent exists and that a prosecution would, in effect, be a miscarriage of justice.

I do not believe that the Magnum transaction comes anywhere near those criteria. The transaction should have been placed before a Court to determine.

On the face of their testimony to the Commission of Inquiry, the SFO and IRD virtually surrendered without a shot being fired.

One such example had already been covered, albeit briefly, in the *Frontline* documentary in May 1994. European Pacific had conceded in the Magnum transaction that it may be breaking s.62 of the Companies Act. It arose because European Pacific Funds Management was effectively financing a second party into purchasing EP Funds' own stock – a move that was illegal under NZ law. As EP executives themselves noted, in the Magnum transaction memo of August 8 1988:

"This money 'run around' from The Issuer [of the preference shares, EP Funds]

to BNZ is likely to be a breach of s.62 of the Companies Act 1955 (New Zealand), as The Issuer will have financially assisted BNZ to purchase The Issuer's preference shares. The result is a $200 fine for the offence and possible ancillary contractual illegality. However, we do not consider this issue to be a serious legal or commercial problem."

As Dr John Prebble, Professor of Tax Law at Wellington's Victoria University, had noted in our documentary, s.62 breaches do normally carry only a $200 fine, but if the transaction involving the breach leads to a loss of money by a third party, criminal charges carrying a maximum of five years jail can be laid.

This was the biggest of the initial tripwires that the Serious Fraud Office had to navigate during the 1994/95 Commission of Inquiry that resulted from the *Frontline* programme.

The SFO had refused to lay any charges in relation to the Magnum deal, in fact the SFO told the Inquiry it had not even formally investigated any of the winebox transactions, despite a reference in internal SFO documentation to the *"deliberate abuse"* of s.62.

SFO Assistant Director John Hicks was asked about the decision not to press charges, during cross-examination by Inquiry Counsel, Colin Carruthers QC.

"We have heard Mr Beattie and Mr Sturt [SFO forensic accountant and SFO Director respectively] give evidence that no one was affected by any breach of Section 62 in the Magnum transaction. Is that your own view?"

"Within the confines of the particular transaction described by Mr Beattie," responded Hicks, *"I am fully supportive of what he thinks about that, yes."* It was a trap, and Hicks had walked right in. Carruthers pressed the point.

"From your analysis of it, is it clear that the transaction could not have been implemented but for this alleged breach of Section 62?"

Hicks squirmed, trying to give European Pacific the benefit of the doubt. *"I have no doubt of it, if that was a stumbling block to the transaction, that ways would have been found to transact or construct the deal in a different manner."*

"I am not talking about other alternatives, Mr Hicks," warned Carruthers, *"In the way in which the transaction was formulated, it required the deliberate abuse of Section 62 that you have spoken of, correct?"*

"Well, I have made a note about that on my papers. It does appear that that took place, yes."

Carruthers pounced. *"And the fact that the transaction was implemented in that way must have had some impact on, for example, the Commissioner of Inland Revenue, mustn't it?"*

I had to admit, Colin Carruthers was sharp. The Inland Revenue Department had lost $2 million in the Magnum deal. What he was suggesting was that the European Pacific staff involved could have been charged with fraud of that amount because of the deliberate breach of s.62.

The IRD had lost $2 million in the transaction, a transaction which SFO investigator John Hicks testified included a deliberate breach of s.62 to make the whole deal work. But the SFO didn't prosecute.

Contrast that with the SFO's prosecution in 1992 of former AIC chief executive Rodney Worn, jailed for three years after being found guilty of 15 fraud charges involving $8 million. The charges resulted from section 62 of the Companies Act. The *Dominion* quoted Justice Temm as telling Worn that while a s.62 breach only carried a $200 fine, the flow-on effects could be grave.

"Where a person breaks the law knowingly and deliberately, that can be strong evidence of dishonest intention."

The SFO must have known how tough the courts were prepared to be on such s.62 breaches – it was an SFO prosecution, after all.

How much of the SFO's approach to the winebox was a result of personal animosity between that office and Winston Peters is unclear, but there's certainly evidence that no love was lost.

Sturt told a parliamentary select committee hearing in late 1994 that he would put his own knowledge and experience of the criminal law against that of Peters and 50 of his assistants.

"One adviser that I'm aware of probably hasn't even seen inside a courtroom," claimed Sturt. He told the committee that he relied on smell in deciding whether to pursue something.

"If what I've ordered doesn't pass the smell test, then I order an investigation."

Perhaps the smell test on European Pacific failed to detect any odour because Winston Peters had managed to get right up the noses of investigators at the SFO. Peters had, in February 1994, sent the SFO copies of the Magnum and JIF documentation at the heart of the TVNZ allegations. In a news release the following month, the MP explained his reasons for doing so.

"The reasons I sent the documents to the SFO upon learning last month that it was applying to the High Court are two-fold.

1. to remind the SFO that it already had the documents

2. to ensure that it could not, once the full ambit of the TVNZ case became known, claim to have been unaware of the facts.

"In short, the SFO is applying for evidence it had been sitting on for 18 months, to minimise the risk of embarrassment should another enquiry disclose what the SFO had not been competent to discover in its own earlier 'investigation'. The SFO have given blanket clearances before that have been found in later Court action to have been totally deficient."

One such case was that of convicted fraudster Peter Roy Jones. In 1993 Auckland police had sent their file on Jones to the SFO to review because of the large sum of money involved – nearly a million dollars. The SFO handed the file back, saying the police allegations were wrong and no serious fraud had taken place. Police pushed on regardless, and secured fraud convictions in the Auckland District Court against Jones. The case was embarrassing to the SFO.

Further embarrassment would emerge for the Serious Fraud Office, however, at the hands of the IRD. The SFO's Sturt, Beattie and Hicks had based their decision not to investigate the winebox or prosecute solely on an examination of the documents themselves, and nothing else. This was in sharp contrast to the IRD's procedure.

"As is *obvious*," IRD Director of Taxpayer Audit, Tony Bouzaid, told the Inquiry, " *the process of collecting evidence, verifying the evidence, analysing the evidence, seeking advice and making a decision is far more thorough and responsible than simply reaching a conclusion based on one or two documents in the 'Winebox'.*

"*It is one thing to investigate the company records, but this may only provide part of the jigsaw. It is also important to examine third party records and to interview people who may have relevant information.*

"*Examples of people we may interview as part of the verification and collection of information process [may include] company officials and advisers . . . bankers, financiers, brokers etc.*"

None of which was done by the Serious Fraud Office.

To suggest that you can make a decision on "criminal intent" – on the state of mind of the accused – simply on the basis of a few documents and without ever talking to any of the accused or other witnesses is plainly foolish.

SFO Director Charles Sturt told the Inquiry that Peters' parliamentary allegations had already had an impact on the SFO's international relationships. If those other international agencies have been keeping an eye on the evidence given to the Commission of Inquiry, I'd be very surprised if they weren't now rolling around the floor in helpless fits of laughter!

CHAPTER 26

The Men From Infernal Revenue

"This is what New Zealand has been like in the mid-eighties: run by cocksure businessmen, with the acquiescence of a tame media, and the apparent enthusiasm of a money minded public."
– BRUCE JESSON, *BEHIND THE MIRROR GLASS*, 1987

IF THE MEASURE OF how much stands to be uncovered can be found in the amount of energy expended to stop it, then the Commission of Inquiry into Certain Matters Related to Taxation promises to be a humdinger. Only days into its first week of hearings in November 1994, the Commission found itself in turbulent seas and in dire need of navigational equipment. At issue: its very raison d'être.

From the beginning of Day One the Inland Revenue Department had signalled that it was not planning to release sensitive taxpayer information in public, because of Section 13 of the Income Tax Act requiring such affairs to remain confidential in the hands of the IRD. This is to protect public confidence in the integrity of the Revenue, a theme echoed in the IRD's boast that even criminals can file tax returns safe in the knowledge that police can't access them. In practice, it meant that more than 70 pages in a 162 page IRD Brief of Evidence to the Commission were blank. The only people to get the full 162 pages of evidence from IRD investigator John Nash were the Commissioner himself, Sir Ronald Davison, and the legal team appointed to assist him, Colin Carruthers QC, Suzanne Clark and Francis Cooke – the son of Appeal Court President Sir Robin Cooke. Everyone else was making do with the censored version.

Normally, briefs of evidence are read out loud by the witnesses presenting them. In this case, however, it was thought that perhaps the witness could read silently when he or she came to a portion of their testimony that the public wasn't permitted to hear.

If there was to be cross examination on a point covered by the secrecy provisions, everyone would have to file out of the hearing except the Commission's lawyers, the IRD and lawyers representing the taxpayer whose affairs were being discussed in the censored portion.

This presented difficulties from a fairness point of view, because some of the censored transactions might involve a number of companies, some of whom might not be aware that the IRD was investigating and who wanted a right of reply in court. In the interests of natural justice, it was argued, all parties to a transaction should have the right to hear the evidence and comment on it.

In addition, because the censoring was sprinkled at random throughout the IRD evidence, it raised the prospect of a "passing parade" of lawyers, journalists, corporates and the public traipsing in and out every five minutes as the Inquiry went in and out of closed session.

It soon became patently obvious that this wasn't going to work, and it also became patently obvious that European Pacific, Fay Richwhite and Brierleys had figured out that if they could keep the IRD evidence secret, then obviously all discussion of their own roles further down the track would also be heard in secret under the same precedent. In effect, it was the best chance they had to turn a public inquiry into a private one where the public, the media and even Winston Peters would be shut out.

The news media got a whiff of behind the scenes negotiations between lawyers representing the corporate taxpayers and Commission staff, apparently trying to broker some kind of compromise that would allow the Inquiry to continue without expensive and time-consuming legal challenges. The compromise was that all the corporates would waive their right to income tax secrecy, allowing them to have access to the IRD evidence about each other, but only if that evidence was given in a closed court.

The *Dominion* of November 8, 1994, put the frighteners on with a front page headline screaming **"Cooks Inquiry to be held in secret"**. This was make-or-break time, and everyone was jockeying for position. Winston Peters' counsel, Colin Pidgeon QC, fired the first shot.

"What is being proposed by counsel for the taxpayers is a waiver of section 13 on a condition that the hearing continues to be out of sight of the media and the New Zealand public banned.

"It must not be forgotten the winebox transactions are now public documents. This Inquiry has been called due to public concerns as to what the state bodies, the Inland Revenue Department and Serious Fraud Office, have done in respect of these transactions which appear to involve huge sums of money that should have been collected by the New Zealand Revenue.

"Taxpayers' details will come out in the course of the Inquiry. All the arrangement suggested by counsel does is buy time, and create a precedent from which to argue for further closed-door hearings. That is not in the interest of this Commission or in the interest of the public. A closed-door Inquiry is no Inquiry at all!"

It was vintage Pidgeon in full flight, and he repeated the point in his closing submission, urging the corporates to totally waive their rights to taxpayer confidentiality *"because if they have nothing to hide there should be no concerns."*

The lawyer for *National Business Review* called the 70 blank pages in Nash's evidence *"a waste of the paper that was utilised"*, using all the venom he could muster. When European Pacific's QC, Richard Craddock, took to his feet, he took a swipe at those who'd gone before.

"I [will] direct my remarks solely to the Commission and not the emotive media," he said ingratiatingly whilst sparing a contemptuous glance for the press bench.

"I will endeavour to address what is purely difficult in principle, but not an unusual problem. It is not enhanced in solution by reference to closed doors and things like that. That is pure media stuff. We are dealing with a question of confidentiality."

All around me my fellow journalists were struggling to hold back their own contemptuous guffaws, but it got more difficult to suppress as Craddock, powered up like the Duracell bunny, began lecturing the Commission on what his client wanted.

"We have got to start, in my respectful submission, with the position that those taxpayers are entitled by statute to have their affairs remain confidential, not because they have anything to hide – that's a stupid thing to say . . . – but because they are entitled to that as a matter of law and because that confidentiality is the foundation of our whole tax system.

"Now you have express power, apart from statutory power, to take some material, some evidence, in private session. It is simply that. It isn't a closed door thing at all. It is a private session."

This too caused titters throughout the hearing room, and I began to wonder whether TVNZ's Graeme Wilson and EP's Richard Craddock were using the same dictionary, presumably one where tax fraud is defined as "tax minimisation" and "private sessions" are not "closed-door hearings".

Sir Ronald Davison decided to have a little fun at Craddock's expense.

"You say private session, Mr Craddock?"

"Not open to the media," Craddock replied helpfully.

"You mean excluding the media?"

"It ought to assist you, sir, counsel assisting and the others here to deal with the matter adequately, without the intrusion of any prurient public inquisitiveness, sir."

The titters became open hoots of laughter, and Craddock fired a withering glance towards the media. The last laugh, however, belonged to counsel assisting the Commission, Colin Carruthers QC. Several journalists and a number of lawyers, including Craddock and Carruthers, ended up in an elevator a short while later. All was quiet, until one of the lawyers teased Craddock.

"I had to go scurrying to the dictionary to find out what prurient meant, Richard."

"Yeah," piped up Carruthers without missing a beat, *"we think it's another word for 'emotive'."* Once again snorts and sniggers rippled through the assemblage. Craddock took it in good grace.

As debate continued on the legal technicalities, it became plain that Section 13 of the Income Tax Act was going to pose a problem. Essentially all information on taxpayers must stay confidential except as required for "carrying into effect" the Inland Revenue Acts.

Previous case law had suggested that "carrying into effect" included defending the IRD from legal action or from *"an inquiry into alleged maladministration"*. The IRD's counsel, Graeme Panckhurst QC, argued strongly in favour of closed hearings.

"*Taxpayer confidentiality is a long established and a very important value which cannot be lightly put aside. It is not possible to afford the general public interest a particularly high value: For the difference between what the public find interesting and the public interest, must not be lost sight of.*"

This suggestion went down like a bucket of manure with the media. It's always good for the public to hear first-hand the general contempt in which they are held by the legal profession and the State. Craddock rose to the occasion again, this time going as far as to suggest that the Commission of Inquiry had no authority to hear the IRD evidence itself – in private or otherwise.

"*I object to the Commissioner of Inland Revenue giving to the Commission, or to anybody else . . . any evidence as to the affairs of any taxpayer.*"

Russell McVeagh partner Gerard Curry, representing Fay Richwhite, took a similar line, prompting Sir Ronald Davison to raise his eyebrows in disbelief.

"*I just query how far is it possible for me to conduct an Inquiry into the competence of the Commissioner [of Inland Revenue], unless I, in fact, do examine examples of the taxpayer cases he has dealt with?*"

The Bank of New Zealand, now owned by the National Australia Bank, took a different line from its former partners in European Pacific. Alan Galbraith QC put it more succinctly.

"*While it is the same bank, it is a bank now owned by different owners and managed under different direction, than the bank at the time of the matters to which you are inquiring. My instructions are to do all the bank can do to make sure that the Inquiry is conducted as efficiently and expeditiously as possible.*"

The BNZ, he said, would have no problem with a "public" inquiry. The Serious Fraud Office, too, wanted all the evidence heard in public.

"*To have any part of the Inquiry into it conducted in private leads to the suggestion that it in some way is an incomplete inquiry into corruption,*" SFO counsel Nick Davidson told the Commission.

Faced with all these submissions and more, Sir Ronald Davison had to make a ruling. Everything we'd done in the previous two years came down to this. If Sir Ronald really was a "tame" judge installed by the Government to sweep the whole thing under the carpet, then he would undoubtedly opt for a closed door hearing.

If, on the other hand, Sir Ronald was prepared to grasp the nettle in his bare hands, and was intent on holding a real Inquiry, then he would call the corporate bluff and rule in favour of full public access.

He proceeded to note some of the parliamentary allegations made by Winston Peters about the Commissioner of Inland Revenue, allegations of incompetence, of lying, of gross negligence, of possible involvement in a criminal conspiracy and corruption.

"*Those allegations,*" said Sir Ronald, pausing to glance around the assembled lawyers and media, "*resulted in this Inquiry, which is directed to inquire into whether the Commissioner of Inland Revenue and his staff acted in a lawful, proper and competent manner.*

"One might think that no more serious allegations could be made against an officer of the Inland Revenue Department and his staff. They strike at the integrity of what must be the major instrument of Government in this country, and the provision of answers to them is a matter of the greatest public concern, as the Government itself recognised by the setting up of this Inquiry."

So far so good, but if I had any doubts they were quickly dispelled.

"The right of the Commissioner of Inland Revenue to defend himself and his officers: in fact the institution of the Inland Revenue Department, perhaps the major institution of Government in this country, against the public allegations made against him – by having his case heard in public – far outweighs any claims the corporates may make to have evidence relating to them heard in secret.

"The comparison to be made is between the defence of the integrity of the major Government department on the one hand, and the secrecy of the tax affairs of some corporate taxpayers on the other.

"The evidence of Mr Nash, and also that of any other Inland Revenue Department witnesses who may be called later, detailing the investigations made into the tax affairs of the corporates, is so fundamental to this Inquiry it should be given openly in public."

The look of horror on the faces of counsel for some of the main players was clearly apparent. They quickly rose to signal intentions to appeal Sir Ronald's ruling. The Commission of Inquiry effectively ground to a halt.

A month later, in December 1994, the arguments were played out again in the New Zealand Court of Appeal, including suggestions that the Commission could hear all the evidence in private without even referring to it in its report to Parliament. In their own decision on the appeal, the three appellate judges took a dim view of the claims put forward by Fay Richwhite, European Pacific and Brierleys.

"Mr Curry [Fay Richwhite's lawyer] submitted that the Commission could exclude the information from its [final] report while still providing a public vindication," Justice Ian McKay wrote in his summary of the case.

"This overlooks the elementary fact that until the Inquiry is complete one cannot say whether the Commissioner of Inland Revenue will be vindicated or not.

"It is certainly reasonable at this stage to predict that details of the investigations and of the information obtained will have to be disclosed if the Commission's report is to have credibility, and one cannot say that that is not a relevant factor to be taken into account."

An alternative argument, rebutting the SFO's demands for a public inquiry, and rejecting the SFO's call for access to all the IRD evidence, was also struck down by the Court of Appeal in the interests of natural justice.

"The terms of reference require the Commission to inquire into the actions of both the Commissioner [of Revenue] and the Director [of the Serious Fraud Office] in dealing with the same transactions, namely those referred to in the winebox papers," said Justice McKay.

"Information obtained by the Commissioner may be information that the Director could and should have obtained. Conclusions drawn by the Commissioner may be conclusions which could and should have been drawn by the Director."

On the general issue of a secret hearing, the Court was equally strong. *"Secrecy for the important and possibly damaging detail, would only arouse public suspicion and put in question the value of the exercise and even the integrity of the Commission itself,"* wrote Justice Michael Hardie-Boys.

The Appeal Court judgement left no room for Fay Richwhite or the other parties to appeal to the Privy Council in Britain and, on February 7, 1995, the Inquiry resumed in Auckland to hear the IRD's John Nash complete his up to now suppressed evidence.

Perhaps the most significant facts to emerge involved the chronology of the IRD investigations. The department received the winebox from the SFO in February 1993, and set up a project team to investigate the deals. A year later, those investigations seemed to have finished.

"I proceeded to sign off all 59 deals, the last being on 21 February 1994, [and] re-examine all the winebox papers for completeness, including all previous analyses signed off during 1993 – this took place from 15 February through to 21 February 1994," Nash told the Inquiry.

Nash obviously felt that he had a good handle on the winebox already, because he also told of preparing a summary report at this stage, a draft news release and a draft report to the Minister of Revenue.

On March 18, after Winston Peters had tabled the winebox in Parliament and made serious allegations about the Magnum transaction, Inland Revenue Commissioner David Henry felt compelled for some reason to publicly defend those Peters was accusing. The winebox had been given by the SFO to the IRD in 1993, he said.

"Inland Revenue routinely audits the tax affairs of companies and individuals using tax havens such as the Cook Islands. The information from the Serious Fraud Office has been fed into the audit process."

The auditors, said Henry, had not disclosed any tax evasion or fraudulent activities, but had disclosed schemes using legal means to try to avoid tax. This is an extremely serious point. Any reasonable person would take it from Henry's comments that the IRD had looked at the winebox and found no evidence of fraud, as alleged by TVNZ or Winston Peters.

Note the date, March 18. Henry was publicly absolving European Pacific of any crime, **before** he got an independent legal opinion on the matter.

On March 21, 1994, David Henry asked barrister Grant Pearson for an opinion on the Magnum transaction. Pearson's deadline to get his head around Magnum and report back was March 23.

On March 22, a day **before** Pearson was due to report back on the legality of Magnum, David Henry reported to Parliament again stating that the winebox had been examined. *"I can confirm to you that the so-called winebox of papers were accessed by my officers in early 1993."*

He also stated that there was no evidence of evasion or fraud in any Cook Islands investigations carried out by his office. He stated 93 investigations had been completed and an extra $55.7 million in tax assessed. A small number of investigations were continuing.

A reasonable person would assume Henry was talking about the winebox, given that his report coincided with Peters' second major speech on the Magnum and JIF deals, and IRD inaction on the winebox. What the public weren't told, was that the Inland Revenue Department had not actually completed a detailed investigation of the winebox at this point in time. Why did the Commissioner of Inland Revenue comment publicly on the issue, allaying public suspicion, even if his minister *had* asked him to?

Why didn't Henry wait until March 23 for Pearson's report on Magnum, especially as Pearson could have decided Magnum was criminal? David Henry compounded the confusion with another report to Parliament on March 30, 1994. Headed *"THE COOK ISLANDS: ALLEGATIONS CON-CERNING TAX"*, Henry's report noted he had now received the winebox tabled by Peters earlier that month and *"I now attach a comprehensive report on this and surrounding issues."*
IRD Commissioner states categorically that they contain no fraud.

"Looking now at the papers as a whole, it is clear that they relate to schemes designed in the late 1980's which are aimed at avoiding taxation imposed by New Zealand and other countries by using the Cook Islands as a tax haven.

"They do not constitute evidence of tax evasion but they do show blatant tax avoidance and cast little credit on the business ethics of the designers. The liability to taxation imposed by Parliament is not however altered by questions of ethics, morality or poor citizenship. I must apply the law as it stands according to the information I have obtained including that arising from my own investigations."

Henry then goes on to detail those *"Cook Islands Investigations"*.

"IRD has been active in investigating Cook Islands transactions. Section 99 has already been applied in relation to tax avoidance through the Cook Islands – 93 investigations have been completed resulting in additional tax assessed of $55.7 million.

"Some investigations are continuing, often as part of wider investigations of the taxpayers concerned. Further assessments can be expected in relation to events which occurred in the late 1980's."

The Government used the IRD's reassurances to try and quash Peters' calls for a public inquiry. Attorney-General Paul East was among the first to his feet after Peters' March 22 speech, defending the integrity of The SFO and the IRD and their decisions.

"The Director of the Serious Fraud Office made a public statement declaring that there was 'no evidence of criminal fraudulent offending'.

"The Commissioner of Inland Revenue has quite clearly placed on public record the fact that he has investigated a number of claims with regard to tax fraud in the Cook Islands and he is satisfied that these investigations have been resolved satisfactorily."

East, relying on the SFO and IRD rulings, later described Peters' allegations as *"baseless"*.

European Pacific was able to use the IRD's assurances to boost the case for a permanent ban on broadcasting the *Frontline* documentary.

The whole affair begins to look even more concerning when you go back to the chronology. David Henry's statement of March 30, 1994 indicated that the whole thing was virtually over from the IRD's point of view.

"*A complete review was carried out in February 1994 by the Manager (International Audit). The purpose was to ensure that all actions taken had been complete and appropriate. The conclusion was that evidence of tax evasion was not established but evidence of tax avoidance was present.*"

The phrasing used by Henry was past-tense. All actions taken, he said, had been "*complete*". The special project team set up to analyse the box was disbanded in mid-February, and little further appeared to have been done until Peters tabled the winebox a month later.

Even so, the IRD testimony to the Inquiry in 1995 confirmed that detailed investigatory work on the winebox didn't begin showing results until June 1994, after the documentary had aired and after Parliament's Finance and Expenditure Select Committee decided to investigate.

These fresh investigations identified potentially tens of millions of dollars of more tax that could be clawed back under the anti-avoidance provisions of section 99, and they also revealed a number of "technical" illegalities, such as the failure by Fay Richwhite to declare thousands of dollars in foreign income and failure to declare an interest in a foreign subsidiary company. The IRD accepted that the failures were unintentional, and issued a written warning.

Nash's evidence revealed that the fresh investigations had turned up new avenues of inquiry into major corporates like Carter Holt Harvey, Fay Richwhite, Lion Nathan, the BNZ, European Pacific and the New Zealand Wool Board.

But, as the *Independent* noted scathingly, "*these activities all took place **after** Henry publicly absolved Fay Richwhite and its winebox clients of tax evasion – and when lawyers acting for European Pacific were using this apparent absolution in the High Court and the Court of Appeal as ammunition in their bid to gag the news media from publishing further details of winebox deals.*"

David Henry had repeated his denials of winebox foul-play in a statement to Parliament on March 30, 1994. Nearly a year later, the newspaper was at pains to remind Henry of his comments.

"*When asked by the Independent how Henry could have absolved Fay Richwhite, European Pacific and their clients of tax evasion on 30 March 1994, when Nash had yet to begin his real work, an IRD spokesman said the department's winebox inquiry should be regarded as a 'progression over time'.*

"*The project team was disbanded in February 1994 after completing its initial analysis of the documents, he said. 'Then it was a matter of completing the investigations'. New evidence had come to light since then and more would possibly be found. 'What could be a certain state of affairs today could be a fraud tomorrow'.* *

---

* In fact, just as this book was going to press in August 1995, the IRD changed its tune on the winebox. It now claims that Carter Holt Harvey may be guilty of tax evasion for allegedly suppressing $63 million of income. CHH denies the allegation. The IRD still believes there is no fraud in the Magnum deal.

"Henry's comments . . . were an accurate assessment of the position at that time, the spokesman said. 'Peters had made a prima facie allegation of evasion on the documents alone, and that just wasn't there'."

Just so the reader is left in no doubt, I shall briefly list some of the dates of the fresh IRD investigations.

29 April 1994:	investigation begins into BNZ $200 million captive "insurance" scheme.
8 September 1994:	investigation begins of BNZ $400 million rps deal (I'll come back to this deal shortly).
15 July 1994:	investigations commence into various Brierley Investments deals.
20 June 1994:	discussion with Russell McVeagh McKenzie Bartleet and Co about the Carter Holt Harvey transaction.
21 June 1994:	meeting with representatives of European Pacific New Zealand Ltd. to discuss Magnum transaction and other matters.

I could go on, but suffice to say that most of the major investigatory work and significant developments appear to date from the latter half of 1994, raising serious questions about David Henry's comments in March 1994 implying nothing of significance was in the winebox. It's pretty clear from the IRD evidence that Henry and others in the department hadn't done enough work at that stage to justify making any comment: if they knew enough in March to say there was nothing there, then they wouldn't have found **new** information and reached new conclusions in June, July or October, would they?

It's a question the Davison Commission looks set to consider as it reviews the Inland Revenue Department's investigatory processes. Regardless of Henry's denials of evasion and fraud in the winebox, the political impact of those statements coming when they did cannot be ignored.

As I've already pointed out, they were immediately pounced on by a Government desperate to allay public suspicion about the winebox, and they were pounced on by European Pacific to argue in the High Court and Court of Appeal that the SFO and IRD had cleared the transactions of criminality, and that those rulings could not be questioned by TVNZ or anyone else.

Indeed, that factor was a major plank in EP's submissions. If the IRD hadn't publicly cleared them, EP wouldn't have known whether it was in the clear and couldn't have used that line of argument.

Back at the Commission of Inquiry, meanwhile, Nash was spilling the beans on transaction after transaction, displaying wiring diagram after diagram, and causing more than a few eyelids to droop. After one particularly long session of listening to John Nash's mind-numbing dialogues on taxation accounting, it was obvious the excruciating minutiae was taking a terrible toll, even on European Pacific and its allies.

"It was easier to understand on the Frontline programme," muttered European Pacific's hired legal counsel Wendy Blennerhassett under her breath, in an obvious reference to the graphically illustrated money trail with its bouncing bags of cash.

"Yeah," quipped fellow EP lawyer Chris Allan, *"Why don't they forget all this crap and just play the bloody video to the Commission – stripped of some of its worst excesses of course!,"* he said, grinning across at me.

It seems other European Pacific staff had also found the *Frontline* documentary enlightening. As I mentioned earlier, Nash testified to the Inquiry that he met former EP executives Anthony McCullagh and Peter Brannigan in June 1994 to discuss, among other things, the Magnum deal.

In particular, said Nash, they discussed the implications of Section 301 of the Income Tax Act which required European Pacific to cough up details of its secret tax refund deals in the Cook Islands.

"Mr McCullagh said that he had never considered the provision and had only learned about it through watching the Frontline television documentary."

McCullagh claimed that he wasn't aware of the structure in the Cook Islands involving promissory notes and had left the tax law side of the deal to European Pacific's legal beagles to sort out. Nash cocked an eyebrow.

"My reaction to these explanations was one of scepticism."

Nash also let slip some other interesting information. One example was his investigation of a Cook Islands company called Halcome Ltd., which he referred to as *"the principal Cook Islands'company of Fay Richwhite."*

"Halcome derived profits from its fixed interest portfolio. Halcome also received dividend income from its 28% shareholding in EPI. These profits were then passed to Fay Richwhite during the 1987 and 1988 income years by way of dividends."

The dividend for 1987 was $25.2 million, and for 1988: $29.8 million. The IRD did not indicate how much of the Halcome income was earnt from its portfolio and how much was earnt via its holding in EPI, but it brings me to an important point.

In 1987, European Pacific Investments posted a total profit attributable to shareholders of only US$4 million, and in 1988 US$13.5 million – nowhere near enough to account for the huge sums earnt by 28% shareholder Halcome and passed through to Fay Richwhite.

It can only be presumed, in the absence of any clarifying evidence at the time of writing, that Halcome was in fact a bigger dealmaker in the Cook Islands than European Pacific was.

The IRD took the same approach to categorising Fay Richwhite as I have in this book: the name is used to refer generically to companies, public and private, in the Fay Richwhite empire.

As Nash noted in his evidence, *"Up to late 1990, the private merchant bank Fay Richwhite and Co Ltd owned approximately 68% of the public company Capital Markets Ltd, ('CML'). CML had two principal subsidiaries, Horizon Oil Exploration NL ('Horizon') and Halcome Ltd, both 100% owned.*

"CML acquired the merchant banking business of Fay, Richwhite and Co Ltd

from principally Sir Michael Fay and Mr David Richwhite, effective as of 1 July 1990. CML then changed its name to Fay, Richwhite and Co Ltd. The former Fay, Richwhite and Co Ltd changed its name to Midavia Group Ltd and continued as the main business vehicle for the private interests of Sir Michael Fay and Mr Richwhite.

"*A limited audit of the taxation affairs of the private business interests of Sir Michael Fay and Mr Richwhite has been carried out by IRD, concentrating on transactions which have been almost inextricably mixed with the financial affairs of the public company, and specific winebox issues have also been addressed.*"

The IRD discovered that Fay Richwhite employee John Balgarnie had acted as an agent for both the public company and the private interests, and Russell McVeagh lawyer Dr Geoffrey Harley had acted on tax matters for both the public company and the private one.

To all intents and purposes, the IRD figured, the two companies were joined at the hip. Incidentally, the IRD claimed its investigation of Fay Richwhite was met at times with outright aggression. In one example, senior investigator John Trezise noted that "*at one point Mr Harley advised Mr Balgarnie not to engage in oral discussions with us – threatened to sue me in person for 'malfeasance in public office', including for exemplary damages.*"

But more was soon to emerge on Fay Richwhite's winebox dealings, dealings that may go to the heart of public calls for an inquiry into the Bank of New Zealand.

CHAPTER 27

The Piggy Bank

*"Huge volumes of cash are remitted every day to and from the
United States from places like Panama and the Cayman Islands
without a question asked, though no one here really believes that
all that cash represents dollars exchanged for local currency
by tourists shopping for rugs or straw hats."*
– JONATHAN BEATY AND S.C. GWYNNE, *THE OUTLAW BANK*, 1993

IN LATE 1993, I had come across what appeared to be some sensational
documents. They appeared to have come from the files of a Dr Brian Perry,
a senior executive within the Bank of New Zealand – or at least he had been
during 1989, which is the period covered by the documents. Page one
virtually reached out, grabbed me by the ears and pulled me in for a closer
look. It was on Bank of New Zealand letterhead, Investment Banking Group,
and it was a facsimile cover sheet dated September 13, 1989.

Brian Perry, Senior Manager, BNZ Investment Banking was writing to
Lindsay Pyne, the BNZ Chief Executive, and the message was marked
"confidential". Being a journalist, this was a guaranteed antennae-tweaker.

*"Maybe this represents a reaction to my 'blowing the whistle' on the level of Fay
Richwhite exposure!?,"* Perry had scrawled across the page. The cover sheet
indicated 10 more pages followed, but I couldn't find them in my pile of
documentation. What I did find was interesting enough, however.

Another letter, dated September 25, 1989, was addressed to Perry from
another senior BNZ Auckland executive Peter Thodey. *"Dear Brian,"* it
began, *"Further to our recent conversations, this letter serves to formally advise
that the Bank of New Zealand has elected to terminate your contract."*

The following day, Perry wrote back, tendering his resignation and
electing to receive three months pay in lieu of notice.

On October 4, 1989, the "Dear Brian" became *"Dear Dr Perry"*. The bank
ordered him to surrender his company vehicle forthwith, before setting out
some other terms and conditions.

*"Your housing finance may continue until 22 December 1989 on the current
preferred terms. At that date however the Bank requires that the advance be
repaid."*

How's that for a sacking – the bank wouldn't even let him remain as an
ordinary customer of the BNZ! I continued reading.

*"Your car loan advanced by the Bank may continue until 22 December 1989
on the current preferred terms. At that date the Bank requires that the advance be
repaid.*

*"Your BNZ Visa Card credit limit will be immediately reduced to the current
level of outstandings. The current preferred interest rate will continue until 22*

December 1989. At that date, however, any debt you may have on a BNZ Visa card is to be repaid, facility will be cancelled and the Visa Card is to be returned to the Bank."

I looked in vain for an *"and by the way, Merry Christmas!"* Another letter, dated January 4, 1990, was addressed to Paddy Boyle and Graeme Pentecost, both General Managers at the BNZ Head Office in Wellington.

"I would like to raise with you both," wrote Perry, *"my disquiet at the manner in which my termination took place, and in particular that no reason was given either verbally or in writing.*

"As no dissatisfaction with my performance was shown in my performance appraisals, and indeed it is only one year since I was appointed Senior Manager, I am driven to the conclusion that the termination took place for one or all of the following reasons."

Reasons 1 and 3 didn't seem to be particularly provocative, but reason 2 caught my eye. *"BNZ exposure to Fay Richwhite group: The other matter which caused comment, particularly from Messrs Diack and Thodey, concerned my disclosure to Mr L.C. Pyne that the bank's exposure to the Fay Richwhite/Capital Markets group appeared to be* **considerably in excess of prudential and regulatory limits** *[author's emphasis].**

"You will be aware that all Central Banks are particularly sensitive to banks' exposures to their shareholders. I continue to believe that my disclosure of this exposure to be in the best interests of Bank of New Zealand."

My mind raced. So a senior executive of the Bank of New Zealand had alleged that too much money had been lent to the Fay Richwhite group, and suddenly found himself sacked, apparently without explanation.

Another document, shown to me but not given to me, contained a reference to an exposure of $900 million. And then the penny dropped.

Back in 1992, Winston Peters had read out an affidavit in Parliament, sworn by a former senior BNZ executive named Larry Johnson. Johnson's affidavit was centred on a loan renewal application being made by Fay Richwhite secured against its Auckland office tower. Johnson was alleging the loan exceeded the permitted size, and was unwise given the Group's existing commitments. The Peters speech had touched on the issue of the BNZ's exposure to Fay Richwhite three times.

"A discussion then took place between Jonathan Arthur and Roger Kennedy and myself [Johnson] in respect of the $900 million current exposure that Fay Richwhite and associated interests had with the Bank of New Zealand.

"In the course of this discussion, Sir Michael Fay became highly agitated and I was called a 'little effing God'. I personally advised Sir Michael Fay that he had a conflict of interest as he had his customer's hat on and asked what he would do when he put on his director's hat.

---

* In testimony to the Davison Inquiry, IRD investigator John Nash said of one Capital Markets/BNZ deal: *"Put shortly, this involved artificial restructuring to avoid Reserve Bank prudential limits. This may be of interest to the Reserve Bank."*

"I told him that I was hired to clean up some of the mess at the Bank of New Zealand, and now he was arranging his own loan which would be far in excess of the loan to value ratios that had currently been fixed by the full Board of the Bank of New Zealand,* and that what he was doing involved a major conflict of interest. At this stage Sir Michael Fay became very irate and told me that it was quote 'my effing bank' and 'I will do anything I want to'."

After the parliamentary allegations, Fay had hit back with a news release calling Winston Peters "a liar and a coward". He also vehemently denied "saying the words attributed to me in Parliament last night. I can categorically refute claims that the meeting was stormy or coercive."

"More importantly, I was not present at any BNZ credit or Board meetings which discussed Fay, Richwhite loans. The BNZ Board is always very particular to ensure no director participates in any credit decision where a possible conflict of interest could arise. Let me state that at no time has Fay Richwhite owed the Bank of New Zealand $900 million or a sum even approaching that amount."

I looked back at the Perry papers in front of me. Finally we had proof that Johnson's allegations weren't the first time the issue of Fay Richwhite borrowing had been raised. I began looking for further corroboration. A source close to the BNZ, who'd also known of the Perry sacking, filled in some of the background. This man told me Perry's story.

"Brian was trying to do a big deal in March 1989, the contract was all but signed. Then, just days before the money was due to be drawn down, Brian was told his deal was being cancelled to make way for another series of transactions. It turned out those transactions were Fay Richwhite group-based. He couldn't find out exactly how much was involved, but he thought it might be between $450 to $500 million."

As the story goes, a furious Perry went back through the files to find out just how much money had already been lent to the Fay Richwhite group. He discovered that "official" lending to the group totalled nearly $450 million, in the form of what's called an "aggregate" or gross exposure. This was **before** these latest preference share deals had gone through.

To me, the $450 million figure was actually quite staggering. I knew from my research that banks in the United States and other western countries were only allowed to lend between 15 and 20% of their capital base to any one customer. It was a rule brought in to prevent defaulting customers from taking a major bank down with them. As early as June 1986, the Reserve Bank of Australia had taken action to make sure Australian banks complied. Those banks were asked to report regularly on "all exposures to individual clients, or groups of related clients, above 10 percent of shareholders' funds of the banking group."

---

* There is some evidence that a 50% loan-to-value limit applied to this particular loan. An internal BNZ memorandum dated 30 November 1989 shows Foenus Investments, the company that owned the Fay Richwhite building, was eligible for a $66 million loan on the building, then valued at $132 million. Fay Richwhite owned a half share of Foenus Investments. Larry Johnson's clash on the issue didn't occur until early 1990.

By 1987, Aussie banks were required to give prior notification of any intention to enter into such large exposures, and be able to show the Reserve Bank that the proposed lending *"would not result in . . . excessive risk."* A glance at the Bank of New Zealand's published accounts told me what I needed to know. In 1988 the BNZ had shareholders funds of a billion dollars. At 10%, lending to the Fay Richwhite group should have been nearer $100 million, not $450 million.

In 1989, the BNZ only had shareholders funds of $92 million!, and by 1990 it had improved again to $770 million. New Zealand, however, was one of the few countries in the western world that didn't have hard and fast rules about the size of loans to clients. So, bearing in mind that BNZ lending to Fay Richwhite group was already excessive by the standards of bigger and wiser countries, how much extra was involved in the transactions Perry had discovered? My source took up the story again.

The transactions had been in the form of preference share deals, and actually added up to about $400 million. If Perry was correct in his analysis, that would take total Fay Richwhite group lending to nearly $900 million. Why preference shares?, I asked.

"Well, the preference share deals produce after tax income for the bank. In other words the bank buys a preference share from a Fay Richwhite group company – in other words Fay Richwhite basically borrows the money from the bank and issues a bit of paper to the bank in return for that.

"But that bit of paper doesn't produce an interest element, it produces an after-tax dividend. So, for example, in a market you might have 15% interest being produced on ordinary overdraft loans, ordinary lending by a bank. Well, if the bank receives that 15% then that's going to be taxable, so you take off your 35% corporate tax and you come down to about 10%. So the bank gets an effective, say 10%, yield on its lending.

"Now on a preference share, the preference share doesn't pay interest, it pays a dividend. It's already been taxed, and therefore the coupon of that preference share can be, let's say, 10 percent, which will give the bank exactly the same yield.

"The bank would be indifferent between receiving a taxable income of 15% or an after-tax income of 15% less the corporate tax rate – 10%. So you see, preference shares are a cheaper form of borrowing for companies, but it really depends on the capacity for the bank to offset that or to use that taxed income."

Easy money if you can get it. If you're a big corporate that is. These cosy deals certainly were not available to the average punter. While it meant nothing to the bank, it meant a lot to the corporate. Instead of borrowing money at an upfront cost of 15%, they could borrow at 10%, invest the sum in another bank, and presumably make a profit on the margin of one or two percent.

Just as in the Magnum deal, the burden of paying tax on its investment transfers from the lender BNZ (Magnum) to the borrower Fay Richwhite (European Pacific Funds Management Ltd.) As long as Fay Richwhite can prove to the IRD that it's paying a preference share dividend to the BNZ out of taxable profits, then the deal will work.

"*The other thing Brian said was that the deals weren't done directly in Fay Richwhite's name. They were using little $100 shell companies set up by some lawyers in Wellington, and the BNZ was lending each of these tiny one hundred dollar companies $50 million in the form of a preference share purchase.*

"*They will have legally ensured that everything was OK and it was well isolated, but the point that Brian made was that – despite all the legal protection you want to give it – it's clearly Fay Richwhite/Capital Markets borrowing because they're using Fay Richwhite securities.*

"*Anyway,*" said my source, "*when Brian discovered these deals didn't appear on the Fay Richwhite account summary, he fired a memo down to Lindsay Pyne – in July I think – expressing concerns about lending and prudential limits.*

"*The regional manager here in Auckland came streaking down the stairs, shouting at Brian 'Did you tell Pyne about the Fay Richwhite pref deals!?', and from then on it was World War 3.*"

It was now October 1993, however, and my energies were being directed towards the winebox deals and the production of the *Frontline* documentary. This BNZ story deserved a documentary of its own, and I had no time to do it. Instead, I filed it away for future reference. It wasn't until June, 1994, that I began working in earnest on the story again.

With the European Pacific programme now broadcast and a parliamentary inquiry ordered, it seemed like a good time to dust off the BNZ file. One of the first things we found was that corroborating evidence for the preference share deals existed in the winebox. Four hundred million dollars worth of deals, in fact. The documents showed a series of $100 companies had been set up by the lawfirm Kensington Swan.

In the winebox documentation available, European Pacific executives had named Capital Markets as the client. Essentially the deals worked like this: The Bank of New Zealand purchased $50 million worth of preference shares in each company, which in turn invested that money, via the Cook Islands, in a Japanese bank.

The interest on deposit, probably around 12.8% if other Japanese bank deals were anything to go by, was higher than the dividend that had to be returned to the Bank of New Zealand, say, for example, 10%. The margin, 2.8%, would be the profit on the deal for Fay Richwhite and European Pacific.

Another BNZ document dropped into my lap, which showed that by November 1989 – after Brian Perry's whistle-blowing back in July – all of the pref deals now appeared on the large exposure list. It also listed the names of all the shell companies:

Eodem Securities Ltd
Galverston Securities Ltd
Rhizo Investments Ltd
Primate Investments Ltd
Panachel Holdings Ltd
Potonga Group Ltd
Litmax Investments Ltd

Patmore Investments Ltd

They were all described as companies *"introduced by Capital Markets Limited to facilitate a four-year Redeemable Preference Share transaction"*.

The document also showed the BNZ had security over the loans, and described the security as *"Mortgage and possession of Bearer Securities issued by Prime International Banks/Sovereigns and/or registered securities."* This did not sound, to me, a very specific list of exactly what securities were held.

What made it even more curious was that the BNZ had gone to great pains to specify the securities it held on other companies. The bank's hold over Fay Richwhite Group, for example, included

"L/C/Funding Facility (Gross $57.5M)

"Deed of Lien over 68.896M Capital Markets shares @ $1-90 (top up 120%)M/V $130.902M say L/V $87.3M.

"Guarantee from Fay Richwhite Holdings Ltd (unsupported).

"$25M risk sold down to State Bank of South Australia."

A pretty detailed list, in comparison to the fleeting descriptions for the shell companies. The winebox documents did indicate that the BNZ held securities equivalent to the value of the pref share loans, but let's examine the possible scenarios.

If, by a cruel twist of fate, the $400 million lent out had disappeared down a taxhaven plughole, how valuable would the securities held by the BNZ be? The first problem might be the maturity date for the securities – they may not be able to be cashed up for months or even years, meaning the bank would have had to carry the loss for some time. Even if the bank could sell them to another financial institution, what price would they fetch? In a firesale, a desperate seller doesn't command a premium.

The new BNZ document also provided some other interesting facts: aggregate lending to the Fay Richwhite empire was listed as $487 million, not inclusive of the rps deals. Only giant corporations employing thousands of people, like Fletcher Challenge or the global NZI insurance and banking group, had borrowed more from the BNZ. How many people did Fay Richwhite employ? A couple of hundred?

At least if Fletcher Challenge went belly-up the BNZ would have bricks and mortar to hold onto in the form of manufacturing subsidiaries. What real security did Fay Richwhite – a paper shuffler and deal-doer – have at this time?

In fact, my questions were answered in evidence to the Davison Commission in August 1995. Ron Diack, still a senior BNZ executive, testified of events leading up to the pref share deals.

"We gave an indication to CML [Capital Markets Ltd.] that we would go through with a total of $400 million RPS deals in approximately October 1988. The debate that occurred resulted from the Bank's worsening financial position at this time. Redeemable preference share transactions are only beneficial to an investor [BNZ] when it is in a taxable profit situation.

"The RPS investor gets a tax-free return at a better rate than a taxable investment after tax. However, if an institution is in a loss situation, and tax is not

being paid, then there is no benefit in entering redeemable preference share transactions. Indeed, when a company is in a loss situation, it is in its best interests to maximise its taxable returns to eliminate the loss as soon as possible."

And the BNZ was certainly on a collision course with a massive loss, more than $600 million. Arguably the bank should not have done the deals, and instead should have charged the money out at full rates of interest. From Diack's testimony, the Capital Markets RPS deals were obviously a bone of contention within the BNZ over the coming months.

No one, he says, appeared to be keeping an eye on who was doing what. Instead, various divisions of the bank stumbled on, assuming that *"if we were doing transactions that were not in the best interests of the Bank we would have expected a message to come down from the upper level of management. We would expect to be told not to do them.*

"There was some considerable debate within the Bank about whether it was appropriate to do the transactions, but I don't think there is any evidence we actually debated the issue with CML."

Instead, Bank staff pushed on, and Capital Markets got the $400 million it was seeking, earning some considerable fee benefits in the process. At the same time, taxpayers were having to bail out the BNZ. It was not the end of the bank's troubles on the matter, however.

To have that much money appearing on the Fay Richwhite group's account would cause problems with the Reserve Bank and its prudential limit ratios. According to Diack, his boss Peter Travers ordered him to disguise the lending so as the loans didn't appear under Capital Markets' name.

"This," Diack told the Commission, *"was a prudential ratio problem."* This was where the idea to use $100 companies set up by the Kensington Swan law firm came from.

"The introduction of these companies was for no other reason than to avoid the necessity of the transactions being reported as CML exposures."

Although they deliberately set out to keep the Reserve Bank in the dark, Diack says the BNZ was happy with the "prime bank" securities put up by the Fay Richwhite group, and didn't regard the loans as an exposure to Capital Markets.

The IRD appears more sceptical, and was critical that many of the deals appear to have been done over the phone with no hard documentation on securities.

"I find it very difficult to accept," John Nash told the Inquiry in 1995, *"that a major financial institution could invest some $400 million in RPS [redeemable preference shares] on the basis of nothing more than a sprinkling of preliminary correspondence concerning the pledging of securities.*

"My scepticism is heightened by the involvement of senior executives of the BNZ Investment Banking Branch in the operations of EPI (including EPBC) and their frequent contact with executives/directors of Fay Richwhite," said Nash. He testified that the IRD had decided the deals were part of *"wider tax avoidance arrangements."*

BNZ Investments Ltd. had its income from the deals reassessed up to an extra $136 million, and BNZ Finance Ltd. an extra $26 million. The IRD now wants those companies to pay tax on that extra income. The BNZ is challenging the assessment.

On a roll, Nash claimed BNZ Investments Ltd. had "*invested in 57 issues of RPS between 1986 and 1991, but only in the RPS transactions executed with Fay Richwhite companies were up-front fees not received by BNZ. That is internal recognition that the RPS transactions under investigation were different from the substitute lending transactions undertaken by way of RPS for non-Fay Richwhite issuers.*"

It all illustrates an apparently close relationship between Fay Richwhite group, which purchased – via Capital Markets – a 30% stake in the BNZ in July 1989, and the Bank of New Zealand.

The original Brian Perry memo that I'd spent a year and a half looking for also turned up in Ron Diack's brief of evidence. Sure enough, Perry had indeed "*blown the whistle*", claiming in his letter that "*I was informed that the transactions did not appear on this [large exposure] reporting list. It would appear, however, that the risk is undoubtedly Fay Richwhite/Capital Markets.*"

Further on, Perry added "*this would raise our gross exposure to the Fay Richwhite group to a level in excess of $1 billion.*"

While the pref share deals themselves had not been hidden from the BNZ Board, there is evidence that directors were not really sure who was behind them. In January, 1989, director Len Bayliss asked at one point who the $100 companies are and "*what is the relationship with Capital Markets?*" At a BNZ Board meeting in July, 1989, the issue came up again. The minutes record:

"*The schedule of exposure levels in excess of 5% of Shareholders Funds was received by the Board. Mr Pearson noted that exposures to Brierleys, FCL etc, are greater than the Bank's Shareholders funds and Mr Bayliss drew attention to rules elsewhere prohibiting this.*

"*Dr Lojkine queried the names at the bottom of the list (Patmore, Potonga etc) and asked that the Board be advised who is actually behind these companies, i.e. to whom is the Bank actually exposed.*"

The minutes record that "*Mr Fay left the meeting at this point 12.55pm.*"

I did get hold of Brian Perry, now in Southeast Asia. A former Vice-President of Citibank New Zealand, former managing director of First Governors Merchant Bank and a onetime Vice-President of the Irving Trust Company in London, he refused to comment on the matters. Which was disappointing. That someone with such credentials, plus a Ph.D in corporate investment strategies and a Master of Architecture degree, should blow the whistle on lending practices within New Zealand's state bank, is clearly a factor of major significance.

The Aftermath

*"While dubious deals may be buried in the detail, it will be the
headline that determines whether Winston Peters' papers will have
the consequences of Daniel Ellsberg's Pentagon papers. If it ever
appears, that headline will contain the amount of tax that big
businesses avoided, possibly legitimately but probably immorally.
If it's tens of millions, it will be the story of the year. If it's hundreds
of millions, it will be the story of the decade."*
– TOM FREWEN, *NATIONAL BUSINESS REVIEW*, 1994

THERE IS A SAYING: What goes around comes around. It is August, 1995, and
the world is closing in on some of those players now familiar to readers. The
Davison Commission has just resumed a full investigation of the winebox
transactions and the companies behind them. The first secret witness has
already been called to testify, and he claims that in one year alone – 1988 –
"we probably did about $2 billion worth of deals."

Treasury estimates New Zealand taxpayers were losing up to $1 billion a
year in the mid-eighties – huge sums which, had they been paid then, might
have paid off the Government budget deficit a lot sooner, allowing more
spending on social issues like education and health. Also being investigated
by the Commission is the role of the Cook Islands Government in the transactions: was it that of a passive tax haven, or that of an active and willing
participant?

As I write this, the Cooks Government has just been firmly embroiled in
another big scandal, this time involving worthless letters of guarantee signed
by the Prime Minister, Sir Geoffrey Henry, and the Cook Islands Treasury
boss, Alistair Rutherford. Each of the 12 letters committed the Cook Islands
Government to pay up to US$100 million *"irrevocably and unconditionally,
without protest or notification"* to a Bahamas shell company or its nominees.
"This guarantee is transferable, assignable and divisible." It would appear that
international American and British criminals were hoping to use the letters
as a gilt-edged, government-guaranteed security for loan applications. They
could then, of course, take the loan money and scarper, leaving an
unfortunate bank holding a worthless Cook Islands guarantee.

The Cook Islands Government has no money: It is a quarter billion
dollars in debt and has had to largely abandon its own currency in favour of
New Zealand's because even its own citizens had begun to regard it as
"funny money". It could never meet the debt if anyone came calling with
even one of the letters of guarantee. The letters were presented to a number
of international banks, who in turn notified central banking authorities like
the Bank of England or the US Treasury.

International alerts have gone out from the latter warning banks to steer clear of *"suspicious transactions"* involving the Cooks guarantees. News of the scandal even reached the pages of Britain's *Observer* newspaper, which mounted its own investigation. All part, it seems, of the Cook Islands declaration of economic terrorism on the rest of the world.

The former Cook Islands Treasury Secretary, Michael Fleming, testified to the Davison Commission that while he was there – up until late 1988 – *"there was a problem in the Cook Islands with issues of fraud and mismanagement."*

He added that in 1987 the Cook Islands Government had been making $1 million a month from a withholding tax credit scam it was directly perpetrating on the Australian Revenue. Unwitting Australian taxpayers were subsidising the Cooks at an annualised rate of $12 million – one third of the entire Cook Islands budget, if Fleming's maths was correct. New Zealand was providing the Cooks with another $13 million each year in foreign aid payments. At the same time, Fleming revealed, Cooks politicians and civil servants were feathering their nests with "travel allowances".

"Another issue was the travelling allowance per diem called the 'multiplier'. The effect of the multiplier was that a Government minister or official who incurred expenses while on Government business overseas would receive payment of his costs multiplied by the multiplier applying to him.

"For example, if the Prime Minister stayed in a hotel in Paris that cost $1000 a night, he got paid $2500 as his multiplier was 2.5. My multiplier was 2.25. I was against the multiplier as there was no deterrent on spending. For example, there was no policy to say that you should not stay in expensive hotels. Given a system like that, people were encouraged to stay in the most expensive hotel that they could."

Fleming said that he was often pressured, as Financial Controller, to approve *"a particular course of action that I felt was wrong. One example of this was the Italian hotel project which I did not support from day one. Norman George was the Minister in charge of the project and I received a threat from his personal assistant to the effect that if I did not support the proposal, harm could come to myself and my wife and children."*

Shortly afterwards, Fleming found his contract had been terminated, and he was booted out of the Cooks. One of the only records he kept, a diary he maintained during his time at the helm.

"I subsequently returned to the Cook Islands for a court case where my diary was used in evidence. It was not returned to me, and then the Courthouse was burnt down and my diary disappeared."

A TVNZ investigative team, including myself, spent some time in the Cook Islands looking into the Letters of Guarantee case. For me, the personal highlight had to be the discovery that Trevor Clarke, a key player in European Pacific, had also been an adviser to the Cook Islands Government on the Letters of Guarantee. During our previous visit to the Cooks on the EP case, we had unwittingly forced Clarke into hiding when we spent a while in the midday sun filming some nearby buildings.

According to local officials, who'd watched the whole thing from a second story window, our presence left Clarke lying down on the floor of his car, quietly baking in an oven of glass and metal – such had been his apparent fear of being filmed by us. It was particularly amusing to me, because we hadn't been looking for Clarke at all.

This time around, I was determined to catch him. After interviewing the Cooks Prime Minister one morning, we bumped into Trevor Clarke coming in as we were leaving. When he realised we were reaching for the TV camera, he backed his vehicle out and rapidly disappeared down the road.

Subsequently, cameraman Owen Goodwin and myself hid in a hedge overlooking the PM's office and Clarke's car, which had slipped in via a back entrance, hoping Clarke would reappear. We weren't disappointed. Half an hour later he emerged. Unfortunately in his excitement, Goodwin turned the camera off instead of on so, as I leapt out of the hedge at a crucial point to yell *"Gotcha!"* triumphantly, Owen was muttering *"No, you haven't,"* behind me.

Not to be beaten, we hid later that day outside Clarke's office for two and a half hours. Goodwin was stationed beneath the shelter of a footbridge across the road, whilst I was poised in a nearby cafe kitchen with a clear view of his vehicle, a new Honda Legend.

People came and went, but no sign was there of Clarke. Finally, convinced he'd spotted us and given us the slip, I summoned up the nerve to go and peer through his office windows. No sign of him. I crept from flax bush to flax bush across the open ground behind his office. Still nothing.

Running back across the road to Goodwin, I was just suggesting we pack it in when Clarke appeared out of nowhere. The shot was priceless – more so when Clarke suddenly realised he was being filmed. If looks could kill.

Our excursion incurred the wrath of the Cooks Government, however. Sir Geoffrey Henry labelled TVNZ a front for the CIA, and accused us of plotting with the Americans to overthrow his Government. He then expelled a TVNZ current affairs crew. Where will it end, I wonder.

The Davison Commission shows no sign of ending. Instead, week by week, it continues to gain momentum. As I write this final chapter, former European Pacific chairman David Richwhite has been taking the stand in his company's defence. The issues he raises are pertinent to the issues in this book, so I believe it is only fair to note them.

Firstly, he explained that while the wine box mentions both Fay Richwhite the private company and Capital Markets Ltd. – the public one – there is a basic rule of thumb as to which was involved in what.

"Any advisory/fee earner work was done by the merchant bank, Fay Richwhite, and anything that incurred or required capital or principal risk was done by Capital Markets."

In addition, as we had already suspected, he confirmed that Sir Michael Fay did not play an active role in the tax haven business.

"Historically I ran the merchant banking side. Michael, even in the early days, was not involved in that. He was very much involved with the big picture planning

and strategy, marketing the business and investing surplus funds generated from the merchant banking activities.

"Then, of course, Michael left for a fairly lengthy period of time in pursuit of the America's Cup. He was out of New Zealand for much of the period of time of the transactions now in issue."

So who was in control of EP on a daily basis?

"Right from day one David Lloyd took control of the EP operation. Fay Richwhite was a passive investor in it as were Brierleys and the BNZ. Whilst we were interested in the business and direction of things globally, nonetheless it was David Lloyd's baby.

"In terms of governance and control, procedures were very important. David Lloyd, right from day one, insisted that this was an offshore bank and offshore trust company and confidentiality and privacy of client affairs were management issues, and that is where they would stay.

"The board was separately responsible for philosophy, policy and for setting exposure limits and making key strategic decisions."

Richwhite's brief of evidence flagged a number of important and intriguing matters. One of the first was the origin of the tax credit schemes, which appeared to originate in mid-1987.

"The nature and scope of the proposed arrangements were made known to the [Cook Islands] Solicitor-General in about May 1987," wrote a Russell McVeagh partner in a letter to European Pacific managing director David Lloyd. *"Initial consultations involving Mr David Lloyd, Dr Robin Congreve, Mr Richard LeGrice and Mr [Tony] Manarangi were followed by a letter dated 5 June 1987 detailing the arrangements."*

Funnily enough, the Russell McVeagh letter related to an ironical situation. European Pacific, having spent months planning the tax credit schemes and getting Cook Islands Government support for the proposal, had been ambushed by rivals, including Euronational Corporation.

Somehow, European Pacific alleged, someone within the Cooks Government had leaked details of its tax credit scheme, and its rivals had lobbied the Cook Islands Government to do the deals themselves.

At the same time, European Pacific was fighting a bushfire involving the Government itself, which apparently planned to do a "bond issue" into Australia. European Pacific reacted swiftly, in a letter from chairman David Richwhite to the Cooks Prime Minister, Pupuke Robati.

"The position is that the Government has received a proposal to issue bonds and Parliament has enacted legislation to enable that issue to occur. The Government has taken a role under which it will use the legislation specially enacted to take an active and direct role in a transaction that, irrespective of technical niceties, will in our view be perceived as a transaction designed to defraud the tax revenues of Australia."

What made the whole thing extremely amusing to me was the follow-up correspondence the following week.

"You have learned," wrote the Russell McVeagh partner to EP, *"that a competitor has now presented to the Cook Islands government an arrangement*

regarding foreign tax credits which is in all material respects identical to your proposed arrangements. In the light of this discovery you have sought advice from two taxation experts and they have informed you that it would be impossible for another party to have devised the arrangements without having prior knowledge of your proposed arrangements."

Unfortunately, it's not clear from the evidence to the Inquiry just why European Pacific felt the bond issue would be fraudulent, or just how different it was from the Government role in the tax credit deals.

Richwhite conceded that it appeared his letter alleging the scheme would be perceived as an attempt to *"defraud"* Australia was related to the scheme that European Pacific was itself claiming the credit for – no pun intended. Serious Fraud Office counsel, Dr Willie Young QC, then suggested to Richwhite that when he used the word "defraud" he didn't really mean it.

"You have been rather 'twitted' in cross-examination so far with the suggestion that your letter was effectively acknowledgement by application that your own scheme was fraudulent," said Young, *"I think that is the proposition that has been put?"*

Richwhite looked as if he wondered where all this was heading.

"I think that has been put to me a number of times."

"The actual wording you use," continued Young helpfully, *"is a 'transaction that irrespective of technical niceties, will in our view be perceived as a transaction designed to defraud the tax revenues of Australia'.*

Dr Young suggested that a literal translation could allow the description to be applied to the Magnum transaction in New Zealand, but he then highlighted the word "perceived".

"So is it fair to say that is one view of your letter – perhaps a literal view – is that what you are talking about is perception rather than necessarily reality?"

"Perception is always important in these transactions," Richwhite replied confidently, *"but it is quite a different thing from the actual technical legality of the particular financing."*

The Serious Fraud Office lawyer also suggested that the use of "defraud" was simply *"hyperbole and exaggeration, because you were really trying to warn [the Cook Islands Prime Minister] off the course."*

Richwhite told the Commission that the Magnum tax credit deal had not come before European Pacific's board. *"I saw the Magnum transaction for the first time in its entirety on television,"* he testified. *"At the time when the controversy over Magnum began to mount, David Lloyd confirmed its existence to me and advised that no similar transaction had taken place in New Zealand.*

"At that time I was most concerned about the legitimacy of the transaction. I was involved with European Pacific's decision to obtain independent legal advice and with the conduct of its claim against Television New Zealand."

Under cross examination, Richwhite stated that he obtained legal advice that nothing European Pacific had done was anything other than legal or proper. The man who gave him that advice was Lindsay McKay, a tax barrister who was later used as part of European Pacific's arsenal in the injunction against TVNZ.

McKay was subsequently appointed as the independent legal adviser to the Finance and Expenditure Committee's short-lived winebox inquiry, to my mind a possible conflict of interest.

But the issue of illegality may be more complex. Richwhite admitted that one European Pacific executive, Alex Adamovich, was worried the tax credit deals were fraudulent and raised the issue at board level.

The Commission's "Witness A" says he too was worried and raised it with Trevor Clarke. European Pacific sought legal advice from an Australian criminal barrister, Brian Oslington QC, who stated that the schemes were indeed fraudulent.

Unhappy with that, its lawyers then sought further opinions from two more QCs who concluded that the tax credit deals were not a fraud. In summary, EP executive Mark Jones warned *"there remains the chance that if the matter ever went to court it may well be that a judge could side with the view taken by Mr Oslington."*

In cross examination, Richwhite stated that the directors had certainly had the issue of criminality drawn to their attention, and had discussed it at some length. Board minutes record there were *"mixed feelings"* on the issue.

"With tax matters like this," he said, *"the devil is in the detail, and the detail as to how the structure was structured would have been very important as to its legality or otherwise."*

Counsel Assisting the Commission, Colin Carruthers QC, asked why the directors didn't place more weight on the Oslington opinion, given his experience as a QC specialising in criminal law.

"One would expect that he would know something about the way in which the criminal law would operate, agreed?"

"Yes, but we were probably more interested in taxation law."

Perhaps the EP directors weren't told, but Oslington had prosecuted a number of Sydney's "bottom-of-the-harbour" frauds in the mid-eighties for the Australian Tax Office. He was not exactly unfamiliar with tax law.

At day's end, said Richwhite, the decision to proceed with the tax credit deals was a commercial one, based on a number of factors including legal input. He stated that if directors had believed a proposal was criminal, it wouldn't have gone ahead. He also lashed out at the allegations of fraud made against him in Parliament.

"As past Chairman [of European Pacific] and the person who has come under most attack, along with Fay Richwhite and Sir Michael Fay from Mr Peters in Parliament, and the attention that the media has chosen to focus on our company in particular – as against the other participants – we have definitely borne the brunt of this particular saga.

"In our business, clearly it is based on reputation. I think I talked in my brief about human capital, we have nothing else to sell other than the merchant banking business. You don't have to be an Einstein to work out what effect that might have."

* * *

THIS BOOK RAISES A number of issues that may or may not eventually be considered by the Inquiry, but which for now lie solely with you, the reader, to ponder.

For the sake of clarity, so that no one is under any misconception, I shall summarise clearly what is being alleged and what isn't.

I have attempted to preface all such allegations with the word "alleged" or similar, out of fairness to those who have been accused. Failure to slip in an "alleged" here or there is not to be taken as an indicator of definitive guilt – it's simply an oversight on my part. The circumstances of writing this book precluded tipping off any of the parties involved – at least I learnt something from the TVNZ/European Pacific debacle – undoubtedly some will make comment on the claims contained within.

The purpose of *The Paradise Conspiracy* was not to prove beyond all reasonable doubt that crimes have taken place. I honestly do not know whether anything illegal has – I'm not a lawyer and I don't profess to be. Instead, this book provides the reader with the circumstantial evidence that the law enforcement agencies had access to, and asks why at least one of them didn't bother lifting a finger sooner to actually investigate.

This issue is even more serious than the actual alleged crimes: New Zealanders have come to believe that our civil service is independent and upstanding, that our regulatory authorities apply the law evenly to all, without fear or favour. You be the judge.

In regard to the death of Paul White, I allege that his death was not investigated fully, with regard to all the possible scenarios. The New Zealand police refused to accept the possibility of a homicide despite the allegations made at the time, and subsequently did not take as much care in the investigation as they would have in a murder case.

I **do not** allege, and nor do I personally believe, that Citibank or any employee of the bank had anything to do with the death of Paul White, nor should the reader draw that conclusion.

There is, in fact, no hard evidence to suggest White was murdered. His wrecked car was long ago sold for scrap, taking with it the scratched paintwork that may have indicated interference from another vehicle.

I do allege that the Serious Fraud Office failed to fully or competently investigate Paul White's disks, given that the SFO never laid a finger on Paul White's disks, but issued a press statement claiming to have examined the information on them.

I also allege that the New Zealand Police failed to protect the perceived integrity of evidence seized under a criminal warrant. These latter two matters are certainly worthy of further inquiry.

It is of course entirely possible that White's accident was caused by his drunk driving. There is no hard evidence to the contrary. Such a finding does not negate the inadequacy, in my opinion, of the official investigations into the matter, nor does it explain that inadequacy.

If he was murdered, then the evidence points to the involvement of state security organisations – either the Security Intelligence Service or the Special Air Service. There is always the possibility that he could have been killed by a foreign entity for reasons as yet undiscovered, but that is venturing well and truly into speculation cyberspace.

In regard to European Pacific, the legality of the deals and the conduct of the IRD and SFO are finally in front of a full, public, Commission of Inquiry, headed by a former Chief Justice.

One final housekeeping matter, the BNZ, as the bank's new owners have already noted publicly, is no longer controlled by the same people who controlled it during the late 1980's and early 90's. It is, to all intents and purposes, a different bank, and people should bear that in mind.

The Paradise Conspiracy has international ramifications. It goes to the heart of the struggle between democracy – Government of the people, by the people, for the people – and plutocracy: Government by the rich and powerful. A weapon in that struggle is the court system, more often than not used to greatest effect by the plutocracy. An example is the series of injunctions taken out by European Pacific to prevent these matters being exposed.

In defamation law, injunctions are now almost impossible to get prior to publication. If the media organisation tells the Court that it is standing by its story, the Court will allow publication on the basis that the two sides can slug it out in Court later if the item is inaccurate.

It's my submission that the law in the breach of confidence area needs to change to reflect the defamation situation. The European Pacific injunctions against the media should never have been able to be granted. The news media were arguing that they were prepared to disclose iniquity or illegality, and the Courts should be able to accept that at face value, for the same reasons that if European Pacific had simply been pleading defamation the Court would have probably struck out the injunction before it got to first base.

European Pacific always had the right to sue afterwards, and it's not as though they were a struggling corner dairy taking on news media "Goliaths". Instead, the media was strung out for up to 18 months, facing more than a million dollars in legal bills, for the right to run stories that were clearly in the public interest. The right of the Court to determine whether a matter is in the public interest or not – *before* the actual publication takes place – should be removed.

The law should be altered to take into account that if the media plead a public interest defence to a breach of confidence injunction, the injunction should immediately be lifted on the clear understanding that if the subsequent publication does not meet the public interest criteria, damages may be imposed.

After all, is the release of confidential, true information any more damaging than the release of untrue, defamatory information? If logic dictates that it isn't, then obviously there shouldn't be a higher burden on media organisations wishing to publicise confidential information.

There was a phrase in one of the winebox documents – a $100 million BNZ pref share deal – to the effect that if the media or the Inland Revenue

Department began snooping around, EP's lawyers were to run legal interference and objections for as long as possible to give time for the transactions to either keep making profits, or presumably alternatively so they could be wound down and evidence wiped out – bearing in mind that IRD would find it virtually impossible anyway to penetrate tax haven secrecy laws in the Cooks. The exact wording:

"Although Capital Markets Limited have agreed to take put options over the New Zealand companies in the off balance sheet side of the structure they have requested that should the structure ever be contested by the New Zealand Inland Revenue that we run with any objection procedure for as long as possible so as not to jeopardise the commercial justification for the structure . . . a reputation risk is present once the Tax Department are involved.

"A 'poison pill' is also built in. It is understood that if the New Zealand revenue or the media investigates the ownership of any of the companies involved, EPTBGL will receive a further fee."

It is this arrogance that manifested itself in the injunction process, with objections and delays being thrown up every step of the way. Former European Pacific Chairman David Richwhite admitted at the Inquiry that part of the reason for the injunction against TVNZ was that the JIF deals were still running and still profitable.

The fact that politicians were prepared to add to the delays, by refusing to allow the publication of a Pandora's box of dirty deals, merely adds to the abhorrent nature of the whole process.

As borders shrink and multinational corporations increasingly take control of the world's economic destiny, it becomes easier for those in business to impose their wishes on Government whilst bypassing the ballot-box, which is why this story is relevant not just to New Zealand but to nations around the world.

Every now and then a whistle gets blown and, even more rarely, the citizens of a country sometimes get enraged enough to take back control of their own affairs.

Here endeth the lesson.

*   *   *

POSTSCRIPT:

In August, 1995, just as the author was finalising the publishing of this book, his car experienced multiple brake failure on the Auckland motorway. A subsequent investigation by mechanics and brake specialists revealed the vehicle's brake fluid contained a strange *"silicon-like substance"* which had turned the fluid into a lumpy *"glue"* and wrecked the power braking system, causing the rubber seals to rupture and disintegrate. The Mitsubishi dealership and the brake specialist reported they had *"never seen anything like it, ever!"* Virtually the entire braking system had to be replaced, and the brake lines had to be flushed three times to get rid of the contaminant. Police are investigating, and the opera obviously ain't over yet.

Acknowledgements

MY OWN ROLE IN proceedings could accurately be described as that of "cheerleader" and "chief mousetrap setter". While others in the media and political arenas were diverting attention, my colleagues and I were able to continue quietly baiting the traps and waiting for a catch.

The investigation has been very much a team effort from the beginning, straddling two rival television networks in an at times rare show of solidarity.

My thanks go to TV3's Peter Stones and Steve Christensen, for having faith and working tirelessly to crack it; to TV3 Vice President Rod Pedersen for having slightly less faith but still managing to sign off on the expense cheques; to TVNZ's new Director of News and Current Affairs, Shaun Brown, Paul Cutler and Paul Norris, for their courage in hiring a rampaging conspiracy theorist and setting him loose, and for managing to sign off on up to a million dollars worth of expense cheques; to Tony Townsend and Steve Bloxham for constantly rearranging staff rosters to accomodate the investigation, and to Steve in particular for his unwavering support and keen editorial eye; to Carol Hirschfeld for taking a dream and making it a real television programme, and in particular for reminding me so graphically why I hate gin and tonic; to Michael Wilson for his business reporting acumen, cool head and his professionalism under extreme conditions; to Mark Champion for helping to keep the programme alive under hostile fire and for his ability to focus in on the main issues faster than a fox to a drumstick; to videotape editors Will Kong and Nic Craig for sitting through dozens of recuts and still managing to produce award winning television; to Heaton Dyer and the *Eyewitness* team for indulging me and shouldering the burden during 1994; ditto Johnny Graham and the *One Network News* team during 1995; to the legal team at Simpson Grierson Butler White – Willie Akel, Helen Wild and Gary Muir – for seizing the day and winning the battle (and above all for playing the "get out of jail free" card on my behalf); to Warren Berryman and Jenni McManus of the *Independent*, and Fran O'Sullivan, Graeme Colman and Barry Colman of the *National Business Review*, for providing early inspiration and ongoing support in print; to Peter & Maureen White, and Stephanie Perry and family for their help, and in recognition of the pain and suffering they've had to endure; to Chris Dickie, Tony Molloy, John Prebble, Brian Tyler, Brian Henry and Bill Hodge for their expert assistance where appropriate, and their recognition of the public interest; to Winston Peters for continuing to take the punishment, day after day; and to Brent Harman and TVNZ for ultimately broadcasting probably the most expensive one-hour investigative documentary they've ever made.

My appreciation goes out to Juliet, Harriet, Graeme and Michael for advice and opening doors. Thanks also to Tim Allan at the Grove Darlow law firm, a medal is in order, and to Neville and Dianna, without whom *The Paradise Conspiracy* could not have been completed.

To those who cannot be named, my thanks also. Without you, and your willingness to risk everything – careers, marriages or more – in order to blow the whistle, this story would never have been told. The world needs more people willing to take those risks, to reclaim their dignity in the face of corporate or political muscle.

Finally, to my wife and family: thank you for being there each day and sharing the load. I know what the cost has been.

Ian Wishart,
August 14, 1995

References

In most cases the reference material quoted in this book is sourced at the time of quotation. Briefly, however, I shall list the newspapers and periodicals drawn upon throughout the investigation. The reader should consult the index for specific information.

The Australian
The New Zealand Herald
The Dominion
The Evening Post
The Sunday Star
The Sunday Star-Times
The Dominion Sunday Times
The Christchurch Star
The National Business Review
The Independent
The Sydney Morning Herald
The Los Angeles Times
The Cook Islands News
The BBC
Agence France Presse
Reuters
Offshore Investment magazine
Metro magazine
North and South magazine
The Listener magazine
Radio New Zealand
Television New Zealand
TV3 Network
ABC Australia
Compuserve Pacific: US Newspaper database

The following books were used during research into these matters:
Distant Voices: John Pilger. Vintage, 1992
A Secret Country: John Pilger. Vintage, 1990
The Feather Men: Ranulph Fiennes. Bloomsbury, 1991
Spycatcher: Peter Wright. William Heinemann Australia, 1988
The Crimes of Patriots: Jonathan Kwitny. Simon & Schuster, 1988
False Profits: Peter Truell, Larry Gurwin. Houghton Mifflin, 1992
The Outlaw Bank: Jonathan Beaty, S.C. Gwynne. Random House, 1993
Where's the Gold?: Ray Smith. R.M. & J.A. Jensen Ltd, 1994
Air America: Christopher Robbins. Corgi, 1988
Inside Out: Dennis Levine, William Hoffer. Random Century Group, 1991

Unholy Babylon: Adel Darwish, Gregory Alexander. Victor Gollancz, 1991
Under Fire: Oliver North, William Novak. Fontana, 1991
Profits of War: Ari Ben-Menashe. Allen & Unwin, 1992
Behind The Mirror Glass: Bruce Jesson. Penguin, 1987
The Ariadne Story: Bruce Ross. Greenhouse, 1988
The Death Lobby: Kenneth Timmerman. Fourth Estate (UK), 1992
Enemies of the State: Gary Murray. Simon & Schuster, 1993
Washed in Gold: Ann Woolner. Simon & Schuster, 1994
Michael Fay — On A Reach For The Ultimate: Iain Morrison, Grant Cubis, Frank Haden. Freelance Biographies Ltd, 1990

OTHER REFERENCES

New Zealand Justice Department, Companies Office
New Zealand Stock Exchange
New Zealand Police: "Paul White File"
New Zealand Defence Force
The European Pacific winebox
The "second" winebox
The New Zealand House of Representatives: Hansard records
The Davison Commission of Inquiry: transcripts of evidence

Appendix

RUDD WATTS & STONE

BARRISTERS & SOLICITORS

17 December 1993

Refer to:
Mr Hurd

**BY HAND
AND BY FACSIMILE 375 0918**

The Group Chief Executive
Television New Zealand Limited
Cnr Hobson & Victoria Streets
AUCKLAND

Attention: Mr B Harman

Dear Sir

EUROPEAN PACIFIC GROUP

1. We act for the European Pacific Group of companies.

2. We are aware that there have been recent discussions between yourself, Mr Geary and others concerning a proposed current affairs television programme on, inter alia, the European Pacific Group and some of its business activities. Mr Lloyd of the European Pacific Group was contacted today by Mr Wishart to discuss aspects of the proposed programme. If our client's understanding is correct, then it has understandable concerns that anything said in the proposed programme about its activities should be accurate and balanced, and that nothing in the proposed programme should in any way contravene the interim injunction orders made by the High Court.

3. You will recall that on 30 October 1992 and 12 November 1992, we wrote to you advising that the High Court at Auckland had granted certain interim injunctions in favour of two European Pacific Group companies against a number of parties, including two newspapers, prohibiting the publication, dissemination, use and copying of certain confidential documents belonging to, and stolen from, European Pacific Group.

4. The grant of those injunctions had been much publicised in the press and in the media. A number of the documents covered by the High Court injunctions were then unlawfully copied and disseminated. The purpose of our letters was to indicate to you that:

    (a) if a copy of any such document came into your possession, it should be returned to the European Pacific Group;

(b) the unauthorised use or copying of such a document or dissemination of any confidential information contained in such a document could render the person or organisation concerned liable to both civil and criminal sanctions; and

(c) any person or organisation, although not a direct party to the injunction proceedings, who, having become aware of the injunctions, acted in contravention of the orders might well be in contempt of Court.

5. We now enclose copies of the injunction orders made by the High Court for your further information. Although Television New Zealand might not be a party to the present High Court proceedings, it may well be liable for contempt of Court if it acts in a fashion which subverts the Court's orders, after receiving express notice of the terms of the injunctions.

6. During his telephone conversation with Mr Lloyd today, Mr Wishart mentioned a particular transaction involving Magnum Corporation Limited. We wish to point out that documents concerning that transaction, and which belong to European Pacific Group Limited, are specifically covered by the interim injunctions. Having said that, our client wishes to advise that it would be more than happy to meet with a representative of Television New Zealand to discuss the application of the injunctions to any European Pacific material which may be the subject of the proposed programme. To this end, we look forward to hearing from you. We would also be happy to discuss any aspect of this letter with you should you wish to do so.

Yours faithfully
RUDD WATTS & STONE

D Hurd
Partner

cc   Mr Ian Wishart

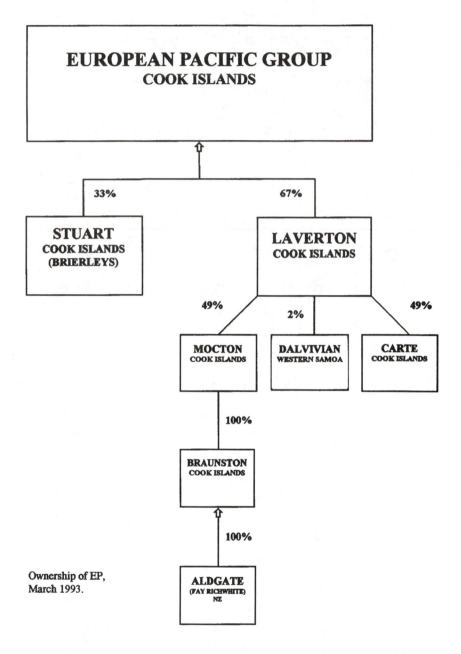

Ownership of EP,
March 1993.

Our Reference **920806/1147**

POLICE
Nga Pirihimana O Aotearoa

11 September 1992

The Officer In Charge
Company Fraud Squad
AUCKLAND CENTRAL

CITIBANK NZ LIMITED : COMPLAINT OF THEFT BY CONVERSION AND DEMANDING WITH MENACES AGAINST WHITE & BLOMKAMP

1. I refer to the minute and previous report of Detective Sergeant CHURCHES.

2. I have attached a copy of Justice Blancher's decision and Justice TOMPKINS' order in relation to Civil Proceedings taken by Citibank.

CRIMINALITY OF WHITE & BLOMKAMP

3. The primary issue to be resolved has always been who has ownership and/or possessory rights over the items delivered to WHITE on the 24 June 1992 by the Office Clearance Company and in particular, the computer disks and literature which contained banking information.

4. In these circumstances WHITE, acting as the New Zealand director of Growth Computers offered, by way of a faxed letter dated 22 June 1992, to purchase "the complete lot" of items offered to him, including "the boxes of cabling and assorted disks and literature". This offer to purchase was accepted and the items were sold to WHITE under invoice. This invoice described the items as "assorted computer equipment". As a result, there can be no doubt that the Office Clearance Company intended to sell to WHITE and that WHITE intended to purchase assorted disks and literature. Any ownership and/or possessory rights which the Office Clearance Company had in relation to the disks and literature therefore passed to WHITE upon the sale occurring.

COPY SUPPLIED
TO ..WISHART..

2 9 SEP 1993

PURSUANT TO
OFFICIAL INFORMATION ACT

5.   Whether the Office Clearance Company had ownership and/or possessory rights to the disks and literature is a separate issue. This question does not need to be definitively answered in assessing criminal liability as in the above circumstances WHITE, in any criminal proceedings, would successfully claim that he believed he had ownership or possessory rights over the disputed items.

6.   It should also be noted that Justice BLANCHARD in his judgement, at Page 7, was prepared to assume for the purposes of that Application "That Mr. WHITE has legitimately become the owner of the tapes themselves." This aspect is important as any dishonesty charge must relate to the physical disks and literature as under current New Zealand law information cannot be stolen.

7.   My reference above to "dishonesty offences" includes all offences which contain the ingredient of either "dishonestly" or "intent to defraud."

8.   Any proposes criminal charge against WHITE or BLOMKAMP must fail and no further investigation should be made in that direction.

THE RIGHT OF POLICE TO INSPECT THE DISKS AND LITERATURE

9.   The disks and files are legally in Police custody under the authority of a search warrant. There is no statutory fetter on how the Police may deal with such property except that it must remain in the custody of a constable.

10.   The Injunction obtained by Citicorp relates to BLOMKAMP, WHITE and "any associated person or company" and prohibits all dealing with the relevant disks and literature. Any associated persons or company must relate to those associated to the defendants, namely BLOMKAMP and WHITE and also to others associated to the Court Action, namely Citicorp. It can therefore be argued that the injunction itself does not relate to the Police and the phrase "otherwise dealing" does not limit Police inspection of the disks and literature.

11.   However, what must now be considered is that if there is now no criminal offence being investigated, then there is now no reason for the Police to inspect, or in any other way deal with the disks and literature. As a result the Police should not now inspect the disks or literature. This does not however address any investigation into the circumstances surrounding WHITE's death.

OTHER CONSIDERATIONS

12.   Due to further developments in this case over the last 24 hours I will comment on the following:

   (a)   Official Information Act implication if the tapes are viewed by the Police.

   The Act will have no effect as although applicable, any disclosure would be refused under s9(2)(a) which relates to the protection of the privacy of a person.

   (b)   Police response to the Serious Fraud Office requesting to seize the disks.

   While there are specific statutory provisions allowing the Serious Fraud Office to access or seize property, the Police should initially refuse to allow them to so as this would be in breach of our statutory obligation under s199 of the Summary Proceedings Act 1957, which requires property seized under a search warrant to remain in the custody of a constable. As the Police are currently the legal custodians of the items then we should be scrupulous in ensuring that any request or demand from the Serious Fraud Office is made with valid statutory authority. As a result any request to seize the items must be referred to the Legal Section, prior to any further action being taken.

CONCLUSION

13.   Neither WHITE nor BLOMKAMP have committed any criminal offence and the investigation into their actions should now cease.

14.   While the Police have a right to inspect the disks and literature in their possession, there is no valid reason for them to do so and therefore should not do so unless the circumstances surrounding WHITE's death necessitate such inspection.

15. The Official Information Act has no practical effect on our dealings with the disks and literature.

16. Any request from the Serious Fraud Office to seize the disks and literature must be immediately referred to the Senior Legal Adviser, Region One Headquarters to assess the validity of the request prior to any action being taken.

[signature]

D.G. FORDYCE
Legal Adviser
Region One HQ

[handwritten notes]

N.Z. POLICE

REPORT FORM

SUBJECT: Citibank and PGE White

TEXT: FRAUD INVESTIGATION

15 September 1992

Detective Inspector Rutherford
AUCKLAND CENTRAL C.I.B

1.   COMPLAINT

Citibank made their complaint to the Police following a lengthy discussion between their solicitor, Sheila McCabe of McIlroy Milne, and Dennis Payne, Deputy Director of the Serious Fraud Office. Mr Payne, a former District Court Judge, obviously considered that there was sufficient evidence to warrant a criminal investigation as he suggested that the matter be referred to the Police.

On 16 July 1992 a complaint was made to the Police by Citibank. The complaint was taken by Peter Preece, Fraud Squad, who then referred the matter to me.

Having read the various affidavits and correspondence supplied by Citibank I was of the opinion that an offence had been committed and therefore that a criminal investigation should be undertaken.

Mr Preece and I discussed at some length the possible criminal liability of White and/or Blomkamp, his solicitor.   Two offences seemed appropriate, Theft by Conversion (in respect of the discs) and Demanding with Menaces (In respect of the demand of $50,000 made by Blomkamp on the bank).

Various checks were made in respect to where White was working and living from and it became apparent that he was working and living at 1 Rugby Ave, Birkenhead.   Blomkamp's office was at Birkenhead Law, 98 Mokoia Rd, Birkenhead.

2.   LEGAL SECTION

Due to the unusual nature of the complaint and the fact that it was contemplated that we would apply for a search warrant for Blomkamp's office, Mr Preece and I spoke with Legal Adviser Dave Fordyce on 18 July 1992.

The result of our discussion was that there was sufficient evidence to make application for a search warrant for both White and Blomkamp's addresses.

The matter of the interim injunction (which had been granted at that time) was discussed and our advice was that the existence of the injunction was not a bar to obtaining a search warrant.

I then prepared an affidavit and search warrants in relation to White's address and Blomkamp's office. It became apparent however that the discs were probably not held by Blomkamp, and therefore the application for a search warrant for his address was abandoned. A copy of my affidavit was sent to Dave Fordyce.

3.   EXECUTION OF SEARCH WARRANTS

On 23 July 1992 I went to the Auckland District Court and made application before a Deputy Registrar for a search warrant in respect of White's address, 1 Rugby Ave, Birkenhead. My application was granted. It should be noted that I attached a copy of the High Court Interim Injunction to my affidavit.

The same afternoon I executed that search warrant on White's address with Mr Preece. Details of what was said are recorded in my job sheets attached to the file, but in essence a full search of the premises was not made and White eventually disclosed that the discs were held at Brambles Record Management Ltd, Mt Wellington.

White had contacted a Thomas Cotter who runs New Zealand Guard Services Ltd, and had contracted him to arrange secure storage of the discs on his behalf. This was evidenced by a document, a copy of which is attached to the file, which was an access authority from Brambles.

Enquiries with Cotter revealed that within days of lodging the discs at Brambles record Management on 7.7.92, Brambles had contacted him and instructed him to uplift the property. This was due to several newspaper articles about the matter. Cotter did this and lodged the discs at Armourguard, Nelson Street, Auckland, for whom he used to work.

A second application was then made on 6 August 1992 for a search warrant in respect of Armourguard's premises and arrangements were made with Cotter to attend and retrieve the property and then hand it over to me at the premises, which duly took place on 6 August 1992.

The discs were taken to the Auckland Central Police Station and lodged in the Property and Exhibit Store under reference F268/124.

4.   COPYING OF DISCS

On 7 August 1992 I contacted Citibank, Mike Farland, to advise him that the discs had been seized under warrant. He requested permission to inspect the discs and make a copy of each one. To that end he attended my office with a bank solicitor, Mark Fitzgerald, a computer technician whose name I do not recall, and Louise Perkins, Solicitor from McIlroy Milne. I remained in their presence while the copying was completed. On one occasion I left the office to go to the public counter. Before I left everybody left the room and in my absence Det. Sgt Hollewand ensured no-one entered the room.

Prior to any copying being done we discussed what the implications were in terms of the High Court Injunction. It was generally considered that we would not be breaching the injunction because it applied to White and Blomkamp only.

The request by the bank seemed a reasonable one in the circumstances. It became apparent that there were literally hundreds of files contained on the discs and to go through each file would take hours. It also seemed to me to be entirely proper and appropriate for the bank to have of a copy of the information contained on the discs as it was after all their information to start with. It was not as if they were copying something which was foreign to them and I believe they had a right to know what it was Blomkamp and White were threatening to disclose to the media if the demand was not met. Any suggestion that files were deleted is spurious.

Allowing Citibank to copy the discs did not breach Section 199(1) Summary Proceedings Act 1957 because the property remained in the custody of the police.

Mr Carter, Solicitor for White, wrote to the police on 11.8.92 and expressed his surprise at a second search warrant having been executed, particularly in light of my having received a second affidavit from David Palmer of the Office Clearance Company, before the execution of the second warrant. In fact I did not receive Palmers second affidavit until Friday 7 August 1992, and in any event it did not in my view alter the position.

Attached to the file is a letter I received from Carter following a telephone conversation I had with him on 9 September 1992. During the course of that conversation I raised the matter of Citibank taking a copy of the discs. I assumed that he already was aware of this but obviously he was not. He assumes that this somehow confirms some sort of conspiracy between the bank and the police, namely myself, and refers to 'ulterior motive and an abuse of process'. Nothing could be further from the truth and my actions were I believe in the interests of natural justice and fairness.

5.   INVESTIGATION INTO WHITE'S DEATH

I have not been involved in this investigation other than to provide background information.

6.   CONCLUSION

Citibank's complaint was treated and attended to no differently from that of any other dealt with by Fraud Squad. As with all complaints I deal with I take a dispassionate view of the complaint and evidence in support of same. It is my duty to investigate any complaint made if I have good cause to suspect an offence has been committed. Any suggestion to the contrary is spurious and patently untrue.

M R CHURCHES
Detective Sergeant 5301

QUESTION FOR WRITTEN ANSWER 431

(For Rules see back)

Name: .... WINSTON PETERS .... (Tauranga)....

to the Minister of .... Police: ....

With respect to the Citibank tapes seizure by the police and access by Citibank, how many laptops were used in the ~~supplier~~ copying process, ~~and~~ what was the capacity of those laptops, and were the files transferred into compressed or uncompressed state?

QUESTION FOR WRITTEN ANSWER 431

ANSWER:

Two laptop computers were used.

Further information will be obtained from citibank as to the exact specifications of those computers.

QUESTION FOR WRITTEN ANSWER 431

ANSWER:

Two laptop computers were used to copy the disks seized by police under search warrant. One laptop computer had a 40 megabyte hard drive capacity and the other had a 20 megabyte hard drive capacity.

Approximately 90% of the files were uncompressed when copied and the remaining 10% of files were in backup format in a compressed state and were uncompressed at a later time by Citibank officials. All the files were merely backup word processing files.

QUESTION FOR WRITTEN ANSWER   434

(For Rules see back)

Name: ....WINSTON PETERS.. (Tauranga)

to the Minister of......Police...

With respect to the Citibank disks was a police seizure of, and later Citibank access to were the disks copied and; if so, how were the disks copied, and what was the software used in the copying proce

QUESTION FOR WRITTEN ANSWER 434

ANSWER:

Further information coming from Citibank

QUESTION FOR WRITTEN ANSWER 434

ANSWER:

The disks seized by police were copied onto a combination of hard disks and floppy disks using two external disk drives. The software used to copy them was a standard DOS command called XCOPY which ensures all files, directories and sub-directories are copied.

Index